THE CUNNING OF RECOGNITION

THE CUNNING OF RECOGNITION

Indigenous Alterities and the Making

of Australian Multiculturalism

ELIZABETH A. POVINELLI

Duke University Press   Durham & London   2002

© 2002 Duke University Press

All rights reserved

Printed in the United States of

America on acid-free paper ∞

Designed by Amy Ruth Buchanan

Typeset in Minion by Tseng

Information Systems, Inc.

Library of Congress Cataloging-

in-Publication Data appear on the

last printed page of this book.

CONTENTS

ACKNOWLEDGMENTS

This book is the result of conversations with a number of people who were generous to share with me their insights on problems addressed in the following pages. Gillian Collishaw, Francesca Merlan, Deborah Bird Rose, and Alan Rumsey provided critical conversation on indigenous social life from an anthropological perspective. Wendy Asche, Ross Howie, Tom Keely, Jessica Klingender, Maria Lovinson, Ken Lum, and Ben Scambari and others working at the Northern Land Council played a vital role in deepening my thinking about the legal and institutional mediations of indigenous recognition. The staff working at the Australian Archives in Darwin, Sydney, and Melbourne, with the Elkin papers at the University of Sydney, with the Stanner papers at the Aboriginal and Torres Strait Islanders Council library, and at the Northern Territory Archives provided patient, vital help navigating the historical record on which much of the following depends. Geoff Gray in particular provided invaluable help. Two research projects—the Center for Late Liberalism at the University of Chicago and the Center for Transcultural Studies—have been vital to my thinking through of some of the problems of liberal forms of recognition and obligation. Whether they fully realized it or not, the following people from these projects critically informed this book: Ackbar Abbas, Lauren Berlant, Craig Calhoun, Vincent Crapanzano, Dilip Gaonkar, Elaine Hadley, Charles Hirshkind, Ben Lee, Leo Lee, Michael Leff, Patchen Markell, Saba Mahmood, Mary Poovey, Michael Silverstein, Charles Taylor, Rolph Trouillot, Candace Vogler, and Michael Warner. Their intellectual guidance was matched by the vigorous conversations—inside and outside Haskell Hall, by door jambs and in cars, over food and the phone—with Nadia Abu El-Haj, Arjun Appadurai, George Chauncey, Lisa Cohen, Jean and John Comaroff, Ray Fogelson, Susan Gal, Neville Hoad, John Lucy, Danilyn Rutherford, Marshall Sahlins, Saskia Sassen, and Siobhan Somerville. Audiences at a number of institutions also were critical to the emergent structure of my argument, especially at Berkeley, Harvard, Emory, Australian National University, LaTrobe, Cornell, McGill, Johns Hopkins, Northwestern, Rutgers, Columbia, the Arena Center, University of Technology Sydney, and the University of Pennsylvania. Finally, Ken Wissoker and two anonymous reviewers for Duke University Press provided constant encouragement and challenge to the form and content of this manuscript.

There are several people who deserve more than thanks, in particular my friends and family at Belyuen and Port Keats with whom I have shared lives for the last seventeen years, especially Marjorie Bilbil, Ester Djarem, Ruby Yarrowin, Alice Wanbirri, Anne Kunggul, Gracie Binbin, and Theresa Timber, and the deceased Betty Bilawag, Tommy Barradjap, Maggie Timber, Agnes Lippo, and Maudie Bennett. Equal to them are Stacey D'Erasmo, Susan Edmunds, and Sharon and Chris Povinelli.

Research for this book was funded by the National Science Foundation, the Wenner Gren Foundation, and the Adolph Lichstern Faculty Research Fund.

Early versions of several of the chapters in this volume have appeared in previous publications. "Mutant Messages" appeared as "Settler Modernity and the Quest for an Indigenous Tradition," *Public Culture* 11.1 (1999): 19–48, special issue: Alternative Modernities," ed. Dilip Gaonkar; ed. "Sex Rites, Civil Rights" appeared as "Native Sex: Ritual Sex, State Rights, and the Making of an Aboriginal Civic Culture" in *Gender Ironies of Nationalism: Sexing the Nation,* ed. Tamar Mayer (London: Routledge, 2000), 163–86; and "Shamed States" appeared as "The State of Shame: Australian Multiculturalism and the Crisis of Indigenous Citizenship," *Critical Inquiry* 24.2 (1998): 575–610, special issue: "Intimacy," ed. Lauren Berlant.

I been panic. I been have to get up.
I been have to get up, talk now. "No.
No. You not going to forget them
Dreaming. You can't forget. They still
there. They still going. They danger-
ous, that mob. You say, 'No.'"
— Betty Bilawag, conversation with
the author, 1993

INTRODUCTION / Critical Common Sense

JUST BE YOURSELF

In his 1958 essay "Continuity and Change" anthropologist W. E. H. Stanner reflected on whether the indigenous population of Australia should assimilate into mainstream settler society. Stanner's discussion would probably not surprise those familiar with mid-century public debates on indigenous assimilation in Australia or, for that matter, in the United States, New Zealand, or Canada. But Stanner writes something that we might easily pass over, rushed, as we often are, to get to the point. He states: "Let us leave aside the question that they may not want to [assimilate], and the possibility—I would myself put it far higher than a possibility—that very determined forces of opposition will appear. *Suppose they do not know how to cease to be themselves.*"[1]

Thirty-five years later, long after Australian state indigenous policy had shifted from assimilation to self-determination and then to reconciliation, Betty Bilawag described to me the feelings of panic she experienced when she attended a meeting to discuss whether mineral exploration should be allowed in Marriamu and Marritjeban country, a small area of land on the northwest coast of the Northern Territory of Australia. When she realized younger Marriamu and Marritjeban family members were about to vote in mass in favor of mining near a particularly sacred Dreaming site, she described her actions to me in this way: "I been panic. I been have to get up. I been have to get up, talk now. 'No. No. You're not going to forget them Dreaming. You can't forget. They still there. They still going. They dangerous, that mob. You say, No.' "

Is it surprising to find younger members of Bilawag's family seriously considering a mining venture as a means of relieving their structural poverty; or to find her feeling "panic" in opposing their desires? This panic acts as a corporeal index of the various contradictory orders and levels of obligation she and her family face as they move across—and within—now complicatedly intercalated discursive and practical spaces of capital, the Dreaming, and, as we will see, state law in relation to them. Wadeye (Port Keats), where many Marriamu and Marritjeban live, is the sixth-largest town in the Northern Territory, a fact often obscured by its nonwhite population and geographic remoteness, located as it is off the main highway that runs from Darwin south to Alice Springs. Wadeye is also, by far, one of the poorest of these Northern Territory towns, with all the incumbent health and social problems of endemic poverty: high childhood mortality, high substance abuse, suicide and depression, and low life expectancy. Mining ventures in the region might alleviate some of this poverty, but there is a hitch.

If capital ventures like the mining proposal are able to relieve certain conditions of poverty these women and men face, such ventures also can create impediments to some of their other territorial and economic aspirations. Just two years after my conversation with Bilawag, I was working with other Marriamu and Marritjeban, preparing for a sea claim to be lodged under the Native Title Act, 1993. As part of the application process, we had to produce a report and map demonstrating the continuing existence of their traditional laws, customs, beliefs, and practices. These traditional customs give their native title application its legal efficacy under Australian statutory and common law. Most jurists loosely agree with an understanding of traditional customs as outlined by one of the first land tribunal justices in the Northern Territory. Justice Olney, who had also served as a land commissioner under the Aboriginal Land Rights (Northern Territory) Act, 1976, described traditional customs as a set of laws, beliefs, and practices that are "integral to a distinctive culture" rather than a mere "description of how people live," how their ancestors once lived, or how a portrait of their lives might be opportunistic to the law.[2] But although state courts and publics demand evidence of the continuity of traditional beliefs, practices, and dispositions as the condition of cultural recognition and, through this, land title, some features and practices of "customary law" are prohibited by common and statutory law and by a public sense of moral decency—what constitutes the socially and culturally repugnant and the limits of recognition.

It is not necessary to conceptualize a coherent subject nor completely separate discursive orders in order to conceptualize the vital sociological consequences of moments in which indigenous and nonindigenous subjects (or any subjects for that matter) experience contrasting obligations to reasoned argument and moral sensibility—and, most important, are called upon to performatively enact and overcome this impasse as the condition of recognition. Moreover, as Bilawag's reminiscences suggest, the subjective embodiment of reason and moral sensibility varies, often significantly, across age and social groups within a community—her younger family members were poised to vote "yes" to the mining venture after all. Is it surprising, then, that the embodiment of "culture" reflects the variations, slippages, dispersions, and ambivalences of discursive and moral formations across the variegated terrain of indigenous and nonindigenous social life? Two types of social risks arise in these moments. First, discursive norms and legal codes are placed at risk as subjects like Bilawag and her family creatively engage the impasses they face, generating new forms of social life. Second, the subject herself—Betty Bilawag—is placed at risk. Numerous people throughout the northwest coastal region have described to me the personal consequences of not being able to reconcile these various orders. They identify people as *piya wedjirr* (literally, "head-rotten") or "silly," made so by their inability to reconcile the competing obligations and desires that make up local lives. These people could neither be nor cease to be themselves in social conditions that maximize the impasse of discursive and moral orders. Whatever else might be said about Betty Bilawag's "panic," this much seems true—it points to and expresses the contradictory mandates she inhabits and embodies. But she is not the only one inhabiting the impasses of late liberalism. In other words, the contradictions and impasses of late liberalism are not found only in and among minorities and subalterns. They are a total social fact.

Nonindigenous Australians must now grapple with what constitutes a felicitous version of "traditional custom" in the context of these legal, public, and moral binds. Nonindigenous jurists and other national citizens face the question of whether commercial cultures are incompatible with the image of distinctive traditional cultures and whether they are incompatible with other capital ventures hinged to traditional cultural forms, such as cultural tourism, ecotourism, and New Age tourism. (Wadeye bark and canvas paintings are auctioned at Sotheby's in Melbourne for thousands of dollars and can now be perused on the Web.[3]) In these uneven cultural fields how do jurists and other nonindigenous citizens discern a real indigenous subject from a "more or less" diluted subject? Is it sufficient for indigenous persons to assert that they know customary beliefs or must they demonstrate some internal dispositional allegiance to that belief? How does one calibrate an internal disposition? Does Betty Bilawag's panic, her seeming concern first and foremost for the lifetime of the Dreamtime, indicate an internal disposition truer to a traditional outlook than that of her younger family members, no matter what they might say? Does her panic place her closer to traditional nonsettler values? The possibility of entertaining this thought has real material and social consequences in the law of recognition.

But the problem of cultural difference is not merely whether commercial cultures are incompatible within legal and other commercial imaginaries or whether an assertion can be distinguished from a dispositional allegiance. It is also a question of whether they are incompatible with personal and public senses of the moral and the criminal. From this perspective new questions surface. On what basis does a practice or belief switch from being an instance of cultural difference to being repugnant culture? How does one calibrate differences across cultural distinctions in order to decide what counts as evidence of continuing culture as opposed to what counts as evidence of criminal conduct?

No less than Bilawag, nonindigenous liberal Australians are confronted with a set of historically variable and seemingly irresolvable obligations. Settler Australians face a central irresolvable tension in the simultaneous obligation to public reason and moral sense; in a multicultural context, to value diversity and to repudiate immorality, to understand the practices of another person or group and to accept them as viable neighbors. In other words, the generative power of liberal forms of recognition derives not merely from the performative difficulties of recognition but also from something that sociologists and philosophers have called moral sensibility, of the social fact of the feeling of *being obliged,* of finding oneself under an obligation to some thing —

or to a complex of things. A person might find herself or himself obliged to a feeling, a practice, a person, or an idea. In this book, I am especially interested in moments in which persons find themselves simultaneously obliged to their moral sense and to reason, especially instances in which the two are not reconciled, and in the new social imaginaries and formations that unfold from these moments. Betty Bilawag, for instance, found herself obliged to the Dreaming inspite of the socioeconomic sense of the mineral exploration or any reason that might arise from public debate. In chapter 3 I discuss instances in which administrators in northern Australia in the 1930s and 40s found themselves opposing federal policy on "tribal customs," not because they did not understand its economic or political rational but because they thought it violated their *sense* of decency. They knew they ought to oppose federal policy, although if asked why they might not say much more than "because it is the right thing to do." In moments like this, persons face most starkly the fact that following one law means violating another. They discover that their reasoning and their affect are out of joint: I should be tolerant but you make me sick; I understand your reasoning but I am deeply offended by your presence.

The experience of what analytic philosophers describe as deep epistemological and deontological differences may well create irresolvable cleavages, not simply between two social groups but within one of them which, prior to encountering radical alterity, was tacitly accepted and experienced as a collectivity. For instance, the intimate "We" of the national "We the People" can come precariously close to being refashioned as a collection of strangers who turn not toward but away from each other in the neighborhood of radical alterity. "We" identifications are refashioned as third-person attributions: they, them; their ways, moralities, and cultures; their liberal or conservative prejudices. National subjects find that no matter the heroic rhetoric of enlightenment understanding, "their ways" cannot cease to make "us" sick. And this sickness scatters the self (I, us) across contrasting obligations to public reason and moral sensibility. It is this cauldron of competing social impulses that interests me, because of the way it generates new ethics and metaethics of national and international social life.

LIBERAL DIASPORAS

In this volume I critically examine Australian liberal multiculturalism as an ideology and practice of governance, a form of everyday affective association and identification, and a specific discursive incitement across the variegated contexts of national and transnational life. I do not comment on Australian multiculturalism in a general way, but rather only in the specific way it emerges in the neighborhood of indigenous subjects and societies.[4] And I am interested in a very particular legacy and moment of "liberalism" within what I call the liberal diaspora. By liberal diaspora I mean to gesture at the colonial and postcolonial subjective, institutional, and discursive identifications, dispersions, and elaborations of the enlightenment idea that society should be organized on the basis of rational mutual understanding.[5]

To understand how liberal discourses and identifications are elaborated in colonial and postcolonial worlds, I think it is important to differentiate postcolonial struggles from multicultural ones.[6] Frantz Fanon and members of the school of Subaltern Studies have suggested how colonial domination worked by inspiring in colonized subjects a desire to identify with their colonizers.[7] The Australian example suggests that multicultural domination seems to work, in contrast, by inspiring subaltern and minority subjects to identify with the impossible object of an authentic self-identity; in the case of indigenous Australians, a domesticated nonconflictual "traditional" form of sociality and (inter)subjectivity. As the nation stretches out its hands to ancient Aboriginal laws (as long as they are not "repugnant"), indigenous subjects are called on to perform an authentic difference in exchange for the good feelings of the nation and the reparative legislation of the state. But this call does not simply produce good theater, rather it inspires impossible desires: *to be* this impossible object and to transport its ancient prenational meanings and practices to the present in *whatever* language and moral framework prevails *at the time of enunciation.*

Although on the one hand I am interested in liberal forms of multiculturalism as a form of domination, I am also interested in these forms both as a response to previous discursive impasses of national life and as a place within which minority and subaltern subjects creatively elaborate new social imaginaries. In this way this book is a partial story, as stories and analyses always are. In it I try to understand how a discursive, affective, and institutional calculus of citizenship and nationalism — the liberal aspiration for a rational nonviolent form of association based on competing knowledges and moral values — is intercalated in legal, public, and state assessments of indigenous claims for material compensation for colonial harms. I am especially interested in these issues as they occur in land and native title claims and in public assessments of state-based indigenous welfare programs and benefits.

At the book's core, then, I attempt to analyze critically a liberal aspiration for a critical rational foundation to national and transnational cultural hermeneutics. I try to understand what this aspiration is — its immanence in real-time "multicultural" social life — and how it acts as a social ethics and social technology for distributing the rights and goods, harms and failures, of liberal capital democracies, and for making sense of who and what ought to be held responsible for the successes and failures of these personal and national dreams. As I do so, I try to understand, on the one hand, how the real hopes and optimisms invested in a particular form of national association — liberal multiculturalism — divert social energy from other political and social forms and imaginaries; how they make certain violences appear accidental to a social system rather than generated by it; and, most important, how they attribute and distribute failures arising from a social system to conflicts between social systems. And I try to understand, on the other hand, how indigenous subjects creatively engage the specific logic of liberal multiculturalism.

Long ago I was humbled by the task of capturing analytically or sociologically the stakes on indigenous life of something so seemingly vague and ephemeral as an aspiration. What model of the social could concretely capture and demonstrate the social effect of this aspiration on Bilawag and her family and on indigenous politics and public assessments and national economies and social poverty? What could demonstrate the response of her and her ancestors to these changing aspirations? Moreover, I worried that something very unusual, hardly representative, might be happening along the northwest coast stretching south from Darwin, in the Northern Territory, to Wadeye, near the Western Australian border, where I had been working year in and year out since 1984. Several important land claims had been given hearings throughout the 1970s, 80s, and 90s. The unusual nature of one, the Kenbi Land Claim (which covered lands on the peninsula just across the Darwin Harbor), was hardly reassuring. To date it has been heard twice and has generated four often-competing indigenous claimant groups, each with their own legal and anthropological counsel. The case concerns the limits of historical transformation in the context of legally mandated customary continuity. Here is an example of how indigenous people critically and creatively engaged the often brutal history of a liberal diaspora, elaborating local imaginaries and translocal economic, political, and social facts, only to meet the law of recognition that places a limit on exactly this type of creativity.

Perhaps only this context would have motivated local indigenous people to speculate that the failure of the claim was the result of their failure to have

and hold onto their "traditional culture" after 120 years of often brutal colonization. Maybe only this particular scene would elevate to sociological significance the impossible demand placed on these and other indigenous people:
namely, that they desire and identify with their cultural traditions in a way
that just so happens, in an uncanny convergence of interests, to fit the national
and legal imaginary of multiculturalism; that they at once orient their sensual, emotional, and corporeal identities toward the nation's and law's image
of traditional cultural forms and national reconciliation and at the same time
ghost this *being for* the nation so as not to have their desires for some economic
certainty in their lives appear opportunistic.[8]

To understand the social sources of these social conditions I began looking
for whatever signposts I encountered along the way. One was found in liberal accounts of obligation. This much seems certain: a range of obligations
strike people throughout the course of their lives in a variety of social settings. Statements invoking obligation address different persons and scales of
personhood: first person, second person, third person (I, we, you, she, he, it);
Everyone or Manyone or Someone. And these obligations encompass a wide
range of social values from justice to cleanliness, and rituals from formal to
informal. Philosophers and sociologists working in the legacy of the Enlightenment have been occupied by the striking nature of obligation — the force
with which an obligation imposes itself on one — and the seeming differences
among the feelings of obligation (of being obliged to something or to someone), the justifications provided for abiding by this or that obligation, and
the procedures for reaching shared understandings. One set of obligations
in particular have exercised western scholars: the seemingly unconditional
nature of ethical and moral obligations and its relation to the enlightenment
obligation to public reason (critical rational discourse).

One can immediately see why this domain of obligation would be so interesting to philosophers and sociologists confronting the question of social and
cultural difference in postcolonial and multicultural contexts and yet be so
difficult for them to resolve analytically. Although reason and moral sensibility are often said to coincide in the last instance, moral obligation becomes
philosophically and sociologically interesting exactly where it seems to differ
from reason — or is strained to the point of extreme tautology. Why . . . Because . . . Why. When people have moral obligations, they seem to have them
independent of the way they arrive at critical rational conclusions. People
seem to be had by them rather than to have them. In the procedural ideal of
critical rational discourse, reasoned public debate occurs prior to a judgment

(judgment is a posteriori to public reason). But moral sensibility works as an a priori type of "knowledge." People feel like they know what is morally right prior to arguments concerning why; they might subsequently change their minds after a long talk, but they know first. Kant was not the only person to be bothered by this. The deconstructive philosopher John Caputo puts the outrage of obligation this way: "I know that I am under an obligation, that the call is received, that I am laid claim to." But if you pressed me for an answer why I am obliged "I will develop a serious cough and ask to be excused."[9]

All this gets a little complicated, especially when liberal obligations to moral sensibility and critical rational discourse are examined as discursively constituted social facts. We do well to remember that "rational critical discourse" and "moral sensibility" are discursive characterizations not presocial facts. On the one hand, rational critical discourse refers to and describes a procedure of interaction (that is, how one should do this thing called rational critical discourse in the process of stating what it is), and is itself a metadiscursive characterization of a social interaction—namely, what type of talk (rational, self-reflective) counts as an instance of public reason. People may well disagree whether or not an exchange should be characterized as critical rational, public, reasoned, or reasonable. In any case, this form of talk and the characterization and valuation of this form of talk arose historically. On the other hand, moral sensibility refers to and characterizes a form of knowing, often described as moral intuition or embodied insight. Other societies have, however, characterized this form of social insight in other ways, perhaps as evidence of the divine working through the human, or a moment of revelation. Given this minor historiography, note that although both moral reason and public reason are metadiscursive characterizations, each also refers to a different aspect of social life. Rational critical discourse refers to a type of talk, so it is a form of language used to refer to an instance of language. But moral feeling, or moral sensibility, refers to a social phenomenon outside or other than discourse—even though, technically, it may be a form of inference. And insofar as it refers to something other than itself, what moral sensibility "is" is always in excess of what enunciates it and what is enunciated.

There is nothing intrinsically anthropologically interesting or socially problematic about this difference between moral sensibility (deontology) and critical rational knowledge (epistemology). The difference between moral sensibility/feeling and rational critical discourse could be and is viewed with indifference in many cultural contexts. The difference is interesting only and exactly because of the way it works as a generative impasse in liberal discourses about and institutions of cultural recognition. A core obligation of liberalism is to decide public matters on the basis of autonomous, reasonable, and rational subjects ("private persons") bracketing the social differences that exist among themselves and presenting to their fellow citizens the most robust, true, sincere, and legitimate argument they can muster. And yet moral obligation proper is otherwise in nature than this obligation to reason. Moral obligation—moral sensibility—is exactly where critical rationality is not.

Seemingly far afield, the American pragmatist Charles Sanders Peirce's understanding of the inference of "perceptual judgment" gestures at the intractability that obligations present to critical social practice—especially that aspect of critical social theory addressing the liberal aspiration to ground national and transnational cultural hermenuetics in the procedures of critical rational discourse—even as it points to the horizon where public and moral reason converge. In "The Three Normative Sciences," Peirce presents, as an example of perceptual judgment (also called "extreme abduction"), Legendre's proof that if a line abuts upon an ordinary point of another line, thereby forming two angles ∠, then the sum of the two angles is equal to the sum of two right angles. This can be shown by drawing a perpendicular line at the point of abutment. This perpendicular will always fall within one or the other angles ∠. Peirce focuses on the transparent truth of this fact, noting that, although we only ever see a specific case of this argument, "the pupil is suppose to *see* that . . . it will be so in any case."[10] Even leaving aside the ninety degrees, we see that the perpendicular will always fall within one or the other angle. This is a "truth" whose self-evidence is guaranteed by the visual field. What separates such instances of extreme abduction from ordinary abduction is the fact that, in Peirce's words, the former feels like "a judgment absolutely forced upon my acceptance and that by a process I am utterly unable to control and consequently am unable to criticize."[11] Sense certainty: where else would the perpendicular fall if not within one or the other angle in two-dimensional space? How could it be otherwise?

Here we see that moral sensibility is, in fact, the experience of the inference of perceptual judgment. And if this is so, then moral reason is as liable to refiguration in social history as is public reason; indeed, all perceptual judgments are. Even the once self-evident universal application of Euclidean geometry was displaced in non-Euclidean space. In another possible world, parallelism suddenly looked very different. And so we are led to wonder what allowed anyone to imagine this other possible world and thereby disrupt the visual guarantee of this actual world. What introduces irritation and doubt about an object of knowledge or a practice or a sense of morality, their status, self-evidence, and value as true without reserve? What allows anyone to value such critical irritation — what Peirce called "critical common sense" — in what contexts; and to wonder, in the form of a second-order abstraction, whether this critical gesture is *going* anywhere; whether it is *going* in any sense other than figuration and refiguration, subject to social struggle, but not oriented toward anything.[12] Does some "culture" own the critical spirit? Does one historical people or conversation have a type of world historical courage for critique without reserve? These questions are, at bottom, what critical social theorists of the liberal enlightenment have asked, from Kant to Marx to Gramsci, and Luxemburg to Du Bois to Spivak to Agamben and their conservative counterparts, Huntington, Fukuyama, and Bloom.

For Peirce, there was movement and direction in reason. It headed toward truth, with "truth" understood as a real fact corresponding to a proposition, a final interpretant at the end of a long asymptotic curve of reasoned inquiry stimulated by the irritation of doubt. Even if reason never did reach truth, man still needed the notion of truth — the experience of the inference of extreme abduction — in order to continue to search for better understandings. The notion of a truth incited, guided, and soothed man. Peirce also thought that particular forms of society provided the conditions of possibility for the arrival of particular forms of doubt and irritation — not for critique in general but for specific forms and modalities of critique. And I agree to this extent — social institutions and relations incite or mitigate against thinking particular modes of otherwise. They influence whether and when critical thought takes place. For those places where it cannot take place in liberal and illiberal societies, courage, indeed, is necessary to think and live otherwise in contexts that indicate the risk of being various forms of otherwise. The celebratory rhetoric of liberal multiculturalism rests on the grounds that this social form provides the social conditions (discursive, institutional, [inter]subjective) for diminishing the heroics of critique; that it makes thinking otherwise safe for liberal democracies — indeed, gives democracy its unique social vitality. Some go so far as to claim for liberalism an ownership of a universal form of critique in the proceduralism of liberal public reason.[13]

And yet in liberal multicultural democracies, subjects still experience certain truths as self-evident and undeniable, and certain ways of thinking, let alone acting, as dangerous and unreliable. Moreover, subjects who consider themselves to be liberals often hold onto their moral intuitions even when their historical knowledge tells them that these truths are not likely to hold.

11

As I elaborate in chapter 4, an invisible asterisk, a proviso, hovers above every enunciation of indigenous customary law: "(provided [they] . . . are not so repugnant)." This proviso interprets specific instances of cultural practices and indexes where public reason no longer applies. For instance, although Australian law might demand "real acknowledgement of traditional law and real observance of traditional customs" as the basis for a successful native title claim, *real* customary being must be free of any sense of a repugnant that would "shatter the skeletal structure" of state law; that is, provoke an affective relation to a cultural or social otherwise, an experience of fundamental alterity. But national jurists and subjects are not exempt from the very problem posed to Aboriginal subjects: the dilemma of capturing real justice in real discourse and narrative time without prompting the appearance of the same interpretant hovering over judgments of native title, criminal law, or public morality. This judgment is just (unless [although] . . . it may appear retrospectively as repugnant or shameful). Australian history is littered with instances in which a moral sensibility of just action was retrospectively seen as a merely prejudicial reaction. In recent years, the Australian public sphere has loudly lamented this mistaken moral sensibility in a number of cases, most recently that of the Stolen Generation (which I discuss below and at more length in chapter 1). The social implication of this double session of institutionally mediated knowing is clear, and it is perhaps nowhere more clear and seriously encountered than in the context of multicultural pronouncements on the limits of tolerance in liberal society.

This may seem a very strange way to get to a simple point about liberal settler forms of multiculturalism. But it raises, in a particularly visceral fashion, important questions for the stance critical theory should take toward certain liberal social institutional phenomena and regulatory ideals, certainly for how the distinction between the true and the inconceivable (which I rely on) opens itself to being read. And it raises important questions for how we approach the ways people actually experience the regulatory ideals of liberal life. How do we, and why would we, critically engage a seemingly irreducible good and truth — the liberal regulatory ideal of decreased harm through increased mutual understanding of social and cultural differences? Of a liberal aspiration for a world where conflict does not exist across epistemic and deontic communities? We could ask whether this is *actually* the aspiration of liberal multiculturalism or whether this is how people actually experience this aspiration — two questions that greatly interest me — but this is to ask something different from whether there is a point to criticizing it. To ask if we should critique these ideals is to allow for the possibility of conceptualizing the institutional, discursive, and subjective conditions of liberalism outside its own terms. It is to allow for the possibility that liberalism is harmful not only when it fails to live up to its ideals, but when it approaches them.

Let me turn to a book by Michael Walzer (who has thought long and hard about liberal political forms) to clarify what is at stake in asking these questions and in the models we develop to answer them. *On Toleration* (1997) reminds us of a certain set of commonplaces among liberal political theorists: that all liberals acknowledge that "we choose within limits"; that few would ever be so daring as to advance "an unconstrained relativism"; and that not every act should be tolerated.[14] Having said this, Walzer does what theorists of liberal pluralism, multiculturalism, and diasporic nationalism often do, he urges readers to set aside the intractable problems facing national and international life—both within liberalism and across liberal and nonliberal societies—and concentrate instead on the levels and types of disagreement that can be resolved without physical violence. Begin with the doable.

The trouble with this tactic is that in actual social worlds those who consider themselves to be liberal are confronted with instances of intractable social differences that they do not set aside—that they do not feel they can or should set aside. They encounter instances of what they experience as moments of fundamental and uncanny alterity: encounters with differences they consider abhorrent, inhuman, and bestial, or with differences they consider too hauntingly similar to themselves to warrant social entitlements—for example, land claims by indigenous people who dress, act, and sound like the suburban neighbors they are. Moments in which subjects are prompted to calibrate the forms and modes of difference confronting them occur in large and small scales, in political and intimate settings; they startle and are long-expected. Courts dismiss the juridical viability of these moments. Governments and public spokespersons denounce them as the limits of good law and good society in a multicultural framework. More important, these moments are not moments at all, but somebody's life. They mark the site where indigenous persons struggle to inhabit the tensions and torsions of competing incitements to *be* and to *identify* differentially. And I mean incitements. Difference does not simply exist out there in nonliberal beliefs and practices. Particular people and communities are also called on to perform particular types of liberal and nonliberal differences for a variety of other persons and communities, be they tourist attraction, ceremonial man, or bush-tucker guide.

Rather than setting aside the intractable, I have decided to give attention to these moments of seemingly irresolvable liberal judgments and indigenous struggles in order to understand their generative social force. In this volume I am particularly interested in a specific nonpassage between discursively and morally grounded ideologies of justice. My discussion is centered on social encounters in which a judgment about what constitutes a viable neighbor is experienced as moral irrespective of its "reasoned" grounds or institutional supports. I seek to understand how this experience is subjectively, textually, and institutionally mediated in the given time of constitutional liberal democracies, and how this ideological and experiential nonpassage — rather than dilemma or contradiction — is deferred rather than resolved into a new national ideological formation — namely, multiculturalism.

I ask: What minimal analytical foundations are necessary for an examination of the social consequences of liberal ethics and anxieties, of the unresolved and irreducible tensions within liberal national settler institutions and ideologies? How do these exact moments — too much and too little difference in indigenous Australia — generate new local and national discursive, affective, and institutional forms and incitements across diverse social fields? How do indigenous persons and communities struggle within and across these discursive, subjective, and institutional fields? At what point does the indigenous become dangerous rather than good to think?[15] Building up from these questions is a second-order series of inquiries; namely, how do these intractable moments form high-order social discourses, social programs, law, and cultural programming?

The critical study of liberal diaspora I propose is not interested in simple critiques of "liberalism," which often move quickly past the complexity of liberal traditions as they have evolved in the context of political struggles within Western, colonial, and postcolonial contexts. Numerous scholars have shown that as emergent social forms and practices were diverted to liberal forms and practices, liberalism itself was dilated and transformed often in strikingly inconsistent ways. One of the great persuasions of liberalism has been its seeming openness, its voracious encompassment. And this is not merely a false front. Liberals do actually value certain forms of thinking and being otherwise, annd it wants to supercede all others in order to be the end of history. The aim of public reason seems to be to achieve this end through a nonviolent convergence of minds and hearts. The trouble is that this is not true without reserve. As I hope to demonstrate, in certain contexts the aim of public reason is not to understand, let alone agree, but rather to sequester some often inexpressible felt-thing from reflexive judgment. Under this procedural principle, public debate "ought" to (or in the stronger ethical form, "must") give way to a collective moral sense, and not only that public debate must give way but that collective moral sense should be protected from the procedures of critical reason. What is considered exemplary of collective morality may be open to public debate or private conscience. My point here is simply that the ideal still formally holds. The algebra of this principle would look like this: $\exists x\,\overline{(\text{Public Reason})}x$.

Let me turn to the representation of procedural reason in an episode of the American television drama *Law and Order* in order to concretize this point. In "God Bless the Child" (22 October 1991), the ailing child of members of a thinly disguised sect of the Church of Christ, Scientist dies because her parents, believing in the healing power of prayer, refuse all medical intervention. The police are faced with the question of whether or not to prosecute the parents for manslaughter. The episode discusses at length whether doubt — a crisis of faith in times of emergency — opens religious belief to legal prosecution. If the parents doubted their faith, but nevertheless withheld medical aid, was the action constitutionally protected in the space of doubt? At the end of the episode, the leader of the church is in the witness stand. In reply to a critical question about church practices posed by the prosecutor, the church leader reminds viewers of the U.S. constitutional separation of church and state so fundamental to liberal democratic proceduralism. The prosecutor has the last word in this exchange, retorting with a set of questions: If child abuse were a religious belief held by some people, should the state stand aside and let the children be abused? If the handling of snakes by children were a religious belief that some people held, should the state stand by? In these statements viewers might hear not-so-veiled references to David Koresh and Appalachian snake handlers.

So why isn't this part of the minor pedagogy of liberal democratic proceduralism? Liberal theorists might hear, and rightfully point to, the prosecutor's conformity to the proceduralism of public reason, opening belief to reasoned and rational argument and placing justification in actual and possible worlds of practice. But this surely would misinterpret the communicative event. These questions are not to be answered (the judge has the last word, ruling the prosecutor's questions "out of bounds"). The questions are performative marks of the line past which the procedures of public reason should not tread, the Pandora's box opened by not heeding our perceptual judgments in moral domains. These performatives issue intolerance in the form of a question, but a question that teaches audiences how to stage the internal limit of liberal tolerance as a reasonable openness to a very open and shut case. When in doubt, drop the bar until critical abduction turns to extreme abduction and your opponent breaks her back (see also *Law and Order*'s episodes "Ritual," 17 December 1998, and "Disciple," 24 February 1999).

Broad characterizations of liberalism, humanism, and modernity fail to capture the complexity of this historical terrain of social and political worlds. They miss the jobs done by minor emotions and discourses such as doubt and irritation and failures of faith and exhaustion in liberal discursive formations — and these are jobs they indeed do. They authorize, authenticate, and guarantee Truth in liberal regimes of critical rational reflection. They indicate that reflexive judgment has commenced, allowing subjects to feel engaged in a social process labeled "justice" and to feel that such mass subject-projections like the nation, the public, and the state are equally engaged. These feelings of moral right provide an excess "reason" beyond the procedures of public reason itself that supports and advances whatever justificatory framework is provided. These feelings superanimate the self-evidence of the justification itself by creating the sense of a "beyond itself."

Far from dismissing the optimisms and aspirations captured in the form of Australian multiculturalism, far from viewing the diverse set of social persons discussed in this book as in silent alliance with the leaders of a grand historical conspiracy, far from casting personal and public crises of identity, tolerance, and material restitution as mere performative maskings, I propose that we only approach a true understanding of liberal forms of multiculturalism by inching ever nearer to the good intentions that subjects have, hold, and cherish and to the role these intentions play in solidifying the self-evident good of liberal institutions and procedures. Many Australians truly desire that indigenous subjects be treated considerately, justly, and with respect, publicly, juridically, and personally. They truly desire a form of society in which all people can have exactly what they want . . . if they deserve it. They do not feel good when they feel responsible for social conflict, pain, or trauma. This is, after all, a fantasy of liberal capitalist society too simply put: convulsive competition purged of real conflict, social difference without social consequences. To provide a sensorium of cultural competition and difference without subjecting the liberal subjects to the consuming winds of social conflict — no more or less is asked of the indigenous subject, the subaltern subject, the minority subject.

In sum, in this book I suggest that before we can develop a "critical theory of recognition," or a politics of distribution and capabilities, we need to understand better the cunning of recognition; its intercalation of the politics of culture with the culture of capital.[16] We need to puzzle over a simple question: What is the nation recognizing, capital commodifying, and the court trying to save from the breach of history when difference is recognized? If Charles Taylor's politics of recognition takes inspiration from Herderian and post-Hegelian notions of recognition, this analysis of the cunning of recognition draws inspiration from Hegel's dark account of reason found in *The Philosophy of History*. In Hegel's hands the cunning of reason was revealed at the same time its brutality was exposed. In this spirit, I ask how late liberal ideology works through the passions of recognition, tries to develop its worth without subjecting itself to the throes of contestation and opposition. I ask how national pageants of shameful repentance and celebrations of a new recognition of subaltern worth remain inflected by the conditional (as long as they are not repugnant; that is, as long as they are not, at heart, not-us and as long as real economic resources are not at stake). I think we should refuse to concede that the answer to the aporias of liberalism is, in the first or last instance, to extend liberalism in ever more radical modes of democracy, but rather we should pause and wonder what it is we are disseminating in actual rather than mere philosophical worlds. Let us look at what various forms of liberalism do rather than decide to be for or against them in their abstraction.

Australia seems an ideal place to examine the generation of a new national metaethics around multiculturalism, both because of the depth of its commitment to this national form and because of the relative rapidity in which it has adopted it. Take Betty Bilawag, for example. Over the course of her lifetime she has witnessed settler Australians shoot her extended family for sport and economic gain, public and state repression of ritual; and national celebrations of Aboriginal culture and regret for past harms.

BANANA REPUBLICS

Much earlier than in the United States, and in response to very different geopolitical conditions, Australian nationalism came to mean something other than descent from the convict, ruling, or immigrant classes who arrived from Britain and western Europe. And more firmly and publicly than the United States and Europe, to varying degrees the various political parties of the Australian state claim to have renounced the ideal of "a unitary culture and tradition" and, instead, now recognizes the value and worth of "cultural diversity within, . . . as the basis of . . . a more differentiated mode of national cohesion."[17] Australian state officials represent themselves and the nation as subjects shamed by past imperial, colonial, and racist attitudes that are now understood as having, in their words, constituted the "darkest aspect" of the nation's history and impaired its social and economic future. Multiculturalism is represented as the externalized political testament to the nation's aversion to its past misdeeds, and to its recovered good intentions.

In short, rather than just some general acknowledgment of shameful past wrongdoings and some limited tolerance of present cultural differences, Australia has putatively sought a more radical basis of national unity. In state and public discourse, the Australian nation aspires to be "truly multicultural." Official spokespersons claim that multiculturalism is an assemblage of the diverse and proliferating social identities and communities now composing the nation's internal population, with no one social position or group's views serving as an oppressive grounding discourse. Cleansed by a collective moment of shame and reconciliation, the nation will not only be liberated into good feelings and institutions but also acquire the economic and social productivity necessary to political and economic hegemony in the Asia-Pacific region—or, at least, to keep the nation from falling further and further behind its northern neighbors.

It was as part of this history that on 14 May 1986, Paul Keating, then treasurer in the Labour Party government of Prime Minister Hawke, described Australia to Australians as a fledging "banana republic."[18] Although an economist, not a Deleuzian, by training, Keating nevertheless acted as if he sought to bend "the outside" inward "through a series of practical exercises"—speech acts, economic policies, and labor practices—in order to reformulate Australian subjectivity along a rationalized spatial economy.[19] He saw this realignment of national identity as a prerequisite to the nation's economic productivity and thus to its social well-being, in the conditions of advanced global capital. Keating was, however, simply eloquently and passionately engaged in Labour's more general campaign to make the Australian public literate in economic rationalism: how "culture(s) and identity (or, better, the processes through which they are formed)" are a "resisting 'environment' of the economic system that has to be made more economically 'rational' and 'productive.' "[20]

Nearly ten years later, as prime minister, Keating proclaimed on national TV: "I am Asian," thereby replacing the banana republic image with a new mapping of Australia in the world to shake what he saw as those national fantasies and complacencies that affected economic growth. Keating's cartographical imaginary aimed to provoke Australians to consider the profits available to them if they would understand their identities and identifications to be flexible and strategic and dislodge questions of ontology from essentialized corporeal and historical grounds. But in reiterating Australian ethnic identity while locating it in Asia, Keating repeated the very assumptions his metaphor was suppose to shake. The addressee of Keating's comments remained, *like* Keating, a loosely defined Anglo-Celtic forced to think of his or her "whiteness" at a double economic margin — at the margin of Europe and the United States and at the margin of the Asia-Pacific.

Social and political-economic conditions in these margins have undergone significant transformations since the emergence of the East Asian so-called miracle economies in the 1960s and 70s and their sudden collapse and revitalization in the late 1990s. Because of these transformations, Keating had good reason to be passionate about the nation and the future of its citizens. He spoke at a moment when Australians already were experiencing a crisis of identity, if not yet a "crisis of authority," owing to significant global, state, and capital realignments.[21]

For the first sixty-odd years of Australian federation, the nation had "the highest living standards and the most equal distribution of income in all the 'developed' nations," primarily as the result of the Labour Accord (the state's direct control over wages, industrial relations, and tariffs).[22] But this economic stability was also a result of Australia's long-standing trading partnership with England, in which Australia provided the primary materials for British industry and imported from Britain manufactured and consumer goods and received capital investment. Most Anglo-Celtic Australians, indeed, were living the good life, beachside and basking in the glow of a well-functioning state and economy. Citizens could, for a while, imagine themselves living in a "lucky country," if they forgot about the indigenous people interned in disease-stricken detention camps in the far north and west of the nation and the Asian laborers and businesspersons suffering from a racialized nationalism.[23] The everyday conditions of these unlucky others did not often puncture public representations in which Australians felt good about themselves, their future, their national self-understanding as a white nation advancing western humanism in the Asia-Pacific.[24]

The Australian standard of living began to change significantly in the early 1970s when England, after a period of economic instability, integrated more tightly into the EEC, leaving Australia bereft of its major historical trading partner. Battered about by a number of global economic crises, the Australian state and business expanded long-standing trading patterns with the so-called miracle economies of the Asia-Pacific, most importantly with Japan.[25] But even as Australia changed economic partners, its economic profile remained remarkably stable. Japan was in need of industrial raw materials and Australia remained in need of capital investment and manufactured and durable consumer goods.

Yet, Australian business leaders discovered that the global conditions of capital had changed by the time they refigured their trading partners. The Asia-Pacific was not simply a new site of capital accumulation but an innovator in new forms of social and capital organization. Japanese businesses, in particular, developed novel production techniques as firms "rationalized" their manufacturing operations by establishing multilayered subcontracting systems and by relocating production facilities to geographical areas unaccustomed to Fordist wage and consumption standards.[26] Subcontracting firms and production facilities increasingly transgressed national borders, leading not only to Japanese economic dominance in the region but to the formation of an interdependent, if not an integrated, Asia-Pacific political economy— the creation of dense linkages among the organization of modes and sites of production, consumer patterns, and material extraction and manufacturing. And while Japan's Southeast Asian trading partners nursed lingering suspicions about the possible emergence of a new Japanese imperialism in the area, a regional bloc nevertheless began to congeal and harden by the middle of the 1970s.

As a result of these changing capital formations, Australia began to face "mounting economic challenges due to falling commodity prices, rising debt burden, and inefficient and uncompetitive industries."[27] The nation was becoming "Latin Americanized."[28] In every financial quarter, it seemed, the national economy shrunk relative to the emerging so-called flying geese of the Asia-Pacific. Jobs were harder to find, although the Labour Accord kept the minimum wage high. Whole generations of Anglo-Celtics, "our kids," were on the dole or on the dole roller coaster. In the midst of this economic downturn, the mass media ran story after story of Asian capitalists buying up choice Australian real estate, along with descriptions of the lifestyles of the new Asian millionaires, and of the "Asian" social and cultural values putatively at the basis of the Asian miracle economies.[29] The mass media rarely discussed the underside of capital transformations, although it did cover the occasional collapsing building and environmental disaster in Malaysia and Indonesia.

What the Australian mainstream media foregrounded were the cultural differences separating Australian and Asian societies, typically Australia's commitment to a notion of universal human rights, rights that appeared to be threatened by these new forms of the economic good. Western humanism's fragility and defensiveness at the double margin of Asia-Pacific and Euro-American hegemony is suggested by the newspaper headlines that greeted my arrival in Sydney on 18 September 1996. In front-page stories, both the *Sydney Morning Herald* and *The Australian* reported that in a speech in Jakarta, Liberal prime minister John Howard defended the Europeanness of Australian nationalism: "We are immensely proud of our distinctive culture, our distinctive history, and our distinctive traditions, and we yield to nobody in asserting their great quality and enduring value."[30] Three years later Howard would oppose the republican movement that sought to divest the state from its formal ties with the British Commonwealth, replacing the Crown with an elected head of state.

The mainstream media weighed these cultural issues against the economic, social, and political profits that might accrue to Australians if they thought of themselves spatially, from a bird's-eye view as a point on the globe, rather than primarily historically, as descended and therefore essentially *being* from another point on the globe. Although Australia may have needed the strong economies of Asia, did the identification with Asia, or as Asians, cross the discursively thin line preserving European culture and its political and social institutions at the nation's core? At what cost would Australians maintain or erase these social and cultural differences and traditions? And, finally, no matter the political-economic sense that his statement might have made, did statements like Keating's "I am Asian" — or, later, an event like the republican movement — constitute a form of race betrayal for those in the nation who still worried whether they would be swamped both by Asian immigration and economic power? Or was it an index of the maturing confidence of Australian nationalism? Rather than a unified stance and a monological voicing of the meaning of multiculturalism, Australian political parties and the public evoke the contestorial field often hidden under this national ideology.

Australia's historical and economic relationship to Asia provided one side of a double margin between which a multicultural national imaginary was to be constructed. On the other side lay indigenous people. As I note in more detail in chapter 3, the 1901 Commonwealth Constitution, which set up the Australian federation government and formally founded the Australian nation, mentions Aboriginal persons in just two places: section 51 (26), which excluded people of the "Aboriginal race" from the special race power of the Commonwealth government; and section 127, which excluded "aboriginal natives" from being counted in the census. Under the 1901 Constitution, states retained the right to formulate their own policies regarding Aboriginal persons within their territories, including the ability to pass legislation excluding them from the franchise; something most states did.[31] Although considered de facto British subjects, most persons classified as "aboriginal natives" were not afforded full citizenship rights in the new Australian nation.[32]

In 1911, a year after the Commonwealth assumed governance of the Northern Territory from South Australia, the Aboriginal Ordinance further eroded the social autonomy of "Aboriginal natives" in the north through the office of Chief Protector of Aborigines. The act granted the Chief Protector authority over Aboriginal employment, movement, marriage, and social intercourse; and it gave the position power as the "legal guardian of every Aboriginal and part-Aboriginal child under the age of eighteen years."[33] It was under this act that between 1910 and 1970, 10 to 30 percent of children of mixed parentage were taken away from their Aboriginal parents — a group that would later become known as the Stolen Generation.[34] Within a few years of the passage of the Northern Territory Welfare Act, 1953, 80 percent of the indigenous population had been declared wards of the state, which they remained until 1963, the year Martin Luther King Jr. led a civil rights protest march on Washington, D.C.[35] It was not until 1962, in the face of persistent, organized, national and international criticism from indigenous activists such as Bobby Sykes and Charles Perkins, as well as nonindigenous groups, that "aboriginal natives" were allowed to vote in federal, Northern Territory, and South Australian elections (Queensland did not follow until 1965).[36] The rise of Aboriginal activism in the 1960s coincided with a more general global phenomenon in which progressive politics splintered into class-based, colonial, and new social movements. In Australia, indigenous and colonial consciousness was raised and deepened by that state's involvement in the Vietnam War.

At the same time that markets in the Asia-Pacific were being restructured from the 1970s through the early 1990s, the state began to shift financial and social resources into Aboriginal communities in response to a national and transnational indigenous liberation movement. This movement highlighted the disjunction between the ideal image of the state as a postimperial exemplar of Western humanism in the region and the actual brutality of the its laissez-faire stance toward its own internal colonial subjects. This would continue to be a problem at the turn of the century. In 1999, after the Howard government

FIGURE 1. "Mr. Howard What Happen with the 'Aborigines'?" (Photograph by AP/Bullit Marquez, *Sydney Morning Herald,* 21 September 1999, p. 12.)

committed ground troops to East Timor, Australian newspapers ran pictures of Indonesian protest banners that read "Mr. Howard What Happened with the 'Aborigines'?"[37] Similar reactions were broadcast during the coup in Fiji in 2000 and after John Howard threatened to withdraw from the U.N. committee system because of criticism by the UN Committee on the Elimination of Racial Discrimination on mandatory sentencing laws in Western Australia and the Northern Territory.

By the mid-1980s indigenous culture and politics had gained a public luminosity, political legitimacy, and economic base unparalleled in Australian history. Almost ten years had passed since the first Commonwealth land rights legislation had been enacted with the Aboriginal Land Rights (Northern Territory) Act, 1976, spawning similar, if less effective, copies in most states and giving indigenous communities, activists, and publics access to capital and bureaucratic and public institutional bases. Aboriginal activists-artists, such as members of the band Yothu Yindi, and popular figures such as Sting and the rock band Midnight Oil, popularized globally indigenous land rights struggles.

Emerging alongside this political revaluation of indigenous social and cultural forms was a vibrant tourism and commodity market in Aboriginal heritage.[38] "Good Aboriginal art" (paintings, sculptures, and artifacts) went on tour, so to speak, and was exhibited in international galleries to critical acclaim.[39] "Bad Aboriginal art" was sold in tourist stalls across Australia and beyond.[40] But both high and low cultural forms contributed to a new global traffic in commoditized indigenous culture, contributing significantly to the national GNP. In the process particular indigenous knowledges were generalized into a natural commercial product, and they contributed to a global resignification of the "indigenous" in relation to social struggle. Indigenousness was unhinged and "liberated" from the specificity of actual indigenous struggles, from their differing social agendas and visions of a reformed social world, and from the specific challenges they posed to contemporary nation-based governmentality and capital.

Freed from specific struggles, the signifier "indigenousness" began to function as an interpretant to be experienced as an aura, naturalizing any struggle or commodity desire to which it was attached. Sydney neighborhood protestors of the Olympic development at Bondi Beach carried banners proclaiming Bondi Beach as a "sacred site." And, when the head of the Australian Children's Television Foundation accused U.S. broadcasters of a "sinister new form" of cultural colonialism, she troped a national counterinsurgency as indigenous and countercolonial.[41] She did this at the cost of effacing the struggles of actually existing indigenous groups against ongoing state colonialism, struggles themselves drawing on transnational discourses and institutions including North and South American indigenous movements. But, in doing so, she demonstrated the elasticity of the notion of indigenous and its function in naturalizing even those social struggles that are potentially to the detriment of actually existing Aboriginal people.

If the indigenous was unhinged from its previous social referent, it was also resituated within a complex field of national and international civil and human rights standards of acceptable and unacceptable social and cultural difference.[42] International bodies produced protocols and held conventions outlining what practices violated human rights, gender rights, racial rights, and cultural rights. Foreign national public debates ensued on the limits of cultural tolerance within liberal multicultural formations, which then circulated through the transnational mass media. Pederasts and gays, religions and cults, cliterodectomies and gential mutilations: national news media struggled to differentiate international forms and their good and bad cultural incarnations, their normative and grotesque referents, their relative values,

FIGURE 2. "Bondi Beach Sacred Site." (Photograph in *The Weekend Australian*, 26–27 June 1999, p. 23.)

and their deformation and reformation of citizenship. Public debate centered, on the one hand, on the question of how courts could prohibit indigenous ritual practices as repugnant to the common law while allowing western sexual practices or religious practices; and, on the other hand, on the question of who deserved the reparative legislation of the state.[43] These debates were driven not so much by the actual amount of land and benefits returned, but by the fact that the process was occurring at the moment when white Australians were suffering from an uncertain future.

When the Australian state, law, and public struggle to piece together a new form of national cohesion in the midst of these modes of difference, they are not acting in bad faith. Nor is Australian multiculturalism ideological in the sense of masking a dominant class interest. Instead, Australian multiculturalism is a deeply optimistic liberal engagement with the democratic form under conditions of extreme torsion as social and cultural differences proliferate and as capital formations change. This engagement is generating, in the words of Slavoj Žižek, " 'utopian' narratives of possible [if, in the end,] failed alternative histories," which, nevertheless, "point towards the system's antagonistic character" and thereby " 'estrange' [the nation from] the self-evidence of its established character."[44] The real optimism of Australian multiculturalism is what I trouble and am troubled by in this book — its affective, not simply discursive and institutional, dimensions.

To be sure, the problems indigenous people face in Australia are not unique

25

to them. But the indigenous does seem to be playing a particular role in debates on multiculturalism. The concept, as opposed to the actual socially embedded persons, seems to be providing the nation an experience of "before nationalism," and an experience of a time before the failures and compromises of national projects. But rather than offering a counternational form, the concept of the indigenous seems to be purifying and redeeming the ideal image of the nation (a problem I take up explicitly in chapter 1). Still, while Australia is an interesting site to explore the conjuncture between indigenous forms of difference and national forms of citizenship, the problem indigenous people face in Australia is faced elsewhere. South Africa, the European Union, Canada: we are witnessing a global adjustment of the constitution of public and legal national imaginaries as state institutions and public sympathy attempt to address the multiplicity of social identities and traditions constituting and circulating through the contemporary nation. Whether the solution is the constitutional protection of a serialized set of social identities (South Africa[45]) or public and constitutional proclamations of the worth of all cultures "that have animated whole societies over some considerable stretch of time" (Canada[46]), we must bear in mind the following: First, the emergence of national formations of toleration need not have emerged in these particular forms. There is no necessary fit or identity between the crisis to which these forms respond and the forms themselves. Second, these emergent national forms have merely responded to, not solved, the crisis from which they have emerged, namely, the stance liberal national subjects should take toward the compulsory aspects of others' "cultures." It is important to repeat these concepts, and to repeat them again and again if we are to quiet the celebratory sounds of the New Society long enough to hear the ideologies of the actual.

The partiality of multiculturalism as manifest in Western Europe, the United States, and the Pacific finds exemplary expression at the tip of the clitoris. In the late 1990s, an economically depressed and politically terrorized France could not agree on the grounds for excluding the North African diaspora living in the country, but could, at least initially, agree on the necessity of outlawing the "genital mutilations" some of the community "inflicts" on its young girls.[47] Moreover, in 1996, the U.S. Congress outlawed North African ceremonial clitoridectomies and directed U.S. representatives to the World Bank and other international financial institutions to withhold billions of dollars in aid to twenty-eight African countries if they did not sponsor education programs aimed at eradicating the practice.[48] A putative prodiversity president signed this bill in a national "post-civil rights" context in which "most Americans believe themselves and the nation to be opposed to racism and in favor of a multiracial, multiethnic pluralism."[49] The U.S. Congress did not pass legislation outlawing individual-based consumerized "mutilations"; that is, the trade in piercing, tattooing, and transsexual surgery. In 1997 some members of the Illinois legislature proposed a bill that would stiffen this federal legislation in the state. The urgency they expressed, which suggested that the Midwest was in the grip of a clitoridectomy epidemic, was perhaps rather more motivated by their anxiety that urban areas like Chicago were haunted by the black Muslim movement.[50] In France and the United States, state officials and public figures struggled to maintain a utopian image of a national culture against the pressure of transnational migration and internal ethnic divisions by holding up this clipped bundle of nerves to public scrutiny as the limit of a "civilized" nation's tolerance of its internal "cultural" diversity.

State and public figures made clitoridectomy and bride murder a commonsense limit of nationalism, and thereby produced a "civil nation" from this limit not simply by referring to the universal principles that the practice violated but by evoking complex affective reactions. They did what Gramsci insisted was necessary to hegemonic projects: they cohered a national will through passionate dramas and experiences of intimate community, not for the most part through pedantic argument. Whereas trappings and dramas of religion were critical to the coherence of a national will in Gramsci's time, now the putative preideological truth of a feeling roused by an encounter with fundamental alterity is critical to "the formation of a national-popular collective will" that the state can use to produce "a superior, total, form of modern civilization."[51] As if they deeply understood these thoughts, state and public figures trumpeted the national shame of allowing *such practices* of savagery and barbarism, of ignorance and superstition, to take place within its borders. The phrase "such practices" acts to expand the field of shame and cast a pall over unnamed subaltern practices where no national-popular collective will would be possible and over entire continents where such practices are imagined to occur.[52] In sum, they took a stance on how a citizen *ought* to understand his or her experience of the fundamental alterity of other moral orders — that is, what is and *should* be the proper attitude of persons to their own and others' modal feelings (what they *should, ought, must* act) — and how these attitudes should determine the distribution of rights, sympathy, and resources in national and global contexts. It is exactly the metamorphosis of these ethical feelings that I track in this book.

For the moment, the above national fetish of severed nerves seems to weld the contradictions and ambivalences of liberal multiculturalism.[53] But when official spokespersons of national culture repudiate subaltern practices by evoking the nation's aversion to them, they encounter the difficulty of discursively grounding their moral claim within a multicultural discourse.[54] And they encounter the double-edged nature of using discourses and affects such as shame as a tool for building national collective wills. On the one hand, as the ban on clitoridectomies shows, certain subaltern practices can produce the experience of a *national* collective will, even in the midst of public debate, by producing an experience of intimate communal aversion to the barbaric, uneducated, and savage practice that *we* as a civilized nation cannot allow to occur within *our* borders. A particular body of belief is, at least temporarily, elevated to the status of a universal principle primarily through pageantries of corporeal shame and revulsion. But in this case as in others liberal democratic societies are now haunted by the specter of mistaken intolerance. They now know that in time their deepest moral impulses may be exposed to be historically contingent, mere prejudices masquerading as universal principles. In particular, past colonial and civil rights abuses cast a shadow over present moments of national and individual intolerance.[55] In the "historical mutation" of the modern liberal democratic society, not only are many "universal grounding[s] . . . contemplated with deep suspicion" but every moment of moral judgment is potentially a moment of acute personal and national embarrassment.[56] Popular and critical thinkers suffer their (in)tolerance; they do not simply decide to be tolerant or intolerant. Liberal members of democratic societies stumble, loose their breath, and panic, even if ever so slightly, when asked to say why, on what grounds, and according to whom is a practice a moral, national limit of tolerance. And, as they panic, they show how the logic of multiculturalism disorganizes the discursive and imaginary field that every limit to it coheres.

It is the contemporary intractability of these questions—and the social generativity of these nonpassages—that interest me in this book. The lost certainty of its moral groundings wracks national hegemonic projects and helps explain the force of national cultural censure in those moments when some national collective will can be found or forged. The nausea created by these shifting grounds becomes especially clear in public debates over particular national intolerances, in which the difficulty of grounding (in)tolerance in specific instances spreads and threatens the general notion of the nation itself, along with a nation-based identity and identification. These anxious national debates circulate through national and transnational mass media and intellectual publics and become much broader crises of modernism, liberalism, humanism, and the democratic polity. After all this history, whose nation is any one nation, after all? Who, after all this history, owns modernity and its hallmarks, humanism and democracy? What groups do humanism, democracy, and the common law serve, protect, and maintain? These questions generate new social discourses, institutions, and subjects.

This is the nerve ending I seek here to understand: how a state and public leans on a multicultural imaginary to defer the problems that capital, (post)colonialism, and human diasporas pose to national identity in the late twentieth and early twenty-first centuries. How do these state, public, and capital multicultural discourses, apparatuses, and imaginaries defuse struggles for liberation waged against the modern liberal state and recuperate these struggles as moments in which the future of the nation and its core institutions and values are ensured rather than shaken; how they recreate a superordinate monocultural referent, chase a transcultural if not transcendental desire, a flickering *something* beyond our differences, even as they purport to be recognizing the cultural subjects standing before them. And, finally, how they open up a space for critical reimaginings of social life as indigenous subjects creatively engage the slippages, dispersions, and ambivalences of discursive and moral formations that make up their lives.

At this switch point, when multiculturalism becomes the grounds for a new transcendental national monoculturalism, the state struggle for hegemony depends on representing and working through liberal practices and intentions in two very different registers. On the one hand, juridical, political, and public spokespersons deploy an abstract language of law, citizenship, and rights—a principled, universalizing, pedantic language. On the other hand, they deploy a language of love and shame, of haunted dreams, of traumatic and reparative memory, of intimacy and desire. Dominant and subordinate social groups draw each other into in an intimate drama of global discourse and capital, of national identity, of history and consciousness. And as they do, shame and reconciliation, a public collective purging of the past, become an index and requirement of a new abstracted national membership. But law and public do not require all citizens to undergo the same type of public, corporeal cleansing, the same type of psychic and historical reformation.

"Suppose they do not know how to cease to be themselves." Suppose your life depends on performing this ontological trick.

THE LAY OF THE LAND

In many ways this volume is the result of a classical anthropological approach to social analysis. I have spent the last seventeen years living with and working on behalf of a small group of people, most of whom live at Belyuen, a small indigenous community on the Cox Peninsula located on the western side of the Darwin Harbor in the Northern Territory of Australia. Other indigenous men and women with whom I have worked live in Darwin and along the coastal communities stretching along the coast from Belyuen to Port Keats (Wadeye), Northern Territory. Year after year I have returned to this small coastal area, acting sometimes as a driver, sometimes as a senior anthropological adviser for land and sea claims, and sometimes as a hunter — shooting more wallabies, pigs, cockatoos, geese, and goanna than I care to remember. At other times I have been a ceremonial actor, a mom, grandmother, wife, kid, and white lady. Children born after I arrived in 1984 are now adults, some with kids. I am an old lady at thirty-nine.

The people I work with go about living their lives within a background both incredibly rich and incredibly brutal. Year after year, I have watched women and men die from the diseases of poverty at ages that would shock those for whom life does not seem a privilege. Tuberculosis, kidney failure, chronic bronchitis, lung cancer: the bodies of those of us who live are mottled with scars from tropical ulcers, fights, and ceremonial practices. I have been asked, and I have asked myself many times, why in the light of so much death and so much life, of the political and economic and social structures of discrimination and poverty most indigenous people face in Australia and certainly in the indigenous communities I live and work in, why the following book is written as an extended, historically and sociologically grounded, theoretical essay.

In other words, several questions faced me as I attempted to write a critique of the liberal diaspora in the context of indigenous Australia. Most straightforward of the questions is where do the people I have lived and worked with over the last seventeen years appear in the narrative of this liberal diaspora? And where do other indigenous actors, agents, and subjects appear in the narrative of how a new metaethics — and critique — of Australian nationalism was generated. As should be apparent from this introduction, the answer is not at all straightforward. These people certainly appear in an explicit way throughout this book. Although I am centrally concerned with settler experiences of the nonpassage between understanding-based ideologies of justice and subjective-based ideologies of morality, this volume continually situates this experience in an actively responsive indigenous social world. Indeed, if I begin the book with a concern for the material mediations of an emergent multicultural Australia, I end it with a concern about how a specific non-passage between reason and morality has been exploited by a particular Aboriginal community. But indigenous persons are the agents of this book in a deeper and more profound sense. They provided the insight and incitement to think critically about the self-evident good of liberalism and liberal recognition.

Second, how do I describe the creative engagement of indigenous subjects with the impasses that liberal diasporas present to them, without their creative response becoming the source for a new heroic rhetoric of liberalism itself? To be sure, many indigenous persons embrace the institutions and ideals of a multicultural form of liberal nationalism. I would just repeat that it does not seem necessary to me to conceptualize a homogeneous social order in order to conceptualize the vital sociological consequences of moments in which indigenous and nonindigenous subjects (or any subjects for that matter) experience contrasting obligations to reasoned argument and moral sensibility — *no matter their various stances toward these impasses.*

Third, how is the story I tell exemplary of a movement in social critique outside this particular social context? If this book gives the story about the generative role the indigenous plays in the emergence and form of Australian multiculturalism, it is not about this story at all. Rather it is about how the social sciences and socially inflected humanities analytically approach the various historical determinations, displacements, iterations, and irritations of contrasting orders of knowledge and obligation in (liberal) societies. It returns to the spirit, if not the conceptual framework, of Durkheim's call for a sociological science of the ought in order to develop an ethnography not simply of existing states of mood and modality, of propositionality and obligation, and of moral possibility and necessity, but also of the conditions of their emergence and transformation as social phenomena.[57] After all, the unimaginable is imagined. And the reasons it is have interested social theorists throughout the twentieth century. In approaching the question of why new modes of knowledge and obligation emerge, I rely on a specific understanding of the trial determinations of social life that I mentioned above — material institutions, semiotics, and (inter)subjectivity. This book is not, however, a theoretical elaboration of the broader conceptual space it relies on.[58]

Nor is this book a standard ethnography of one social group or a standard sociology of a single historical or institutional site. Whatever analytic power such studies have, and such power they do have, in this book I attempt to demonstrate the dynamic of liberal impasses from a different critical perspective, from the perspective of a critique of the liberal notion of self-correction. Liberal procedural accounts of public reason highlight the self-correcting nature of rational argument. The self-reflexivity of public reason leads over time toward a shared and better sense of public opinion because it is supposedly (ideally) oriented only to the best argument, and, as more persuasive arguments arise, they continually renew, emend, revise, and rectify past accounts. This provides the historicity of public reason. But liberal reason is not merely a discursive procedure, it is institutional dynamic. In other words, the dynamic among the domains of liberal society provides for a similar self-correcting movement. In the case I analyze, court members may well represent themselves as making decisions according to precedent and other genre-specific procedures of the juridical domain, but they also understand themselves to be continually revealing the relevance of the common law to contemporary public opinion of what constitutes the good, the tolerable, the abhorrent, and the just and to statutory laws passed by parliaments and congresses (themselves understood as reflecting the public will). Legal readings of statutory law and common law precedent are constantly represented as being corrected by the dynamic among publics, state, and civil society.

As with all pieces of writing this book reflects a decision to approach the conditions of these discriminatory practices in a particular way. It does not, for instance, present a general political economy of land rights or territorial distribution in Australia; that is, how much land has actually been redistributed under the various land rights and native title laws now in existence. Nor does it provide an extended account of the forms of title available to indigenous Australians under the various statutory laws and their specific contradictory demands.[59] Nor does it provide an extended account of how one group of indigenous Australians has grappled with the legal, political, and cultural conditions of Australian multiculturalism, although throughout and especially in the last two chapters, the focus is exactly on these questions.[60]

The chapters of this book reflect an attempt to understand the various discursive, subjective, and material/institutional mediations of liberal social life on the one hand, and, on the other, the manner in which the historical impasse of public and moral reason has generated a new metaethics of national life; namely, multiculturalism. The central rhythm of the text is a return in different contexts and archival materials to an impossible demand placed on indigenous and nonindigenous Australian subjects within the discursive and performative regime of settler multiculturalism and their creative response to these impasses. Different chapters slice into different regions of this impasse. Chapter 1 tracks this impasse across public sphere representations of an indigenous multiculturalism, while chapter 4 focuses on the generative force of this impasse in one state institution — the High Court — and more specifically its judgments on native title. Chapter 1 asks what the state and nation are recognizing and finding worthy when they embrace the "ancient laws" of indigenous Australia: how is this thing socially produced and politically practiced; and why must Aboriginal persons identify with it to gain access to public sympathy and state resources. The chapter tracks public debates over the worth of ancient aboriginal law, legal mandates on the form traditional culture must take, and mass-mediated commercial portraits of traditional indigenous culture. Chapter 4 turns to two High Court cases, *Eddie Mabo v. the State of Queensland* (1992) and *The Wik Peoples v. The State of Queensland* (1996) to examine how liberal legal subjects manage to protect themselves from experiencing, in the moment of cultural discrimination, the experience of future negative judgment. How is judgment possible in multicultural contexts? And how do judges escape as individuals, and as the authors and proponents of social projects, the unconditional of the future perfect proposition: We will have been wrong.

Chapters 2 and 3 examine the ways in which particular forms of indigenous corporeality (ritual sex) superanimated liberal self-reflection, causing Australian non-Aboriginal citizens to experience their intolerance as their moral and intellectual limits, thereby helping to precipitate the discursive grounds for a new national ideological formation. These chapters view the social generativity of the impasse between public and moral reason from the perspective of indigenous and settler everyday life, as do chapters 4 and 5, which return to the present and shift the perspective from settler to indigenous Australians. Chapter 2 takes up the theme of the repugnant and the uncanny in the writings and research of Baldwin Spencer and Frank Gillen as they lived among the Arrente and other central Australian indigenous groups at the turn of the century. It examines the ways in which particular forms of indigenous and settler corporeality, corporeal relations, and corporeal practices (public, violent, playful, ceremonial, noncouple, retributive) superanimated liberal reflection; caused a crisis of reason in Australian non-Aboriginal citizens; caused these citizens to experience their intolerance as their moral and intellectual limits; and helped to precipitate the discursive grounds for a new national ideological formation. Spencer and Gillen's writings are read not to produce a historiography of settler sexuality so much as to situate the problem of the indigenous difference in the national archive. Chapter 3 continues this examination of the nonpassage between understanding and obligation played in the emergence of the Australian indigenous multicultural. It examines administrative, public, and anthropological debates about how indigenous and settler sexuality should be administered in the Daly River region in order to examine the emergence of a new multicultural metaethics of Australian nationalism in the field of indigenous and settler interaction in the 1930s and 40s. Both chapters foreground the problem of the national archive of the repugnant in contemporary indigenous efforts to secure an acceptable form of cultural difference.

The last two chapters discuss how the relatives of Betty Bilawag attempt to produce a felicitous form of cultural difference within the shadow of these liberal archives, institutions, discourses, and subjectivities. They examine how these histories of difference, their institutions of law and common sense, play out in a community's attempt to claim land under the Aboriginal Land Rights (Northern Territory) Act, 1976. Chapter 5 examines Belyuen women and men's reading of the national archive in order to show how they experience, grapple with, and try to produce a legally and morally workable form of locality by articulating local social processes, often themselves contested, with the federal law of land rights and cultural difference. I try to show how these women and men make Belyuen a socially felicitous place as they engage the legal and social forms within which they live; the archived memorial forms of their own histories; the national and transnational circulations of these forms; and their own ambivalences toward the traditions, identities, and identifications of this archive in light of changing standards of the legally and normatively acceptable.

Chapter 6 concludes by examining the fate of Aboriginal belief in the context of three principles of contemporary liberal multiculturalism: that all deliberations that affect the public should be accessible to public scrutiny; that the validity of an argument stands in a negative relation to self-interest (the more disinterested a position is, the more likely it is to be universally valid and rational); and that in certain contexts principled public debate ought to give way to a collective moral sense — and, not only that public debate must give way, but that collective moral sense should be protected from the procedures of critical reason. The chapter asks, in the shadow of these liberal ideals, how Belyuen women and men produce "true beliefs" in the practice of land claims.

"Take into care beings as a whole." And if we attempt to think the whole of beings at once, then we think, roughly enough, this: that the whole of being "is," and we consider what it "is." We think the whole of beings, everything that is, in its being. In so doing we think at first something indeterminate and fleeting, and yet we also mean something for which we find nothing comparable, something singular. For the whole of beings does not occur twice, otherwise it wouldn't be what we mean.
—Martin Heidegger, *Basic Concepts*

1 / Mutant Messages

INTRODUCING (THE THING)

In the 1880 introduction to the ethnology *Kamilaroi and Kunai,* the Reverend Lorimer Fison described a sensation he experienced studying the "intersexual arrangements" of indigenous Australians.[1] He described feeling "ancient rules" underlying the Kamilaroi and Kunai's sexual practices, catching fleeting glimpses of an ancient "strata" cropping up from the horrific given conditions of colonial settlement, sensing a "something else, . . . something more" Kamilaroi and Kunai than even the Kamilaroi and Kunai themselves, a some *thing* that offered him and other ethnologists a glimpse of an ancient order puncturing the present, often hybrid and degenerate, indigenous social horizon. Fison pointed to this ancient order as the proper object of ethnological research, and he used the promised feelings this order produced to prod other ethnologists to turn its way. But Fison cautioned, even admonished, other researchers that to reach this order and to experience these feelings they had to be "continually on the watch" that "every last trace of white men's effect on Aboriginal society" was "altogether cast out of the calculation."[2] Only by stripping from their ethnological analysis the traumatic effect of settlement on indigenous social life could the researcher reach, touch, and begin to sketch the outline of that thing, which was not the present corrupted Aboriginal social body but an immutable form that predated and survived the ravage of civil society.

The emergent modern ethnological epistemology Fison promoted bordered on the paranoid. Every actual indigenous practice was suspect. All "present usages," even those seemingly "developed by the natives themselves" and seemingly untouched by "contact with the white man," might be mere mirages of the investigator's own society. They might be like the "present usages" of the "Mount Gambier blacks," the desperate social acts of men and women who had watched their society be "reduced from 900 souls to 17" in thirty years, and who were "compelled to make matrimonial arrangements as [they could], whether they be according to ancient law or not."[3] But even "present usages" untouched by the ravages of British settlement were little more than mere chimera of the ancient thing Fison sought. They taunted him with glimpses of what he truly desired — a superceded but still signifying ancient society shimmering there just beyond him and them, settler time and emergent national history.[4]

The proper ethnological thing Fison sought would always just elude him, would always be somewhere he was not. Maybe this ancient order survived in the remote interior of the nation, but it was never where he was. Where he stood the ancient rules were submerged in the horror of the colonial present and were mediated by the faulty memory of a "few wretched survivors [who were] . . . obliged to take such mates as death has left them, whether they be of the right classes or not."[5] Or the ancient rules were heavily encrusted with the autochthonous cultural debris generated by the inexorable tectonic shifts Fison's colleagues called social evolution. Not surprisingly, a restlessness pervades Fison's ethnology. Irritation and humiliation punctuate the rational veneer of his text as he is forced to encounter his own intellectual limits and to account for his own conceptual failures. Time after time, Fison is forced to admit that what he feels and desires cannot be accounted for by what he sees, reads, and hears.[6]

Whatever Fison was chasing, Australians still seemed in desperate pursuit of more than a hundred years after *Kamilaroi and Kunai* was first published. At the turn of the twentieth century, most Australians had the distinct feeling that some decisive national drama pivoted on their felicitous recognition of an ancient indigenous law predating the nation and all living indigenous subjects. In two crucial, nationally publicized and debated decisions, *Eddie Mabo v. the State of Queensland* (1992) and *The Wik Peoples v. the State of Queensland* (1996), the Australian High Court ruled that the concept of native title was not inconsistent with the principles of the Australian common law (the *Mabo* decision) and that the granting of a pastoral lease did not necessarily extinguish native title (the *Wik* decision). As a result, native title still existed where the state had not explicitly extinguished it; where Aboriginal communities still maintained its foundation — namely, the "real acknowledgment of traditional law and real observance of traditional customs"; and where those real traditions did no violence to common law principles.[7]

As I will discuss at greater length in chapter 4, in the fantasy space coordinated by these two legal decisions, traditional and modern laws seem to coexist without producing conceptual violence or social antagonism. The legitimacy of native title is granted; its authority is rooted in the ancient rules, beliefs, and practices predating the settler nation. The object of native title tribunals is merely to judge at the "level of primary fact" if native title has disappeared "by reason of the washing away by 'the tide of history' and any real acknowledgment of traditional law and real observance of traditional customs" and to judge whether any of these real ancient customs violate contemporary common law values.[8] This is why the *Wik* decision on pastoral property was so important: the vast hectares under pastoral lease were "the parts of Australia where [native] laws and traditions (important to sustain native title) are most likely to have survived." These places were the spaces perceived as least touched by modern society.[9]

The moral and legal obligation of the nation to its indigenous population was foregrounded in another well-publicized debate; namely, the moral and economic claim of the "Stolen Generation" on the Australian nation. The Stolen Generation refers to the 10 to 30 percent of the total population of Aboriginal children between 1910 and 1970, who were forcibly removed from their parents as part of the state's policy of cultural assimilation. Members of the Stolen Generation filed a federal class action lawsuit against the state, arguing that it had violated their human and constitutional rights. A Royal Commission investigated the intent and effect of these assimilation policies. It found that past state and territory governments had explicitly engaged in what could most accurately be called a form of social genocide, a cultural holocaust as defined by the 1951 Genocide Convention — an analogy made more compelling by the age of the Aboriginal applicants, many of whom had been taken in the early 1940s.[10] Australians looked at themselves in a ghastly historical mirror and imagined their own Nuremberg. Would fascism be the final metaphor of Australian settler modernity? In 1997 the High Court ruled that the 1918 Northern Territory ordinance allowing Aboriginal and "half-caste" children to be forcibly removed from their mothers was constitutionally valid and did not authorize genocide de jure, although in retrospect it was misguided and morally questionable.

This Australian drama would not surprise most liberal theorists of the global travails of liberal forms of nationalism, and settler nationalisms in particular. The works of Charles Taylor, Richard Rorty, Jürgen Habermas, and Will Kymlicka, among others, pivot on the question of whether and how a multitude of modern liberal nation-states should recognize the worth of their interior ethnic and indigenous cultural traditions. In this chapter I turn away, however, from the question of whether and how the settler nation should recognize the worth of indigenous customary law. Instead, I ask more fundamental questions: *What* is the state and nation recognizing and finding worthy when it embraces the "ancient laws" of indigenous Australia? What is it about the thing of "indigenous tradition" that produces sensations, desires, anxieties, and professional, personal, and national optimisms? What is this thing that is only ever obliquely glimpsed and that resists the bad faith of the liberal nation while at the same time does no violence to good civil values, indeed crystallizes the best form of community "we" could hope for? What is the glimmering object the public support of which can produce, as if by magical charm, the feelings necessary for social harmony in the multicultural nation, for good trading relations with the Asia-Pacific, and for a new globally inspirational form of national cohesion?[11] How is this thing socially produced and politically practiced? Why must Aboriginal persons identify with it to gain access to public sympathy and state resources?

To understand what the nation is seeking to recognize, touch, feel, and foreground *through* its recognition of an ancient pre(ter)national order, this chapter tracks (across multiple state and public domains) the public debates over the worth of ancient aboriginal law, legal mandates on the form traditional culture must take, and mass-mediated portraits of traditional indigenous culture. In this chapter I focus specifically on the intersection of mass-mediated public representations and political debates over land redistribution. As I track the transformations of the object "traditional indigenous law" across these public, state, and commercial domains, I map the political cunning and calculus of cultural recognition in a settler modernity. More than ten years ago, Kaja Silverman noted the "theoretical truism that hegemonic colonialism works by inspiring in the colonized subject the desire to assume the identity of his or her colonizers."[12] Perhaps this is what fundamentally distinguishes the operation of power in colonial and (post)colonial multicultural societies. Hegemonic domination in the latter formation works primarily by inspiring in the indigenous subject a desire to identify with a lost indeterminable object — indeed, to be the melancholic subject of traditions.[13]

To understand this new form of liberal power, I examine how recognition is at once a formal meconnaissance of a subaltern group's *being* and of its *being worthy* of national recognition and, at the same time, a formal moment of being inspected, examined, and investigated.[14] I suggest this inspection always already constitutes indigenous persons as failures of indigeneity as such. And this is the point. In certain contexts of recognition, Aboriginal persons must produce a detailed account of the content of their traditions and the force with which they identify with them — discursive, practical, and dispositional states that necessarily have a "more or less" relationship to the imaginary of a "real acknowledgment of traditional law and real observance of traditional customs." What are the social consequences of the noncorrespondence between the object of national allegiance, "ancient tradition," and any particular Aboriginal person, group, practice, memory, or artifact?

INTERROGATIONS

Meaghan Morris noted that 1992 marked a certain watershed in the Australian national stance toward indigenous people.[15] In 1992, in *Eddie Mabo v. the State of Queensland,* the Australian High Court overturned the doctrine that Australian was *terra nullius* (a land belonging to no one) at the point of settlement and ruled that Aboriginal Australians had and retained native title interests in the law. In a subsequent ruling (*The Wik People v. the State of Queensland,* 1996) the court further ruled that the granting of a pastoral lease did not necessarily extinguish native title. In 1993, in response to the *Mabo* decision, public pressure, and its own political strategy, the Labour government passed the federal Native Title Act, which legislated the mechanisms by which indigenous groups could claim land.

A year later the conservative Liberal-National coalition, which promised to protect the interests of (white) miners, farmers, and landowners from delete-rious native title claims, defeated the Labour Party for the first time in nearly a quarter century. During the first session of the new Liberal parliament, Pauline Hanson, an independent minister from Queensland, vehemently at-tacked the basic tenets of the state's twenty-year-old multicultural policy, especially two of its central tenets: self-determination for indigenous Aus-tralians and increased Asian immigration.[16] She claimed that multicultural-ism was a guilt-based ideological program doing little more than partition-ing the country into drug- and crime-ridden Asian and Aboriginal enclaves. In what would provoke a national scandal, Hanson argued that indigenous self-determination was just another name for a massive and massively mis-conceived social welfare program, transferring through taxation national wealth generated by hardworking (white) Australians to socially irrespon-sible (black) Australians. It was time for white outrage. "Ordinary Australi-ans" should reject "the Aboriginal industry's" insistence that they feel guilty for past colonial policies they were not responsible for and, instead, proudly embrace what was for Hanson the obvious point: that white Australians made the modern nation, no matter that present-day white Australians had as little to do with past economic policies as they did with past colonial policies. In hailing what she often referred to as "ordinary Australians" Hanson consti-tuted a political space for all who desired to be such and to have such define the motor of Australian settler modernity.

Pauline Hanson went to the heart of the traditional thing. In a series of public addresses and interviews, Hanson argued the "ordinary" Australians should ignore the romantic image of traditional Aboriginal society and in-stead examine what she believed were the real conditions of present-day indigenous social life: third-world health and housing conditions, dread-fully high infant mortality rates, rampant substance abuse, sexual disorder, and truncated life spans—namely, the horrific material conditions that, she claimed, indexed a tremendous "waste" of "our" tax dollars. In 1998, the Mel-bourne *Age* reported that census figures indicated that one in two Aborigines would be jobless by 2006.[17] What was this thing "Aboriginal tradition," which was never wherever anyone was? What did "self-determination" mean when so many Aboriginal communities and individuals would be destitute with-out massive government financial support? Indigenous social conditions had barely budged, she argued, in the thirty-odd years since Aboriginal men and women had been made citizens, had been removed from ward rolls, and had been given the right to vote, receive social security benefits, and drink. Indeed, she and other conservative critics argued that indigenous social life had gotten worse since full citizenship had been extended to Aborigines. The availability of social security benefits increased drug and alcohol addiction and lessened the incentive for Aboriginal women and men to become working members of the national economy.

Most public and political spokespersons labeled Hanson and her followers "fringe" and "extreme," and called their views dangerously antiquated. They wrung their hands and rang warning bells, cautioning the nation that a line of tolerance was being approached that, if crossed, would bring grave social and economic consequences. But although Hanson was politically marginalized and her views historicized, mainstream political officials were also recorded as publicly questioning the value of an ancient indigenous law for a modern technological society. Just days before Liberal Party Prime Minister John Howard appointed Liberal Senator Ross Lightfoot from Western Australia to the coalition backbench Committee on Aboriginal Affairs, he forced the senator to apologize to parliament for claiming "Aboriginal people in their native state are the lowest colour on the civilisation spectrum."[18] The Liberal Party's Aboriginal Affairs Minister, John Herron, nearly lost his portfolio after publicly supporting the assimilation policies of the 1950s, including the forced removal of indigenous children from their parents. Herron argued that forced assimilation had had positive social effects: "Half-caste" children had been given an economic and social head start over their "full-blood" cousins who were handicapped in the race to civil society by their adherence to outmoded beliefs and practices.

In 1997, claiming that the *Wik* decision on pastoral property threatened to ruin the moral, social, and economic health of the Commonwealth, the Liberal government introduced federal parliamentary legislation exempting pastoral lands from native title claims and restricting native title rights in other contexts. Many public spokespersons and groups swiftly responded, couching their criticisms in a rhetoric of principle and passion, finance and freedom, and modernity and its moral encumbrances. Labour opposition leader Kim Beazley; two former prime ministers from opposing parties, Paul Keating (Labour) and Malcolm Fraser (Liberal); and church and business leaders urged the public to look beyond "simple property rights," beyond their pocketbooks, and beyond the actual conditions of Aboriginal social life. They should consider, instead, the question of national honor, national

history, and national shame looming just beyond these economic and social struggles,[19] and recognize that the value of ancient indigenous law would
finally free the settler nation from its colonial frontier and confirm its contemporary reputation as a model (post)modern multicultural nation. So suggested Beazley in a nationally televised address explaining the Labour Party's
support of existing native title legislation: "There's more bound up in this
than simply property rights. We face here a question of our history and our
national honour. We have a diverse and vibrant community which we will be
putting on show in three year's time at the Sydney Olympics. We won that
bid because nations around the globe believed rightly our better instincts lead
us to coexist effectively with each other in a way in which a torn world finds
inspirational."[20]

In giving over the self-image of the nation to the world's aspirations, "Australia" would be reaffirmed, strengthened, and deepened by the very multicultural forces that Hanson thought threatened, weakened, and undermined
it. Mourning a shared shameful past would do no more, and no less, than pro-
pel the nation into a new cleansed national form. Besides, Beazley reassured,
native title was materially minor if not outright meaningless: "Native title will
only ever be able to be claimed by a small minority of Aboriginal and Torres
Strait Islander Australians — those who can evidence some form of ongoing
traditional association with the land in question."[21] And, "Native title itself
will very often mean not much more than the right to access for hunting, fish-
ing and traditional ceremonial purposes: only in a small minority of cases will
it ever involve anything like rights of exclusive possession."[22]

Indeed, rather than subtracting from the nation's wealth, the primary purpose of native title legislation was to provide the symbolic and affective conditions necessary to garner financial investment in the new global conditions of
late modern capital. In the global reorganization of finance, commerce, and
trade, cultural intolerance was a market matter. The world, especially Asian
and Southeast Asian financial and tourism industries, was listening into the
national conversation about Asian immigration and Aboriginal human and
native title rights. Moreover, Aboriginal traditions were a vibrant sector of the
economy mark(et)ing the Australian difference to national and international
cultural consumers. Major regional newspapers presented a daily tally of the
political and financial stakes of Hansonesque rhetoric — lost trade, lost financial investment, lost international political influence and tourism, and lost
jobs due to uncivil, intolerant talk.[23] These financial stakes took on height-

ened significance as regional financial markets began to collapse in the first half of 1998. The Australian economy maintained moderate growth, but in a general field of financial anxiety.

National spokespersons did not simply point to juridical principles of common law, abstract notions of national honor, or the public's pocketbooks. They also spoke of the pleasures produced by concentrating on the vibrant ancient laws found not only in remote interior indigenous communities but also in public classrooms and curricula; on major networks and cable channels; in concert halls and art galleries; in the glossy magazines leafed through on airplanes, couches, and toilets. An ancient law was now thoroughly intercalated in public, intimate, even scatological spaces of the nation. If the good Australian people could look past the current bad material conditions of much of Aboriginal Australia, if they could strip away the incrustations of two hundred years of engineered and laissez-faire social neglect and abuse, they would catch a glimpse of the traditional values that remained, persisted, and survived state and civil society. Shimmering off this traditional mirage they would catch a glimpse of their own best selves.

But this shimmering surface would prove to be a complicatedly reflective and refractive one. As Hanson's political party, One Nation, rose to national prominence in the mid-1990s, Australians were forced to ask themselves, and ask themselves publicly: Has a malignant intolerance lodged itself in the liberal body of the contemporary Australian nation? National spokespersons and ordinary citizens pointed to both worrisome symptoms and hopeful signs. In May 1998, a "National Sorry Day" was held to atone for the nation's treatment of the Stolen Generation. The day was organized after a federal inquiry, published in a volume titled *Bringing Them Home,* shocked the nation with graphic details of the liberal state's inhuman treatment of generations of indigenous families. Believing they were acting for the good of both indigenous people and the nation, Anglo-Australian government officials tore Aboriginal families apart between 1910 and the late 1960s and interned thousands of Aboriginal children in horse paddocks, abandoned army barracks, and worse. State and territory officials were intent on severing the generational transmission of Aboriginal traditions and, thereby, speed up the process of cultural assimilation. In the process many children were psychologically, physically, or sexually abused. According to Ronald Wilson, the author of *Bringing Them Home,* this massive government-initiated social experiment was carried out "because the Aboriginal race was seen as an embarrassment to white Australia."[24] But no longer. By 1998, most Australians believed that they themselves and their right-minded fellow citizens not only tolerated the nation's indigenous heritage but recognized its worth.[25] They encouraged Aboriginal men and women to embrace the wealth of their cultural traditions and to preserve and pass down these traditions to their children.

But as much as Australians might wish, racial prejudice would not remain consigned to the history books. Not long after the last Sorry Book was closed, the One Nation Party—staunchly opposed to Asian immigration and Aboriginal land and social welfare rights—stunned the country by capturing nearly a quarter of the vote in the Queensland state elections.[26] The racial rhetoric and policies of One Nation shocked and shamed many Australians. They saw the liberal credentials of the nation threatened, and they feared an unwitting repetition of the very racist history that had led to *Mabo* and to contemporary pageants of atonement like National Sorry Day. Attacks on Aboriginal rights and multiculturalism prompted grassroots groups to organize large and small antiracist rallies wherever the leader of One Nation, Pauline Hanson, appeared. An outpouring of high school students in Sydney, Melbourne, and Canberra renewed a nation's pride. Labor Party leader Kim Beazley described the student demonstrations as "one of the most moving affirmations of basic Australian decency I have ever seen."[27] For many Australians, the student demonstrations were the literal embodiment of more than a decade of social and civil rights struggle.

But not all protests against One Nation and not all aspects of Aboriginal customary law and culture deepened Beazley's patriotism and sense of decency. Nor did these protests immediately modify or lessen the appeal of One Nation's rhetoric. School administrators warned parents to be on guard for a socialist infiltration of the student movement. Cameras caught protesters spitting, shoving, kicking, and screaming at older, frail-looking women and men—everybody's grandmother and grandfather. Northern newspapers and street gossip circulated descriptions of "traditional" Aboriginal customs that shocked liberal sensibilities.[28] And One Nation continued to threaten the electoral hold of both Labour and Liberal-National party candidates even as its racial rhetoric intensified. Not long after the Queensland victory, at a fundraising dinner in Adelaide, Hanson claimed that the "Australian people [would] have thought twice about casting" their vote to give Aboriginal people full citizenship rights "what they knew today was foreshadowed for them."[29] Although acknowledging that Australians had voted overwhelmingly in a 1967 referendum to give "the Aboriginal race equality," she claimed most Australians now believe "the pendulum has gone too far the other way and now there is so much discrimination, so much inequality in our society that it is causing resentment among all people."[30]

Numerous outraged public spokespersons, including Liberal Party Prime Minister John Howard, described Hanson's speech on Aboriginal citizenship as "sinister," "abhorrent, undemocratic, ignorant and inaccurate."[31] Public spokespersons pointed out that the 1967 referendum did not give Aboriginal people voting rights, as Hanson had claimed, but rather gave the federal parliament powers to enact race-based legislation; that is, it was about social justice not citizenship. In the late 1960s, the sound of social justice struck a convincing national and international chord. The chant for Aboriginal rights resonated with the protests of African Americans in the United States and de-colonialized people throughout the world. The Australia public responded to the call from Aboriginal activists for social justice by registering the largest affirmative majority in a national referendum (90.8 percent).[32]

Yet, nearly a decade passed before the lofty ideals of the 1967 referendum were translated into any economically meaningful piece of federal legislation. It was not until the federal parliament passed the Aboriginal Land Rights (Northern Territory) Act of 1976 that Aboriginal groups were allowed to claim vacant Crown land in the Northern Territory, an area with a low nonindige-nous population. The more populous states followed with much weaker legis-lation.[33] Another decade and a half passed before the Australian High Court ruled that native title still existed over all Australian lands and seas where it had not been explicitly extinguished and where Aboriginal people main-tained a "real" acknowledgment of traditional law and "real" observance of traditional custom. And it was not until 1993, twenty-six years after the 1967 referendum, that the federal Native Title Act (1993) brought home to most Australians the economic costs of social justice and the potential social costs of multiculturalism.

These costs proved too high for many Australians. Editorials published in northern papers confirmed Hanson's claim that federal legislation designed to give Aborigines a "fair go" was simmering a politics of resentment. In a letter to the editor of the Northern Territory *Sunday Territorian,* Andrew Harvey de-scribed the compensation claims of the traditional Aboriginal owners of land on which the Alice Springs to Darwin railroad was to be built as "a greedy ploy to bleed taxpayers for monies not earned, nor justified." He warned Aborigi-nes to "wake up to yourselves before you lose everything and have to save for the majority of your life to purchase land, like every other Australian."[34] Ted

Hagger, One Nation candidate for Parliament in the Northern Territory, argued that "only people who have undergone traditional Aboriginal initiation rites should be regarded as Aborigines" for the purpose of social welfare and land rights. All others should be viewed as "yellow fellas . . . rorting the (welfare) system."[35] Preparing for what many feared would be a race-based federal election campaign, the Liberal government amended the Native Title Act restricting native title over pastoral lands and seas, while Aboriginal Affairs Minister John Herron of the Liberal Party attacked Aboriginal land councils and the Aboriginal and Torres Strait Islander Commission for gross misuse of funds and disregard for Aboriginal health and welfare. Monoculturalism re-emerged as a legitimate form of national desire. Howard and Hanson publicly claimed that Australia remained monocultural (and European) in its core institutions and beliefs and retained the right to defend its unique traditions and identity from Asian or Aboriginal incursion, although neither gave specific content to their view of "the Australian way of life."[36]

In the darting shadows cast by these social actions and reactions, the public media asked a number of questions: How does a person, a party, a nation know when they are acting for the Good, for Justice, but not intolerantly? How does a person and community distinguish between discriminatory prejudice and moral conviction? Between good forms of (in)tolerance and bad forms of (in)tolerance? Between social justice and social discrimination? Is there some essential Liberal Good, some form of Social Justice, that neither time nor cultural perspective can defile? History had provided few answers to these questions, and little comfort. Given time, deeply held moral convictions had reappeared as simple parochial beliefs, as good intentions gone awry. Government policies meant to promote social health and welfare ended up producing individual and social trauma (the Stolen Generation). Citizens protesting violent and intolerant speech turned into the very things they protested — violent and intolerant thugs. Federal social justice legislation that required Aboriginal land and native title claimants to demonstrate a "real" acknowledgment of traditional law and a "real" observance of traditional customs was transformed into a demand by One Nation members that social welfare and land rights intended for Aboriginal Australians be restricted to "real" initiated "tribal blacks" and exclude "yellow fellas." How do citizens distinguish the beliefs of the nation's judiciary that native title is tied to cultural difference from the beliefs of a One Nation member who believes there are "real blacks" and "yellow fellas"? Likewise, how do courts and ordinary non-Aboriginal citizens distinguish between indigenous traditions that deepen and strengthen liberal national traditions from indigenous, but nevertheless, repugnant practices?

In 1998 a coalition of senators from both Labour and Democratic parties refused to pass the Howard government's new native title legislation. As a result, Howard threatened to dissolve both houses of parliament and call a new election. If he had done so, the Australian government would have been decided in large part on the basis of its citizens' belief about the extant value to the modern nation of an enduring ancient prenational tradition. In the end, however, Howard did not act on his threat, and the election did not focus on indigenous issues. Indeed, many political pundits considered Howard's focus of the campaign on whether or not a Goods and Service Tax should be implemented rather than the issue of a race-based election to be a brilliant maneuver to refigure the grounds of public debate in order to defuse the major issue of the One Nation Party. Thus, the election was about indigenous justice only in a negative sense—that social justice mattered less than taxation. But in discussing whether or not the election should focus on the support of indigenous land and entitlement legislation, what did the public and its politicians think they were recognizing or rejecting?[37]

EXCITATIONS

We can begin to answer this question by examining the difference between the traditions to which a cacophony of public voices pledge their allegiance and the indigenous people who are the alleged sociological referent of these traditions. Simply put, what does "indigenous tradition" refer to and predicate, what does the nation celebrate? Answering this question entails examining the relationship between indigenous tradition, identity, and subjectivity and their discursive, affective, and material entailments. Let me begin with a set of commonplaces; in other words, with what might be described as the hegemonic status of "indigenous traditions" in Australia.

Most people would probably not spontaneously describe indigenous subjectivity, or other social subjectivities, as a passionate attachment to a point in a formally coordinated system of semiotic presuppositions and entailments; nor would they call it the ongoing regimentation of semiotic practices as people, consciously or unconsciously, articulate gaps and differences in an unfolding relational network itself part of the "historical reality of the intertextual, multimedia and multimediated modern public sphere."[38] But most Australians would have a strong sense that indigenous subjects are more or less like other social subjects as a result of shared or differing beliefs, characteristics, and practices (often experienced as characterological essentialisms) and that the loss of certain qualities and qualifiers would narrow the difference between contemporary social groups. For instance, they might not be able to say why, but they would "feel" that ethnic and indigenous identities share the common qualifiers of "race" and "tradition-culture." And they would feel that these qualifiers somehow differentiate their social location from the other social positions, or identities, crowding the symbolic space of the nation— say, whites, homosexuals, women, or the disabled. But an indigenous identity would not be considered the same as an ethnic identity because traditional indigenous culture has a different relationship to national time and space.[39]

Indigenous modifies "customary law," "ancient tradition," "traditional culture," and so forth by referring to a social practice and space that predates the settler state. Commonsensically, "indigenous people" denotes a social group descended from a set of people who lived in the full presence of "traditions." I would hazard that in contrast to the concept of, say, a "unicorn," most Australians believe that to which "tradition" refers existed at some point in time and believe some residual part of this prior undifferentiated whole remains in the now fragmentary bodies, desires, and practices of Aboriginal persons. And I would also hazard that most non-Aboriginal Australians think indigenous people are not only distinguished by their genealogical relation to the nation-state but also by their affective, ideational, and practical attachment to their prior customs. To be truly Aboriginal, indigenous persons must not only occupy a place in a semiotically determined social space, they must also identify with, desire to communicate (convey in words, practices, and feelings), and, to some satisfactory degree, lament the loss of the ancient customs that define(d) their difference.

I mean here the awkward "that to which" to evoke the strategic nonspecificity of the discursive and affective space of "indigenous tradition" in the contemporary Australian nation, a point I will elaborate later. And I mean my constant use of conditionals—"to some satisfactory degree," "some . . . part"—to mimic the juridical, public, and political conditioning of an authentic Aboriginal subjectivity. And, finally, I intend these mimetic provisos to suggest how the very discourses that constitute indigenous subjects *as such* constitute them as failures *of such*—of the very identity that identifies them (differentiates their social locality from other social localities) and to which they expected to have an identification (affectively attach).

In their discursive passage into being, then, indigenous people are scarred by temporal and social differences. These scars are the difference between any actual indigenous subject and the full presence promised by the phrase "indigenous tradition" and thus the identity "indigenous." At the most simple level, no indigenous subject can inhabit the temporal or spatial location to which indigenous identity refers—the geographical and social space and time of authentic Ab-originality. And no indigenous subject can derive her or his being outside a relation to other social identities and values currently proliferating in the nation-state. The category of indigeneity came into being in relation to the imperial state and the social identities residing in it, and it continues to draw its discursive value in relation to the state (and other states) and to other emergent national subjects (and other transnational subjects). To be indigenous, therefore, requires passing through, and in the passage being scarred by the geography of the state and topography of other social identities. Producing a present-tense indigenousness in which some failure is not a qualifying condition is discursively and materially impossible. These scars are what Aborigines are, what they have. They are their true difference; the "active edge" where the national promise of remedial action is negotiated.[40] Legal and popular questions coagulate there: Is the scar small or large, ancient or recent, bleeding or healed, breeded out or passed on? What institutional suturing was and is necessary to keep this lacerated body functional, and for whom and for what? These questions are asked in a practical political sense in the context of public debates about the allocation of resources to various Aboriginal cultural, social, and political organizations.

The gap existing between the promise of a traditional presence and the actual presence of Aboriginal persons is not simply discursive. It also produces and organizes subaltern and dominant feelings, expectations, desires, disappointments, and frustrations sometimes directed at a particular person or group, sometimes producing a more diffuse feeling. For instance, as early as 1951, while advocating the forced assimilation of "half-castes"—to make them "white" by forcibly removing them from their Aboriginal mothers—the Liberal Party leader Paul Hasluck counseled the nation not only to tolerate but to take full "enjoyment" of the traditions of its indigenous "full-bloods."[41] Likewise, mid-century liberal educational films like *Art of the Hunter* promoted traditional Aboriginal "culture" as a critical contribution to the production of a unique, distinct Australian nationalism and, thus, to the global relevance of the nation—its "artistic and social contribution to the history of mankind."[42]

49

By the 1990s the nation seemed to have fully incorporated Hasluck's suggestion. In certain commercial and cultural domains the Australian public took pleasure from representations of brightly smiling Aboriginal persons, thereby forgetting the trauma of three decades of Aboriginal activism for the most part archived in remote land council offices, personal homes, and private memories. Businesses took advantage of this shift in public attitudes, regularly using images of traditional Aborigines to establish an identification between consumers and commodities. Citations of nonabrasive indigenous "traditional culture" saturated the mass-mediated public sphere. In Coke, Telecom, and Qantas Airline commercials, in popular novels and songs, Hasluck's command, *enjoy their traditions,* was translated: enjoy our product *like* you enjoy their traditions. And, as the public consumed indigenous traditions in the form of art, music, and cultural tourism, the national economy came to rely increasingly on the popularity of the simulacra of indigenous culture to fuel the internal combustion of national private capital. It would only be in the late 1990s that the national mainstream Australian media would begin to question whether some of the profits from the art and tourism industries were being fairly returned to indigenous communities, an issue of fairness researchers and advocates had been arguing about since the emergence of the market in the 1980s.[43]

The listening public probably needed little urging to imagine the ancient traditions of Aboriginal people as a powerful, pleasurable, persisting force predating the nation and defining its historically specific difference in modernity's global diaspora. A generation of film and music (for example, *Walkabout,* 1971; *Picnic at Hanging Rock,* 1975; *The Last Wave,* 1977; *The Chant of Jimmy Blacksmith,* 1978; *The Adventures of Priscilla, Queen of the Desert,* 1993; Yothu Yindi, and Midnight Oil) refigured Australian modernity through an archetypical ancient law sensual and perduring, lying under the physical and social space of the nation and gestating in the bodies and practices of Aboriginal people living in remote bush, in fringe communities, in urban centers. Traditions were a level, a layer, a strata, existing before but now thoroughly intercalated in the present symbolic and material conditions of the multicultural nation. Ecofeminism, ecotourism, and New Ageism, as well as mass popular books like *Mutant Message Down Under, Crystal Woman,* and *The Songlines,* elaborated and ploughed into the national consciousness a commonsense feeling that this ancient order made Australia a special country.

RECITATIONS

Given the public commotion and commercial promotion, it might surprise us to learn that most Australians know very little about the actual social conditions of indigenous Australia. Many Australians acquire an outline of "Aboriginal culture" in school and from mass-media and multimediated images — glimpses of traditional culture garnered from popular books, movies, television talk shows, commercials, audio tapes, and CDs. But although many Australians have heard Peter Garrett of the rock band Midnight Oil sing the lyrics from "The Dead Heart" ("we carry in our heart the true country and that cannot be stolen, we follow in the steps of our ancestry and that cannot be broken") few know to what these musically moving evocations of "ancestry" refer.[44] Likewise, after the *Wik* decision on pastoral property and the threat of the Howard government to extinguish native title, The Body Shop stores in Melbourne began selling armbands bearing the message "Coexistence, Justice, Reconciliation." Most Australians knew that the colors of the armband (red, black, and yellow) referred to the Aboriginal flag. But few Australians knew to what the nation was reconciling itself, nor how specific legislative, juridical, or constitutional principles had already figured the sign "tradition" as a rights-bearing instrument in a series of federal, state, and territory acts of land rights, social welfare, and cultural heritage. Still fewer had any sense of the local, national, and transnational political and social struggles entextualized in law and legislation.

Most people did not know, for instance, that the federal Aboriginal Land Rights (Northern Territory) Act, 1976 defined "aboriginal traditions" as "the body of traditions, observances, customs and beliefs of Aboriginals or of a community or group of Aboriginals, and includes those traditions, observances, customs, and beliefs as applied in relation to particular persons, sites, areas of land, things or relationships."[45] Or that this definition became the blueprint for most major legislative references to "aboriginal traditions." Nor would most people know that if Aboriginal persons are to be successful land or native title claimants, they must not only provide evidence of the enduring nature of their customary law but also evidence of their "degree of attachment" (dispositional orientation) to these ancient laws and lands. Likewise, although they might know that the federal Native Title Act, 1993 stipulates that an Aboriginal group must continue to observe "traditional laws" and "traditional customs," most Australians would not know that the content of these traditional laws and customs are left undefined even as others are altogether excluded from legal recognition. Still fewer Australians have had the chance to appreciate the breathtaking rhetorical skill with which the High Court in *Mabo* and *Wik* simultaneously castigated previous courts for their historically and morally laden refusal to recognize the value of Aboriginal beliefs and customs and reconfirmed the function of dominant morality in deciding issues of cultural recognition.

Why then should we be surprised to learn that Pauline Hanson knew little more about indigenous traditions than the average non-Aboriginal Australian when she urged the public to avert its eyes from the mesmerizing image of indigenous tradition and to wake up from the spell cast by a materially motivated "Aboriginal industry"? Hanson should make us pause, but not for the usual suspects lurking in her rhetoric: specters of racism, intolerance, and bigotry. We should pause because embedded in this racist rhetoric is a call for "ordinary Australians" to look at the real conditions of Aboriginal social life.

What if we were to do the unthinkable and agree with Hanson that there is something fishy about the nation's enjoyment of ancient Aboriginal traditions? About the national celebration of a social law preceding the messiness of national history? About the tacit silences surrounding the content of Aboriginal traditions? About legislation written to support an ancient law predating anything present-day non-Aboriginal Australians are responsible for and anything present-day Aboriginal Australians could know about? To appreciate Hanson's uncanny insight while refusing her political or social analysis necessitates taking seriously the claims of many public spokespersons and ordinary Australians that they are honestly celebrating the survival of indigenous traditional culture. When they think about it, many Australians are genuinely moved by the miraculous persistence of an Aboriginal law in the face of centuries of traumatic civil onslaught. There in the distance, although never wherever an actual Aboriginal subject stands and speaks, the public senses a miracle of modern times, a sublime material impossible to define but truly felt, an immutable and indestructible thing that predates and survives civil society's social and corporeal alterations. *The Last Wave, Picnic at Hanging Rock,* and numerous other popular films and books strive to evoke this affective state. The nation truly celebrates this actually good, whole, intact, and somewhat terrifying *something* lying just beyond the torn flesh of present national social life. And it is toward this good object that they stretch their hands. What is the object of their devotion?

In part, this object is the easily recognized wounded subject of the modern liberal state.⁴⁶ The political drama of an ancient law's battle for recognition is refigured as a series of personal traumas suffered by innocent indigenous citizens. This figuration accounts for why, in the Australian edition of *Time* magazine, a psychiatrist rather than a politician or constitutional lawyer explained the social meaning and import of the Stolen Generation's moral claim on the nation: "The grief echoes through generations. With no experience of family life themselves, many find parenthood difficult—one woman told how she had to be taught how to hug her children."⁴⁷ Not surprisingly, given the ages of the plaintiffs, in its investigation of the forcible removal of Aboriginal children from their parents, the report *Bringing Them Home* likened cultural assimilation, the Australian liberal state's final plan for Aborigines, to physical annihilation, the German fascist state's final plan for European Jews; that is, the meaning of an indigenous cultural holocaust is figured metaphorically in relation to the global archetype of holocaust. The report, and many Aboriginal men and women, noted the irony that as Australians were fighting fascism abroad they were perpetuating it at home.

Bringing Them Home was not alone in raising the specter of a creeping fascism secreted in the heart of Australian nationalism. It was widely feared that popular support for Hanson's xenophobic political party, One Nation, signaled a potentially apocalyptic failure of historical consciousness—an actual amnesia of the social costs of the infamous mid-century white immigration policy. While commenting on the need for federal recognition of indigenous native title, former Labour Prime Minister Paul Keating explicitly figured opposition to native title in the commonsense formula of antifascism: first they came for X . . . finally they came for me. "If we start wiping out indigenous common law rights, when do we start wiping out non-indigenous common law rights? This is what this game is about."⁴⁸

This really *is* what the game is about or, at least, is *also* about—the rightness and authority of "our" common law, its defense, and in its defense the defense of the liberal subject of rights. Another wounded subject stands behind the scarred indigenous body: the liberal subject who wielded the frontier blade and nearly fatally wounded himself in the process. Explicit ongoing intolerance of the indigenous population threatened to reopen the wound and finish the job. Beazley and other public spokespersons suggested that mitigating the ongoing failures of the liberal common law through acts of public contrition and atonement simply provides a means of building a newer, deeper form of national self-regard and pride, a form freed from its tragic siblings—imperialism, totalitarianism, and fascism.

In short, national subjects are not pretending to celebrate the survival of indigenous traditions while secretly celebrating their necessary discursive and affective failures, returning again and again to wound and to worship the wound. Liberal supporters of indigenous traditions really want them to have survived, at least in part. They want to worship a traditional order stripped of every last trace of bad settlement history, at least in part. This real desire makes it even more difficult for Aboriginal men and women not to see the failure of cultural identity as their own personal failure rather than as a structure of failure to which they are urged to identify. Aboriginal persons I work with often turn their critical faculty on themselves or become trapped between two unanswerable questions: "Were my traditions taken from me?" or "Did I, my parents, and my children abandon them?"

We might here ask: What national reformations are accomplished by this traditional survival? A perduring ancient law wiped clean of the savage history of modernity burnishes the tarnished image of the settler nation and the torn imaginary between it and its citizens in four important ways: (1) The survival of good indigenous traditions transforms liberalism's bad side into a weak, inconsequential historical force. The very social weakness of Aboriginal people reinforces this fantasy. If even *they* could survive liberalism's bad side, this bad side must be weak indeed. (2) When good traditions appear before the nation, liberalism's good side also appears as a strong supporting force. The trauma of settler history is revealed to have been an unfortunate transition on the long road to a new, triumphant national: "We cannot really celebrate the triumphs of our history if we're not also prepared to acknowledge the shame of our history."[49] Of course, much depends on Aboriginal persons censoring "those laws and customs . . . repugnant to natural justice, equity and good conscience" so that the nation does not have to experience its own continuing intolerance, its own failures to achieve a truly multicultural national formation without recourse to discipline and repression. (3) Resilient Aboriginal traditional law provides a fantasy space for non-Aboriginal subjects to imagine their own resilience in the face of the brutal conditions of liberal capital and to hope that things will get better without the painful process of social transformation. In other words, resilient Aboriginal traditions provide the grounds for popularized fantasies like *Mutant Message Down Under*, which, while critiquing commodified culture and capital formations, perpetuate these same forms in being itself a commodity. (4) And, finally, the survival of some Aboriginal traditions confuses the question of who or what is responsible for the loss of other traditions. If some Aborigines were able to resist the "tides of history," why weren't most? Responsibility for the continuity of native title is shifted from the state to the "activities and will of the indigenous people themselves."[50] The social conditions in which Aboriginal subjects must maintain their law is not a matter that law and nation need consider.

As the nation stretches out its hands to an ancient aboriginal law in order to embrace its own ideal body, indigenous subjects are called on to perform a complex set of semiotic maneuvers in exchange for the good feelings of the nation and the reparative legislation of the state. Indigenous subjects must transport to the present ancient prenational meanings and practices in *whatever* language and moral frameworks prevail *at the time of enunciation;* the rights and resources that the state and nation extend are intended for the *indigenous* subject — that imaginary prenational subject haunting the actions of every actual Aboriginal person. If conjuring this impossible indigenous subject were not itself an arduous enough semiotic task, Aboriginal men and women are also called on to give national subjects an experience of being transported from the present to the past, including the nation's failed promise to the very persons carrying them along. The demand for this dual transportation is captured in the most banal of public and private queries to Aboriginal persons: "Tell us what was it like before us."

Aboriginal subjects should, in short, construct a sensorium in which the rest of the nation can experience the sensations described, at the opening of this chapter, by Fison. They should model a national noumenal fantasy. But every determinate content of Aboriginal culture — every propositional content — forecloses the imaginary fullness of ancient law. Every time indigenous subjects provide content to their traditional practices, they do so in present time — linguistic time — and this marks their alteration by history. Thus, no matter how strongly Aboriginal persons identify with these now lost but once fully present customary practices, all Aboriginal subjects are always being threatened by the categorical accusation: "You are becoming (just) another ethnic group" or "You are becoming a type of ethnic group whose defining difference is the failure to have maintained the traditions that define your difference."

So?

What I am saying is hardly news, nor do I mean it to be. In their nature as socially produced and negotiated abstractions, all identities fail to correspond fully with any particular social subject or group and are propped up or undermined by their relation to other social identities and institutions. But all failures of identity are not the same; they are not related to state and capital institutional structures in the same way, and they do not produce the same discursive and affective results. Each one arises from and is situated in a particular set of social practices and relations, each constitutes a particular set of social problems and organizes a particular set of social desires, horrors, and hopes.

My ultimate interest is not in these discursive and affective aspects of indigenous subjectivity nor in their commercial tracks. The goal of understanding the necessary failure of indigenous identity is to understand how national and state recognition of that identity supports and strengthens the nation and capital, not indigenous peoples, or not primarily indigenous peoples. The real goal of this chapter and this book is to understand better how power operates and is configured in multicultural settler nations like Australia. The abstraction "indigenous tradition" is a critical relay point through which immanent critiques of dominant social formations, institutions, values, and authorities are transformed into identifications with these same formations, institutions, values, and authorities. This socially practiced *idea* translates national failures to provide even basic economic and social justice into local failures of culture and identity. It organizes commonsense notions of who (or what) is responsible for the social inequalities characteristic of the late liberal Australian nation.

If for non-Aboriginal Australian subjects indigenous tradition is a nostalgic memory-trace of all that once was and now is only partially, for Aboriginal subjects ancient law is also a demand: You Aborigine establish an identification with a lost object. Strive after what cannot be recovered. Want it badly. We do. See us celebrating it. The social consequences of "the nation" embracing indigenous traditions is quite different from the consequences of indigenous people embracing the same. Embracing its shameful frontier history allows the nation to begin bit by bit to unbind itself from the memories and hopes once associated with that history, and allows the nation to get on with its business, find new ideals and images to identify with. But something very different happens with the indigenous subject. For not only are indigenous people scarred by loss in their discursive passage into being, the historical and material pressures on them to identify with the name of this passage (tradition) affectively constitutes them as melancholic subjects,[51] and the risk of producing a melancholic subject increases; that is, the more they believe publicly mediated incitements that the nation is embracing them. This melancholia acts as a communicative vehicle for distributing, and confusing, *feelings* about who is responsible for present-day social maladies, for the state's failure to curb the excess of capital and to provide equitable health, housing, and education. Non-Aboriginal Australians enjoy ancient traditions while suspecting the authenticity of the Aboriginal subject; Aboriginal Australians enjoy their traditions while suspecting the authenticity of themselves.

And so, in the following final section, I examine an all too clear calculus coordinating the material stakes of an Aboriginal person's or group's claim to be traditional and the determinate content and passionate attachment that they must produce to support their claim. When capital resources are only indirectly at stake, the content of the "ancient order" often remains vaguely defined. But when the material stakes increase, particular indigenous persons and groups are called on to provide precise accounts of local social structures and cultural beliefs that necessarily have a "more or less" relationship to the ideal referent of "traditional customs and laws" and to anything actually occurring in their day-to-day lives. At some "to be announced" boundary, the "less" becomes "too little" and the special rights granted to indigenous persons give way to the equal rights granted to all groups in the multicultural nation.

SPECIFICATIONS

Managing this discursive gap is clearly the semiotic challenge, dilemma, and irony of urban Aborigines, many of whom have served at the frontline of political action, arguing for land rights, social entitlements, and basic justice. How does an urban Aboriginal person become a convincing indigenous subject and thus secure the social, discursive, and affective resources available through this convincing performance? We find a clue in an ordinary article published in the *Sydney Morning Herald* on 7 August 1997. The story featured Lydia Miller, "a very modern manifestation of Aboriginality . . . a city power broker . . . in charge of nine staff and an annual $3 million budget." Miller is described as an Aboriginal activist from "one of Australia's best-known indigenous families," a family composed of lawyers, activists, artists, and actresses. What makes Miller's Aboriginality compelling is not, however, (or not simply) her biological heritage, but rather that heritage plus her identification with the "diplomatic protocol of ancient Australia." She becomes authentically Aboriginal only at the moment she willingly alienates her discourse and identity to the fantastic claim that she is able to transport from the past an ancient practice.

Lydia Miller, until recently the head honcho of indigenous arts funding in Australia, and current Olympic events organiser, has a particularly Aboriginal view of the political geography of this nation. "I think of it as something like 301 nations—300 indigenous nations and one nation called Australia." This view of the world makes life infinitely more complex for Miller than for your common or garden variety bureaucrat. For example, during her two and a half years as director of the Australia Council's indigenous arts board and now, as a project head with the Olympic Festival of the Dreaming, she has meticulously followed the diplomatic protocol of ancient Australia.[52]

Some readers of the original story probably passed over the strange passage, "she has meticulously followed the diplomatic protocol of ancient Australia," without much thought. Others might have imagined sun-drenched, clay-painted *black* bodies dancing a sacred corroboree, or sacred ritual objects passing from *black* hand to *black* hand. If they did, they imagined bodies and hands whose color coding is otherwise than Miller's own, a reading that the *Sydney Morning Herald* foregrounds with a large photo of Miller. Still other readers might have smirked, believing the entire article to be a product of public relations machinery. If she said anything like what was quoted, Miller might have thought she was donning an "ideological mask" for a variety of political reasons.[53] In any case, the *Sydney Morning Herald* does not elaborate to what "the diplomatic protocol of ancient Australia" refers.

This referential nonspecificity is not the result of a lack of knowledge or a failure to report it. Rather, "ancient protocol" is experienced as maximally symbolic at exactly the moment when it seems minimally determinate.[54] This semiotic hinge allows readers to fantasize a maximal variety of images of the deserving indigenous subject at the very moment the description of the content of the social geography approaches zero. In other words, nineteenth-century social models of a male-dominated family and clan walk side-by-side twentieth-century models featuring crystal woman, and ad infinitum. This proliferation of possible "protocols of ancient Australia" fits neatly in the consumer-driven capital, especially in the modern protocols of global tourism (of which we can now understand the Olympics to be a part).

Of course, the seemingly simple statement "the diplomatic protocol of ancient Australia" projects national and state forms and practices into this empty geography (diplomatic, protocol, and ancient *Australia*). A landscape actually emptied of all meanings derived from settlement history is the real unimaginable, unrepresentable ground of "indigenous." All *representations* of this ground must pass through whatever narratives of national history exist at the time. But it is this fantastic, unrepresentational social ground where the truly deserving Aboriginal subject(s) stand(s) — the social state against which the legal apparatus and the jury of public opinion measure whether contemporary Aboriginal persons are deserving of national sympathy and special state reparative legislation. Every actual Aboriginal subject produces personal and national optimisms and antagonisms because in speaking and being they *stand in the way of* this unrepresentable good object in the dual sense of being merely metonymic of it and a material barrier to it.

When material resources are directly at stake, the distance between unknowable prenational social geographies and present social, linguistic, and cultural practices are more closely scrutinized in the press and are more precisely measured in law. In these instances, nation and law demand that Aboriginal subjects produce maximally concrete cultural and social referents, diminishing the symbolic range and potency of every particular contemporary practice. For example, in the midst of the Kenbi Land Claim in the Northern Territory, Rupert Murdoch's *Northern Territory News* featured an interview titled "Topsy Secretary — Last of the Larrakia."[55] This interview came amidst a stream of editorials detailing the large cost (to white Australians) of the Kenbi Land Claim and the amount of land that would be taken out of the "Territory's future," a region defined as white insofar as it defines the allocation of land to Aboriginal Australians as taking this land out of Territory hands. A breezy piece, the article pivots on a series of racial, cultural, and ideological differences between the ancient Aboriginal past and the unfolding Aboriginal present. The interview begins by describing Topsy Secretary as "the last full-blooded Larrakia," while it acknowledges the existence of other "fair-skinned [Larrakia] descendents."

Although the article describes Topsy Secretary as a "pure" Larrakia in a racial sense, it suggests she is not a pure Larrakia in her material and cultural desires. While seemingly celebratory of Topsy Secretary, the article describes her everyday desires in a way that marks her as just another national hybrid cultural subject undermining the political cause of which she is cast as a symbol. The article is able to undermine the Kenbi Land Claim by suggesting that this last real Larrakia is *really* no different than the average Australian (white) citizen. Topsy Secretary only retains "knowledge about traditional foods," an enthusiasm shared by many settler Australians. Her other pasttime pleasures are on par with many middle-brow "white" Australians — sitting on her veranda, watching *Days of Our Lives* and *The Young and the Restless*. The hall-

59

mark of Aboriginal high culture, men's ceremonies are now " 'All forgotten,' she said. 'No old men—they're gone—no-one to teach.' " Finally, her political views, the very fact that she has political views, differentiate her from her own parents, the site of real precolonial Aboriginality: "Topsy said her father never worried about land rights. He accepted the Europeans as friends and never wished them to go away. But Topsy had lived to see her country shrink with the passing of generations. She wanted to see freehold title over the Kulaluk land and was hopeful the Larrakia would be successful in the long-awaited Kenbi land claim" (16).

A knot of speculative enjoyment is captured in this interview, inciting questions about the *deserving* Aboriginal subject: Who should receive the benefits of reparative legislation? How to measure the line between the polluted and diluted present and the pure ancient past? What line demarcates an Aboriginal subject from a national ethnic subject? The article does not answer these questions, rather it simply raises the stakes of any particular decision a land commissioner might make regarding what will constitute legally felicitous indigenous traditional cultural difference. Should someone who watches *Days of Our Lives* and *The Young and the Restless* receive valuable land on the basis of their traditional beliefs and practices?

All major pieces of cultural heritage and land legislation in some way mandate such felicitous traditional cultural differences and promote to some degree the paranoid epistemology of Fison's modern ethnology. Most land legislation restricts claims to "traditional Aboriginal owners." And they demand that claimants demonstrate a genealogical connection between their present and past customary beliefs and practices (the more specifically the better) and, further, that they identify with those customs (the more passionately the better). Those few pieces of legislation based on history, or on a combination of tradition and history, reaffirm as "unchallengeable" the commonsense notion that tradition provides the true economic and cultural value of Aboriginal society to Aborigines and to the nation. In New South Wales, for instance, land rights legislation is not restricted to traditional owners. It allows Aboriginal groups to claim land on the basis of their historical attachment. But the goal of the legislation is the "regeneration of Aboriginal culture and dignity . . . at the same time [that it lays] the basis for a self-reliant and more secure economic future for our continent's Aboriginal custodians."[56]

When Aboriginal persons disrupt the fantasy of traditional identity by rejecting it as the authentic and valuable difference of their person and group or insisting on its alterity to common law values, they risk not only the material values available to them through this *idea* but also the ability of future generations to stake a claim based on its semiotic remainders. The following few interlocutions between lawyers and their Aboriginal clients drawn from the Kenbi Land Claim suggest the microdiscursive nature of these attempts to disrupt such fantasies. The first example is taken from a legal proofing session held right before the Kenbi claim was first heard in 1989, the second from public testimony given during a second hearing held in 1995–96, and the third from a videotape I made with two younger claimants during a lull in a young men's ceremony. In the third sequence, Raelene Singh and I tease each other about the basis of the Belyuen claim: conception relationships (*maruy*) with the Belyuen waterhole and by extension a spiritual tie to other sacred sites in the claim area; a physical relationship to each other and the claim area by the fact of a shared substance (sweat *ngunbudj*); and a familial relationship with the spirits and graves of deceased ancestors (*nguidj*) throughout the claim area.

(1)

KENBI LAWYER: What was it like before the white man?

TOM BARRADJAP: I don't know mate I never been there.

KENBI LAWYER: Yeah, right, ha ha ha, but what was the traditional law for this place? We need to know what was the traditional law for this place.

(2)

ROBERT BLOWES: Right. And when you were talking to Mr. Howie here you said that's the native way to call him brother?

TOPSY SECRETARY: Yes.

ROBERT BLOWES: Yes. Was that really brother?

TOPSY SECRETARY: Well, in your way it's cousin brother, but my way we call him brother, and sister.

ROBERT BLOWES: So he had different father and different mother?

TOPSY SECRETARY: Yes, but it's still, we call him brother and sister.

ROBERT BLOWES: And he's still Larrakia?

TOPSY SECRETARY: Yes.

ROBERT BLOWES: And he's still the same country?

TOPSY SECRETARY: Yes.

ROBERT BLOWES: Okay. And what about your father and Tommy Lyons; is that the same way, then? Your father Frank—

TOPSY SECRETARY: Yes, it's the same way.

ROBERT BLOWES: So he's not really brother.

TOPSY SECRETARY: Well, they all brothers.

ROBERT BLOWES: That native way.

TOPSY SECRETARY: Real brothers.

(3)

BETH POVINELLI: What you? Are you for this country?

RAELENE SINGH: He taping for pretend report.

POVINELLI: Ngambin (cousin's daughter), you for this country?

SINGH: Yes. This is my country. It's like my life.

POVINELLI: Oh, it's like your life from the Dreamtime ancestors?

SINGH: Yeah. And I come out of that Belyuen waterhole.

POVINELLI: Oh, you been born from there now?

SINGH: Yeah, that's the dam. That old man Belyuen gave this mob kid here now, us here now, like today where we walk around.

POVINELLI: Yeah, walk around.

SINGH: It's like a gift from God.

POVINELLI: From which one from on top way?

SINGH: Yeah, well, we got our own, we got our own thing, gift, ah, we got our own father, see.

POVINELLI: We got him from here now?

SINGH: From Belyuen from our ancestors.

POVINELLI: And do you believe that?

SINGH: Yes.

POVINELLI: Oh, you do?

SINGH: Yes. That is true.

POVINELLI: And are you teaching your kids?

SINGH: Yes.

POVINELLI: Oh, which ones?

SINGH: I am teaching my niece, there, Chantelle.

POVINELLI: You call him daughter isn't it?

SINGH: Yeh, my daughter from my little sister.

In this case as in other land claim cases, lawyers, and the anthropologists who help them, practice the law as if knowing that their asking Aboriginal witness to embody an imaginary and discursive impossibility were irrelevant to the very organization and operation of power they intend to be challenging. Keeping with *local* speech practices, Barradjap uses humor to jolt the Kenbi lawyer back into social present time—to think about what he is asking. But speaking the "truth" to fantasy, such as Barradjap tries to do, or creating an

FIGURE 3. Belyuen traditional owners.

ironic hypertext about law and identity, as Raelene and I do, does not upset the practice of primarily valuing Aboriginal subjects in relation to their ability to afford for national subjects a language and experience of "before all this." It only shifts the register, only sets into motion a chain of signs whose object is to forestall the collapse of the fantasy: o.k., right, but what about "before the white man," about "traditional law," about the "real Aboriginal way."

The Kenbi lawyer is no fool. It is not a lack of knowledge that prompts his query. He knows he is asking the impossible of Tom Barradjap. He and I have laughed about these types of questions, yet he asks anyway. The utterance of the Kenbi lawyer registers a desire that, *if only for a moment,* reality be torn, that what he knows is true not to impede what he wishes for *nevertheless,* that the social consequences of violent settler history be suspended *even if only for this private moment,* especially in this *intimate interpersonal moment.* And in this movement from knowledge to its refusal we see the contours of the desires and suspicions constantly circulating around Aboriginal men and women, an affective topology in which they are formed and to which they must respond. These personal and national needs, desires, and demands disturb every Aboriginal enunciation. In the logic of fantasy, Barradjap's insistence that the Kenbi lawyer "get real" is reinterpretable as Barradjap withholding from the Kenbi lawyer the *real* truth, a form of truth existing somewhere beyond this fragmented and corrupted social reality. In the linguistic fragments "yeah, right, ha ha ha, but," the Kenbi lawyer marks the irresolvable tension between a barred desire (his desire to refuse knowledge and gain entry to a traditional land) and a barring agent (Barradjap's refusal to act as a discursive passage to that land).

Like the first Kenbi lawyer, so is another Kenbi lawyer, Robert Blowes, very knowledgeable about Aboriginal social relations. Along with numerous land claim cases, he served as counsel assisting in the presentation of the *Wik* case before the High Court. Yet, again, something intrudes and interrupts his knowledge. If the utterance of the Kenbi lawyer indexes some desire for his knowledge of national history not to bar his access to the prenational, Blowes's utterance seems to index some desire for his support of indigenous customary difference to remain just a matter of words. Although Topsy Secretary refuses to orient her understanding of family to Blowes's description, Blowes's micro-management of the truth value of various kinship systems is an example, and just an example, of the historical and still pervasive microsociological inter-actions that produced in Raelene, Topsy Secretary's brother's granddaughter, the (mis)recognition of her daughter as her niece. Moreover, the evidence of

Topsy Secretary suggests how any determinate content of local traditions up-sets the fantasy of "ancient law" as a form of otherness that is deeply recogniz-able and does not violate the core subjective or social values of settler society. Raelene and I may pun the micromanagement of discourse necessary to main-tain the core fantasy of land and native title claims, but our discursive play also marks the migration of this fantasy. My own reminder to Raelene to de-scribe Chantelle as "daughter" rather than "niece" provides further evidence of the microdisciplinary tactics constantly operating within the Aboriginal social field.

The desires and suspicions circulating around Aboriginal women and men are not confined to formal legal hearings. In the now-numerous commer-cial venues commodifying Aboriginal traditional culture, national and inter-national consumers approach indigenous men and women expectant, opti-mistic, and cynical. They hope that *this time* traditional culture will appear before them (which it always does *more or less*) and that *this time* they are buy-ing sight unseen the real thing (which they always are *more or less*). But before they have even purchased their ticket, every consumer of culture is already disappointed by what they know: what they are about to see is a commercial product. They, like Fison, leave the scene of cultural performance frustrated. Why aren't traditions wherever I am? Who is withholding them from me? I bet there are none here. Who is to blame for their disappearance?

This is why the "real law man," and to a lesser extent the "real law woman," fixes the attention of the nation, law, and commerce, publican and politician. Law men and women are simultaneously what the nation viciously ghosted and where it hopes it can recover a previously unstained image. The nation looks not at but through contemporary Aboriginal faces, past where every Ab-original and non-Aboriginal Australian meet, wanting the spirit of something promised there: "Tell us something we do not, cannot, know *from here* — what it was (you and we were) like before all this. What our best side looks like." In the moment before any particular answer, ears and eyes are transfixed by the potential of indigenous knowledge, by what might be unveiled, and by a more general possibility of experiencing the new, the ruptural, the truly transfor-mative. This moment is filled with horror, anticipation, excitement. Of course no Aboriginal person can fulfill this desire, be truly positively alterior, nor if they could would they *make sense* to the institutional apparatuses necessary to their livelihood. This "first speaker, the one who disturbs the eternal silence of the universe" would in fact be experienced as stereotypically psychotic.[57]

These semiotic figurations and mediations of indigenous spirituality are not simply in language but in space. They present travelers with a set of expectations about what they might and have a right to expect from the people and places to which they travel. At the heart of these textual mediations is the expectation of an experience of being in the presence of the spirit. And this expectation is manifested spatially — it interprets physical space and is extended into social interactional space. Compare, for example, Belyuen and Wadeye. Remember Belyuen lies on the Cox Peninsula on the western side of the Darwin Harbor. Ever since the British settlement of Darwin, the proximity of indigenous camps on the peninsula has provided visiting dignitaries, international celebrities, film-makers, writers, and academics with access to Aboriginal culture.[58] Periodically between the 1930s and 50s Belyuen served as a base for national radio programs, films, and anthropological studies; and traveling dignitaries, scholars, and celebrities desired and were provided with a variety of cultural performances, productions, and artifacts produced there. However, as the transportation infrastructure between the Cox Peninsula and Darwin improved, Belyuen has gotten closer to Darwin and, in the process, lost its aura of distinctiveness. In 1984, when I first arrived at Belyuen, the ferry ride between Darwin and the Cox Peninsula took upwards of an hour. Nowadays, it takes fifteen minutes. Likewise, the drive from Darwin to Belyuen now takes roughly seventy minutes, rather than the two to three hours it previously took, depending on the condition of the dirt road.

The legal status of Cox Peninsula lands has also contributed to a sense that the culture of the area has whitened. Under an unresolved land claim for the last twenty years, most of the peninsula remains Commonwealth land, a no-man's land of economic and political practice. Capital investment for large- and small-scale business ventures continues largely to be unavailable until the claim is resolved. And no Aboriginal group has any clear, legally sanctioned mandate for excluding non-Aboriginal people from the country or restricting their activities in certain places. In late September 1999, non-Aboriginal campers defiled a women's ceremonial ground. Several residents of a small residential development nearby responded by saying that, as Commonwealth land, the area was open to everyone for any type of use. It was considered "white land" as much as "black land." The lack of legally enforced Aboriginal title encourages and discourages particular types of visitors. Middle-class families on package tours are not likely to visit. But self-described freaks, New Age travelers, ferals, or sportspersons camp on beaches or in the scrub by themselves or in areas next to those of Belyuen men and women.[59] These forms of interactions have their own economy of scale, resulting in small-scale exchanges of beer, food, shirts, or cigarettes for small informal conversations, song performances, or tours to sacred sites.

If physical and regulatory space has fashioned Belyuen as a place too close to white society to profit from the commodification of the spirit, Wadeye has been too isolated. Located off the Stuart Highway and in the middle of a large Aboriginal reserve, Wadeye is physically hard to reach. Several Aboriginal communities lying closer to the main highways profit from the tourist trade. The regulatory environment likewise impedes tourism. Wadeye lies within the Daly River Aboriginal Land Trust, as designated under the Aboriginal Land Rights (Northern Territory) Act, 1976. The community can and does require that nonresidents obtain permits before visiting; and, indeed, all non-Aboriginal people traveling within the land trust are supposed to have a permit issued for some designated community. Even as they impede travel to Wadeye, the difficulties these physical and regulatory environments present to travelers function as an interpretant of that space as more authentically Aboriginal. The question facing those building regulatory and physical environments at Wadeye is how to capture the tourism market now serviced by other Aboriginal communities without, in the very process, deauthorizing space. Let me put it this way: as Wadeye becomes a bridge to geist—as it forms material space in the spirit of consumer capitalism—it risks installing the deauthorizing signs of Western commerce.[60]

If popontology, law, and economy provide critical texts by which space and thus its capital manifestations are formed and interpreted, they also orient visitors' expectations of what will be found in these spaces. These expectations include an understanding that a visit to an Aboriginal community is not about: (1) the horror, exhaustion, and anxiety of being in the world of capital spacetime, but rather the experience of geist in the midst of this spacetime; (2) Aboriginal people nor their lives but rather an experience only Aboriginal people can afford; and (3) the aporia of truth, ethics, or moral action in the face of fundamental alterity, but rather the experience of a shared movement of human spirituality in spite of this alterity. Law and capital and publics and politicians do not need to be colluding in some way—engaged in a concerted mass conspiracy—to be seen as producing in different forms and for different purposes certain human beings as valuable insofar as they afford passageway to an enchanted spiritual being, away from the conditions of the spirit of capital. Indeed, these various discursive contexts and practices disperse common-sense understandings of indigenous spirituality and themselves constitute the dispersed sites in which this spirituality is produced.

And yet the people who are charged with transporting visitors to this enchanted realm, to an experience of being-in-dwelling, themselves dwell within the legal and economic debris of advanced capital. They inhabit a form of poverty that makes well-intentioned visitors afraid, physically ill, or subject to panic. It is a type of poverty that can place such visitors in limits similar to those in which Betty Bilawag and her family found themselves. Tourism in these limits risks (and promises) opening experience not to the spirit that capital commodifies, but to the overwhelming presence of liberal capitalism's bad faith, its dirty corners, its broken covenants.

Legal practitioners may hope to disambiguate themselves from these other cultural markets, but economic and symbolic logics articulate them, as do the Aboriginal subjects who move between them. Aboriginal subjects field similar desire-laden questions from tourists, anthropologists, and lawyers: Is this how it was done before white people? And they hear legal and commercial consumer reports—satisfied consumers grateful to be shown a part of real traditional culture; dissatisfied consumers grumbling that what they heard and saw didn't seem real *enough*. As did their ancestors, Tom Barradjap, Topsy Secretary, and Raelene Singh must orient themselves to the multiple symbolic and capital economies of "traditional law" if they are to gain the personal and material values available through them—if they are to alleviate to some extent the social conditions to which Hanson alluded and produced. As they navigate among mass-mediated and multimediated fragments of public discourses about the value of Aboriginal traditions and about the limits of cultural alterity, Aboriginal men and women like Topsy Secretary and her granddaughter Raelene Singh are left to grapple with how to present a form of difference that is maximally other than dominant society and minimally abrasive to dominant values. The hot potato of multicultural nation-building is dropped in their laps.

The ever-widening stretch of history never seems to soothe the desires or irritating suspicions of white subjects that somewhere out there in archives or within a withholding Aboriginal subject is the knowledge that would fill the fantasy space of "tradition." At the time Fison wrote *Kamilaroi and Kunai*, one hundred years had passed since the settlement of Sydney. At the time Tom Barradjap spoke, over two hundred years had passed and Aboriginal traditions had long since become a politicized and commodified form of national identity. Raelene Singh, her sister, and nieces (or daughters) had literally grown up under the shadow of the Kenbi Land Claim. For the entire span of their lives they heard their grandfather, grandmother, and mother publicly valued primarily for their traditional knowledge and role. Now they must be that impossible thing of national desire. And if the Kenbi Land Claim were ever to end, other land claims, native title claims, and cultural heritage claims are over the southern horizon. The external suspicion that somewhere out there someone is withholding a valuable thing is transformed into an internal local anxiety: Which of "our" old people is withholding information from us? What will they say or not say? How will the lives of the next generation be altered on the basis of a speaking or withholding relative? What if someone reveals a "real tradition" repugnant to the common law?

For external as well as for internal reasons, I shall select as the basis of this comparison the tribes which have been described by anthropologists as the most backward and miserable of savages, the aborigines of Australia, the youngest continent, in whose fauna, too, we can still observe much that is archaic and that has perished elsewhere.
—Sigmund Freud, *Totem and Taboo*

Australia is the present home and refuge of creatures often crude and quaint, that have elsewhere passed away and given place to higher forms. This applies equally to the aboriginal as to the platypus and kangaroo.
—Baldwin Spencer, *The Arunta*

This ethical problem of the definition of practices of freedom, it seems to me, is much more important than the rather repetitive affirmation that sexuality or desire must be liberated.
—Michel Foucault, "The Ethics of the Concern for Self"

2 / The Vulva Thieves (*Atna Nylkna*):
Modal Ethics and the Colonial Archive

EMPTY CITES AND MODAL ETHICS

A simple empty square confronts the reader on page 231 of Michael Taussig's "Maleficium: State Fetishism." An empty site captivates, holds, and is meant to hold the reader's attention. It is captioned with the following: "This empty space is where I would have presented Spencer and Gillen's drawing of the frog totem because it seemed to me next to impossible to get the points about representation across without this amazing image. But my friend Professor Annette Hamilton, of Macquarie University, Sydney, tells me that to reproduce the illustration would be considered sacrilege by many Aboriginal people—which vindicates the power not only of the design but of the prohibitions against it being seen."[1]

What Annette Hamilton says is true, I think. And, insofar as this modifies the textual practice she proposes, it positions both writer and reader on the side of an anthropological ethics arising from a modal architectonics; that is, a professional textual ethics built up from a grammatical structure that indexes the relationship between a predicate and the interior "mood" of a subject—here, a class of subjects. In the English language, mood is marked by auxiliary verbs such as "would," "should," "must," and "might." Hamilton's promotion of a specific text-building (or demolition) practice is dependent on delicate calibrations of knowledge and belief that these grammatical structures signal not only a person's attitude (epistemic modality) but the multiple obligations that arise out of that attitude (deontic modality). In short, Hamilton's ethics of the colonial archive is built on her sense certainty about how compulsory aspects of attitude should translate into compulsory aspects of behavior. In this case, a hypothesized Aboriginal subject "would be" offended or, worse, be fundamentally violated by the textual reproduction of the frog totem. Anthropologists should not, therefore, indeed must not—perhaps more interestingly *cannot*—reproduce the image. Something holds back the hand. Indeed, the "proper" of anthropology discovers itself retrospectively in each anthropologist's discovery that she or he is subject to an obligation.

In the broadest sense, in this chapter I reflect on the substitution of a practice of textual deletion, ellipsis, and paraphrase for a fuller social theory of the politics and ethics of alterity and similarity. In the narrowest sense, I analyze the material emergence of ritual sexuality as such in the colonial context of "radical interpretation" and examine why sexuality was the site in which an emergent ethical relationship to colonial cohesion and the customary was played out. Thus, I meditate on the emergent metamodality of liberalism motivating these textual practices, a philosophy not merely of the ought but of the emergence of a new normative relation to liberalism's own and others' moral philosophies, their oughts. At the same time I attempt to understand the limits and possibilities of "radical interpretation" in colonial contexts and its retroactive inscription in present political and social imaginaries, as discussed in the last chapter.

I do not mean to question here Hamilton's good intentions or, for that matter, her ethical project. As an ethics of respect this text-building project is, for the present, unassailable. Rather I want to understand who and what are being protected, saved, and recuperated from the breach and shadow of the settler archive and colonial history. My point is simple: something other than the Aboriginal subject risks being fundamentally violated when parts of the colonial archive are cited *verbatim*. Reading and reproducing the colonial archive risks the liberal subject's experience of the necessity of liberal intolerance and its translation into domineering force. And yet these uncitable sections continue to play a vital role in the evaluation of contemporary indigenous subjects and groups (as we will see in subsequent chapters) and the national celebration of tradition (as discussed in the last chapter). Land commissioners, native title tribunals, and formal and informal students of indigenous society read them and use them as the grounds from which contemporary practices are calibratable deviations.

I begin by situating these meditations in Baldwin Spencer and Frank Gillen's representations of Arrente sex acts and conclude by resituating them in the politics of cultural recognition and material distribution in contemporary Australia. Although I analyze the when and how of the textual constitution of a sex act qua sex act, and analyze how these acts subjectify persons, I am not so much interested in sex, ritual sex, or sexual violence per se in this chapter, or in the next. Rather both chapters examine the ways in which particular forms of corporeality, corporeal relations, and corporeal practices (public, violent, playful, ceremonial, noncouple, retributive) superanimated liberal reflection; caused a crisis of reason in Australian non-Aboriginal citizens; caused these citizens to experience their intolerance as their moral and intellectual limits; and helped to precipitate the discursive grounds for a new national ideological formation.

In short, this chapter, like the next, is only obliquely a history of sexuality. It examines the emergence of "sex" as a distinct act, of sexuality as a form of desire, subjectivity, and identity, and of the puzzling "manner in which what is most material and most vital in [bodies] has been invested" in indigenous Australia.[2] I hope to suggest how the superanimation of liberal discourse lifted "sex" out of local corporeal practices and to gesture toward the legal and cultural consequences of this artifactualization. But the chapter does not examine sex; instead it examines a feeling that radical interpretation chases, produces, and aspires to incite: the feeling of a destabilizing indeterminate "something" that lurks beside and rattles liberal understanding; a teetering into the sublime that this indeterminate something threatens and promises; and the deferred ethics of alterity haunting the politics of freedom and cultural difference in Australia. This chapter thus primarily examines what Spencer and Gillen were chasing in the Arrente desert; what they found; what they missed, foreclosed, and destroyed. And what, in foreclosing, they set in motion and what they helped to weave into the fabric of national discourse. This chapter is, in short, an attempt to understand why one form of nationalism rather than another developed in Australia, and how this form of nationalism figures a form of social coercion as a moment of cultural recognition and translation.

Why do I examine the Arrente case, or, for that matter, why do I examine in the next chapter the 1936 Daly River case of so-called ritual rape? They are, after all, simply two case histories among numerous colonial encounters that animated liberal reflective judgment in Australia between 1896 and 1936. I could fairly easily be accused of a somewhat haphazard methodology — of grafting grand theories and social teleologies onto all but forgotten, trivial, and nonrepresentative encounters. Worse yet, readers might wonder what temporal, spatial, or social dimensions connect the two case studies when actually they are separated by forty years and refer to two different Aboriginal groups in two different social, ecological, and cultural regions and to settler Australians across two very different periods.

A few preliminary responses are in order here. First, the two cases take up the theme of the social productivity of radical alterity (the repugnant and repulsive) and uncanny similitude from two different angles and aspects. This chapter focuses on the question of how to read the colonial archive as well as how to write a genealogy of the present in its shadow, a problem of hermeneutics and historiography. I do not advocate a shift back to a critical theory of reading from a critical theory of writing, but rather I suggest a regrounding of Althusser's insightful notion of symptomatic reading — reading "an answer without a question" — in a critical, pragmatically informed practice of historiography.[3]

Second, the cases reflect two types of encounter between settlers and indigenous people and two ways in which these encounters affected national and global understandings of Aboriginal Australia and Australian nationalism. It is these two types and modes that interest me. Spencer and Gillen's account of the corporeal practices of Arrente men and women would have a significant impact on how non-Aboriginal people inside and outside Australia imagined traditional indigenous culture and society. The administrative and juridical memos I examine in the next chapter would themselves reflect this history, though they themselves would not have the same circulatory range or impact. But the Daly River case suggests the variety of events and eventfulness that provided the conditions of possibility for the emergence of state multiculturalism. The struggle among police, administrators, ethnologists, and indigenous men and women to fix the proper meaning of a practice — and fix their own careers in respect to this positioning — is exemplary of the minor encounters, personal struggles, and ethical dilemmas that constituted, and constituted as compelling, the theoretical and administrative problems that scholars, government officials, and other state citizens addressed in texts like Spencer and Gillen's *Native Tribes of Central Australia* and, later, A. P. Elkin's *Australian Aborigines: How to Understand Them,* and still later, *Mutant Message Down Under; The Adventures of Priscilla, Queen of the Desert; Labor's Lot;* and *Eddie Mabo v. the State of Queensland.*

Finally, both chapters theoretically foreground, through historical and ethnographic material, how the emergence of a broad multicultural perspective was subjectively, textually, and institutionally mediated. Thus I use these two cases, on the one hand, to reflect on the expectations, exhilarations, frustrations, and tediousness of moments of "radical interpretation," or the fantasy of being in a moment of radical interpretation. On the other hand, I use these cases to question a persisting liberal model of communicative rationality, perhaps best and most radically summarized by Jürgen Habermas's notion of ideal communicative action (communicative versus practical reason) and Richard Rorty's poetic proposition for liberal society, namely, that liberal society treat as "true whatever can be agreed upon in the course of free discussion and waving aside the question of whether there is some metaphysical object to which the result of such discussion might or might not correspond."[4]

So let us begin.

OPENING VEINS

It is 1896. The desert heat is oppressive; the flies a constant annoyance on mouth, nostrils, and eyes. Baldwin Spencer and Frank Gillen are camped just outside of Alice Springs. Gillen had arranged for Arrente men and women and their surrounding Aboriginal neighbors to gather nearby to perform a repertoire of their rituals in exchange for food, tobacco, tea, and protection from pastoralists and police. At the time of their research, Baldwin Spencer was a zoologist and Frank Gillen a telegraph operator, but both men aspired to be the intellectual heirs of Lorimer Fison and A. W. Howitt's emergent late Victorian discipline of anthropology in Australia. And so, every day they took photographs, scribbled notes, and sat with now-nameless older central desert men and perhaps some central desert women, who themselves sat and struggled to answer the river of questions Spencer and Gillen directed at them about the ceremonies they were performing.[5]

At times Spencer and Gillen's eyes must have wandered from their writing and passed over the distended, malnourished bellies of Arrente children or the buckshot-scarred backs of Arrente men and women. When Spencer and Gillen helped their Arrente informants map out their kinship relations and marriage classes they must have heard full or fragmentary stories of the epidemics, poisonings, and massacres that accounted for the dead ends of numerous Arrente family groups. Gillen's later letters to Spencer periodically refer to this sexual and physical violence, a fact of frontier social life (as I'll discuss in more detail below) in which he critically intervened.[6] Their coauthored work *Native Tribes of Central Australia* (1899) also mentions the traumatic social and physical consequences of British settlement on Aboriginal society. But the purpose of the text was not to explore the traumatic effect of British colonialism, liberal bodily techniques and practices, pastoral capitalism, privatization, or Christian mortification on Arrente society, but rather to make sense of Arrente practices as such.[7] Thus, they sought — as had their mentors Fison and Howitt — to excise "every last trace of white men's effect on Aboriginal society" so that they might better get at Arrente practice or, perhaps more precisely, the *ideas* that organized it.[8]

No doubt Spencer and Gillen were engaged in grueling physical and mental work; at times the heat must have overwhelmed everyone. But they were happy to sweat, to inhale flies, to stretch a cramped leg. They knew the unprecedented nature of what they were witnessing.[9] The corpus of central desert male culture was unfolding before their eyes as "unspoilt Arunta [Arrente] men" and their Aboriginal neighbors performed and described nearly every one of their initiation, increase, and totemic ceremonies.[10] Spencer and Gillen hoped that the ethnography they wrote based on this field trip would become a bestseller in Europe, the Americas, and Australia, as well as a touchstone for ensuing generations of anthropologists.[11] It did, and their names will long be remembered for their work among the Arrente. In some deep and fundamental way, Spencer and Gillen made most social scientists Australianists, no matter their geographical or theoretical bent, insofar as critical foundational texts in structural-functionalism, structuralism, Marxism, and psychoanalysis were all refracted through *Native Tribes of Central Australia* on their way into public and private circulation and consumption.

To read Spencer and Gillen's texts is to understand why audiences were so captivated by them. As they detail the corporeal *praxis, techne,* and intensity of Arrente ritual life, the reader glimpses something of the multiplex and intense intercourses the Arrente maintained with one another and the animate landscape through elaborate and mundane techniques of rubbing, cutting, encasing, burying, swallowing, washing, and severing body parts, ritual objects, and ritual grounds. Few academics could imagine a better social site for testing the powers of Western rationality. These "primitive savages" provided an impediment against which multiple scholars and administrators could figure and test their intellectual powers. These natives frustrated and attracted; incited rage and respect, despair and regret. As Gillen would write to Spencer: "D——n them, they puzzle me and I doubt whether we shall even succeed in learning much about them."[12]

The question *how do we make sense of these practices* was not only of interest to academics but gained an international urgency in the context of debates about whether or not the white Australian colony was mature enough to become a sovereign Australian nation-state. How the indigenous was situated within extant discourses of the wild and reasonable and the civil and savage would affect the formulation of state policy in relation to Aboriginal persons and white settlers. During the Federation Conference of 1890, Australian Federalists like Sir Henry Parkes and Sir Samuel Griffith continually referred to the moral and economic maturity of the Australian colony as grounds for statehood, and they encouraged increased social and communicative networks between the colonies in the belief that the then current "want of knowledge which one colony possesses of another" impaired the health of the entire national body.[13] Were the "crude cults" ascribed to the Arrente and other indigenous Australians and the carnal and economic arrangements between indigenous groups and settlers the private affairs of a society apart or were they public matters of national import?[14] What were the shared symbolic bases for rational communication and debate between indigenous and settler society that might provide the grounds for a peaceful resolution of these differences? Did the lack of a common language or shared moral universe between settler and indigenous groups threaten the very notion of an Australian nation before there was a nation in fact? As I discuss in the next chapter, indigenous subjects were excluded from federal protection; indeed, they were barred from being included in the national census. But the treatment of indigenous persons by various colonies—especially by Queensland and the Northern Territory governments—put at peril the unity notion of "we the people."

Throughout, *Native Tribes* and *Northern Tribes* address these national anxieties, broaching the topic of the public secret of Aboriginal "marriage" and suggesting (and modeling) the form that a modern moral judgment should take in the scene of cultural alterity. Gillen, who was urged to run for local government in Victoria, was centrally involved in some of these public and government arguments. In 1898, he advocated the establishment of a federal Department of Aboriginal Affairs that would collect and record the customs and beliefs of indigenous groups.[15] But he opposed a proposed bill that would regulate the "carnal" relationship between white men and "any female Abgal or Half Caste" because he feared that such a bill would encourage false accusations against whites who offended blacks or their white employers.[16]

As for intra-Aboriginal sexual practices, "yes," Spencer and Gillen wrote, it is true, "considerable license is allowed on certain occasions, when a large number of men and women are gathered together to perform certain corroborees. When an important one of these is held, it occupies perhaps ten days or a fortnight; and during that time the men, and especially the elder ones, but by no means exclusively these, spend the day in camp preparing decorations to be used during the evening. Every day two or three women are told off to attend at the corroboree ground, and, with the exception of men who stand in relation to them of actual father, brother, or sons, they are, for the time being, common property to all the men present on the corroboree ground."[17] But, "in regard to their character it is of course impossible to judge them from a white man's standard. In the matter of morality their code differs radically from ours, but it cannot be denied that their conduct is governed by it, and that any known breaches are dealt with both surely and severely."[18]

We should not move too quickly past these and other reflections on emergent modern forms of national moral judgment. Statements like the ones above register the propositional form that emergent moral standards would take in the scene of customary difference and alterity and register the displacement of older normative conventions. Simply put, the text is a dialogical register of Spencer and Gillen's assumption of the moral stance their readers would take toward these acts: repugnance and attraction, repulsion and titillation. Indeed, they specified some elements of this reaction as a perfectly natural human response in need of a counternormative modern cultural pedagogy; namely, modern men should judge the compulsory forms and practices of other societies from the perspective of perspective.

To successfully incite readers to take up their positions (repulsion and reconciliation) depended in part on a number of successful textual maneuvers. In the first instance, Spencer and Gillen had to forestall the reading of their own writing as simply sensational ethnopornography. In short, rather than being repulsed only by Arrente practices, readers might be repulsed by the prurience of Spencer and Gillen. Spencer and Gillen were well aware of the potential for this representational and moral reversal. The debates between the "anthropo-logicals" of the Anthropological Society of London and the "ethnologists" of the Ethnological Society pivoted in part on the stance scholars should take toward sex (how it should be treated and talked about); and the emergent discipline's relationship to a politics of respectability.[19]

Several of Spencer and Gillen's colleagues provided graphically detailed accounts of Aboriginal sex acts and were subsequently accused of trafficking in pornography.[20] Others used different textual strategies to signify the scientific nature of their sexual discourses and thus protect themselves and their writing as ethnoscientigraphia from similar interpretations that the material was mere ethnopornographia. In treatises on circumcision and subincision, W. E. H. Roth and Herbert Basedow included line drawings of Aboriginal men and women engaged in sexual intercourse. But Roth placed an author's note at the head of the last chapter — suitably titled, "Ethno-Pornography" — of his ethnological study *Ethnological Studies among the North-West-Central Queensland Aborigines,* which read, "The following chapter is not suitable for perusal by the general lay reader."[21] And Basedow drew on the metalinguistic properties of code-switching — from English to Latin and German — to frame his investigations as "scholarly."[22] But this textual practice did not save his text from the market in ethnoporn — his extraordinarily dry and dusty treatise on subincision was reprinted along with Roth's by a small, private New York publishing house specializing in *ars erotica.*[23] Indeed, social scientific treatises on Aboriginal sexuality emerged in and circulated through a textual field saturated with fictional and nonfictional accounts of savage lives and times.[24]

By 1937, M. F. Ashley-Montague would observe that "such was the delicacy of feelings of the correspondents to the editors that rarely were they able to permit themselves to make more than the briefest references to those [sexual] customs and beliefs which it was their habit to dismiss with some such caliginous epithet as 'disgusting', or 'bestial.'"[25] In his private letter to Spencer, Gillen himself worries about how others will judge his accounts of Arrente sexuality: "This is hardly the sort of subject to write about so fully in a letter, old man, but I have drifted into it."[26] However, once Spencer notes the scientific value of such "unsavory material" Gillen promises to pursue its sense in detail.[27]

Still, by and large, Spencer and Gillen stop short of graphically positioning the Arrente in sex acts in their published writings. Instead, they use various techniques of textual implicature to prompt readers to infer the positions and practices of ritual sex. Forcing readers to draw their own inferences about what were the sex acts to which the elliptical passages referred at once and the same time qualified the moral character of Spencer and Gillen (as men being constrained by decent, proper, and scientifically oriented concerns) while maximally expanding the possible referent of sex. In other words, by conveying less information about the actual sex acts, Spencer and Gillen's increased the possibilities of what the sex acts might be.[28] For instance, in their more popular volume, *Across Australia* (1912), Spencer and Gillen describe the Arrente as "naked, howling savages" engaged in bodily acts that were "crude in the extreme."

Let us leave this textual field for a moment and ask instead what Spencer and Gillen saw or heard that they thought could or should be described as "considerable license" and "sexual intercourse" between "women" and "men"? To answer, let me turn to the following passages that purport to describe exactly what takes place "when a large number of men and women are gathered together to perform certain corroborees."[29] The first passage is taken from *Native Tribes* (1899); the second from *Northern Tribes* (1907).

A man goes to another who is actually or tribally his son-in-law, that is, one who stands to him in the relationship of *Gammona* [mother's brother], and says to the latter: "You will take my *Unawa* [wife] into the bush and bring in with you some *undattha altherta*" (down used for decorating during ordinary corroborees). The *Gammona* then goes away, followed by the woman who has been previously told what to do by her husband. This woman is actually *Mura* [wife's mother] to the *Gammona*, that is, one to whom under ordinary circumstances he may not even speak or go near, much less have anything like marital relations with. After the two have been out in the bush they return to the camp, the man carrying *undattha* and the woman following with green twigs, which the men will wear during the evening dance, tied round their arms and ankles. There will be perhaps two or three of these women present on each day, and to them any man present on the ground, except those already mentioned, may have access. During the day they sit near to the men watching but taking no part in the preparation of decorations. The natives say that their presence during preparations and the sexual indulgence, which was a practice of the Alcheringa, prevents anything from going wrong with the performance; it makes it impossible for the head decorations, for example, to become loose and disordered during the performance.[30]

There are further, in addition to this particular time, other occasions on which intercourse with women, other than those allotted to them, is allowed to the

men. It is very usual amongst all the tribes to allow considerable license during the performance of certain of their ceremonies when a large number of
natives, some of them coming often from distant parts, are gathered together —
in fact on such occasions all of the ordinary marital rules seem to be more
or less set aside for the time being. Each day, in some tribes, one or more
women are told off whose duty is to attend at the corroboree ground, — sometimes only during the day, sometimes only at night, — and all of the men except
those who are fathers, elder and younger brothers, and sons, have access to
them. When an ordinary corroboree is performed, which often occupies two
or three weeks, the women are close to the ground, as there is usually nothing sacred which they might not see, but in the case of sacred ceremonies they
are generally brought up during the evening. In the Arunta, when an ordinary
corroboree is in course of progress, an elder man will say to his son-in-law,
"You go into the bush with my *unawa* and bring in some *undattha altherta*"
(ordinary corroboree decorating material). The younger man then goes out
with the woman who is his *mura,* and to whom under ordinary circumstances
he may neither go near nor speak, much less have marital relations with, as
he does upon this occasion. The man and women return to camp, the former
carrying the down and the latter green twigs, which will be worn by the men
who perform the dance in the evening. When all is ready the women who have
spent the day with the men are painted with red ochre, and go to the lubras'
camp to summon the other women and children. The idea is that the sexual
intercourse assists in some way in the proper performance of the ceremony,
causing everything to work smoothly and preventing the decorations from falling off. In some tribes this sexual intercourse is much more noticeable than in
others.[31]

Critical understanding pauses over the meaning of the sentences: "The
natives say that their [women's] presence during preparations and the sexual
indulgence, which was a practice of the Alcheringa, prevents anything from
going wrong with the performance; it makes it impossible for the head decorations, for example, to become loose and disordered during the performance"
and "the idea is that the sexual intercourse assists in some way in the proper
performance of the ceremony, causing everything to work smoothly and preventing the decorations from falling off "? What might the Arrente men have
said and meant that Spencer and Gillen paraphrase as "it makes it impossible
for the head decorations, for example, to become loose and disordered during
the performance"? In other words, what were the socially mediated networks

of meaning and practice that makes the explanation "sexual intercourse prevents decorations from falling off" sensible? More particularly, why was it necessary for *Gammona* and *Mura* to bring *undattha altherta* into the proximity of this awkwardly phrased thing—"anything like marital relations"? We might ask what sex refers to in this ritual context; whether sex is a category always already independent of language and context, social relations and practices; and, more narrowly, whether "sex" or "sexual indulgence" is the proper interpretant of what *Mura* and *Gammona* did out of sight of Spencer and Gillen. The point of this series of questions is to understand whether these rituals were elaborate symbolic representations of male reproduction as Spencer and Gillen suggest, and many subsequent anthropologists claim, or whether it is possible to interpret the distinctiveness and value of these corporeal acts relative to some other set of acts and meanings. For instance, could sex be a minor form of bloodletting?

Let me try to be clear. I have little doubt that Spencer, Gillen, and most of their predecessors and successors took it to be self-evident that what they saw (or heard about) on or off to the side of corroborree grounds was "sex" between "men" and "women"; that when they and the Arrente pointed to a "sex act" they were pointing to the same act and field-of-action; that this act had a social syntax (men sexually exploiting women); and, finally, that an indigenous gender hierarchy could be read off this social syntax. Indeed, as had Fison and Howitt, Spencer and Gillen played a critical role in the development of a modern social science of kinship and descent whose difference lay in integrating the acts into a broader "intersexual arrangement" to use Fison's phrase. That is, not only did they see sex, Spencer and Gillen and their American, British, and French colleagues and students—from Morgan to Radcliffe-Brown to Lévi-Strauss—sought to formalize these elaborate corporeal intercourses into multiple models of heterosexually regimented familial organization (originally figured as kinship classification and marriage classes). Out of their and subsequent researchers' work would come the characterization of kinship, marriage, and descent as universal and necessary core features of tribal (and human) society.

But Spencer and Gillen saw and heard more than can be captured by the "mock algebra" of emergent studies of human social and sexual organization.[32] Indeed, they describe in some detail the corporeal *praxis* and *techne* of Arrente ritual life and the manner in which, for their Victorian sensibilities, these rough rituals bled into the brutish, bordered on the traumatic, became at times indistinguishable from the lewd. Blood flowed from veins, sweat

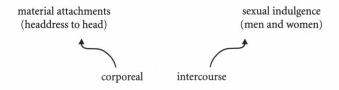

material attachments
(headdress to head)

sexual indulgence
(men and women)

corporeal   intercourse

FIGURE 4. Attaching headdress to head.

from pores, words from throat. These secretions of the body were rubbed into human bodies, ritual objects, and ancestral sites. Words and sounds, spoken and sung, softly or at a deafening volume, communicated to and penetrated into initiates and ancestral sites. Young initiates were encased in a wall of human flesh as their bodies were cut, their teeth knocked out, their skulls bitten. Arms, backs, chests, genitals, and other body parts were repeatedly punctured or seared with fire and fire-sticks, sometimes voluntarily, sometimes not. As Spencer and Gillen pile detail upon detail, European and Arrente socially mediated semiotic orders begin to peel away from one another. The more Spencer and Gillen describe exactly what took place and exactly how central desert men described their practices, the greater the two orders of denotation and predication flayed apart (figure 4).

If Spencer and Gillen did not explicitly question the sexual referent of these ritually elaborated corporeal discourses, their writings suggest some discomfort with the simple equation of Arrente and settler understandings of sexuality. As Fison and Howitt argued for the Kunai and Kamilovai, Spencer and Gillen argued that Arrente sexual acts were premised on marriage and the family, although not in the British or European sense of these terms. Bronislaw Malinowski, cofounder of British functional anthropology, would later lament Spencer and Gillen's "quite illegitimate silent assumption" that sexual acts were diagnostic of the relevance of monogamous heterosexuality to central desert people. He argued that although "the sexual aspect of family life is very important, nevertheless, it is only one side of the picture, and that to outline this picture correctly, we may not exaggerate one side of it."[33] Malinowski did not, however, question the silent assumption that Arrente were engaged in sex acts. He simply wished to mitigate the challenge that nonmarital, nonnormative sex posed to a universal family form built up from, he believed, the natural intimate bond a man and a woman felt for each other and for their children. Spencer and Gillen hardly questioned the self-evident nature of this normative socially mediated embrace. They ordered Arrente sexual practices in nested and ranked hierarchies of normative upper-class British sexual values: "The first is the normal one, when the woman is the private property of one man, and no one without his consent can have access to her, though he may lend her privately to certain individuals who stand in one given relationship to her. The second is the wider relation in regard to particular men at the time of marriage. The third is the still wider relation which obtains on certain occasions, such as the holding of important corroborees."[34]

Although the above description of sex may seem rather pedestrian to contemporary ears, such descriptions of Arrente sociality were interlaced with graphically detailed accounts of rites and customs most Australians did and would find appalling. Indeed, *Northern Tribes of Central Australia,* a slightly revised version of *Native Tribes,* opens with "a word of warning" that the rituals described therein were "eminently crude and savage in all essential points."[35] This warning echoes a passage from Sir Henry Maine's *Ancient Law* (1864), which warned scholars that if not properly approached the "strangeness and uncouthness" of ancient social practices could lead to the annulment of reason.[36] To put it simply, the ethnographic texts of Spencer and Gillen are not for the weak of stomach or mind. Nor can the challenge that their representations of indigenous corporeal intercourses pose to liberal theoretical and national formations be easily resolved through the comforting lens of sexual difference and gender masquerade.[37] Arrente customary practices really did shock and offend many British settlers, and not merely those who saw and experienced scenes such as Spencer and Gillen saw or heard described but also those who read about them in texts like *Northern Tribes* and *Central Tribes.* Spencer and Gillen's descriptions would have produced strong or weak affective responses, but their responses would have been physical for many readers — chills, palpitations, critical reflections, horror. Spencer and Gillen knew the possible affective destabilization of their text, as did their contemporaries in Britain. And they registered their knowledge of the physicality of textual reception in passages such as the one above in which they comment on what should be the proper and improper forms, contexts, and purposes of the judgments of modern man.

If Spencer and Gillen provided shocking, graphically detailed descriptions of Arrente body techniques, they were not interested in these details in or for themselves. This much charity we should extend to them: Spencer, Gillen, and other Victorian ethnologists sought primitive sex not for the "sheer pleasure of recounting the bizarre and eccentric," nor for the capital profit this pleasure garnered in the marketplace (that is, in the capital-generating genres of colonial memoir, travelogue, and ethnoporn), nor simply to make a name for themselves and their disciplinary interests.[38] On the contrary, Spencer, Gillen, and their contemporaries were captivated, at least in part, by what gazing on these acts of carnal spirituality seemed to provide a glimpse of—the idea and experience of a shared human supersensible moral realm, a *something* that linked what the Arrente called *Alcheringa* to what Europeans called Morality, Customary Law, and Justice.

Counterintuitively, perhaps, descriptions of these sex acts were intended to convey this supersensible moral experience across its textual mediation. Rather than what impeded the development of a humanistic science of culture and society, the impasse to reason presented by the "brutal and often revolting severity" with which the Arrente lawfully treated one another, along with the judgment that these actions could be—indeed should be—considered part of a single "lawful order," were the grounds of the emergent sociology of morality, and of sociology and anthropology more generally. These acts presented ever more forcefully, if ever more precariously, the awe-inspiring nature of the *thing* that the emergent science of man sought.[39] The feelings of repugnance and abhorrence that these acts produced in settler subjects prompted a calibration of the difference between their and their indigenous neighbors' notion of the moral and good life, the just and right life. The founder of modern sociology, Emile Durkheim, would posit that a general sociological theory of religion was possible exactly and only through the scholarly experience of two contrasting if not contradictory deontic systems. Only by experiencing the horror of moral alterity could the science of man sketch a sociology of morality itself, the real of human(e) society. The moral repulsion of Westerners in the vicinity of the cults of "primitive" and archaic peoples and the judgment of them as violations of human being confronted the moral authority that these same practices had in the society itself. It was in this hypermorally animated scene that reason was forced to—and writers promised reason could—discover a "convergence," a "horizon," a great arc, a superordinate realm, a metaphysical substrate, a final interpretant, a synthetic a priori where a universal idea resided connecting these human orders into human being, though wherever this idea abided it is nowhere that anyone ever stood, a moment no one has ever experienced.[40] This manifestation of the Spirit of Man depended, of course, on settlers considering the Arrente as human. And such a view is what Spencer and Gillen advocated.

We should not underestimate the intellectual stakes behind the gauntlet thrown down by this neo-Kantian wager. The challenge was issued as a simple proposition and a simple interrogative to Victorian ethnologists and colonial administrators: They are men. Are you man enough to know them? Both answers could well be "no." Victorians could fail in two obvious ways. First, Victorian man might simply fail to understand primitive man, his practices and their meaning and import. Researchers, state administrators, and private citizens often tasted the bitter failure of their effort to understand "tribal" practices, to make sense of them without a nagging remainder exceeding the analysis, teasing and tempting the mind, inciting counterargument. For instance, Reverend Fison described as "humiliating" his inability to make sense of Aboriginal terms of reference. And although he remained "perfectly sure, that there is a good reason for every one of the inexplicable terms" used to describe "inter-sexual relations," he was also irritated and angry at the Aboriginal and European men who he thought had deliberately impeded his understanding.[41] Throughout his letters to Spencer, Gillen also referred to the frustration of reason he experienced in the proximity of Arrente social and ritual orders. Their impediment to his reason had to be confessed, it caused anxiety and excitement, and it kept him awake at night animated by its puzzle.[42]

Second, in the end civil man might not be so different from colonized man. Apparent differences might be little more than ideological conceit, as Freud would quip, no more than the narcissism of minor differences — an uncanny, and uncomfortable, similitude. The *Northern Territory Times and Gazette* signaled this anxiety of identity in its defense of a police massacre of Aboriginal persons living among or near the Arrente twelve years before the arrival of Spencer and Gillen: "Justice is being sternly dealt out to the blacks in the Northern Territory." The information supplied by Inspector Beasley, which we publish elsewhere, gives an account of the way in which proceedings were carried on. Those who read the report will doubtless think that the trial and execution was somewhat quickly dispatched, and that there was an element of revenge about the affair which is inconsistent with our civilised notions of justice. But the writer of the report insists upon the fact that notice was given to the accused and the whole party was called upon to surrender. They may or may not have understood the meaning of the warnings, but certainly it appears that the officer in charge did all he could to prevent the wanton waste of life."[43]

Although we should not underestimate the gauntlet that rational understanding was forced to run in social contexts such as Spencer and Gillen's experience among the Arrente, we should also not move too quickly past the real hope and optimism motivating the Enlightenment belief that clarity of mind and language could release man from the force of internal and external coercion, from the force of unfreedom itself. What a monstrously optimistic fantasy: man might crawl out from the web of blind necessity through his understanding of himself and others. Kant's call for man to resolutely and courageously make use of their reason in public took on a spectacular — and specular — form in the colonial world as scholars faced the annulment of public and private reason on the *engwura* grounds (the site for the final initiation ceremony of young men). But the threat of reason's euthanasia rededicated ethnologists to the struggle.

Finally, we should not underestimate how deeply the wager of Enlightenment understanding is embedded in modern sociology, anthropology, and comparative law, in national and transnational political and public rhetoric, and in the common sense of communicative reason. From Emile Durkheim to Claude Lévi-Strauss to Pierre Bourdieu, to Donald Davidson and Richard Rorty, sociologists, anthropologists, and liberal philosophers have leaned on the idea, and proclaimed the faith that, as Lévi-Strauss argued, "there is a reason in what agents do and that the human sciences work most effectively when the ideas of a peoples are clear or are made so by the process of reasonable reflection.[44] The analytic philosopher Donald Davidson went a critical step further by arguing that "if we cannot find a way to interpret the utterances and other behaviors of a creature as revealing a set of beliefs largely consistent and true *by our own standards,* we have no reason to count that creature as rational, as having beliefs, or as saying anything."[45]

If the utterances and behaviors of our fellow creatures are to be judged as human (rational) only insofar as they meet *our* standards, then the gauntlet thrown at *our* feet by Arrente practices is no less intimidating now than it was during the lifetime of Spencer and Gillen. Arrente ritual practices have not become less shocking or more palatable over time for either settler Australians or Arrente. As contemporary Euro-American and Australian readers, whether of a more or less radical or conservative bent, move through *Native Tribes* and other documents in the settler archive they are likely to feel more or less uncomfortable, more or less shocked. These readers will probably notice a certain moral stance, perhaps framed as "uncertainty," they are taking toward certain represented acts. They might wonder: What effect would general public knowledge of these practices have on general public support of Aboriginal culture? Perhaps, if forced to refer to these texts these readers, now writers, will use various citational techniques that allow them not to reproduce the offending passage — a passage that offends the reader or their imagined audience — but instead rely on indirect reference. Or, perhaps they will reproduce verbatim Spencer and Gillen's words, then try to frame and guide judgment: *That was then, this is now; from their perspective this makes sense.*

Let the reader beware. Gillen noted in a letter to Spencer on 7 April 1902 that their description of the "death and burial ceremonies make interesting if gruesome reading."[46] I paraphrase here: Young male and female initiates are encased in a wall of human flesh as their bodies are cut, their teeth knocked out, their skulls bitten by objects and their flesh opened by other objects. Arms, backs, chests, genitals, and other body parts are repeatedly punctured or seared with fire and fire-sticks, sometimes "voluntarily," sometimes not. Older men and young women — what most non-Aboriginal Australians, perhaps many Aboriginal Australians, would probably consider "girls" — engage in "sex acts" with objects, sometimes the woman providing evidence of what Spencer and Gillen understood as "consent," sometimes not, often one woman the sexual object of multiple male partners, or so Spencer and Gillen describe the exchange. "Consent" being that without which freedom is difficult to imagine in a liberal framework, and thus without which coercion must be assumed, the liberal reading subject will be bothered, irritated, or enraged; again no matter their radical or conservative bent. To say, "but what is consent or voluntarism in such a scene?" is not to solve the social problem but to deflect and disperse its effects. The same can be said for the attempt to disperse the problem with textual technologies like footnotes and page references, ellipses and paraphrase.

Reason was not shocked solely by ritual. It reverberated against other revelations; for instance, what should be made of the fact that these natives seemed to demonstrate little interest in the conjunction of the carnal and spiritual; that they did not experience the trauma they were producing in us? In the glare of the Arrente sacred, the comforting narrative of the progress of liberal cultural tolerance and understanding shows its crevices, fault lines, and wrinkles. The question might be asked: What has changed since the days of Spencer and Gillen? Have liberal subjects become more tolerant as the power of publicly mediated understanding has progressed? Or have the people, practices, and textual referents that irritate liberal understanding simply been footnoted or deleted altogether? Is liberal understanding progressing, or are its disciplinary effects?

Let us turn away for a moment from the glare of the contrast of these semiotic and social orders and, instead, return to the question of what Spencer and Gillen witnessed from the perspective of the central desert men with whom they spoke. Why did Spencer and Gillen assume that the acts they witnessed or heard about were sex? If sex it was not, how did Spencer and Gillen come to believe they were seeing "sex" as such? As I explore these questions, I turn away from the terminal bind of semiotically oriented linguistic relativism. Rather, I want to focus on the function of power in the pragmatics of radical interpretation in settler contexts. I begin to answer the above questions by turning to the communicative conditions in which Spencer and Gillen gathered their ethnographic materials.

"THAT" DEMONSTRATIVE MOMENT OF "SEX"

Let us examine the explanation that Spencer and Gillen gave for why the Arrente engage in ritual sex: "The idea is that the sexual intercourse assists in some way in the proper performance of the ceremony, causing everything to work smoothly and preventing the decorations from falling off." What could this statement possibly mean?

I can begin by noting that whatever this sentence meant it is unlikely that Arrente men produced it. According to one account, Baldwin Spencer arrived in central Australia believing Frank Gillen to be a fluent speaker of Arrente, only to find his "knowledge of Arunta (and several other Aboriginal languages) was in fact rather less fluent than Spencer had assumed."[47] As a result, when they spoke to Arrente men about their ritual practices, Spencer and Gillen probably utilized utterances such as, "Why do you do *that* during your rituals?" Or, they might have used a pidgin equivalent "What for thatem?" or "What for youfella doem thatem longa corroboree?" (Gillen provides various examples of pidgin he reports hearing indigenous men speak in central Australia, many of which refer to sexuality.[48]) As they asked these questions they no doubt pointed to or diagrammed on paper, ground, or their bodies the action Spencer and Gillen understood to be "doem sex." Spencer and Gillen may also have used an Arrente term they understood to mean "copulate."

It is unlikely that the Arrente men responded with a series of utterances like, "that business now was done in the *alcheringa.* It was the same then. You cannot miss a step if you do that business. You cannot make a mistake. The headdress stays secure to the head." It is more likely that they spoke a pidgin version that in Gillen's transcription might look something like, "that business wefella must do em, em do same, em same longa *alcheringa,* em same, from thatem em make em right, cant mistake, thatem make em properly longa head." These complex communications were entextualized as "sexual indulgence, which was a practice of the Alcheringa, prevents anything from going wrong with the performance; it makes it impossible for the head decorations, for example, to become loose and disordered during the performance."

For the moment and for the sake of argument, let us agree that the Arrente men said something like what Spencer and Gillen report and that what the Arrente men said was "true" in the sense that they believed that the state they described was a result of the acts in which they engaged.[49] We can ask then, in a loose way, not what makes the headdress stick to the head, but, first, what makes the Arrente stick around to explain the rationale of their action to Spencer and Gillen; and, second, what makes Spencer and Gillen so interested in this rationale? To answer these two questions let me bring the linguistic lens even closer and pause over what could be considered the most minor, indeed, strictly speaking, the most meaningless of colonial communicative exchanges — the historical substitution of the lexical noun "sex" for the demonstrative pronoun "that." If "sex" secured headdress to head, it did so only after "that" (or its English-based pidgin equivalents, "det" or "detem") secured, and in the process refashioned, two very different semantic fields to one another.[50] At some point in time, whether before or after Spencer and Gillen arrived in Central Australia, indexical signs like demonstratives and finger pointing opened a coherent enough communicative channel between Arrente and settlers. We can see this rough coupling if we treat the above sentence, "sexual indulgence . . . ," in its indexical signal capacity rather than in its sense meaning. The indexical capacity of these utterances secures two very different semantic realms of sense by first securing each semantic realm to an agreed-on point of reference (to the same event, object, or field of action) *before* any actual or significant meaningful exchange or (re)alignment. In other words, these indexes create the delicate semiotic bridges across which sense and social meaning can be conveyed, and because of this are the prerequisites for liberal goals of agreement, disagreement, and consensus. However, they themselves remain, strictly speaking, neutral in relation to these meanings.[51] I sketch out this indexical architecture in figure 5.

In real-time moments of radical interpretation, even these strictly speaking non-sense indexical forms would have taken time to secure as an entity of action was slowly, delicately detached from its local semantically and pragmatically embedded field of action. Gillen repeatedly comments on the time its takes to secure an agreed-on point of reference.[52] Thus, figure 5 is profoundly misleading, if ever so unintentionally. At first contact, or its imaginary projection, understanding has yet to secure itself to sense or referent.

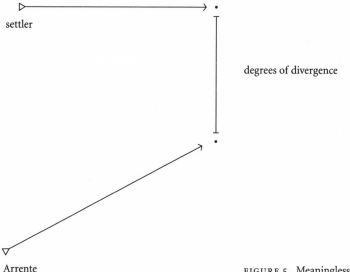

settler

degrees of divergence

Arrente

FIGURE 5. Meaningless indexicality.

Even non-sense presuppositional indexicality is not initially secure (if it is ever finally secure) in moments of radical interpretation any more than is presuppositional meaning because the point of reference, the thing itself, is not yet (does not yet exist), because it is still embedded in two different fields of denotation, predication, and practice (figure 6).

Meaning rocks. A back-and-forth indexical motion slowly detaches an entity—a point of reference. It produces this entity, this point of reference slowly draws in semantic meaning to provide the world with border, dimensions, weight. In this case, Spencer and Gillen might have pointed to an action and asked its purpose or meaning. The Arrente may have responded in such a way that Spencer and Gillen realized that Arrente were referring to an action at an oblique angle to their interests, and from this response narrowed their own query. Or Spencer and Gillen might have thought their subjects to be lying.[53] Back and forth, pointing and questioning, repointing and requestioning. At our most generous, we can imagine Spencer and Gillen listening patiently, attentively, and respectfully to how Arrente *put things.* And we can imagine the Arrente men trying their best to explain their beliefs and practices *to* Spencer and Gillen.

At this point my description may not seem so far afield from Richard Rorty's description of communicative action. After all, Rorty has argued that "what matters to the search for truth [is] the social (and in particular the political) conditions under which that search is conducted, rather than the

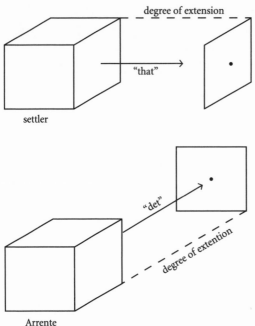

FIGURE 6. Indexical extensions.

deep inner nature of the suspects doing the searching."[54] In a context stripped
of force no communicative suspect can be found guilty of a crime of mis-
translation. But if we turn to the social and political conditions in which the
search for Arrente truth proceeded, we see that the conversations in which the
Arrente were engaged mock liberal ideals of a rational communicative event
excisable from its complex fields of force. This is an odd claim because Gillen
and Spencer seem to have gone out of their way to remove force from the
ethnographic scene. Certainly, they misled the Arrente men in serious ways,
promising the men that they would describe the ceremonies (only) to "two
oknirabata (men of influence) of south eastern Australian tribes," who were
in fact Fison and Howitt.[55] But in exchange for allowing them to record their
rituals, Gillen and Spencer offered the Arrente and surrounding Aboriginal
groups food and protection from police and settlers for the duration of the
ceremonies.

In addition, Gillen was well known to many Arrente and regional groups
as a settler who could be trusted to stem the worst of colonial violence. Historical descriptions of this violence are not for the weak of stomach or mind.
While stationed in a telegraph station in Adelaide in 1874, Gillen received
the dying transmissions of the Barrow Creek stationmaster who was under

fatal attack by local Kaititja men. Fifteen to fifty Aboriginal men, women, and children, virtually an entire Aboriginal community, were shot in retaliation. Shocked and appalled by the savagery of the white response, Gillen began humanitarian efforts to protect the indigenous population soon after he was transferred to overland telegraph stations in and around Alice Springs in 1875. He became locally famous for bringing to trial Constable W. C. Willshire, a notorious advocate of the severe treatment of the indigenous population. Soon after Willshire was appointed mounted constable to the Alice Springs region in 1882, rumors began of his gross physical and psychological abuse of local Aboriginal men and women. By 1891 it is estimated five hundred Aboriginal men, women, and children had been shot to death within a three hundred kilometer radius of Alice Springs, well within the range of the Arrente and their neighbors. Along with physically eliminating the indigenous population, Willshire sought to destroy the authority of Aboriginal men and their law. Police archives record him forcing local Aboriginal women to walk across men's sacred grounds. By 1890, after collecting testimony from Aboriginal men and women, as well as from Christian missionaries at the nearby Hermannsberg Mission, Gillen charged Willshire with the unjustified murder of local Aboriginal persons. Although Willshire was exonerated by a Port Augusta jury, he left the area and never returned.

We see then that no matter how the Arrente responded to specific requests from Spencer and Gillen for information, or to their general request to hold their *engwura* near Alice, they were not simply speaking among themselves or with other regional indigenous groups. They were attempting to communicate across significantly different semiotic orders under real-time, often brutal, conditions of social, physical, and psychological domination, exploitation, and humiliation. As they danced and talked, the Arrente and their neighbors were in the midst of being physically exterminated, having their ritual objects stolen, lost, or destroyed, and watching their lands be appropriated and, with them, their life-sustaining material and spiritual resources. Gillen himself would come to understand the deadly implications of the white theft of Arrente men's ritual *churinga* (totemic objects): "Martin tells me—this is between ourselves—that an old man out in his locality has been killed for divulging locality of Churinga to Cowle—This upsets me terribly, I would not have had it happen for 100 pounds and I am going to write Cowle strongly about the Churinga business, there must be no more ertnatulinga robberies. I bitterly regret ever having countenanced such a thing and can only say that I did so when in ignorance of what they meant to the Natives."[56] As they talked and danced in Spencer and Gillen's presence, Arrente men introduced formal, functional, and meaningful changes to these rituals and to the social relations they diagrammed and entailed in response to these settlement conditions. Indeed, as is well known, the form and function of the *engwura* performance Spencer and Gillen organized and recorded was novel — never before had so many rituals been performed together and never for the purpose of "demonstration." These questions were also novel in signaling the past tense of Dreamtime: How would you *have* done it? How *did* you *do* it?

In this context, force can be said to have been removed from the scene only in the most superficial and banal sense. Force was the very condition of communicative action, of practical reason. The Arrente would have been all too aware that one aspect of colonial power was being bracketed by another equal and opposing colonial force; that Spencer and Gillen were holding police, settlers, and starvation at bay.[57] Little wonder that the Arrente extended the length of the event to several months rather than the few weeks Spencer and Gillen had planned for. These significant inequalities of power provided an incentive for the Arrente to orient their utterances, if ever so delicately, to the semantic and pragmatic contexts in which Spencer and Gillen were embedded and which they were creating. And it incited the Arrente to detach, if in the beginning ever so slightly, a segment of their semiotic "life-world" and to use this segment as a means of building a somewhat coherent common language between themselves and these European men (figure 7).

As the Arrente struggled to understand the referent of "that," the multi-functional effect of "that" slowly worked its way into the sense-making structures of Arrente lives — across the preexisting contested fields of Arrente social life. Spencer and Gillen were not the only people trying to decipher a complex foreign semiotic system. Whether in their presence or out of their range of hearing, we can minimally assume that the Arrente discussed what Spencer and Gillen could *possibly* mean by their questions, what their questions suggested about European views of humans and their environments. And it is likely that they discussed what they could and could not discuss with Spencer and Gillen as a matter of ceremonial law and interethnic "etiquette," and what practical information these formal and informal conversations conveyed about settler economy, police, and morality. Over time, the domain of excluded improper talk would include the very actions Spencer and Gillen were so fascinated by and were, I suggest, creating: ritual sex, sex in public, sex out of the institutions of monogamous "marriage." Arrente and other indigenous groups learned what *that* was and learned simultaneously not to discuss

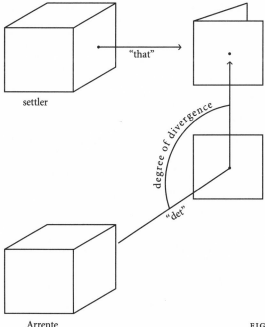

settler

Arrente

FIGURE 7. Degrees of detachment.

that. Indeed, Gillen would comment on the quickness with which the Arrente and other northern indigenous groups assessed white cultural assessments: "In doing work such as we are engaged upon one has to be careful not to let the savage perceive that you disapprove of or disbelieve in his ideas for if he once gets that idea into his head he will shut up like an oyster and wild horses will not drag reliable information out of him."[58]

To be sure, Spencer and Gillen were hardly the only or even the first pedagogues of sex in central Australia. Arrente men and women would have had contact with white settlers since the early 1860s, nearly forty years before Spencer and Gillen carried out their research. The Macdonnell Ranges running through Arrente territory were named by John McDouall Stuart as he passed through the territory on a surveying expedition in 1860. And although the white population was hardly formidable in the early years after Stuart's survey, its physical and psychological effects were formidable — as they were intended to be in many instances.[59] For instance, the missionaries of the Lutheran Hermannsberg Mission, established in 1877, intended to reshape the exteriority and interiority of central desert Aboriginal men and women, including their linguistic practices, the results of which Gillen mercilessly lampooned.[60]

Over time and in the multiple and varied encounters that Arrente men and women had with settlers, a particular corporeal act and its value in relation to other corporeal acts would lay out social space and organize social relations not in terms of ritual and nonritual space, nor in terms of the corporeal exchanges I will discuss in the next section, but rather in terms of notional themes like the public and private, the intimate and economic, the secular and sacred, the rational and passionate. Physical spaces and semiotically mediated genres organized around "sex difference," "sex acts," "carnality," "sin," and so forth would entail new aspects of the world of the Arrente. New gendered and sexual subjects would be created through these organizing concepts and through the institutions that helped to cohere and reproduce them, as would be the space in which these subjects interacted. And, importantly, the semiotic architecture introduced would be introduced to a social field already itself a field of contestation among and within various Arrente and non-Arrente Aboriginal groups.

In these real-time social interactions *that* appears anew as a grammatical grappling hook and an instrument of seizure as much as it does a means of securing one semantic and pragmatic system to another. That is, a prelude to semantic violence was proffered as the pragmatic means of escaping physical violence, corporeal discipline, and governmentality. In this light the question "Why do you do *that?*" can be detached from its original context and redeployed as a metalinguistic commentary on the act and orientation of translation in colonial contexts.

M. M. Bakhtin noted long ago what I am getting at here—namely, that utterances do not simply express propositional content but instead presume, predicate, and entail their contextual sites of occurrence. Utterances cite and express a form of power that does not issue from within the semantic features of the utterance, that strange mysterious force of illocution. Instead they express the social forces that make communicative sense possible in the first place. They are aimed and shaped, if ever so delicately, by the desires and expectations within or giving rise to a scene of communication. They can be subtle desires like the desire to understand. Or they can be crude desires like the desire to live. To live may well necessitate quick understanding. When I said that indexes are neutral in relation to sense and social meaning, this did not mean they do not express the social value of their production. Indeed we can understand these indexes to be simultaneously signaling an emergent object or field of action and expressing, or pointing to, the social source and power of their production.

Why should we pay attention to these delicate features of colonial communicative practices? I offer the following modest answer. By submerging into the recesses of linguistic action we begin to locate the excitement and horror generated by efforts at radical interpretation. And in doing so we begin to inch nearer to the thing Spencer and Gillen chased in the form of radical interpretation. Spencer and Gillen imagined, sought, and engaged a form of thinking whose value lies in its overcoming a repulsion; a being thrown back against itself; a being repelled. The repulsive in this sense animates investigation and excites reason insofar as it has not yet been cast into a determinate outline, insofar as understanding has not completed its announced task: comprehension. As long as that which radical interpretation seeks has not yet made an appearance, possibility reigns. Determinate judgments are postponed. A seemingly infinite progression of possible, if ever so delicately differentiated, worlds present themselves. In the domain of this indeterminate possibility awareness is heightened, the senses accentuated, attention fixed on the most minute of motions. No object is self-evidently itself. This *undattha altherta* might be either just the discarded remains of an Arrente fowl dinner or the portal to the *alcheringa*.

Such excitement. Spencer and Gillen found themselves continually thrown back onto themselves, faced with the "mysteries of Aboriginal life" and thrown against the question of whether they would "ever succeed in learning much about them."[61] A superanimation of the mind made the time memorable, a psychic memorial, worth telling, lingering over, and remembering. In a letter to Spencer written years after their Alice Springs trip, Gillen wrote longingly of their field research and his sorrow that "we could [not] live our Engwura life over again," though he noted "it was an anxious time," in which there was "always a danger of the thing bursting up."[62] In other letters, Spencer and Gillen remember the intensity of focused but frustrated thought, the exhilaration of destabilized understanding, major and minor moments of misunderstanding, and the anxiety of reaching and feeling the limits of their intellectual capacities, of the prognosis of their "ever getting to the 'why' of things."[63]

There are two very different ways we can understand Spencer and Gillen's description of their subjective state in the *engwura*. We can understand them, as George Stocking has, to be "confessing" an experiential state external to the scene and goal of radical interpretation and cross-cultural communication—in other words, that their anxiety was the by-product not the goal of radical interpretation. Spencer and Gillen were saying that *in spite of* the anxiety and *no matter* the feeling that they would never get to "the why of things," the time was memorable. Or, we can understand Spencer and Gillen to be saying that what made the time memorable was that they were forever deflected from the why of things. The Arrente afforded for them the experience of an object only existing in the deferred—Man, Humanity, something other than themselves and the experience of their desires as particular, banal, and ordinary moments in a desert.[64]

If we understand the memorial aspects of Spencer and Gillen's *engwura* experience in this way, then their experience of radical interpretation can be understood as a form of, or akin to, trauma. By "trauma" I would not deviate radically from the way that Cathy Caruth has defined a traumatic event; namely, as an event in which excitations from the outside are powerful enough to alter "the mind's experience of time, self and the world."[65] I do not intend to be dramatic, nor to claim that all cross-cultural communication is traumatic or that history is traumatic. Instead, I merely wish to unsettle a commonsense liberal notion that *liberalism* figures corporeal and subjective trauma as bad, to be avoided at any cost; as something external to liberal forms of self and communal governance, to *Aufklärung*. Further, I want to suggest that by paying attention to this excitement we begin to understand what secured Spencer and Gillen to the scene of radical interpretation as opposed to what secured the Arrente. Spencer and Gillen chased a desire to be challenged but not undone; and what they demanded of their Arrente informants was to challenge but not to undo them.

There is a final reason why I think we need to pay attention to these delicate features of communicative action. Rather than assuming that the emergence of shared meaning is a moment of cultural conservation, an *Aufhebung*, we must ask whether radical interpretation's relationship to alterity is one of foreclosure, and whether it was the effect of this foreclosure that Spencer and Gillen also felt and chased. Liberal theorists of cultural communication sidestep the issue of what is both lost and set into motion in moments of radical interpretation. They postpone or shunt a discussion of the here-and-now conditions of communication into a future ideal context. Derrida put it elegantly in his analysis of the "future modality of the living present" that belies the liberal gospel; namely, that the de facto "good news" of its "effective, phenomenal, historical, and empirically observable event" is always yet again deferred in the form of "an ideal good news, the teleo-eschatological good news, which is inadequate to any empiricity."[66]

SEX AS A MINOR FORM OF ATTACHMENT

I have postponed long enough a direct discussion of what the Arrente men might have said and meant by Spencer and Gillen's paraphrase "it makes it impossible for the head decorations, for example, to become loose and disordered during the performance"; of the possible networks of meaning and practice that makes the explanation "sexual intercourse prevents decorations from falling off" sensible; and of whether sex actually was on these ritual grounds or any others. Of this much I think we can be relatively certain: Spencer and Gillen lifted sex out of a field of ritual action complexly carnal and corporeal and severely misunderstood by the rush to sex.[67]

To understand what may have been foreclosed in Spencer and Gillen's determination that Arrente *engwura* corporeality was ritual sex necessitates distinguishing between forms of corporeal and mental trauma that might have been a vital aspect of Spencer and Gillen's practice and those that might have been a vital aspect of Arrente practice. In other words, we must attempt the difficult. We must resist negatively valuing illiberal physical violations and physical heteronomy (lost autonomy). We must resist imposing on Arrente bodily acts extralocal values like "good" or "bad." They were neither. Nor were they "torture" or "self-shattering." The "soul stirring" that settlers and their metropolitan brethren felt when witnessing or reading accounts of casual or violent and individual or group "sex" and "genital mutilations" depended on ideas not in the scenes themselves. These feelings originated from the very source that drove Spencer and Gillen into the *engwura* in the first place, and that animated them to make sense of the ritual forms they faced.

When we bracket how Spencer and Gillen classified corporeal practices and mythic narratives and concentrate instead on their descriptions of them, the narratives they re-present take on a different focus. They foreground the corporeal and ontological transformations that occur when a body is under a heightened state of physical and mental stress or stimulation — at least from the perspective of the Arrente men they talked to.[68] Take, for example, the myth of the *Unthippa* women. According to Spencer the *Unthippa* women were said "to have sprung into existence far out in the *Aldorla ilunga* (the 'west country') from where they began their travel across the central desert," dancing "all the way along." The *Unthippa* women started their journey as half-women and half-men, "but before they had proceeded very far on their journey their organs became modified and they were as other women." Their account continues:

Somewhere out west of the River Jay the women changed their language to Arunta and began feeding on mulga seed, on which they afterwards subsisted. Upon arrival at a place called Wankima, about 100 miles further to the east their sexual organs dropped out from sheer exhaustion, caused by their un-interrupted dancing, and it was these which gave rise to well-known deposits of red ochre. The woman then entered the ground, and nothing more is known of them except that it is supposed that a great woman land exists far away to the east where they finally sat down.[69]

An emphasis on the transformations that *engwura* landscapes and beings are subject to consequent of their extreme stimulation and stress is common to the mythic genre throughout the desert region. This genre may be called the "left behind" stories, the "plot" of which could be summarized as "they came; they suffered enormous stress or experienced extreme stimulation; they left behind a piece of themselves." Indeed, in 1976 the minister of Aborigi-nal Affairs elevated this narrative genre to a pan-Aboriginal cosmogony when describing traditional Aboriginal cosmology in his second reading of the Ab-original Land Rights (Northern Territory) Act, 1976:

> Traditional Aborigines associate identifiable groups of people with particular "countries" or tracts of territory in such a way that the link was publicly re-puted to express both spiritual and physical communication between living people and their "dream time" ancestors and between the "country" as it now is and the "ancestral" country which had been given its names, its physical features, its founding stocks of food and water, and its owners and possessors by the ancestors themselves. It is believed that ancestors left in each "country" certain vital powers that, used properly by the right people, make that "coun-try" fruitful and ensure a good life for people forever. Everywhere there was a plan of life — a good and satisfying life — based on an identifiable and unmis-takable group of people forming a descent group or "clan," living with relation to an identifiable territory publicly recognised as the "country" of the group because of the actions of the ancestors who had left in each "country" sacred memorials — the totems and totemic sites of which we hear so much — as proof of entitlement for, and to guide and discipline, their descendents.[70]

Extreme corporeal stress is not just issued in reports about the mytho-history of the *engwura*. It is recreated in the Arrente rituals that Arrente men showed Spencer and Gillen. In virtually all the Arrente rituals, Spencer and Gillen describe totemic substances being forced into human bodies, human substances into totemic bodies, and human substances into other human bodies. The directional flow of substances described in myth is often reversed: The substances the *Unthippa* women — and numerous others like them — left behind are forced back into the human body. The force with which these substances are inlaid into the body might appear quite weak to an outside observer. That is, the violation and stimulation of the human body of ritual action may not appear to be sufficient to cause any serious physical or psychic disruption, and certainly are not sufficient grounds to create a traumatic reaction.

For instance, in the witchetty grub *Intichiuma* ("increase ceremonies" relating to a specific food source, the grub), the ceremonial leader (the *alatunja*) "takes up one of the smaller stones" that constitutes the witchetty grub totem and "strikes each man in the stomach saying, *Unga murna oknirra ulquinna* ('You have eaten much food')."[71] In a photograph of this event we see a younger adult man, his hands behind his back and braced against the ground. Kneeling, his torso is thrust out toward the senior man who is rubbing the witchetty grub stone against his chest. The Arrente believe, the authors tell readers, that this action will ensure the plentiful supply of witchetty grubs, a staple in the desert food economy. In a like manner, in the final stage of the initiation of young men, *churinga* are brought out of a local storehouse and are examined and redistributed among the men. During the ceremonial handing over of *churinga,* ochre is rubbed over the sacred objects. The hand of the young man who will be responsible for this sacred object is then "pressed down on the Churinga [and] rubbed . . . up and down upon it," while the senior man "whisper[s] to him, telling him to whom the Churinga had belonged, who the dead man was, and what the marks on the Churinga meant."[72] These ritual practices hardly seem to warrant the designation traumatic.

Churinga were not the only objects pressed into human bodies during rituals. Fats, charcoals, ochres, blood, and sweat were rubbed into or injected by initiates and their elders, again in ways that might not immediately appear to the non-Arrente observer to warrant the characterization as traumatic. For instance, "to promote the growth of the breasts of a girl, the men assemble at the *Ungunja* or men's camp, where they all join in singing long chants, the words of which express an exhortation to the breasts to grow, and others which have the effect of charming some fat and red ochre which men who are *Gammona,* that is, brothers of her mother, have brought to the spot." At daylight the young girl, accompanied by her mother, is brought close to the men's camp. There "her body is rubbed all over with fat by the *Gammona* men, who then paint a series of straight lines of red ochre down her back and also down the centre of her chest and stomach. . . . When this has been done the girl is taken out into the bush by her mother, who makes a camp there at some distance from the main one, and here the girl must stay until the *ilkinia* or lines on her body wear off, when, but not until when, she may return to the main camp."[73] Spencer and Gillen discuss this action in purely representational or ornamental terms, figuring the body as a canvas on which the designs slowly wear away. But we could also understand the men to be rubbing fat *into* the young girl's body in order to prepare her body to be able to *absorb*—or embody—the costume and designs. In this view, bodily massages, incisions, and ornamentation become a vital part of an Arrente's corporeal substance through absorption, slowly rearticulating its nature and the orientation of the body from the outside in. If this was how Arrente viewed the events then these seemingly mundane scenes may well have been extraordinarily intense for the initiate, powerful enough to alter "the mind's experience of time, self and the world."

Arrente men and women sometimes used *churinga* and other materials and objects to carve or impress the totemic designs into the body of initiates in ways more recognizably traumatic.[74] In one ritual, the thumbnails of Arrente men were ripped off with an opposum tooth immediately after the men were shown sacred ground designs. They were then lain on top of the sacred design while "eight deep close-set, wavy lines" were carved in their foreheads, the blood of which was pressed into sacred objects associated with the design and then poured on the ground design. The manner in which these corporeal practices permanently orient the initiate's body and mind to the ritual scene is suggested by Spencer and Gillen's observation of the mental state of a senior man, Reraknilliga, who is recalling the ritual. Spencer and Gillen note that when Reraknilliga "described what happened to him, he evidently retained very vivid recollections."[75]

Not only were the "leftovers" of the traumatized bodies of *engwura* beings forced into contemporary humans, as the last example suggested, human substances were forced into *engwura* object-beings. In a witchetty grub ceremony "the *Alatunja* [leader of the local group] begins singing and taps the stone with his *Apmara* [soft wood seed carrier] while all the other men tap it with their twigs, chanting songs as they do so, the burden of which is an invitation to the animal to lay eggs."[76] The substance pressed into the stone is language (song). Singing to the stone penetrates the object; it is simultaneously a semantic conveyance, a social act, and a bodily emission like other bodily emissions—sweat, blood, spit, language, and genital fluids—*all these substances flowed out of human corporeal tunnels,* the throat, veins, pores, vagina, penis. These substances literally mixed with the *engwura* being in the design space. During the *emu* ceremony, for instance, the ceremonial leader

> and a few other men, amongst whom were his two sons, first of all cleared a small level plot of ground, sweeping aside all stones, tussocks of grass and small bushes, so as to make it as smooth as possible. Then several of the men, the Alatunja and his two sons amongst them, each opened a vein in their arms, and allowed the blood to stream out until the surface of a patch of ground, occupying a space of about three square yards, was saturated with it. The blood was allowed to dry, and in this way a hard and fairly impermeable surface was prepared, on which it was possible to paint a design.[77]

Once again, rather than simply a primitive gesso, blood taken from the human body comprises an integral part of the *engwura* being expressed and entailed *rather than represented* on the ground—the human blood materially integrating, indexing, and mediating human and *engwura* corporeal and ontological orders.

At this point we begin to see how the material intercourse between human and *engwura* seems to have been a critical component of the general logic of central desert initiation practices. Year after year, decade upon decade, human substances and *engwura* substances were exchanged between and embedded into each other. Blood lost during young men and women's initiation rituals—circumcision, subincision, menstruation, vulvation—was not "disposed" in ritual grounds, nor were other human bodily parts.[78] Rather, through the practices of burning, burying, soaking, singing, rubbing, sweating, smoking, being born from a place (*erathipa*) and sinking back into it at death (*ulthana*), Arrente men and women came to share a corporeal substance with the *engwura* earth, problemizing any simple distinction between human and *engwura* bodies.

In a similar way to how *engwura* substances were forced into the human body and human substances into *engwura* bodies, so human substances were forced into other human bodies, a circle of exchanges that leads us back to the public scandal of ritual sex. We return to this scene, however, with a new set of questions, perhaps the most fundamental of which is who or what was engaged in "ritual sex"? The answer to this question is not clarified from the perspective of Arrente grammar.

Some forty years after Spencer and Gillen journeyed to Alice Springs,

T. G. H. Strehlow published the first full-length treatment of the Arrente language (*Aranda Phonetics and Grammar,* 1944). T. G. H. Strehlow was the son of one of the founders of the Lutheran Hermannsberg settlement. He grew up among the Arrente and was a fluent speaker of their language. The purpose of *Aranda Phonetics and Grammar* was to outline the major phonemic and grammatical features of Arrente and, along the way, to dispel widespread negative stereotypes about Aboriginal languages. But Strehlow is significantly bothered (indeed, a bit scandalized) by one feature of Arrente grammar—the absence of gender distinctions. He writes: "The Arrente nouns know no distinctions of gender: masculine, feminine and neuter are all meaningless terms to the Central Australian tribesman. Not even the common animals of the chase are differentiated according to sex."[79] According to Strehlow, the Arrente do not merely *lack* gender distinctions in the noun phrases of their language, but they "*refused* to acknowledge in [their] grammar the primal distinction of the genders," a state of mind reflected in grammar that Strehlow refuses to believe had always been the case.[80] We must qualify the conditions of Strehlow's outrage.

It is true that in the Arrente language as currently understood, nouns are inflected as agents or nonagents in given propositional contexts and are classified on the basis of the distinctions among human, animate, and inanimate rather than on the basis of gender distinctions.[81] But gender is not an absent semantic feature. Once qualified as human or agent a noun phrase can then be modified by the unmarked (*orea,* male), the marked (*mala,* female), and two neuter forms. Arrente pronouns and kinship terms are marked by gender as are ritual and developmental terms, designating the status and rank of persons who have progressed past the crawling stage (figure 8).

Arrente classifications of noun phrases cannot tell us, however, what we wish to know—namely, whether or not the Arrente thought that "humanness," "animateness," or "inanimateness" were essential qualities of subjects and objects or ontological domains through which the "same" object traversed. The ethnographic data suggest the latter condition was the case. According the Spencer, Gillen, Strehlow, and others, Arrente men and women believed that their bodies were composed of various still-animate *engwura* ancestors.[82] In certain ritual contexts, human beings not only took on the costume of totemic ancestors, they became those ancestors.[83] We do not know whether or not the human body was reclassified as an animate body during rituals, nor whether speakers referred to performers as animated *engwura* beings. But this much we can say with some certainty: at least two

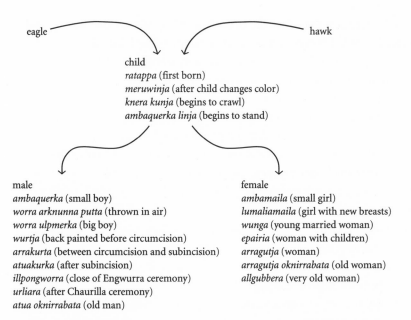

FIGURE 8. The social history of sexual difference. Based on Baldwin Spencer, *The Aruntz: A Study of a Stone Age People,* vol. 1 (London: Macmillan and Co., 1927), 582.

context-presupposing and entailing classifications (human and animate) of the (human) body coexisted in the Arrente language. In a ritual space Arrente speakers may have used the Arrente language in such a way that the former may well have given way to the latter. The semiotic and linguistic entailment of the Arrente body at least "remains *indeterminate* until one places it in the framework of a context, where 'context' entails intersubjective contracts, ongoing discourse, and a horizon of background experience."[84]

I do not wish to reduce the event of *engwura* ritual to any of the above semiotic forms, even if these forms were relevant frames for the Arrente. Instead, the *engwura* practices might be better understood as a total environment in which older men's physical weight, verbal intensity, and spectacular intricate knowledge intimately and intensively enveloped the initiate, destabilizing the prior cartography of his body and the integrity of his body as *his* or *the* body as such. What body, where, and whose? Did the Arrente consider themselves as most intimately in their selves, their skins? Did the surface of the body separate them from the world, or provide a sensuous medium of contact with it, a potential site of heightened mental and corporeal stimulation?

Spencer and Gillen, and other ethnologists of the period, provide suggestive hints. Clay designs are carefully rendered on young men's bodies. Older men take sweat from from their armpits and groins, massaging it over, around, and into the young men's body. Various totemic objects — *churinga,* each carefully covered with ochre, are pressed into the palms, bellies, backs, buttocks, penises, and brows of the young men. Preparatory songs are sung, sometimes soothingly, intimately into the ear of one boy, sometimes intensely, intimidatingly, a deafening chorus bearing down on the young men huddled together. Older stronger hands clasp young limps. The skin crawls. Adrenaline is produced. Awareness and the senses are heightened. A cut is made. Blood flows from it, is collected in a shield, is buried. More *churinga* are pressed on the wound; more men embrace and encase this intensified initiate surface and stimulate the production of a formally differentiated interiority. As a young man is being cut, other men and women are cutting deep wounds into their own bodies, on their and their relatives' backs and limbs. Or they are opening and extending previous incisions, the length of the scar a spatial calibration of ceremonial time, an indexical icon of human bodies becoming *engwura* bodies. The young men do not move; they stare ahead; they listen or not to the songs resounding in their ears. They are overcome by their environment.

All these corporeal practices fashioned and reoriented the body, fastening it to a place, a memory, a people. Trauma may well have been the necessary condition for the production of an *engwura* orientation, indeed an *engwura* body. For trauma would turn mind and body again and again to the *engwura,* sticking headdress to head. In other words, the interiority and exteriority of the initiates' body was remade in rituals, not simply symbolically but compulsorily, the body and mind returning to the scene not simply because the ideas of the *engwura* are compelling in and of themselves, but because the body and psyche *were* as a result of *being* compelled by the scene. These men are not men any more than this body will ever be a singular human self again. Rather than producing the homogenous collective consciousness of modernist accounts, these rituals might well have fashioned a particular orientation to the grounded condition of Arrente being — literally the geography of the *engwura.* The rituals particularized persons and groups. Words, songs, hands, and flint knives provided a new diagram of the psyche, the social, and the surface of the body as the body was extended into the social, into the environment, and was itself an extension of the social contours of that environment.

In this economy of the body, sex may have been just another form of attachment, a fastening, a fascination; an incitement through intensity; a subjective restructuring based on some *engwura* operation other than "sex." Further, was sex one form of incitement and attachment, or was it not in the above scenes at all? Can we imagine a corporeal practice and discourse that would displace "sex" and replace it with another model of the body's excitement based on tunnels, flows, and intercourses through veins, vaginas, waterholes, tunnels, throats, voices? What would the material and social stakes of this refashioning be? It may not have been possible for Spencer and Gillen, or indeed for us, to believe that sex was not sex; for them to believe that these other corporeal penetrations they witnessed actually reproduced human life, let alone for them to believe that the Arrente men ceased being men in the "Dreamtime." Perhaps these corporeal transformations still can only be "fantasment" and "metaphorique" for contemporary readers.[85] If so, these interpretants stand forever between the Arrente, Spencer, Gillen, and us.

CRISIS

The preceding discussion of Arrente corporeality is what makes anthropology so "interesting" for its writers and readers—the cultural difference that anthropology conveys simulates our senses and sensibilities without dissolving our deepest sense of our selves. The "ethnographic magic" lies in part in the anthropological transcoding of moral horrors into reasoned/reasonable difference; that is, alterity into difference. All of what I have said is fairly understandable; and insofar as it is, my description entrenches the idea that cultural translation occurs without loss or violence and supports the fantasy *that we can think our way out, that thinking is the way in and out*. In the process this description reinforces the monstrous optimism of Lévi-Strauss: "Every human mind is a locus of virtual experience where what goes on in the minds of men, however remote they may be, can be investigated."[86]

But let the reader beware. Surely the precolonial meanings and techniques of Arrente ritual have not been captured by the above description. I have merely created a way of thinking about central desert ritual practices. And my description is simply one small chapter in a history of chapters that have returned to the scene snapped by Spencer and Gillen. And it is this *returning* rather than the content of the return that might capture something more essential about Arrente ritual corporeality for settler subjects and their enlightenment; namely, that it continues to provide a limit-experience for settler understanding, an experience of something-I-know-not-what, a sublime object forever refusing the enclosure of narrative.

Even if I had captured without remainder the true meanings of Arrente ritual practices, there remain in *Native Tribes* and *Northern Tribes* passages that describe "things the Arrente do" that would be hard for a contemporary reader to think her way out of. These passages suggest the whimsy of the optimistic "I can move forward because I can think," and suggest in what contexts this whimsical statement is transformed into a declaration of cultural warfare. Throughout these texts corporeal acts—"sex acts"—are described in ways that continue to incite negative critical judgment. In the face of these acts, liberal readers would experience an "ought," a moment in which the micropower of teleological thinking becomes apparent and presents us with an apparently impossible impasse to liberal multicultural thinking. The "things" that provoke the compulsory feelings of morality do not put morality "in limbo"— that ne'er-do-well nowhere; that bracket between heaven and hell. Rather these "things" make morality appear, vitally. They make liberal readers experience the compulsory nature of their moral sense and obligation, even as these same readers struggle to maintain their liberal ideal of cultural "tolerance" and "rationality." This compulsory, visceral reaction was long ago noted by Spencer and Gillen, who remarked "it is one thing to read of these ceremonies—it is quite another thing to see them prepared and performed."[87]

Here I return to the questions with which this chapter began: How do we develop an anthropological ethics of the colonial archive? What is being saved through the textual form of deletion and ellipsis? What attaches itself to textual practices of respect? I myself have not quoted the disturbing passages I allude to above, though this empty textual space is where I would have presented Spencer and Gillen's description of sex because it seemed to me next to impossible to get the points about the authority that moral hegemony exerts on our citational practices across without these "amazing images." And yet, hovering over my reading and writing is the proviso of liberal multicultural recognition of the Aboriginal customary as cited in the High Court decision *Edie Mabo v. the State of Queensland:* "provided those laws and customs are not so repugnant to natural justice, equity and good conscience." Why would the High Court insert this rider to their recognition of customary law as the basis of native title? Why would these justices—or ordinary Northern Territory residents writing letters to the editor of the *Northern Territory News*— think that some Aboriginal customary laws might be repugnant? I will examine both of these questions at more length in chapters 4, 5, and 6. Indeed, the shadow that the colonial archive casts over every performance of Aboriginal traditional culture, over Aboriginality itself, as a conceptual, identificatory term, will haunt the rest of this book as it does indigenous lives.

Let me note here an obvious point: books like *Native Tribes of Central Australia* have an artifactuality. Land commissioners, native title commissioners, anthropologists, writers, and filmmakers read, refer to, and defer to such texts as that which captured "unspoilt Arunta men." The simple semiotic technology of the book's table of contents and index allows any and every reader to find practices and acts from which they would recoil in horror. In many ways the colonial archive is more shocking now, supplemented and interpreted as it is through mass-mediated representations of sexual perversion, child abuse, posttraumatic subjectivities, sin, the soul. It is doubtful that my claim that these women are not women, men are not men, would salve this wound. This colonial archive makes a mockery of liberal claims about the progress of tolerance. The tolerance manifested by multicultural forms of liberalism has not advanced appreciably. The state and its unwitting publics simply have demanded that someone delete what irritates them.

If I cannot present passages that would continue to horrify liberal readers, how can I convincingly demonstrate how these same liberal subjects are now haunted by the specter of historically mistaken intolerances, and by the severed grounds of any and every modal imperative? How can I produce in the reader the impossible conditions of being rent by the two moral imperatives of late liberalism: I must be tolerant of cultural difference; I must not allow the repugnantly illiberal? If I cannot produce this effect then I cannot adequately convey the impossible conditions of being an Aboriginal subject in a multicultural state; namely, the demand that they span the contradictory imperatives of late liberalism and protect the liberal subject from experiencing the (ir)rationality of their intolerance.

The phenomena which early societies present us with are not easy at first to understand, but the difficulty of grappling with them bears no proportion to the perplexities which beset us in considering the baffling entanglement of modern social organization. It is a difficulty arising from their strangeness and uncouthness, not from their number and complexity.
—Sir Henry Maine, *Ancient Law*

The old printed record concerning Aboriginal custom is replete with misunderstandings of the religious symbolism. Observers vested mere externals—the vehicle or symbolizing means—with intrinsic significances. Preconception usually ensured that the attributed meanings were deprecatory, often odious. For example, ritualized acts of sex, which seem usually to be but ecstatic means of symbolizing non-sexual things, were taken as evidence of bestiality. Hence, probably, the view of the amiable Mr. Dredge, the early nineteenth-century protector who described the Aborigines as "men of Sodom, sinners exceedingly." But the more recent Freudians have also given the sexual symbolisms a grotesquely exaggerated significance.
—W. E. H. Stanner, "Religion, Totemism, and Symbolism"

3 / Sex Rites, Civil Rights

INTRODUCTION

Baldwin Spencer and Frank Gillen were hardly the first settler Australians to reflect publicly and privately on the "ritual sex acts" of indigenous men and women. Nor would they be the last. They had long been praised and buried when on 11 June 1936 the administrator of the Northern Territory of Australia, Robert H. Weddell, sent an urgent telegram to the Commonwealth Department of the Home and Territories in Canberra:

CONSTABLE PRYOR FROM DALY RIVER ARRIVING ON 12TH JUNE WITH 6 ABORIGINES CHARGED WITH RAPING LUBRA [white slang, Aboriginal woman] STOP UNDERSTAND OFFENCE IS MORE OR LESS TRIBAL CUSTOM WHEN FEMALE ABORIGINAL WALKS ON SACRED GROUND RESERVED ONLY FOR MALES SUCH FEMALE BEING REQUIRED [TO] HAVE SEXUAL INTER-

COURSE WITH ALL AND SUNDRY STOP MORE NATIVES WOULD HAVE
BEEN IMPLICATED BUT FOR THE TIMELY ARRIVAL OF PEANUT FARMER
HARKINS[1]

Rather than praise the investigative promptness and moral sense of northern police, the secretary of the Department of the Home and Territories (Interior), C. A. Carrodus, reprimanded the police for their actions and implicitly threatened their careers:

YOUR TELEGRAM 11TH JUNE WAS CHIEF PROTECTOR CONSULTED BEFORE
APPROVAL GIVEN FOR ARREST OF NATIVES STOP ON INFORMATION GIVEN
BY YOU MATTER APPEARS ONE IN WHICH THERE SHOULD HAVE BEEN NO
POLICE INTERFERENCE.[2]

In a strongly worded follow-up letter sent six days after this telegram, Carrodus continued his criticisms of the northern police and the administrator: "It is considered that the action of Constable Pryor in arresting the natives and bringing them to Darwin was at variance with the spirit of the instruction given by the Minister and conveyed to you in my memorandum of 10th February, 1936. It is also considered that steps should have been taken to prevent the departure of Constable Pryor from Daly River with his charges when details were known in Darwin."[3] Carrodus said that the spirit of administrative policy was clear. Neither settlers nor police should interfere with "more or less" Aboriginal practices where "tribal laws only are concerned and where no white person is involved."[4] Only those Aboriginal men and women who were less rather than more culturally, racially, or spatially distinguishable from settlers were to be subjected to state police, juridical, and welfare institutions, have their children removed; and have their employment and movements restricted. The general administrative policy in which "tribal blacks" would be left undisturbed had been formulated in 1935 on the recommendation of a board of inquiry appointed by the Australian governor-general to inquire into allegations of the ill-treatment of Aboriginal men and women by Northern Territory patrol officers like Constable Pryor.[5]

These were but a few of the documents among many that passed between state agencies about this case. Other memos argued the facticity, legality, practicality, and morality of the policy of noninterference that Carrodus cited. Citations of this case and other similar ones also circulated outside the strict confines of the state. With more or less detail, accuracy, and directness, popular and academic presses (newspapers, chapbooks, travelogues, memoirs, ethnographies) described and debated similar frontier events and the local and national state policies meant to control them. Settler men and women who witnessed, heard, or read about such events debated the meaning and rightness of Aboriginal practices and government policies in local bars, over domestic kitchen tables, on horseback, and after church. From the textual debris they left behind we can surmise they asked each other moral, epistemological, and practical questions about the troubling status of "a nation within a nation" and about how to include or exclude fairly and justly indigenous people and practices in the relatively new Australian nation. How could a modern, civil nation condone a state-sanctioned space of sexual immorality, perversion, and violence? How could the indigenous population be integrated into the nation and be given equal citizenship rights and responsibilities while they maintained customs antithetical to civil society? And how could the state enforce a policy that so clearly violated the commonsense limit of human right and decency? If the state could not do so, was a period of mute, irrational force the necessary physical and communicative first conditions for the emergence of a morally integrated civil Australian nation? "Myall blacks" were by this time understood to be abiding by customary law when they engaged in these practices (the colloquial phrase used to refer to Aboriginal persons who had not encountered settler society).[6] Many Aboriginal women and men did not know settler laws. Punishing indigenous groups for crimes that had no local name might forever link Australian nationalism to the savagery of its birth.

In this chapter I examine the emergence of a new metaethics of Australian nationalism in the field of indigenous and settler interaction in the 1930s and 40s. I ask how struggles over indigenous policy in the north helped to create a new language of national consociation in the middle half of the twentieth century. I pay particular attention to the material conditions and the material conditioning of this emergence. And I argue that the "material" critical to these discursive emergences includes aspirations and feelings and identities and identifications, as well as the institutional structures of state and civil life. My intent in this chapter is not to understand or adjudicate ritual sex as a true or false moment of alterity, assimilable or not to liberal forms of nationalism. Nor is it to insinuate that the Daly River case—or cases like it—is the ur text of Australian multiculturalism. Nor, finally, is it a judgment on ritual practices.

Instead, in this chapter I intend to use the historical archive surrounding this case to make three broad points about the genealogy of Australian multiculturalism. First, this case, and other cases like it, caused settler Australians

113

to experience a nonpassage between understanding-based ideologies of justice and subjective-based ideologies of morality in the given time of constitutional liberal democracies. Second, this type of experience was subjectively, textually, and institutionally mediated. Failure to understand the social specificity of each of these forms of mediation and their interaction leaves us with a very shallow account of the historical sociology of metaethical discourses like multiculturalism. Finally, these cases suggest that this ideological and experiential nonpassage — rather than dilemma or contradiction — was deferred rather than resolved. Multiculturalism would not relieve the nonpassage but simply figure its relation differently. Strictly speaking, then, this chapter is genealogical in form and conceit. In it I do not seek to show multiculturalism lurking in emergent mid-century cultural relativisms, but rather I wish to sketch one aspect of the condition of its emergence: the (still) unresolved and irreducible tensions within liberal national settler ideologies in the context of indigenous agency. The tension that lay at the historical ground of multiculturalism, I argue, neither aimed at nor ended with the logic of extermination but rather with what I will call a logic of a prohibitive interest — a practical, and legal, form of ambivalence still apparent in the contemporary law of recognition.[7]

Although in this chapter I am centrally concerned with settler experiences of the nonpassage between understanding-based ideologies of justice and subjective-based ideologies of morality, I continually situate this experience in an actively responsive indigenous social world. This responsive indigenous world, as I hope to show in more detail in chapters 5 and 6, faced its own experience of nonpassage between contested local deontic and epistemic forms and the material institutions of national life. But, if I begin this chapter with a concern about the material mediations of an emergent multicultural Australia, I end the book with a concern about how a specific nonpassage between reason and morality was layered into Aboriginal worlds and how settler fears became indigenous truths. The historical archive I seek to understand in this chapter is also used by Aboriginal activists and their opponents in contests over the authenticity of contemporary cultural heritage and land rights claims.

ADMINISTERING SEX

The simple question of why C. A. Carrodus sent the telegram quoted above recalls the observation of Jürgen Habermas that "institutionalized action" is always "the selective realization of cultural values under situational constraints."[8] As secretary of the Department of the Interior, Carrodus was charged with carrying out the minister's Aboriginal policy in the Northern Territory. This bureaucratic role, and the concomitant notion of the "proper functions" associated with this role, safe-guarded his prose to a certain degree from the potentially troubling discourses of morality and justice raised by the policy. The form of his memo — a directive — reflects its institutional location and frames Carrodus's action as a simple (re)iteration of previously announced government policies that are, in turn, framed as previously agreed-on interpretations of the constitutional status of "Aboriginal natives" within the Australian Commonwealth. Figuring the state of "agreement" in the past tense, Carrodus sought to stifle ongoing debate about the status of the policy and of indigenous people under federal administrative law. He was, he could say, simply doing his job.

The constitutional and common-law status of Aboriginal natives was, however, a matter of ongoing legislative, legal, and administrative debate, as was the meaning of the seemingly transparent phrases "Aboriginal native" and "tribal custom." The referential and interpretive indeterminacy of "Aboriginal native" and "tribal custom" was indicated by the phrase "more or less" throughout the memos that Carrodus dictated — and, for that matter, also throughout the memos, ethnographies, and editorials others wrote referring to native customs. Why was the referential object of the Aboriginal customary still indeterminate, perhaps indeterminable, in 1936? What did it matter that no one could say exactly who was who, what was what; and that, in regard to the Aboriginal question, everything was always modified as more or less?

Nothing in the 1901 Commonwealth Constitution, which set up the Australian federation government and formally founded the Australian nation, would suggest this referential trouble. The Constitution uses the phrases "aboriginal race" and "aboriginal natives" sparingly and does not mark them as particularly problematic concepts. Two places mention Aboriginal persons: section 51 (26), which excluded people of the "Aboriginal race" from the special race power of the Commonwealth government; and section 127, which excluded "aboriginal natives" from being counted in the census. Under the 1901 Constitution, states retained the right to formulate their own policies regarding Aboriginal persons within their territories, including the ability to pass legislation excluding them from the franchise; something most states did. Thus, although considered de facto British subjects, most persons classified as "aboriginal natives" were not afforded full citizenship rights in Australia.[9]

The few Aboriginal persons who did obtain the right to vote in South Australia were effectively barred from the Commonwealth and state vote by the Commonwealth Franchise Act, 1902, which enfranchised white women.[10]

In 1911, a year after the Commonwealth assumed governance of the Northern Territory from South Australia, the Aboriginal Ordinance further eroded the social autonomy of "Aboriginal natives" through the office of Chief Protector of Aborigines (the act was significantly strengthened in 1918). The act granted the chief protector authority over Aboriginal employment, movement, marriage, and social intercourse; and it gave the position power as "legal guardian of every Aboriginal and part-Aboriginal child under the age of eighteen years."[11] It was under this act that between 1910 and 1970, 10 to 30 percent of children of mixed parentage were taken away from their Aboriginal parents.[12] The Welfare Ordinance Act, 1953 further authorized the government to designate as its "ward" any person who by reason of "(a) his manner of living; (b) his inability, without assistance, adequately to manage his own affairs; (c) his standard of social habit and behavior; and (d) his personal associations, stands in need of such special care or assistance as is provided by this Ordinance."[13] As Alan Powell notes, though the ordinance applied equally to all Territorians, in fact it was almost solely applied to Aboriginal persons. Within a few years, 80 percent of the indigenous population had been declared wards of the state, which they remained until 1963. In 1936, indigenous Australians remained a legally defined disenfranchised subject population, an unfree and unequal race within a nation founded on the liberal notion of human freedom and equality. Their bodies, movements, intimacies, and consumption practices were subject to state control.

The unproblematic way in which the Constitution mentioned "Aboriginal race" and "Aboriginal native" is not surprising if we consider the performative nature of the text, which was meant to found, not administer, a nation. The smooth functioning of the massive state apparatus that this performative founded (what it did and demanded be done in the shadow of these words) depended, however, on the administrators' ability to differentiate the social identities of national subjects and to allocate citizenship rights, resources, and duties accordingly. Take, for instance, gender discrimination, which was also being contested at the time. Should women have suffrage? Although types and levels of citizenship based on gender were debated, the categorical and referential clarity of the notions "woman" and "man" were not. "Native" was otherwise.

Between 1901 and 1905, the federal attorney general's office referred to the commonsense idea of racial difference as the ground on which social groups should be differentiated, constitutional rights be distributed, and administrative policies be based. Put bluntly: people and rights were determined by the same principle, a racialized notion of blood. In 1905, Robert Garran, the secretary of the Attorney General Department, advised the government that "half-castes are not disqualified [from voting], but that all persons in whom the aboriginal blood preponderates are disqualified."[14] He argued similarly two months later that the Immigration Restriction Act was intended to limit racial rather than national groups. As a result, Joseph Bakhash, born in New York, but with a "Syrian" parentage should be, and was, denied entry into Australia.[15] Racial identity was understood at the time to be fixed at birth and altered only by generation-time—that is, miscegenous sex. Miscegenation was thereby transfigured into a technology of national (racial) reintegration.[16] So persuasive was the rhetoric stating that conflicts at the frontier could be bred away that W. E. H. Stanner, an anthropologist who would play a significant role in determining representations of Daly River indigenous ritual culture, published an article in the *Sydney Morning Herald* in 1933 arguing against miscegenation as an administrative policy: "Miscegenation is neither escape nor solution. The attitude of most people towards the mixed-blood is made up of vague sympathy, prejudice, and incomprehension. In the face of this, any scheme of miscegenation cannot be regarded as even a partial solution [to the 'Aboriginal problem']. It also runs the risk of raising a wretched border colony of lost souls."[17]

Stanner was right. Physical and cultural miscegenation presented administrators with more problems than it solved. Reading off the notes and queries they sent, we find administrators continually returning to a general set of quotidian but nonetheless nontransparent linguistic and epistemological questions about the referential confusion of the notion "native": What did "Aboriginal native" and "Aboriginal race" refer to and predicate? What made an "Aboriginal native" an "Aboriginal native" as such? If there were types of Aboriginal subjects or degrees of Aboriginality, should the entire cline be treated in the same way? In concrete instances: was *this* an "Aboriginal native"? Embedded within such questions were formal distinctions among identity as a formally coordinated differential system of signs; the characteristics or qualities considered more or less vital to one or the other of these identity designations in one or another context; and the felicitous nature of each of these identities and qualities from the point of view of state administration.

Citizenship was initially understood in racial terms, but over the course of the 1920s and 30s the means by which identity was determined was pulled away from the means by which state rights, resources, and duties were allocated. A number of Aboriginal advocates used a series of public scandals and spectacles to detach citizenship qualifications from racial characterizations — to make race an impractical grounds of citizenship and to substitute for race an underdefined notion of civilizational achievement.[18] For instance, the Aboriginal Protection League and the Aborigines' Protection Association (APA) staged a number of public protests calling for citizenship and economic rights for *civilized* Aboriginal men and women. In 1938 in the background of frontier massacres and violence, the APA sponsored a Day of Mourning held on the 150th anniversary of the white settlement of Australia.[19] Grounding citizenship in racial differences was characterized as a "baseless assumption"; that is, an interested justification for an irrational prejudice. Three years after the above telegram was sent federal government policy reflected this more general movement away from race and toward civilizational achievement as the basis for citizenship rights. John McEwen, minister of the interior, announced the government's "New Deal" for Australian Aborigines, promising to treat "Aboriginal natives" in such a way as to raise "their status so as to entitle them by right, and by qualification to the ordinary rights of citizenship, and enable them and help them to share with us the opportunities that are available in their own native land."[20] The form and language of the "New Deal" was critically influenced by Adolphus P. Elkin, chair of anthropology at the University of Sydney from 1934 to 1956, and also by C. A. Carrodus.[21] By 1944, Elkin could convincingly claim that all people had the capacity to "make progress towards civilization [if] a sound native policy designed with that end in view" were formulated.[22]

Racial topologizing did not cease in the 1930s, nor cease to be relevant to the reckoning of citizenship. What changed between 1905 and 1939 were the discursive procedures by which the state could legitimately link race and citizenship in its Aboriginal policy. Experts on "primitive people" still defined human types in terms of racial characteristics, but they argued that a superordinate *human* capacity for internally rational social and cultural systems made all people potential candidates for modern citizenship. These same experts argued that citizenship should be hinged to nothing other than an Aboriginal persons' achievement of (white) human civil culture. Permanently denying the benefits and responsibilities of citizenship to a group of people based on nothing but their racial heritage called into question not the civil status of the primitive people but the modernity and civilizational capacity of the white nation. Ten years after the first telegram was sent to Carrodus, W. E. H. Stanner addressed a national radio audience, stating that "it would give Australians a shock to know how often the fate of our blacks is flung up against an Australian abroad despite our excellent record in New Guinea and Papua. We are very widely thought of as a callous, hard-boiled people in such matters. I have heard some awkward conversations between Australians and Americans, Japanese, Italians, and others on matters of race policy."[23]

As part of their argument, Aboriginal experts insisted that all aboriginal groups had their own civilizational type animated by general and rational social principles — the hallmark of human rationality — which provided their life with meaning, purpose, and moral order. To this end W. Lloyd Warner titled his influential 1927 ethnography of the north Arnhem Land Murngin people, *A Black Civilization,* describing the purpose of his ethnography as "not only to present the civilization of the Murngin in the description of the various parts of tribal life, but to attempt to discover some of the general principles which govern their social life."[24] By 1936, most British-trained anthropologists, and the British administrators and police they trained, shared the general sense that the social order of primitive society consisted of delicately balanced local systems of heterosexual reproduction and its regulation — or, in the disciplinary rhetoric, its prescriptive and proscriptive rules, forms, and sanctions of kinship, marriage, and descent.[25]

According to the first and second chairs of anthropology in Australia, A. R. Radcliffe-Brown and A. P. Elkin, this preexisting, fully rational, principled, and meaningful indigenous social order made the government dependent on anthropology. To begin to understand the indigenous social order, it had to be apprehended in purely rational terms or, more exactly, apprehended from the perspective of *sympathetic* reason.[26] Although this argument was counter-intuitive, Elkin argued that the willingness to understand the sense made by ritual sex and violence provided the nation with a just and socially healthy means for doing away with it. Such an understanding was something only anthropologists could provide; that is, it itself depended on the proper division of social roles (especially a division among the faculties of scholar, administrator, missionary, and police) and on rigorous training in interactional and textual methods — how to talk to Aborigines and how to create specific types of texts, genealogies, moieties, ethnographies, and field notes. Only after anthropological reason had established the rationale of Aboriginal social practices and cultural beliefs through proper text-building practices could Aboriginal culture and Aboriginal people be made practical for the modern nation; could the "strangeness and sordidness" of their native customs be transformed without destroying the fabric of their civilization. In short, the fledging discipline of anthropology in Australia leaned on the scandal of indigenous ritual sexuality as the constitutive grounds of its own self-evident institutional necessity—and life, since Australian anthropology was dependent on government financial support.

Although arguing for a leading role of anthropology in the administration of the indigenous population, Elkin, Stanner, and other mainstream anthropologists sharply distinguished "understanding" proper to the academy from the practical political and social "judgment" proper to civil man, the categorical being more proper to national humanity.[27] Understanding the diversity of human culture and society may be the proper orientation and aim of the faculty of anthropology, but, in the end, the human faculty of moral feeling not only *may* but *should* curtail this understanding, driving it from the field of practical action. In other words the "human" as a categorical imperative of emergent modern nationalism could contain indigenous people but not all their practices in civil society. In his landmark ethnography, *The Australian Aborigines: How to Understand Them* (1938), Elkin wrote:

> Any people whose history, tradition and beliefs are different from our own is almost sure to have customs that seem strange and puzzling to us. We may even feel that these customs are not so good as ours, that they are degrading and should be abolished, but before we pass such opinions or act on them, we must first understand what those customs are, the traditions and beliefs on which they are based, the meaning which they possess for the individuals who practice them, and the social function which they perform. But while such an understanding undoubtedly makes another people's customs less puzzling to us, it does not necessarily commend them all, and we may still feel constrained to use our influence or authority to have some of them abolished or modified.[28]

In the national brand of anthropology these men advocated, speculative reason lacked practical autonomy.

What anthropologists had that missionaries, bushmen, and government administrators did not, and thus what made the arguments and discipline of Radcliffe-Brown and Elkin compelling to the degree that they were, was an undisputed purchase on the discourse of scientific epistemology and methodology. This epistemological and methodological perspective promised a rational ground for understanding Aboriginal practices, though not, we will see, moral assessment. A sympathetic and rational orientation to the social practices and beliefs of indigenous groups differentiated absolutely anthropological expertise from all other competitors — including Aboriginal men and women themselves.

In this spirit, Elkin ended an essay in the 1936 chapbook, *White and Black in Australia,* with this practical blueprint for the civilizational imperative: "The task of the missionary or other civilizing agent who desires, as he *must* do, to change various native practices, is, therefore, very difficult, for it involved his getting beyond the practices concerned to the secret sanctions involved, and endeavouring through the old men, the custodians of native sanctions, to modify or substitute fresh sanctions."[29] The trouble with missionaries, A. P. Elkin argued, was not their lack of good intentions, but their lack of a scientifically oriented and trained understanding of Aboriginal "cosmology" and "philosophy." As Elkin's colleague W. E. H. Stanner would later put it, rather than men of cosmology, missionaries saw only promiscuous women and "men of sodomy, sinners exceedingly."[30] Missionaries were right, Elkin argued, to see ritual sex acts and some other customary sexual practices as antithetical to the goal of Aboriginal citizenship. He himself made a similar argument in a short text, *Citizenship for the Aborigines.* But, Elkin argued, missionaries were wrong to confuse Aboriginal customs and cosmology with Aboriginal sexuality. Aboriginal sex acts and Aboriginal customary law and ritual were not identical, and Elkin promised that anthropology would demonstrate the difference to Australian publics, missionaries, state administrators, *and* Aboriginal elders.[31]

It was a fantastic vision, really, and one that was outlined earlier by Bronislaw Malinowski before the British Social Hygiene Council and the Board of Study for the Preparation of Missionaries.[32] If ritual sex was really about social and cosmological reproduction, then Elkin and his legions of trained administrators could disambiguate sex from customary law without destroying the fabric of Aboriginal society, and in so doing could produce a sanitized, sex-free culture conversant with a tourist economy, a privatized native sexuality conversant with Aboriginal citizenship, and a morally reintegrated nation. Armed with their scientifically trained understanding, anthropologists would sit with "tribal elders" and through critical rational conversation — the magic of words rather than the machinations of force — persuade them to alter those aspects of "social organization and custom" that were objectionable to civil society. (Note: Most anthropologists never actually reached more or less tribal people, but rather worked in leper colonies, on missions, or in government settlements.) By focusing their notes and queries on local practices and beliefs about sex and social organization, pursuing its meanings, contexts, types, positions, and variations, anthropologists would persuade Aboriginal men and women to devalue some of the "bad objects" of culture that, in critical ways, anthropologists themselves were valuing by showing such intense interest in them. Sympathy, nonprejudice, respect: these emotional stances would provide the affective tools for establishing a bridge of trust between native and anthropologist, an emotional architecture necessary for communicative reason to proceed. Sympathy would dilate local culture to anthropological and national persuasion. The "good objects" of sexual difference would remain; namely, familial organizations of sexuality as the basis of property, religion, and meaning understood through models of kinship and descent such as patrilineality, matrilineality, cognation, ambilineality, and so forth.

At the same time that they debated with Aboriginal elders, anthropologists conversed with the national public, calming their fears, explaining away the "strange and puzzling," the "degrading," and the disgusting of Aboriginal social life, even while reassuring the public that these "bad objects" of Aboriginal social life were being systematically eliminated. In both his monographs and his "practical"[33] tracts, Elkin extols his readers to remember that "puzzling marriage customs . . . objectionable to us" were "either practiced by Europeans or by peoples of early historical times, for whose contribution to civilization we have great respect."[34] Reasoned analogy is not, however, sufficient. Elkin further soothes the troubled reader by adding, "many important changes have been made in social organization and custom, and also in the ceremonial life; but they have been made after consideration by the elders, who are the custodians of law and tradition, and in time mythological (that is, 'historical') sanction or authority has grown up to account for that change."[35] Yes, Aborigines' civil progress depended on their acquisition of Western forms of masculinity and femininity, but this transition must be accomplished slowly and in a way compatible with local beliefs.

The affective technology of sympathy was not used as a persuasive tool exclusively on indigenous subjects. Because anthropologists were people of good will—people who could demonstrate a real sympathy, knowledge, and passion for Aboriginal society—they could reassure the public that whatever disciplinary protocol they advocated for Aboriginal society was advocated humanely, tolerantly, and on its behalf. It would be just and moral. Sex is (soon to be) nothing (to fear): anthropological understanding would provide not only a rational explanation for Aborigines' strange sexual customs, but also a means for doing away with them and, thereby, doing away with a whole host of horrors threatening the Australian nation's claim to be a modern, civil, and humane society.

These complex scholarly and national orientations created deeply dialogical ethnographic texts. As Elkin, his colleagues, and his students addressed heterogeneous academic and nonacademic publics, they moved across different discursive registers, citing the voices of neutral and objective science, of a horrified and traumatized public, and of their readers' national desires and shames. Insofar as they succeeded in convincing the public of the scientific grounding of its good intentions, anthropology not only salvaged indigenous culture, but also saved the ideal of nationalism and dispassionate reason from its miscarriage at the nation's frontier, and instantiated itself as the premier discipline of indigenous social life. The social price of a failure to appreciate the proper roles of the faculties was high. Untrained interference in local social processes, and, especially, interference in systems of religious social sanction, risked unwinding the social fabric — the result of which was a "remedy worse than the disease"; namely, the horrors of settler dysfunction, including drunkenness, veneral disease, poverty.[36] Throughout the first half of the twentieth century, the Australian press published claims that Christianity, the standard-bearer of Western colonialism, ruined rather than raised native peoples.[37]

Even if anthropological understanding was constrained by moral judgment rather than reason — a morality that aspired to be world historical and practically relevant — insofar as anthropologists figured their practices as dispassionate social scientific assessments of indigenous practices and beliefs, and insofar as they assessed Aboriginal beliefs as reasonable from a culturally internal perspective, they intensified the problem of administering national law across civilizational boundaries. The anthropological view that indigenous culture was rational, that it made sense, circulated in the mass media as in this *Northern Territory Times* editorial: "One of the most fatal mistakes that can be made in dealing with the blacks is to laugh at their secret superstitions and beliefs [for] below the surface" is reason not irrationality.[38] Public and administrative debates ensued about the fairness and justice of trying "more or less tribal" Aboriginal people under British law. These debates were grafted on to earlier ones. As far back as 1837, the British House of Commons Select Committee on Aborigines observed that expecting "wild natives" to observe British law was "absurd," and punishing "the non-observation of them by severe penalties" was "palpably unjust."[39] Based on what principle of fairness and justice could an Aboriginal man be tried and condemned to death for a crime he has no language for or understanding of? How could "full justice . . . be done" and what did "legal justice" mean in a colonial context in which no common language connected indigenous and settler communities?[40] When Aboriginal persons were brought to trial for customary practices where no white person was involved, the absence of a common language and practice between settler and indigenous groups and the presence of a rational cultural order within indigenous groups further blurred the line between force and justice, trial and torture, civil and savage law, the frontier and modern nation. Civil law was opened to accusations of barbarity. Because of this, sixty jurists from the Northern Territory called on the Darwin Supreme Court in 1933 to try Aborigines according to their customary laws where the offense was of a "more or less tribal" nature. To do otherwise would expose "white" law to shameful charges of savagery, injustice, and inhumanity.

This nonpassage between justice and morality, and between rational assessments and practical governance of cultural difference, irritated public discourse. And it demonstrated one manner in which indigenous subjects in the north were nation-makers. Indigenous subjects prompted and moved public debate. And, perhaps, in ways that still irritate the membrane of liberal democratic nationalism. Take, for instance, the public exchange between Joe Croft and W. E. Davies. Although Croft morally condemns Aboriginal men's ritual sex acts he also castigates the "authorities" — not, as we might imagine, for shielding these acts from state and private interference, but for failing to shield other violent native customs. In reply, Davies suggests how liberal anthropological models were being taken up and recirculated in the public sphere. Here is the extract from Croft, followed by the statement by Davies:

"The Old People and Their Tribal Affairs." I maintain we should not interfere with them. If we do we should start in Darwin. I can take the authorities to the Compound and charge fourteen of the aboriginals with bigamy. Then I can take them to the Daly River and charge aboriginals with cutting their fingers off. Then we can go down to the McArthur and Roper River and charge the natives with inflicting torture on young girls. This horrible rite is practiced for the sole purpose of forcing maturity on girl children so the old men of the tribes are kept supplied with wives. Just after this ordeal 10 and 11 year old girls can be seen newly operated on like calves in a branding yard. Then I can take the authorities further out to the Hubert River where natives perform the surgical operation on the males which prevents any possibility of propagation. Now I maintain that if these outrageous offenses are permitted by the aboriginal in their tribal affairs the fights between them should be allowed and that we of the English speaking race have not the right to interfere in their tribal affairs.[41]

Sir, — In reference to the above I am writing more especially to acknowledge Mr. Joe Croft's suggestion. I shall ask the Rev. Mr. Warren to deal with the letter at his discretion, or you may arrange an interview with him regarding his views. I myself send my mite of explanation to your contemporary. Croft speaks from a wide experience and there is a power of sense in what he says. I would not agree with him in maintaining that no effort should be made to raise the aborigines of Australia above crude practices. To my mind the aim should be to moralize or christianize the traditional customs and lore (without destroying them) as has been done with other peoples and tribes. In the tribal stage the "individual" is non-existent and non-moral, Your and &c. W. H. Davies.[42]

SPECULATIVE SEX AND THE LIMIT OF REASON

It was in the context of the nonpassage between justice and morality and between reason and practical settler governance that academics and government officials suggested a (usually three-) tiered system for the administration of indigenous groups. In a letter to Carrodus about a related Daly River case, the first director of Native Affairs in the Northern Territory, E. W. P. Chinnery, who had previously held the positions of government anthropologist and commissioner of Native Affairs for Territory of New Guinea in 1924 and 1928, respectively, advocated the official adoption of the "Murray System" in the Northern Territory. Chinnery described the Murray System as noninterference with "relatively untouched natives who live more or less permanently in remote areas, both inside and outside the reserves."[43] In effect, national space would be divided, not according to commonsense notions of the public and private and state and family, but rather according to socially, if not geographically, separated, functionally integrated national and subnational (tribal) groups.

Put simply, Aboriginal groups would be distinguished on the basis of their civilizational achievements. In practice this judgment was little more than a measurement of an Aboriginal group's proximity to the edge of the frontier. "Relatively," "more or less": the emergent civilizational grounds for citizenship rights and administrative policy did not do away with the uncertainty of identity. Nevertheless, the idea was that, if treated scientifically, the structure and function of primitive society would serve as an organic administrative apparatus until "permanent Government stations have been established within such areas and European ideas of law and order have been introduced gradually by methods of peaceful penetration."[44] Until that time, anthropologically trained men and women would work the social alchemy of sympathetic understanding.

The government policy of relative noninterference in the affairs of "more or less" tribal natives who lived in "more or less" remote areas was not adopted by government administrators simply because of its anthropological fashion—although anthropologists studiously, and effectively, worked to make their discipline indispensable to government deliberations. A hands-off policy for more or less tribal groups had independent symbolic, economic, and bureaucratic appeal. To begin with, the policy mitigated the symbolic and economic costs of frontier violence, and it especially lessened the cost of police patrols and patrol justice by lessening the occasion for settler violence. Settler violence was in the news. In 1929 the Australian parliament published a comprehensive and scathing report on the atrocious economic, sexual, and social degradations of white Australians.[45] This report was prompted by Australian public outrage over the massacre of Aboriginal men, women, and children in the Kimberley region to the southwest of the Daly River, which circulated across the regional press. In the Northern Territory, for instance, the *Northern Territory Times* reported that the author of the inquiry, J. W. Bleakley, former Chief Protectorate of Aborigines in Queensland, saw indigenous persons, not settlers, in need of protection, and recommended the protection of "full-blooded" Aborigines from "contaminating . . . outside [white] influences."[46] In the same year Bronislaw Malinowski published *The Sexual Life of Savages* (1929), describing Trobriand Islanders as having "definite [sexual] laws, stringent in their application and enforced by punishments" and "also a sense of [sexual] right and wrong and canons of correct behavior not devoid of delicacy or refinement,"

The Kimberley massacre was hardly an anomaly. Memoirs and newspapers described the treatment of Aboriginal men and women in terms that "no earnest student of humanity can read without a shock of disgust, and a fervent desire that some, at least, of the white ghouls may find retribution at long last."[47] Settler memoirs like *Cattle Chosen* (1926), *Memoirs of Simpson Newland* (1926), and *Life in the Bush* (1939) told tales of frontier massacres and ritual mutilations, as did anthropological memoirs such as Baldwin Spencer's *Wanderings in Wild Australia* (1928). In 1932, after carrying out research in

Western Australia, Ralph O'Reilly Piddington embarrassed the government by describing in a newspaper interview specific "sexual violations of Aboriginal women, beatings of Aboriginal men and women . . . [and] the misappropriation of government rations designated for aged and infirmed Aborigines."[48] The Kimberley massacre, the Coniston massacre, the Forrest massacre: the horrors of the frontier roiled public debate and threatened to turn Australian nationalism wild, revealing its native policy as motivated by nothing so much as brute force and sexual predation, oriented toward nothing so much as profit, abuse, and extermination—not rational communicative reason, not social reform, not civil advancement.[49]

The idea of a self-regulating, self-reproducing native group also provided to government and business an economically expedient excuse for the use of Aboriginal men and women as a disposable labor pool.[50] Although virtually every Aboriginal person would have had some form of contact with settlers by 1936, either directly or mediated by trade with neighboring groups, many northwestern, central, and western desert groups maintained some relative autonomy and some relative expressive difference (local language, dress, ritual practice) from white populations. Employers used these commonsense indexes of tribal function to justify their practice of paying Aboriginal laborers meager rations, arguing that a worker's extended Aboriginal family could forage for any extra provisions that might be needed during the work season and during periods when no work was available.[51] Governments likewise justified paltry budgets for indigenous health, housing, and welfare by referring to the fantasy of the tribal function. Even when government compounds ("reservations") were established in the far north in the early 1940s, administrators envisioned them as serving as "refuges or sanctuaries of a temporary nature" where "the aboriginal may . . . continue his normal existence until the time is ripe for his further development."[52] This all but free labor pool was critical to capital accumulation in the north, where profit margins were thin at best, especially during the global depression of the 1930s.[53]

Traditional expressive culture was emerging as the ground of a very different type of symbolic and economic value. In 1930, the *Northern Territory Times* printed "A Plea for the Abo" in which it reported that the British Association for the Advancement of Science considered the "Australian aborigines as being among the most valuable living people for the scientific study of the early history of mankind."[54] Christian ministers echoed the argument that "our aborigines are a national asset"; and this theological imprimatur was circulated in the national press.[55] Aboriginal expressive culture (rather than

Aboriginal people per se) slowly emerged as a national value, as something that belonged to the nation and thus merited federal protection. Although noting that the Commonwealth government had no constitutional authority to intervene in state indigenous policy, in the shadow cast by these reevaluations of indigenous worth, the *Northern Territory Times* called on the federal government to provide state and territory governments with trained anthropologists to study local people.[56] In other articles, the *Northern Territory Times* called on ordinary settlers to provide their own ethnographic insights on the ways of "our Abo."[57] Similar themes were sounded in short educational films such as *Art of the Hunter.*[58]

Certified as world historic by such internationally recognized scholars as Freud and Durkheim and by esteemed institutions like the British Association for the Advancement of Science, Aboriginal culture lent Australia a symbolic value and luminosity. Anthropologists were not the only settler subjects converting this symbolic capital into economic capital. Two years after announcing the scientific value of Australian Aborigines, the *Northern Territory Times* ran a four-part series, "Smoke Signals from the Never-Never," reporting on the novel transformation of the rural economy from pastoralism to tourism. In the serialized articles, the emergent voicings of a global cultural tourist market can be heard: "Quite genuine old timers are neglecting the raising of stock or giving it second place in the great new industry of shewing [*sic*] sightseers round. . . . For a few sticks of tobacco stone age savages will doff the rags of civilization and perform weird rites in full panoply of feathers tuck on with blood. Spears up-raised, they will charge madly down on the row of loaded— cameras, and rejuvenated business men can take back irrefutable evidence of the tough time they had against the blacks."[59]

Simultaneously an administrative technique and a fantasy of liberal appropriation, the Murray System promised a seamless and peaceful transition from a state of national economic, racial, and civilizational separation to a lucrative business of cultural commodification. As the frontier was absorbed into the nation, Aboriginal people and their customs would gradually lose their "wildness." No longer wild, Aboriginal men and women would no longer be recognized as "more or less tribal." The full force of state law would then be extended in concert with the full benefits of citizenship and full panoply of business initiatives. Until that time, the more indigenous groups maintained the native customs that signified and were thought necessary to produce a self-regulating Aboriginal group the less state and private capital had to be expended to maintain and reproduce the Aboriginal labor critical to the appropriation of Aboriginal lands and resources.

Far from ungrateful, many northern citizens praised Aborigines in the reading republic of national newspapers, broadsheets, and books for their generous contribution to private and national wealth. In 1930, the editors of the *Northern Territory Times* celebrated the "generous kind-hearted loyal . . . outback black [who] lightens the labour of the outback worker [and is] almost indispensable" to the pioneer.[60] These publicly oriented national testimonials to the generous character of northern "tribal" Aboriginal men and women, when properly treated, included prescriptions for maintaining this blessed state of affairs that drew directly from emergent mainstream British anthropological discourses.[61] The object of public and administrative interpretation was the appropriation of lands at a minimal cost; the means of acquisition was the same sympathetic understanding anthropologists sought.

The addressee of these messages was neither the Aboriginal Australians nor any specific Australian citizen. Nor were these texts instances of "mere" ideology. They were the textual voicings of the good national subject addressed to the same imaginary, semiotically figured, mass subject that many actual Australian citizens desired as a counterfactual self to the shockingly real factual actions and attitudes of their neighbors.[62] Factual images of this specifiable, and specifiably, bad national subject circulated beside these good images in press and conversation. Insofar as Australian settlers successfully entailed a sharp and clear division in textual space — the good and the ghoulish white subject — they then sought to position themselves in respect to it. In other words many, though not all, citizens desired to be the imaginary national subject they sought to entail in texts, to have been all along acting for the best (or at least the betterment). Even if the ability of the militarily and economically powerful to take the territories of the weak might reflect nothing more than the natural order of things, many settler subjects desired that this natural order be issued in a civil register; to have taking be a form of gift bestowal; and that the physical, moral, or social pharmakon of Western civilization be medicine not poison.[63]

The attempt to write a portrait of a well-intentioned frontier and then to identify themselves with it was an attempt to write over a violent, vicious settler history that would not historicize itself and that seemed to produce merely degrees of variation, more or less, among settler and indigenous practices. We should not take lightly the aspiration for some other national poetics than the pitiless pastoralism that inspired a tortured national meter, haunting Australian nationalism with the horrible shapes and specters of its frontier history.[64] Take, for instance, this poem published in the *Northern Territory Times and Gazette:*

> A lubra fled with her screaming child through
>   the line of pitiless rifles.
> And I galloped away to kill the two for their
>   lives to me were trifles.
> As my horse strode after the dusky pair, like
>   beasts, I could heard them panting,
> I shot them both as they fell fatigued, 'neath a
>   light wood gently slanting.
>
> We dug a trench in the golden sand where the
>   wattles skirted the river,
> And we buried the slaughtered side by side and
>   left them to rest forever;
> And those were the blacks who had speared my
>   sheep and maimed and destroyed my cattle,
> And I reckon we slew them fair as fair that day
>   as soldiers in battle.
>
> But in tortured dreams, when I fall asleep, I
>   can hear the lubras weeping,
> And spectral blacks through spectral woods are
>   always toward me creeping;
> And ever and ever they beckon me on to strange
>   and mysterious places,
> Where, in fancy, I see their comrades lie with
>   the blood on their ghastly faces.
>
> Like the miserly men who oppress their kind to
>   make heavier still their purses,
> I walk through life a detested thing, and a mark
>   for a thousand curses;
> And, although I feast on ambrosial fare and
>   imbibe my winy nectars,
> I'll be hunted down to my grave at last by
>   horrible shapes and spectres.[65]

The national haunting of white sexuality was not restricted to the poetic public sphere. W. E. H. Stanner's field notes provide some evidence of the personal and professional anxiety that white sexuality generated in the Daly River region during the 1930s. Stanner remarks that during his fieldwork a local farmer, Ridsdale, sometime slept with him because he was sure that "blacks" were going to murder him for "cohabitating with wife of Tuckerboy." Stanner continues, "many local whites in secret fear of natives. Various symptoms: over cruel handling; fear of being too close with them; note what Byne boys said on m[y] return from Port Keats through the Moill country (yet old Parry is different). Great many men in bush seem to believe that they will 'collect' in the end." Stanner describes the relay of paranoia created by these frontier conditions: "Will never forget fright when Ridsdale first came. I was asleep. He crept down through shadows from his tent (just imagine that walk: in darkness, thinking blacks were after him). I woke out of my sleep with dreadful fright. Shall not lightly forget those few seconds. Might have shot him."[66]

These, in short, were some of the institutional, subjective, and discursive constraints and values that shaped Carrodus's telegram. When the customary practices protected were minimally dissonant with normative values, the policy of noninterference in tribal customs where no white man was involved meshed a maximal set of overlapping academic, administrative, and settler aspirations. The state's tolerance, even narcissism, of minor cultural differences reinforced the imperial fantasy that colonial appropriation was a form of paternal recognition and gift bestowal, casting the settler nation in the role of ward, protector, and pater; and casting liberal colonization as a "more or less" gradual and peaceful transition from savagery to civilization. In other words, it reflected the real optimism of mid-century liberal humanism; namely, that critical public conversation, premised on and oriented toward rational understanding, provided the means for a peaceful, progressively integrated society. And, insofar as something that could be figured as progress did occur, this fantasy reinforced public identifications with and idealizations of the white Australian nation as a civilized nation. In these moments, the state seemed little more than the political-administrative prosthesis of this nationalized subject — the apparatus of its well-intentioned republic of good will.

But the tiered system of indigenous administration did not resolve the nonpassage among reason, practical morality, justice, law, and administration. Although the policy may have made administrative, economic, and discursive sense, many non-Aboriginal Australians raised practical, legal, epistemological, and moral objections to it. They argued, as did mainstream anthropologists, that reason and administrative practice should be limited by collective morality. For instance, in the Daly River case the question of whether or not Constable Pryor knowingly transgressed department policy quickly turned to the practical problem of implementing it. Informed of department policy, A. V. Stretton, superintendent of Northern Territory police, wrote to Robert H. Weddell, administrator of the Northern Territory of Australia, advising him that the directive was legally "too wide, covering as it does capital crimes committed in settled areas" and practically unmanageable. "It is also pointed out that if the Police Officer is compelled to wait for approval from the Chief Protector before securing the offenders and witnesses, it will probably mean that by the time such instruction is received offenders and witnesses will have scattered over a wide area increasing the difficulties of arrest where necessary considerably and involving probably hundred of miles of patrol."[67]

If the vast frontier terrain made it enormously difficult to rearrest indigenous subjects once released, it also made it difficult to capture the civilizational meanings and origins, even more or less, of the practices they were being arrested for. But when patrol officers asked how they were to know whether or not a practice was more or less tribal, Carrodus dismissed their epistemological concerns. In his memos, critical faculties and duties are presented as matters of professional competences, capacities, and sympathies, and of proper bureaucratic technique. According to Carrodus it was not up to an untrained patrol officer to determine whether an act they or others stumbled on was "more or less" tribal involving "more or less" wild men (though his repeated use of the qualification "more or less" iterated the central crises these men faced). Police constables were simply required to take careful notes from which other people would form critical judgments.[68] Underlings collect. Anthropologists assess. Courts make judgments. According to Carrodus: "The question of whether ritual rape and certain other rites and customs should be suppressed is one which should be determined in the light of the advice given by anthropologists or officers trained in anthropology. It is suggested that the degree of civilization reached by the natives performing the rites would be a material factor."[69]

Carrodus may have dismissed their epistemological concerns, but we should not underestimate what was being asked of ordinary settler subjects—those holding government jobs, designing and administering state policy, plowing fields. Those like Constable Pryor had to decide quickly whether peanut farmer Harkins had collided into the vibrant core of indigenous culture or stumbled on the perverting effects, "more or less," of a Christian colonialism gone terribly awry. Was an indigenous practice part of the group's precolonial traditions? Or was it a response to the "type of white man" living in the frontier, to Christian missionaries proselytizing across the outback, or to the very laissez-faire entrepreneurs the policy was in large part designed to protect and support? More troubling is the question, at what point did a white person become "involved"? Was knowing that these things were occurring in the back forty enough to involve a white man? Even if state workers were to protect "more or less" customary practices, as a primitive administrative means toward the eventual end of Western civilization, they had to make critical cultural and moral judgments on the spot which might have much wider social ramifications—a murderer hung rather than set free; a rapist allowed to wander at will; insurgents ready to mobilize the native population.

If these practical aspects of government policy were not troubling enough, A. V. Stretton, the superintendent of police in Darwin, raised legal questions about department policy, anchoring his criticisms in normative bureaucratic distinctions among the administrative, legal, and police functions of the state. While notifying all police stations in the Territory that they must abide by the policy of the minister, Stretton pointed out the illegality of the directive in a separate letter to the Northern Territory administrator.[70] Carefully drawing on the indirect function of speech to avoid any accusation of insubordination, Stretton deployed the same discourse of proper state function against state policy that Carrodus had deployed to uphold it: "I desire to direct Your Honour's attention to the fact that whilst I am prepared at all times to give effect to instructions, in this case it is pointed out that the instructions are in direct opposition to the Statute law which it is my duty to see is properly enforced. It is suggested therefore that in lieu of the instruction an amendment of the existing Statute law is desirable."[71] The idea of zoning nonnormative sex and nonstate violence might make administrative sense, might even be the just thing to do. Nevertheless, it was unlawful.

Regarding matters of dominant legal interpretation of the time, Stretton was right. While many courts questioned the justice of applying English law to "wild" or "uncivilized" natives, time and again Australian courts and governments would rule that as a matter of legal fact "Australian law, civil and criminal, substantive and procedural, was to be applied to Aboriginals to the exclusion of their own laws except in the rare cases where legislation made specific provision to the contrary."[72] Indeed, Commonwealth and state governments established the office of aboriginal protector in the 1830s in lieu of state recognition of indigenous customary law and the establishment of native courts.[73] Carrodus was impeded by this dominant juridical opinion when he replied to Stretton's legal challenge by noting that the Aboriginal Protector had the authority to decide if an Aboriginal person should be charged and prosecuted no matter whether the crime was tribal or not, or involved a white person or not. In response, a Northern Territory judge submitted a legal opinion to the minister of the Department of the Interior that the policy breached the proper separation of police and administrative powers: "Under the law as it stands, it is the duty of the police to take immediate action with respect to breaches of the law which come under their notice, without respect to colour or race of the parties concerned. If it is desired that this position should be altered, such alteration should be brought about by amendment of the law, and not by Ministerial direction."[74]

Finally, whether or not the directive was constitutional, legal, or practical, some opposed it simply on moral grounds. Acting Chief Protector of Aboriginals W. B. Kirkland wrote that the criminal status of an Aboriginal practice should not be based on its relative tribalness. If tribal practice was morally reprehensible then it should be "suppressed." Simple, principled, and just law should give way to the collective moral foundation of the nation as should the moral perspective of the natives. "Certain rites and customs of the aboriginals should be suppressed and it may be argued that the only method of suppression justifiable is the application of the white law. Notwithstanding the opinion expressed in the Department's memorandum of 18th June, it is respectfully submitted that ritual rape is such a custom."[75] Unlimited by moral feeling, reason was like rape — a specter haunting governance in the frontier.

I could end this section with the final verdict in the Daly River case: the Malakmalak men were found guilty and sentenced to jail in Darwin. But to close the case at this point would be to repeat a national fantasy not to analyze it.

THE SUBJECT OF SEX

This brief history of the mid-century administration of indigenous people in northern Australia reminds us that state policy is a complex voicing of the immanent form and content of society. In the shadow of Marx, we remember that all voicings (social genres) are the debris of past standardizations of space, people, and talk that makes communication meaningful in the here and now. In this case, this debris includes constitutional texts, anthropological texts, administrative memos, and juridical opinions and their complicated national and transnational circuits, imaginaries, and desires. These genres, as Bakhtin noted, are embedded in formal and informal institutions that dictate the varying degrees of risk that varying types of people face breaking generic frames.

But knowing these things about genre and context does not tell us why genres are moved, invaginated, defended, or left exposed; why, for instance, a Northern Territory magistrate took the time to write a note correcting the legal assumptions embedded in Carrodus's administrative memo. No genre coordinates itself outside the field of interpretative practice. That is, knowing that Carrodus's telegram and policies were "the selective realization of cultural values under situational constraints" does not tell us why particular men and women emphasized rather than mitigated particular generic spaces; why they bent the generic spaces and discourses of government, publicness, modesty, law, and justice to change state policy and, in doing so, generated new policies, rhetorics, and dispositions of national citizenship. The fact of the loose coordination among the formal legal, administrative, and police arms of the state is not sufficient to explain Stretton's or Kirkland's objection to state policy—is not really an explanation at all. The incommensurateness of practical, moral, and legal genres is endemic to national formations. Likewise, statutes exist in liberal democracies that are rarely if ever enforced and that do not become the site of social struggle and protestation; ditto administrative policies that skate the thin edge of legality. Texts do not transform *themselves* from the tacit to the tactical. Texts lay dormant until some person has a stake in raising them or, perhaps less intentionally, until some person accidentally moves them while trying to move something else.

In other words, people wield the law of genre against each other during moments of what linguistic anthropologists call explicit and implicit metapragmatic discourse; respectively, moments in which speakers, texts, or discourses indicate to others how to speak or produce proper or improper social forms and the means by which speakers, texts, and discourses signal a sense of ending or beginning, of narrative form and flow and of the routine and remarkable, and thereby indicate what we should do or say or act if we know what's good for us.[76] We saw, for instance, in the grammatical debris of their texts, Stretton, Carrodus, and Kirkland indicating to each other how to talk in particular types of places with particular types of people; and saw how these signals acted as indexical hinges, plotting contexts (this spacetime) into discursive types (this genre) into subject types (this social role)—and vice versa.

Whether implicitly or explicitly these discursive frames indicated how each of these men should calculate and calibrate the stakes, pleasures, and risks of taking a certain stance in a certain type of formed space.

Any genre can be plotted into any other genre as a means of building new provisional standardizations of thought, perspective, and expectation: a love plot into a work plot, a sex plot into a math plot, an identity plot into a literary plot. Stretton, for instance, wielded a discourse of proper state function against Carrodus's own. Kirkland graphed a discourse of morality into arguments about proper state function. But we must always remember that this emplotment occurs within the social institutions of personal and group risk. The social and economic risks people took criticizing government policy and policymakers in the first half of the twentieth century were real and widely known. Ralph O'Reilly Piddington was effectively banned from further research in Australia after embarrassing the Western Australian government with his allegations of specific settlers' physical and economic abuses. His blacklisting had a formative effect on how Australian academics couched their criticism of the government.[77] Bronislaw Malinowski was likewise subjected to research and employment restrictions due to his outspoken views on colonial life.

And here we see the difference between the conditions of agency for settler and indigenous subjects. Their practices may have incited this governmental anxiety. But very few indigenous men and women could play levels of state bureaucracy against each other. Although they could not, specific indigenous subjects and practices were nevertheless an immediate cause of governmental fission. Even a superficial reading of the Daly River case suggests the provocative nature of the administrative policy before and after 1940. Carrodus demanded that Constable Pryor of Daly River either forfeit his job or hold back the hands of peanut farmer Harkins. That he do no more than look on as the "female [was] required [to] have sexual intercourse with all and sundry." The internal stability of "wild natives" might depend on "the free exercise of their native customs," but the majority of white Australians understood sacred acts of bestiality, ritual masturbation, same sex, and group sex as incommensurate with a modern civil society's understanding of sex and intimacy as a private, normatively monogamous heterosexual affair. And the reading public had a full fair of ethnopornographia to incite this understanding—textual representations that as often as not had little to do with the attitudes or intentions of any indigenous subject or group. The public and semipublic sacramental sexuality of indigenous groups narrated in such salacious ethnographies as

Herbert Basedow's *The Australian Aboriginal* (published in 1925 and reprinted in 1929) conjured images of profound immorality, the absolute limit of a civilized nation's tolerance of cultural difference, even as this sexuality became a source of public incitement and excitement, private capital, and personal advancement.

What I want to understand, in other words, is not simply the discursive and textual frames within which the policy made sense to the Department of the Interior, nor simply *that* various people drew on genres and linguistic forms to index various state functions and authorities, but rather *what* prompted people like Stretton and Kirkland to act, to risk their economic livelihood or advancement, by making explicit the ongoing incommensurability of state policy and personal and national morality? And how to conceptualize the agency of indigenous subjects in this field of risk. To answer these questions in even a minimal way we need to examine how persons inhabited the policy; how they experienced the mandate to carry it out, including their experience of institutional mediations of their moral sense.

Let me summarize where we are. The difficulty the Daly River case posed to liberal national democratic ideology was twofold. On the one hand, as I discussed above, while most white Australians agreed that Aboriginal ritual sex defied the ideal of a normative national collective morality, they quarreled in administrative domains and in the critical public sphere about whether or not this moral judgment should invalidate normative notions of justice and right that ideally subtended state law and practice. On the other hand, the case raised the question not simply of how to administer law justly across maximally heterogeneous cultural fields, but whether there was any meaningful difference between indigenous and settler sexual morality and practice. The real problem that ritual sex posed to many settlers was not its transparent difference from white sexuality but the rending of that difference.

This is not to say that settlers did not experience something best described as radical alterity. It is, however, to question its source and to demand a finer differentiation in the meaning of subjectivity and agency. Alterity does not uniquely refer to moments of experienced or understood maximal heterogeneity across socially or culturally differentiated groups (paradigmatically found in colonial settler encounters), though we should not ignore or shy away from the fact that fundamental differences do exist between real and imagined means and modes of producing a good life. Even when such social heterogeneity exists, what is experienced as radical difference is not interior to the social forms themselves but exterior, so to speak, or emergent in the spaces of their intersection — what Georg Simmel called sites of contact.[78] Moreover, this experience may well create irresolvable cleavages not between the two groups but within one of them, which had previously tacitly accepted and experienced itself as a collectivity. In this case, the intimate "we" of the nation came precariously close to being refashioned as a collection of strangers who turn not toward but away from each other. Likewise, the interior space of the subject may be rent, the "I" of myself lost in the field of irreconcilable moral injunctions. This is, I want to suggest, what occurred during events like the Daly River case. Society and subjectivity were revealed to be a collectivity that depended on the taken-for-granted, the tacit, the unexamined life. Once again, indigenous agency is vital in understanding this movement, even if the mode of motion is different from the settlers' own.

To get at the source and dynamic of these rendings, let us turn to an archive of a police case compiled four years after the above "ritual rape." This case ("Murder of Jesse") once again involved a group of Malakmalak men. Rather than rape, the charge was the murder of a woman ("Jesse") from the "Brinken" tribe after her alleged violation of sacred Kunapipi grounds. The Daly River police officer at the time, Constable J. T. Turner, compiled a folder consisting of two typed letters in which he outlined the case, a set of "confessions" taken from the Malakmalak suspects, a map of the area where the murder occurred, and an anthropological assessment. The anthropological submission was written by Bill Harney, a staff member of the Native Affairs Department, who informally trained under A. P. Elkin and who wrote, with Elkin's encouragement, a number of memoirs and travelogues about Aboriginal and settler life in the Northern Territory. The popularity of these books helped to establish him as a national radio personality.[79]

In his two typed submissions, Constable Turner provides details of the psychological state of the Malakmalak men he apprehended ("they both seemed proud of their killing"); the shocking nature of the material evidence ("I looked at the Shovel Spears in the hands of each and found them covered at beyond Shovel Point with fresh blood"); and the quoted motives of men ("That dead fellow Lubra and War-wool (Lubra) been walk on Sacret Groun takem my things. . . . That two lubra been alonga my Sacret groun come back from Chinaman takem my thing").[80] The Malakmalak men are reported to claim that the murder was the lawful outcome of the woman's transgression of sacred Kunapipi grounds. The ritual itself was said to have been introduced to them four years previously by a Wagaman man — the same year of the above "ritual rape."[81] But these same letters report conflicting testimony from other

Aboriginal groups. Another Brinken Aboriginal woman who had witnessed the attack disputed the existence of a "Sacret Groun" in the area in the company of Brinken men who did not deny her claim.[82]

In his submission, Bill Harney provided a short ethnographic and comparative history of the "Big Sunday cult," the colloquial term for the Kunapipi (or Karwadi) ritual. Harney testified that "gang rape" and "murder" were two customary penalties for the violation of men's sacred grounds by uninitiated women.[83] Harney argued that the sanctions were wholly within an ancient Aboriginal law. But he also noted that the rate with which they were being used had risen dramatically because "contact with civilization tends to make the native women disobey the laws and taboos of the tribe, and they would pass over or near these taboo spots knowing they are protected by the law, or the white people of that part, and so the natives seeing their greatest weapon for law and order (increase, regeneration and clearing up of tribal disputes) becoming useless by these women, become annoyed and use force."[84] In Harney's submission "contact with civilization" euphemistically figures a host of material, sexual, and social exchanges occurring in the frontier, exchanges the Malakmalak men also note as relevant to their actions ("come back from Chinaman takem my thing").

Harney's views about Big Sunday were influenced by emergent professional anthropological perspectives on Kunapipi and related men's "high cults." Baldwin Spencer first described a regional variant of Kunapipi in 1914, detailing its mythological dimensions and sexual imagery, but not mentioning any ritual sex acts.[85] It was not until 1937 that W. Lloyd Warner, a student of the American anthropologist Robert H. Lowie and the British A. R. Radcliffe-Brown, situated a full ethnographic account of Kunapipi in its broader mythological and ritual contexts. Based on his fieldwork from 1926 to 1929 among the Murngin of Arnhem Land, Warner argued that the ritual use of sex was both a legal sanction for the violation of the sacred ground and a part of the sacred cult itself. Warner's ethnography exemplified the means by which anthropology deferred, rather than resolved, the sense of ritual sex. Loosely following the lead of Emile Durkheim and Bronislaw Malinowski, Warner cosmologized ritual as he desexualized sex, refashioning it as a symbolic, but unpleasurable, part of ritual cosmogony. Warner argued that Kunapipi rituals, and the Wawilak myth and ritual to which it properly belonged, were "fertility rites" designed to "aid nature" in the reproduction of the conditions of social life. Sex during these rituals was not about pleasure or violence. And it certainly was not an index of the Aboriginal male psyche—indeed, men had to be forced into practicing it. This is why, Warner argued, "the young man who refuses to copulate with the woman in the fertility rite of Gunabibi is scolded and told that he will be sick and make his partner ill" and that "scarcity and sickness" were "likely to result."[86]

In the 1940s, the first students of A. P. Elkin, Ronald and Catherine Berndt, followed up Warner's initial studies. Ronald Berndt devoted a full-length monograph (published in 1951) to the ceremonial and mythic complex. Ronald and Catherine Berndt jointly authored another text on the sexual practices and beliefs of Western Arnhem Land groups.[87] In the latter monograph, the Berndts supported Warner's general view of sex and sexual meanings in Kunapipi and his detachment of ritual meaning from ritual practice, the referential and cosmological from the carnal and corporeal: "The sexual content of [religious] dogma, as represented in its mythology and enacted through ritual, is obviously extensive; but its basis of sex refers principally to fertility and to the increase of the natural species, and not to eroticism."[88]

Perhaps the most radical attempt to displace sexual pleasure and violence as the goal and referent of ritual sex was made by W. E. H. Stanner in his essay "Religion, Totemism, and Symbolism." This essay was based on his fieldwork in the Daly River and Port Keats regions in the early 1930s but was not published until 1965, some thirty years after the Daly River cases were closed. In this work, Stanner confronts and attempts to counter public perceptions of Aboriginal ritual sexuality as erotic in nature or end. His aim was to distinguish between sex acts and customary law and ritual acts and ritual meanings. To do this he differentiated the cosmological aspects of Aboriginal high culture from what he called its "vehicle or symbolizing means."[89] According to Stanner, from Aboriginal men's perspective, sex was simply a symbolic tool, one of a number of powerful and transformative corporeal and noncorporeal actions and substances of which they chose to vehiculate their cosmological values: "The vehicles or symbolisms are not themselves the symbols . . . the things to which the symbols point are metaphysical objects"; they are about ontological questions such as "man's being."[90] Semen, sweat, blood, songs, and clay penetrated initiates' bodies and sacramentally reformed them into ancestral beings.[91] All these substances created intimate corporeal relations between humans and landscapes, transferred ancestral powers, and conveyed cosmological meaning. In other published and unpublished works, Stanner further questions the inherent sexual symbolism of ritual paraphernalia. He argues that in an indigenous context highly disturbed by European and Chinese settlement, the "bull-roarer has come to signify the phallus, or has come to be associated with sexuality" even though "ab initio . . . the business of the bull-roarer is to roar" not to symbolize the phallus.[92] In sum, sexual products were merely one of many related bodily products. Sexual objects were equivalent to, rather than the general equivalent of, these other bodily exchanges. In portraying sex as merely an equivalent, Stanner enunciated the grounds of a radical critique of the status of sex in the sex acts riveting the nation and discipline.

Although Stanner deprivileged sex as the final interpretant of corporeal and symbolic intercourses in indigenous society, he reestablished it as the final interpretant of bodily and social exchanges in civil society. According to Stanner, neither Aboriginal subjects nor Aboriginal cosmology ("the Dreaming") could take their rightful place in Australian civil society unless a more suitable vehicle than sex for symbolic locomotion were found. Citizenship would elude Aborigines until cosmology and sexuality were separated and properly relegated to their public and private domains. And, in so arguing, Stanner privileged sex in relation to other corporeal substances and exchanges in civil society and removed nonnormative (from the perspective of settler society) sex from public and semipublic semiotic circulations. Stanner reconfirmed commonsense civil distinctions among sex acts, publics, privates, and sacramentalities rather than pursuing the difference of indigenous corporeality and using it to critique dominant forms of intimacy and publicness and, thereby, contributed to the slow reformation of the place and function of sexuality in Aboriginal society. In a civil form, sex would become familialized; would index the difference between the worlds of politics and domesticity; and would be used to create families, clans, and territorial associations through maternal and paternal ties. And ritual would be cosmologized.

W. E. H. Stanner did not, however, share Bill Harney's confidence about the origin of Big Sunday. In 1958, he reported that he had been "the first to see this cult [Kunapipi] in operation" twenty-five years earlier in the Daly River region, "since it had been reported by Sir Baldwin Spencer."[93] In his life history of Durmugam, a Nangiomeri man, Stanner described the spread of Big Sunday services into the Daly River region. Durmugam was born circa 1895, about seventy miles from the Daly River police station. According to Stanner, Durmugam remembered little about his early childhood other than his father and mother dying in the local mines, "endless bloody fights between the river and back-country tribes, and numbers of drink-sodden Aborigines lying out in the rain."[94] As a young man, Durmugam traveled throughout the Daly River region and down to the Victorian River Downs district, a region rife with tensions among indigenous groups about how to respond to the encroachment of whites into their country. Older indigenous men and women knew the stakes could be high. In 1884, just eleven years before Durmugam was born, police and settlers led a massacre on and nearly wiped out the Malakmalak after some members of this linguistic group and others attacked and murdered several white miners. It was in the Victoria River Downs district that Durmugam and other Nangiomeri and Wagaman men "came for the first time into intimate association with an Aboriginal High Culture" and were initiated into "the religious cult, Kunapipi."[95] Durmugam traveled back to the Daly River, playing a key role in the introduction of Big Sunday rituals into the region during the mid-1930s.

Here we see emerging two very different types and modalities of indigenous agency in the Daly River area. On the one hand, the men Stanner worked with used a technology of affect and dignity to persuade him of the sense of their practices and to incite him to produce a new discourse of culture and sexuality embedded in the real-time social politics of the frontier. On the other hand, indigenous men and women struggled among themselves to create a new internal discourse of resistance to settler encroachment. Indeed, in 1965, Ronald Berndt would attribute the spread of the Kunapipi rite into the Daly River region directly to the earlier 1884 massacre, arguing that Kunapipi lent men the means for solidifying a counterinsurgency.[96]

Although Stanner disputed the specifics of Berndt's argument, he generally agreed with him that the culture Durmugam was initiated into was initialized by settlers and reinitialized by local indigenous women and men. Stanner suggests that peanut farmer Harkins did not arrive just in time to see the vibrant core of Daly River culture passing into extinction, but rather to see the evolution of men's ceremonial life under the torsions of a Christian colonialism gone horribly awry. The moniker "Big Sunday" provided an uncanny clue to the origin of the ceremony for those who dared read it. Stanner confirmed a nation's worst nightmares—the "fertility Mother cult" sprouted up, like the flu and venereal disease, in response to European settlement. The good and the bad of this new high culture, Stanner claims, is the miscegenous progeny not of bodies but of beliefs—capitalism, humanism, and Christianity perversely folded outside themselves, mistranslated, misheard, or maybe heard all too well. White men were always already involved in the murders and sexual assaults they witnessed because they had created the very practice that terrorized them. Stanner states:

Before I had heard a word of Kunabibi I had been told that Angamunggi [All Father] had "gone away." Many evidences were cited that he no longer "looked after" the people: the infertility of the women (they were in fact riddled by gonorrhea), the spread of sickness, the dwindling of game among them. The cult assumed the local form of a cult of Karwadi, by which the bullroarer, the symbol of the All-Mother, had been known in the days of the All-Father. Karwadi became the provenance of the mixed but connected elements which I term the new High Culture.[97]

Stanner did not have to refer directly to the other form of sexuality haunting the frontier for his readers to understand who was responsible for the fact that women were "riddled by gonorrhea." As I mentioned above, Aboriginal ritual sex was not the only frontier sex act making national headlines. The sexual relations between white and Asian men and Aboriginal women shocked and troubled the nation. The "half-caste problem" underscored the potential injustice of punishing black men but not white men for their illicit and illegal sex acts.[98] Bill Harney, who had several female Aboriginal lovers, scoffed at the suggestion that interracial sex could be regulated. "What then? Walk around amid the budding belles in a fit of sexual repression, when all the while they laugh at the 'good one' as a stupid fool? Not on your life! The pioneer makes the country by using the gifts within it to his needs."[99] In 1943, this regional problem would become a national scandal with the publication of Xavier Herbert's critical account of the racial politics and hypocrisies of northern miscegenation in his fictional account *Capricornia*. What surprise then that northern newspapers published calls, if not for a public accounting, then for a mass public confession. Inserted into a public register, sex became a public matter, reproduced within the textual strictures of public reason—that public matters be about a hypostacized "we" released from "the world" of interested social status, risking truth. In the *Northern Standard* Nan Utarra remarked: "Each and everyone of us has a dual side to his make up— ah'h'h. The side we would have the world believe us to be -a'h- and the side we know ourselves to be—ah'h. F'r instance -a'h—take the question of the native and his woman—ah'h—there's hardly a man here -ah'h- who at some time or other ah'h has not had dealings with them—ah'h. Yet the vast majority of men -ah'h—would bury their heads very deep in the sand of Dugong Beach -ah'h'h—should their progeny claim -ah'h—their natural fathers -ah'h."[100]

Many state employees were as appalled by white male settler sexuality as by Aboriginal sexuality. In the same frontier where peanut farmer Harkins stumbled onto Kunapipi grounds, Constable Turner stumbled into army barracks. In a memo to the director of Native Affairs dated 28 May 1942, Daly River Constable J. T. Turner strongly protested military conduct in the Daly River region. After military officers complained to Turner that they had contracted venereal disease from local indigenous women, Turner "made enquiries and was informed by the Aboriginals that 'the soldier men were no good.' Four had had connection with the one lubra, one after the other. 'All same Dog.' One soldier finish another 'jump alonga top same lubra.' 'Soldier been catchem every lubra. Every night want lubra.'" Turner was "also informed that some of these 'selected men of this Independent Force' had also been having connections with young girl . . . but 13 years of age."[101]

Savage settler sexuality complicated epistemological, moral, and practical aspects of state function, which most clearly were seen in trials such as the infamous case of *Tuckiar v. the King*. Heard in the Northern Territory Supreme Court, the trial of the Woodah Island indigenous man, Tuckiar, involved his murder of a police officer. Tuckiar spoke no English, and in the course of his arraignment he confessed twice, the second time indicating he had acted in self-defense after the police officer had repeatedly sexually assaulted his wife. Tuckiar was sentenced to death after the presiding judge told the jury that they should discount Tuckiar's allegations of sexual improprieties because they would denigrate the reputation of the dead police officer. In the midst of public outrage, the conviction was eventually overturned by the federal High Court. However, Tuckiar died en route to his home, and many scholars speculate that he was murdered by settlers or rival indigenous men after being dropped by the police just outside Darwin.[102] Rather than what the Northern Territory judge would have liked, the absolutely imaginable possibility that settler sex lay at the root of frontier violence destabilized verdict after verdict. But even this determination was destabilized by the notion of native calculation.

Constable Turner suggests how this might be in his police submissions about the murder of Jesse. He begins by agreeing with Stanner's general position that Malakmalak men's ritual practices have a settler origin and orientation. In letters addressed to his superiors on 7 and 8 August 1940, Constable Turner goes beyond simply describing the suspects and their murder weapons.[103] He adds what he considers to be critical sociological data—the disturbing response of the "Mullick-mullick" men when he informs them that they would be arrested for murder: "They both [the two Malakmalak men] appeared nothing would be done [to them] in the matter and proud of the matter."[104] More sinister yet, the ultimate target of the Malakmalak men's spears may not have been the Aboriginal woman killed. One of her companions, targeted but merely wounded, was the former wife of an Aboriginal police tracker, Bull-bull, who was using his office to protect his own sexuality.[105] "I *may* mention that this is the third murder of Lubras in this District and the excuse has been by the Murderers this Sacred Ground, as they have been or understand nothing will be done to them as considered a Tribal Affair, and this Mullick-mullick Tribe have been known as Blood lustful Aboriginals."[106]

For Turner, the Kunapipi ritual was nothing less than a cunning use of a ceremonial masquerade for disciplining Aboriginal collaborators. The Kunapipi ritual mocked the state's ability to discern culture from connivance and was a testimony to the uncanny ability of Aborigines to take advantage of the good intentions of settlers. These views were not Turner's alone. W. E. H. Stanner would himself describe the ceremonial leader of Kunapipi, Durmugam, as an "agent provocateur of the Daly River" who used "knowledge gained in court and gaol to instruct other blacks in the limits of police power" and who was "adept in playing white against both white and black."[107] When Constable Turner penned his remarks to Weddell he might have been thinking of conversations he had or heard about others having with Stanner in the 1930s and 40s. Indeed, throughout his writings Stanner foregrounds the agency of Aboriginal men and women in refashioning their cultural beliefs and practices in the shadow of an often vicious settlement. But wherever and however Turner gained his opinion, indigenous male rituals were for him little more than the diabolical deceit of "Blood lustful Aboriginals," their "excuse for rape and murder." Aboriginal men's high culture was on the rise not because of the functional integrity, more or less, of indigenous society at the frontier, nor for that matter because women had violated a new high ceremony, but simply because Aboriginal men "understand nothing will be done to them."[108]

Constable Turner provides us with some evidence of the embodied nature of the epistemological and moral dilemma that I am trying to understand here. He did not simply face the problem of knowing whether or not the Malakmalak men acted on the basis of little more than tribal law, nor whether or not this action involved other white men. He and others faced the impossible closure of rational knowledge and moral sense. And he experienced the state's complicity in his epistemological and moral dilemma; the dismissal of his travail by state functionaries who did not *face* the problem *entre-nous*.

Turner's experience of his moral sense as subjected to an immoral state machinery is signaled by his grammar of subordination (*may I*). But the pain and anxiety of his position appears in the register of paranoia and official neglect in other letters.[109] But outside the state machine, Turner might well have used another genre, entailing pubs and police headquarters as spaces of another hypothetical imperative—Canberra should not dictate frontier policy when they knew little to nothing about the real conditions of frontier life. If he did so speak, he echoed similar positions being advanced in the regional press.[110]

What I am getting at here is the need to take seriously the corporeal mediation of state policy. Zygmunt Bauman and others have pointed out that a bureaucratic form of moral mediation made the Holocaust possible. We might deploy this insight in a related way. Turner complied with state policy. But the disjunction between the policy and his embodied moral feeling, exacerbated during moments such as the "Murder of Jesse," incited various forms of speech in various contexts; and, insofar as it did, this disjunction incited a discursive *otherwise* that circulated in the public sphere—a counterfactual national normativity. We do not have to agree with Turner that face-to-face encounters are truer forms of social being to be able to appreciate how these various forms of textual mediation proliferated types of talk that reformed as they moved across provisionally formed social space—letters oriented to private consumption, administrative memos to superiors, or conversations with mates in pubs, church, at work.

"What have we produced?" When all is said and done, Kunapipi and other variants of men's high culture were neither local nor regional, neither indigenous nor settler. They were truly national rituals, international affairs, for which neither anthropological theory nor national ideology was prepared. In suggesting settlement's implication in ritual rape, Stanner and others ripped away the comfortable narrative that settler and indigenous societies were engaged in a clash of values, had different systems of belief, morality, and value, indeed, that there was any simple, morally grounded differentiation between "them" and "us." *Settler* sexuality and *settler* immorality erased the clean line between the "horrible rites" of native society and the quotidian practices of settler society. Settlers did not just think, look, imagine, and feel implicated in indigenous sex acts as critical judges, but they did this also as critical actors: they knew it, they were the condition of it, they did no differently.

Once again I could close with a verdict. In 1940, an unidentified person noted in the court records that, although the "Mulluk Mulluk" murderer was found to have been "provoked" by the women's "deliberate infringement of native custom," the "prisoner [was] found guilty."[111] The judge sentenced him to prison and ordered that the "tribal area [was] to be rid of the influence of a recent introduction the Karawadte ritual."[112] In the same year, C.A. Carrodus modified government policy: "The Minister has now agreed to rescind the ruling referred to in its general application. In future, the directive will only apply in the case of relatively uncivilized natives who live more or less permanently in remote areas, who are not under any form of permanent European control, assistance or supervision, and who depend for internal stability on the free exercise of their own native customs."[113]

But at this point it should be clear that Turner was hardly the only person talking. Similar scenes were repeated throughout the northwest region and beyond. Anthropologists were corresponding with missionary and government agents running the settlements in which they worked. These conversations created a wide field of inter-Aboriginal practice stretching to the far north, including to the parents of contemporary Belyuen (Wagaitj). Belyuen and neighboring land claims open this archive. That is, the case is never closed. It just circulates in a different social space and time.

I should not have been surprised then to learn that not long after the Daly River murder case was closed it reopened to the north of Daly River. The small, understaffed Natives Affairs Branch hired Jack Murray and Bill Harney to round up the Wagaitj camping throughout the Cox Peninsula and consolidate them on a new inland government compound, Delissaville. Harney was appointed soon after as the temporary acting superintendent of the compound. He and Murray became fast friends, and this mateship was no small part of the reason why Murray was appointed superintendent of Delissaville soon after Christmas 1941. Although Jack Murray did not collaborate with any famous anthropologists or write popular memoirs, he did leave behind several daily journals and a trail of administrative memos and letters that suggest some of the personal and practical travails he faced administering state indigenous policy, as well as the personal and practical travails of Wagaitj men and women deemed his wards.

In his journal and personal letters, Murray does not appear to have been an unusually harsh or intolerant man for his time. And he seems to have had a rather average interest in local mythic and ritual life. Anthropologists (including A. P. Elkin), royal dignitaries, war correspondents, public radio producers, international ballet stars—all trooped through Delissaville (later called Belyuen) documenting Wagaitj expressive culture, kinship and marriage customs, and ritual and myth, more of which I will discuss in chapters 5 and 6. Murray notes their activities with a similar set of brief remarks embedded in his notation of the administration of the settlement — digging latrines, planting cassava, repairing motor engines.

(Thur May 14th 1942)
Had a visit from two war correspondents who made some recordings of natives singing and dancing also Mr. Sweeney stopped & went away with same party, taking Jacky Wola & Tommy Immabul with him for a few to help round up lepers.[114]

(Sun Feb 14th 1943)
Had young man's initiation ceremony Military from West & party of officers came to watch same

(Sun April 18th 1943)
[missing text] man Tommy Burradjup was circumcised [missing text] of rations arrived.

Little about local ritual activity captures the writerly attention of Murray. He neither encourages nor discourages informal camp corroborees, young men's initiations, or mortuary rituals. Amid this dense cultural traffic, Murray spent his time motivating local men and women to work in camp gardens and seeking relief from his own boredom and isolation.[115]

Murray's writerly passion centered on the war effort (organizing a Black Watch, patrolling the coastal waters for downed Japanese and American pilots) and on the sexuality of his wards (Aboriginal men "pimping" female relatives, Aboriginal women making "liaisons" with undesirable European men on the peninsula).[116] The sex of his wards made Murray's life meaningful, pulled it from the mire of the everyday, the grinding of routine, boredom. We should not, therefore, be surprised that Murray's interest in Wagaitj culture is pricked when he is told that a number of local men were making "Sunday business . . . demands . . . on three girls" under the influence of visiting Daly River men. If what Turner knew about Big Sunday was gained from Stanner, then what Murray knew he probably learned from his mate Bill Harney over beers at Delissaville or from Wagaitj women themselves who appear as strategic partners in a complex local intra-Aboriginal political field.[117] What we know is that Murray quickly intervened, calling in the Darwin police and a local missionary whom Stanner had also encountered at the Daly River and at Port Keats.[118] But when the missionary requested that Murray send one of the women across the harbor for questioning, Murray responds by citing administrative role and protocol: "Re sending Alice Bruck Bruck over to Darwin for these matters 'we' want to clear up. Personally, I consider any matter concerning this girl are matters that also concern this Dept, and therefore should be dealt with by the Dept or some person authorized by the Dept."[119] In the end, the Daly River men were sent back to the Daly River mission, and the local men were exiled to a distant Aboriginal settlement.[120]

But Murray never mastered the sexual activities of his wards. In 1942, when the Japanese bombing of Darwin began, the Aboriginal men and women stationed at Delissaville were forcibly relocated to Katherine. Here, once again, Murray learns that "blackfella business" has or is about to be started up.[121] And once again Murray tries to suppress the practice by relocating the men he considers the main instigators. This time, however, Murray's supervisor, Vincent White, intervenes, sending a strongly worded memo to Murray criticizing him for interfering in tribal customs: "The removal of these two natives to Alice Springs has caused considerable trouble here . . . [the male leader's] place in the Wargite tribe is such that the old men deem him to be important and indispensable in the excercise of tribal ceremonies, so essential to sustain the community during its period of exile in Katherine."[122]

From the textual fragments he left behind, we cannot say for certain whether or not Murray bitterly reflected about his treatment by his superiors to his friend Bill Harney or others. If he did, it would hardly be surprising not to find such bitterness and frustration in the official memoranda he sent to his supervisors. Even Stretton carefully couches his criticism of state policy in a polite register. But the minor literatures that Murray, Turner, Stretton, and others produced strongly suggest that answering the question of when a white person was involved was neither simple nor simply an academic concern. The ability of Aboriginal men to get away with sex and murder at least frustrated, if it did not *humiliate*, Turner, Murray, and many other mid-level government employees. The fact that their agency was impaired — that their ability to manipulate the state apparatus was impeded by strategically minded indigenous men — may well have made their blood boil and soured their view of many of their fellow white citizens. Of course white people were involved! They knew. They watched, listened. They were constrained from acting. And, insofar as they were, they were symbolically blackened.

THE ARCHIVE OF SYMPATHY

The lure of anthropological reason seems clear. Eliminating the sex haunting the nation through critical understanding promised not only to bolster liberal ideology at a moment of its seeming demise, but also to lift it up (*Aufhebung*) to a new tolerant form. But in their progressive call for the extension of citizenship to civilized natives, anthropologists and liberal government administrators and settlers initiated a double termination. Insofar as civilization was an execution, something to be carried out, conducted, and conduced, this movement, on the one hand, detached indigenous persons from their local social and cultural practices and, on the other, inscribed in a national archive this disciplined culture and social order as the authentic space of a (disgraced) indigenous Australia.

The trouble is that anthropologists, if not missionaries and government employees, did not want to get rid of sex or violence simply, absolutely, and without trace. The ambivalence of anthropology was exemplified in A. P. Elkin's work. Perhaps reflecting his dual career as rector in the Anglican church and professional ethnologist, Elkin evidenced a very conflicted moral assessment of indigenous social organization and cultural belief *because of* its use and configuration of gender and sexuality. According to Elkin, men's ritual treatment of women caused them to "live in terror" and to exhibit a sexual laxity that was easily put to immoral use by whites and Asians.[123] Thus, no more and no less than Fison and Howitt and the wider protectionist community, Elkin was in a deeply conflicted relationship to the perceived gender and sexual economy of Aboriginal ceremony. Back and forth Elkin went, chastising the narrowness of the public's horizon of sexual normativity, even as he reassured that same public that "the worst" of these practices have passed.

After viewing the forms and queries of these settler encounters, the temptation is to see two European worlds in the northwestern Top End region. *Something* distinguishes the practices of social workers, government, and capitalists, bushwackers and ethnologists. For instance, one could distinguish the focus of missionaries, government officials, and capitalists from that of ethnologists, government officials, writers, and filmmakers studying Aboriginal "traditions." The focus of the former seems more on the management of the Aboriginal social self to the end of transforming that self through work and belief. The latter seems, in contrast, to be focused on the Aboriginal management of social life in and of itself; that is, for knowledge's sake. Thus, on one hand, we see whites managing black social relations and, on the other, whites studying black social management. But by now we should see this as *temptation* indeed. For these worlds existed in the same real spacetime and, in critical ways, were interested in the same thing — gathering social data and modifying social relations — and relied on each other for the collection and processing of information and for critical interventions in social praxis.

These government officials, missionary "zealots," ethnologists, bushwack-ers, and capitalists produced a saturated but uneven field of forms and queries, of cultural interventions and evaluations, through which indigenous women and men moved and maneuvered. The memos, camp rolls, clan and kinship designations, and so forth compiled by camp supervisors, medical nurses, and doctors, and the interests and disinterests shown by a host of other per-sons in local indigenous cultural practices, are the past from which indigenous and nonindigenous men and women draw and evaluate contemporary local traditions. Some of these lists and queries survive. Some were never written down. Some are remembered on scraps of paper. Others are remembered by older women and men at Belyuen, Daly River, and Port Keats who have pub-lished their own stories and who have told me and a host of others about their memories of the sexual history of whites and blacks — the latest white men and women working in the thoroughly saturated field of "field notes," many of which lie scattered in boxes on the floors of my offices.

Throughout the long duration of this inquiry, Aboriginal women and men have received neither a "yes" nor a "no" to their cultural practices. They have instead encountered a prohibitive interest in their traditional practices. On the one hand, even by the overt prohibition of certain social practices and ceremonial complexes missionaries and camp supervisors were likely to in-clude a gesture of interest in these same practices. Demands that Aboriginal persons transform sexual and erotic components of ritual practices, abandon polygamy and marriage between much older men and younger women, came via some understanding of those same practices, even in the simple sense of understanding to what they referred. This understanding might be purely in-strumental (seen as the best means of accomplishing a social transformation) or purely accidental (the "against which" the prohibition becomes legible), but in either case it wrote over the prohibition with interest.

On the other hand, interest in traditional social practices and ceremonial complexes frequently included some form of prohibition. Often this prohibi-tion was an overt act of repression. Some aspect of a social practice or cere-monial complex was considered "repugnant," recorded in field notes but sup-pressed in practice and in field reports. Ethnologists had many reasons for these overt acts of suppression. Some scholars seemed to think that it was in the interests of Aboriginal persons to emphasize the philosophical versus the erotic or sexual side of ceremonies — even though ritual uses of gender and sexuality were considered traditional components of Aboriginal (read: male) "high culture." Others, following the lead of Fison and Howitt, seemed to think that the sexual "perversions" they witnessed in ritual and social organization were an effect of colonial contact and, therefore, excisable from discussion of precontact traditions. Still others documented, to the best of their knowledge, the linkages between culture and sexuality. This latter group of scholars would probably not have considered their work an act of prohibition. But if we examine the syntax of their query, the past tense of their interest writes over the present with historical time: How *did* your parents do it? What *were* the old ways?

On the final hand of this grotesque body are the lawyers, police officers, and anthropologists who now scour the national archive to defend contemporary indigenous persons by authenticating a contemporary practice as customary. In June 1980, G. M. Borders, a solicitor defending a Port Keats man against the charge of rape, sent W. E. H. Stanner an inquiry about whether the "passing [women] amongst the men" was a tribal custom carried out among groups living near Port Keats.[124]

What troubles me most is an attitude of mind that could come to prevail amongst white Australians: a feeling of irritation apparently based on a conviction that we are saddled with the responsibility for problems not really of our making, and by their nature probably insoluble. The underlying thought is twofold: no one now alive has hurt the Aborigines or their legitimate interests, and no one contemplates deliberately doing so.
—W. E. H. Stanner, *White Man Got No Dreaming*

Australia's Prime Minister John Howard, a conservative elected in 1996, has rejected the demands of Aborigines for a formal government apology for past mistreatment as well as calls for a civil rights treaty. Today's march started from an intersection near his official water-front residence, but Mr. Howard did not join the gathering. The Reconciliation Council acknowledges that its own extensive research shows majority support for Mr. Howard's position. The surveys show 58 percent oppose special rights for Aborigines to reflect their historic position. Some 62 percent reject an apology now for previous wrongs, some fearing retrospective compensation claims.
—"Australians March in Support of Aborigines," *New York Times*, 29 May 2000

4 / Shamed States

COURTLY RECOGNITION

In 1992 and 1996 in the cases *Eddie Mabo v. the State of Queensland* and *The Wik Peoples v. the State of Queensland,* the Australian High Court considered reasoned arguments and passionate pleas that it decide decisively the legal status of traditional indigenous native title in the modern multicultural state. But supporters and opponents of state recognition of native title, including the members of the High Court, did not confine their rhetoric to a strictly legal discourse. They moved between two different registers, a legal language of national and international precedent, sovereignty, rights, and fiduciary duties and a moral language of national history, memory, responsibility, and compassion. Some of the historical origin and texture of these registers was presented in the preceding chapters.

In the years that followed the 1992 *Mabo* judgment, Australian subjects sent themselves a national postcard addressed to the general question of historical accountability: How should Australian nation-building be remembered and from whose perspective? What would this nation-building look like from the perspective of Aboriginal history? Would it seem a bloody, illegitimate ordeal, a rotten deal forged on the back of blind prejudice and material greed? Indeed, should the eventfulness of colonialism be figured in the past tense? Did colonialism happen or was it happening? In the present, could the nation — or each and every person within that nation — be responsible for events of the past? And could responsibility be decided decisively in the manner of a court case? Could copping the sins of the past liberate the present from that evil, or would it create new problems — opening, for instance, the state's coffers to reparation claims? On radio and television, in beer and parliament halls, in newspaper columns and among columns of cheering and jeering demonstrators, in the midst of the Hanson scandal, the Stolen Generation scandal, the Native Title debates, and the Republic referendum: public pundits, parliamentarians, and other citizens debated a new counterintuitive model of national cohesion registered in these two High Court decisions. They argued about whether a patriotic nationalism could arise from the sackcloth and ashes of a public accounting of a nation's shame and about what the implications of this new form of nationalism on statutory law and private and public property was. Not even the question of whether Australia should remain a part of the British Commonwealth seemed to matter to Australians as much as negotiating the truth and place of their shame. As Meaghan Morris has noted, "if a *popular* national debate was underway by the mid-1990s, then Mabo, rather than the monarchy, was its focus."[1]

Finding native title amid national history was, therefore, not simply a juridical task. It was a national referendum, a litmus test, on whether Australia would finally recognize and take responsibility for a population who had suffered, and continued to suffer, from the dominant national dream. But if, as I will suggest, courts and publics do not blame shameful events on bad people but on the good intentions of good people, how are the good intentions of present people protected? As courts and public lament the long history of bigotry and malice masked as rationality and public reason, how do they negotiate the dilemma of capturing real justice in real discourse and narrative time without prompting the appearance of the same interpretant hovering over native title or criminal law judgments. This judgment is just (unless[although] . . . it may appear retrospectively as repugnant or shameful). How, in short, do court justices side-step the problem of accounting for justice in the breach and shadow of the court's own repugnant and shameful history?

I am moving here from the perspective of the cynical subject as discussed by Peter Sloterdijk. I want, however, to shift away from a discussion of the cynical forms of subjective inhabitations of the law, not because they are unimportant but because they miss a hard stone in the kidneys of liberal multiculturalism. These forms suggest that liberal subjects know the particular interests hidden behind liberal ideology, but perpetuate it through an ironic or cynical stance toward it (a postideological world in which people know what they are doing and do it anyway). Therefore, instead of following a discussion of original forms, I want to build on the work of Slavoj Žižek, Gayatri Spivak, and Jacqueline Rose, who note that the ideals of liberalism are not about knowledge and its exposure to truth and revelation, but about the fantasies necessary to act in a liberal society and how these fantasies are protected and projected into social life through specific textual practices.[2] The critique of liberalism does not begin with where it fails or where subjects know or do not know this failure, but rather where it seems to be succeeding.

In centering primarily on an analysis of the texts and contexts of the *Mabo* and *Wik* decisions, I seek to understand the role that the discourse and affect of shame played in making an expansion of legal discriminatory devices seem the advent of the law of recognition or a rupture of older models of monocultural nationalism and the grounds for national optimism, renewal, and rebirth. I pay close attention to one aspect of national life, the justificatory discourses and functions of the Australian High Court and its genre-specific features. By situating these two decisions in broader national and transnational discourses of postcolonialism and multiculturalism, I try to account for the captivating nature of this specific juridical stance on national life.[3] I hope to demonstrate how liberal legal subjects manage to protect themselves through narrative devices, in the moment of discrimination, from the experience of future negative judgment; how they are able to be optimistic, to believe that this time they've gotten it right, that this time history will be ruptured, and that this will be remembered as a time of social enlightenment. I also discuss the political and social implications of the liberal desire to escape, as individuals or as the authors and proponents of social projects, the unconditional of the future perfect proposition: "We will have gone on record as having spoken and felt our times (lines) in ways and domains we never would have imagined." "We will have been wrong."

At the onset, it is useful to remember several very general points about "native title." Native title is a legal concept from British common law referring to a type of beneficial title or ownership. Native title is distinct from the radical title the Crown claims at the moment of colonization (concomitant of sovereignty). From the perspective of the High Court, neither *Mabo* nor *Wik* concerned the sovereignty of the Crown, but rather only whether indigenous Australians had this form of title and what it was grounded in, and thus what could extinguish it. But note: Aboriginal Australians did not have native title prior to English settlement. Whatever practices and beliefs organized indigenous bodies and lands prior to settlement, these were not the *thing* we now call "native title." Moreover, aspects of the recognition of native title touched on in this chapter are particular to Australian national law and state history, although they are embedded in and address, explicitly and implicitly, international law and world history. The history and consequence of Australian forms of native title recognition differ from other states, which recognize this concept as legally binding. Some of these differences emerged as national courts struggled to rectify emergent common law precedent with emergent commonsense social standards. In Australia, for example, native title is seen as grounded in the customary beliefs and practices of indigenous people, because by the time native title was recognized the anthropological concept of customary law (as discussed in the last chapter) was a commonsense truth. Thus, today native title in Australia can be extinguished if the genealogical and occupancy relationship to land is severed and, *in addition,* if the customary beliefs and practices of the group claiming native title are severed *more or less.* In the United States and Canada, legal proof of native title rests on demonstrating a genealogical connection to the original owners of the land and continued occupancy or use of the land not on demonstrating a cultural continuity with these original owners. This legal grounding of native title reflects nineteenth-century notions of usufruct. But although the law of recognition is not grounded in the performance of cultural continuity in the United States, it is supplemented by public accounts of the justice of granting "special rights" to native Americans who appear to be too culturally and socially like nonnative Americans. Finally, in Brazil courts demand some proof of distinct cultural difference as the grounds for the legal recognition of customary native title rights and interests. The indigenous people of Brazil face the question of the commonsense meaning of difference. But they are not compelled to demonstrate an unbroken connection between contemporary beliefs and practices and the beliefs and practices of their genealogical ancestors.

LEGAL DISCRIMINATION

In *Eddie Mabo v. the State of Queensland* (hereafter *Mabo*), the nation-state's highest juridical body considered a case from a representative of "a people" in whose vicious colonization the common law was implicated and whose continuing structural impoverishment was widely discussed in national and transnational public spheres. On behalf of a Torres Strait Islander group, Eddie Mabo claimed that his native title had never been extinguished and, therefore, that he and his group retained proprietary rights over their land. Up until this case, the Australian court had rejected the claim that indigenous Australians had had sufficient social organization and the proper cultural beliefs to have evolved property interests (native title) in Australian lands at the moment of colonization.[4]

In a defining moment of nation-time, on 3 June 1992 the court broke with tradition in a six-to-one decision that overturned the doctrine that Australian was *terra nullius* (a land belonging to no one) at the point of settlement, and decided instead that Aboriginal Australians had and had retained native title interests in the law. Where the Australian state had not explicitly extinguished native title, Aboriginal Australians had and still held that title if they maintained the traditional customs, beliefs, and practices that created the substance of its difference. The judicial majority argued that it was no longer tolerable to make sovereignty contingent on representing native people as "so low in the scale of social organization" that it is "idle to impute to such people some shadow of the rights known to our law."[5] Indeed, they argued that the manner in which such representations had been used in legal theory to carry colonial dispossession into practical effect constituted "the darkest aspect of the history of the nation."[6]

In response to the *Mabo* decision, public pressure, and its own political strategy, the Labour government passed in 1993 the federal Native Title Act, which legislated the mechanisms by which indigenous groups could claim land based on their native title rights to it. The Native Title Act translated aspects of the High Court decision into statutory law, and in the process acknowledged the validity of native title but demanded, as the condition of its recognition, that claimants establish their descent from the original inhabitants of the land under claim, the nature of customary law for that land, their continued allegiance to that customary law, and their continued occupation of the land. Liberated from its shameful legal history, law could be returned to a more pure form of judicial judgment. The charge of native tribunals would be merely to adjudicate, at the "level of primary fact," whether or not native title had disappeared "by reason of the washing away by 'the tide of history' and any *real* acknowledgment of traditional law and *real* observance of traditional customs."[7]

The justices could have limited their decision to the case at hand — whether these particular people (Eddie Mabo and this group of Torres Strait Islanders) had native title interests in this particular land. For the court to do so, however, a majority of justices would have had to sign, name by name, onto the savage conditions to which most Australian indigenous people were historically and are still subjected, conditions broadcast globally by multinational and transnational organizations like the United Nations, Amnesty International, various nongovernmental indigenous organizations, mass media like CNN World News and the *New York Times,* and major cultural figures like the musician Sting. And the court would have had to sign away the relevance of the nation's highest juridical power to the social welfare of its most discriminated-against people, leaving their fate to state largesse or their own political acumen. And, from most social and economic indicators, their fate was dire. In the Northern Territory in the mid-1990s, 60 percent of Aboriginal Australians earned between $1,000 and $9,000 per year. Nationally, indigenous unemployment hovered around 35 percent. Not only was economic space fragmented based on individual race and settlement history, national generational time was out of joint, a disjunction that would have significant ramifications for a culturally based law of recognition. In the mid-1980s, government agencies reported that the average life expectancy of indigenous Australians was only 52 years. By 1998 it had inched up to 57 for men and 62 for women.

In 1992, six High Court justices would not cast their names into a current of legal history now widely understood to be propelled by racial and cultural intolerance. Writing that the common law was shamed by its racist history and the gaze of the international community, the justices took the occasion to alter fundamentally the conditions of Australian sovereignty. They chose to sign their name under the signifier *social justice* and to differentiate this new version of justice from an older version to which the same common law had subscribed in settlement times. In other words, in these justices' hands the common law was represented as the fertile inner kernel of justice that a selective reading of precedent could release from the inert husks of racial prejudice. The justices relied on the great optimism and utopianism of the common law, which holds that good judgment will in theory always emerge from the archive of precedent.[8] This belief licensed these justices to use the very tools that had legislated and institutionalized racial and cultural prejudice to free national institutions from that prejudice without performing an ideological critique of the institutions themselves. And here, the High Court marked its deep commitment to liberalism, implicitly declaring that good intentions and good precedents are sufficient to make institutions good versions of themselves.

It is here that we come face-to-face with several fundamental questions about liberal law and its public imaginary. What allows the court such optimism about the rightness, or goodness, of its present judgments given the history of past shameful judgments that it reviews and laments? And what allows this confidence to circulate and mobilize public optimism about an obtainable if future-oriented unconflicted national gain? After all, time and again jurists are confronted by evidence of good intentions gone awry, institutionalized optimisms about a good society that led to or were, when viewed historically, acts of harm or evil. We know, for instance, that at least some if not most administrators who formulated and carried out the forced removal of indigenous children from their parents did so with the best of intentions for their "wards." And this is but one example—the colonial law of sovereignty is certainly another. As the justices in *Mabo* noted, not colonial evil but misguided colonial prejudices distorted the root good of the common law.

But isn't present judgment also liable to such distortions, as situated in the future perfect, "We will have been wrong"? As new moral, philosophical, and religious understandings emerge from the proceduralisms of democratic discursivity—public reason—the law is continually forced to reflect on the trail of its own, albeit unintentional, bigotry, prejudice, and malice; and forced to expunge discursively this malice from the common law without implicating the common law in the production of that malice. Equally difficult, the court must sometimes construct a convincing difference between the good of constitutional and common law principles and the misguided, even repugnant, acts able to make themselves at home within those principles. Thus was its task in deciding the constitutionality of the Aboriginal Ordinance of 1911, the Northern Territory legislation responsible for producing a large portion of the Stolen Generation. The court ruled that although Territory law had "authorised gross violations of the rights and liberties of Aboriginal Australians," these gross violations did not abrogate any constitutionally recognized rights and duties. Of what type is constitutional justice when repugnant acts and social harms are not strangers to it? For whom or what does this Constitution operate? These and other questions circulated in public discourse in the build-up and aftermath of the rulings.[9]

Given this history of the mistaken identity and forced cohabitation of harmful acts and good intentions, we might ask how the court achieves any convincing optimism about the social trajectory of its own and the nation's present good intentions, such that the law becomes a site of optimism both for itself and for the very nationalized communities who have suffered from it; and such that it is understood as a practice that could repair a torn life, pull a people out of structural impoverishment, breath life into fathers, uncles, and grandfathers past their mid-fifties, or prevent children from passive and active acts of suicide?

We can begin to answer these questions by noting that neither the High Court justices nor those who supported their decision relied simply on the supposedly universal principles of justice embodied in the common law. They also relied on national passions and affects organized around the imaginary of a shamed and redeemed nation. The High Court argued not only that the common law could not tolerate the racist foundations of *terra nullius,* but also that law and liberal democratic states were shamed by their continued adherence to what the court called the " 'barbarian' theory underpinning the colonial reception of the common law of England."[10] The justices and the Labour Party of Prime Minister Paul Keating, which supported the ruling, argued that "the fiction of *terra nullius*" was a racist, humiliating betrayal of the good that the common law and liberal democratic state was, sought to be, and represented to the nation. Past uses of cultural discrimination were held up as shameful, though excisable, cancers on the root good of the common law. In short, the precedent of the common law's shame or virtue came to figure national history, critical national aspirations and diversions, and national morality. And hegemonic national history and consciousness came to be figured as the archive of precedent.

In sum, the court was engaging in and helping to define public debates over the proper affective response of the nation to its settler past. It was not alone in this project. For instance, an editorial in *The Australian* asked readers to consider whether shame or guilt was the proper and most nationally productive emotional response toward Australia's indigenous groups.[11] In so asking, the editorial reiterated and fixed the social location of the normative citizen as Anglo-Celtic. The addressee of the editorial, the community of anxiety it engaged, remained a loosely defined "Anglo-Celtic" who, *like* the writer, was forced to (re)think its "whiteness" against colonial history and contemporary regional realignments of states and capital in the Asia-Pacific. The editorial anchors public debate in the High Court majority decision.[12] "With justices William Deane and Mary Gaudron, the matter was put as clearly and truly as it could be. The dispossession of the Aborigines was 'the darkest aspect' in the history of Australia. It had bequeathed us a legacy of 'unutterable shame.' While this legacy remained unacknowledged and unrepaired in law, the spirit of our nation was diminished."[13] According to this editorial, to be Australian necessitated not a "collective guilt over the dispossession of the Aborigines" but an "embeddedness" and "implication" in the nation's history "in a way outsiders or visitors cannot be." Pride in national achievements, such as that felt by the nation for the soldiers who fell at Gallipoli, is no better suited for the task of nation-building than shame at national wrongdoings.[14] What is crucial is that the state, law, and public collectively engage in the pride *and* shame occasioned by historically specific and nationally differentiated colonial and civil rights struggles. An embeddedness, implication, and engagement in the nation's historic brutality toward its colonial subjects is rewritten as the necessary condition of nation-building in late modern liberal democratic societies. It is the crucial affective element in the definition of its borders, interiors, discourses, imaginaries, and identities.

A very similar invocation of national renewal through collective acts of mutual implication is found in the 1999 parliamentary debate over the passage of the "motion of reconciliation." Stimulated by repeated appeals for a national apology for the wrongs done to indigenous peoples, and under considerable political and public pressure, Liberal Coalition Prime Minister John Howard agreed to a motion written by Democratic Party Senator Aden Ridgeway, an indigenous Australian, reaffirming the "wholehearted commitment to the cause of reconciliation between indigenous and nonindigenous Australians as an important national priority for Australians"; acknowledging that the "mistreatment of many indigenous Australians" represented "the most blemished chapter in our international history"; and expressing "deep and sincere regret that indigenous Australians suffered injustices under the practices of past generations, and for the hurt and trauma that many indigenous people continue to feel as a consequence of those practices."[15] Howard's regret carefully avoided the performative of a state apology, a speech form that could be used as grounds for reparative claims and that could turn the recognition of the past harms into the redistribution of present economic goods.

While citing aspects of the High Court's decision (darkest history, most blemished chapter) Howard explicitly rejected all attempts "to embroil" the Australian people "in an exercise of shame and guilt," describing most settler atrocities as "mistakes" and assigning these mistakes to a past in which "the overwhelming majority of the current generations of Australians" had "no personal involvement."[16] Of course, his forceful rejection of a shamed state and national people only incited the movement of just such a debate.[17] National newspapers opened editorial space to various visions of national regret and renewal, foregrounding, for instance, author and poet David Malouf's call for the nation "to rethink the strong note of self-pity in our reading of our beginnings and ask ourselves if it, too, does not belong to our contemporary culture of complaint."[18] But although rejecting the politics of shame and guilt in his address to parliament supporting the motion of reconciliation, Howard foregrounded the positive national consequence of affective purges, as had the *Mabo* justices. Indeed, as Howard himself noted, his support for the motion of reconciliation pivoted on the "measure" of indigenous "commitment to the essential unity of the Australian nation" and on the measure to which the motion itself was issued not on behalf of indigenous Australians but of national pride and national achievement.[19] Confronting the uglier, blemished bodies that nationalism wasted was intended to deepen and extend national pride and pleasure; not unlike the manner in which, for Richard Rorty, the external cry of the pained other purifies liberalism. The articulate pain of the other simultaneously allows the liberal subject to feel herself or himself to have been unintentionally causing wrong and to be constantly moving to rectify that wrong. Likewise, a confrontation with the ugly underbelly of national history constitutes the beauty of national time:

> The Australian achievement, as I said, is of a scale that should make all of us proud. This country has achieved enormous things. This country has won itself great repute and great credit around the world. Just as we as a nation are entitled to draw pride from the triumphs and the achievements of Australians, so we must in a completely unvarnished fashion confront both dimensions of our national story. We must not only confront and embrace the dimensions which give us pleasure and pride and a sense of achievement and a sense of satisfaction but also confront the uglier parts of our national history.[20]

Kim Beazley, Labour opposition leader, countered the liberal tense of colonial history, referring to the Royal Commission report on the Stolen Generation (*Bringing Them Home*): "What I read about were events and institutions in my life — my life — and people who had been in those institutions in my house — my house. But, if you go through dates and places and times, you see that

that report takes us well into the 1970s. . . . We are dealing not with far past history; we are dealing with contemporary history."[21] But in no less dramatic terms did the Labour opposition place the fate of Australian nationalism in a shared achievement of mourning, holding out to the imagined publics of its national address a renewed national optimism as the desired end to their honest "atonement."[22]

In this way we see that the High Court decision and public statements supporting it, from the Left and Right, leaned not only on images of the shamed national subject, but also on images of a national subjectivity now fully conscious of its past mistakes. Their statements continually referred to a repaired social body, to an equitable society, and to a tolerant nonracist white subject made possible through the verdict of *Mabo* and the passage of the Native Title Act that was the legislative response to it. Court judgment and legislative act would be the political testament to the good intentions of the state and its normative publics. Repairing the law and national attitudes would rupture the nation's legacy of racial and cultural intolerances. These repairs, however, were primarily made to the torn images and institutions of Anglo-Celtic Australians—the real addressees of the court. That is, the High Court and its supporters constructed their legal act as a journey to a promised land in which the possibility of social discrimination would cease because good attitudes and good legislation would repair the unnatural deformations of the law's good intentions and, thereby, those of the state and its normative citizens. The potential radical alterity of indigenous beliefs, practices, and social organization was not addressed. Instead the court decision and the public discourse surrounding it urged dominant society on a journey to its own redemption, leaning heavily on the unarguable rightness of striving for the Good and for a national reparation and reconciliation. The problem is that discrimination was not exiled from the law, nor the source of intolerance banned from public forums. Court and public reserved the right to sanction— to discriminate against—any practice considered repugnant to common law and public values and to discern when a social or cultural difference has ceased to function as a recognized difference as such. Let me elaborate.

TIDES OF HISTORY

The court's invitation to the nation to enter history anew in a refreshed and cleansed version of a persisting, unchanged ideal image of itself was not extended to the indigenous subjects around whom it organized its shame. I noted above that the court found that Aboriginal Australians retained their native title interests in land *if* they retained the traditional customs, beliefs, and practices that created the substance of their difference and if these customs were not repugnant to the common law. This dual "if" curtailed the history-bearing capacity of indigenous tradition, making the legal standing of Aboriginal traditional customs, beliefs, and practices more limited than might be suggested by the language of the court. On the one hand, in this particular decision, the court stated that Aboriginal traditions could change and adapt to new circumstances but that they had to embody and perform the ideal of "tradition" and "locality."[23] The High Court held that "when the tide of history has washed away any real acknowledgment of traditional law and any real observance of traditional customs," the foundation of native title disappeared and native title rights were extinguished.[24] As if merely substituting the notion of culture for an older version of race, the court argued that if Aboriginal culture interbred with another "heritage" to some underdefined degree, it forfeited these rights. On the other hand, some traditions, some features, and some practices of "customary law" were and remained prohibited under statutory and common law: "The incidents of particular native title relating to inheritance, the transmission or acquisition of rights and interests in land and the grouping of persons to possess rights and interests in land are matters to be determined by the laws and customs of the indigenous inhabitants, provided those laws and customs are not so repugnant to natural justice, equity and good conscience that juridical sanctions under the new regime must be withheld."[25] Do we read these "limits" as simply rhetorical, minor moments in a major judgment, or as an essential discursive architecture of multiculturalism? Two recent native title claim decisions suggest how these legal judgments throw indigenous subjects between the whirlpool Charybdis of distinct culture and the monstrous Scylla of repugnant culture.

The Members of the Yorta Yorta Aboriginal Community v. the State of Victoria (1998)

The Yorta Yorta Land Claim was the first of the major native title claims to come to trial.[26] Thus, perhaps unsurprisingly, Justice Olney, who presided during the trial, reviewed at length the evidential requirements for proving native title rights and interests. Reading across court and parliamentary law, he began his written decision with the judgment of Justice Brennan in *Mabo* that the origin of native title lies in traditional law and that the continued existence of this title depends on the degree to which present descendants acknowledge and observe this law. Four avenues of inquiry present themselves: (1) Are the people claiming native title the descendants of the original occupants of the land? (2) What are the nature and content of traditional laws currently acknowledged and observed? (3) What connections to land and law have been maintained? and, (4) Are the rights and interests claimed under native title recognized under the common law of Australia?[27]

Charged with evaluating the measure to which culture had been frozen or been flooded, Olney faced the problem of adjudicating in a field of judicial metaphors. How does one measure cultural tides, their ebbs and flows? How is the demand to assess cultural drift made practical? These questions lay at foreground in the Yorta Yorta claim. The land in dispute lay in the northern hinterland of Melbourne. The claimants consisted primarily of persons most non-Aboriginal Australians would describe as urban Aborigines. The Yorta Yorta claimed to hold unbroken strands of Aboriginal law passed down from generation to generation. But their concerns about and language of spirituality and country, and ecology and pain, struck many non-Aboriginal observers as stretching the credibility of the notion of cultural distinctiveness. To what should Yorta Yorta present-day claims about their cultural traditions be compared? It was not to the oral histories the Yorta Yorta told that Olney turned, but to the colonial archive; especially the nineteenth-century writings of the ethnologist Edward Curr. It became for him the commonsense repository and transparent referent of real tradition. Temporally closer to and politically removed from the present scene, the colonial archive could and did function as the neutral measure of contemporary social being. Archival texts would interpret and value oral texts: "The oral testimony of witnesses from the claimant group is a further source of evidence but being based upon oral tradition passed down through many generations extending over a period in excess of two hundred years, less weight should be accorded to it than to the information recorded by Curr."[28] What then was noteworthy culture as per Curr as per Olney? Consider these extracts from *Yorta Yorta*:

> But, though there was no government, there were certain important practices among the Bangerang which deserve to be called laws. Some of the principal of these had reference to the transfer of the young from one class to another (particularized hereafter), the knocking out of teeth, making the ornamental scars on their backs, breasts, and arms, and restrictions with respect to food. There were also others which had reference to females. In the latter case only did infractions occur with some frequency, on which occasions, as I have already

noticed, the persons aggrieved, when they chose, made their complaints publicly in the camp, and publicly vindicated their rights, the offender being often constrained by custom to go through the ordeal of having a certain number of spears thrown at him, and so run the risk of death or wounds in satisfaction for injury done.[29]

It appears that in the Bangerang society the role of women was subservient to men. Curr records that in domestic life man was "despotic in his own mia-mia or hut" . . . that children belong to the tribe of the husband . . . and that prior to the coming of the whites the Bangerang, as a rule, "enforced constancy on the part of their wives, and chastity on their unmarried daughters."[30]

Olney found these traditional corporeal disciplines to be too sharp a contrast to the contemporary ecospirituality of the Yorta Yorta. And, what matters in legal hearings is not what matters to the people but what matters to the law.

The applicants readily concede that they and their forebears have long since ceased to observe traditional practices in relation to initiation or to perform other ceremonial activities which are frequently, in other Aboriginal societies, indicative of spiritual attachment to the land.[31]

Preservation of Aboriginal heritage and conservation of the natural environment are worthy objectives the achievement of which may lead to a more ready understanding and recognition of the importance of the culture of the indigenous people but in the context of a native title claim the absence of a continuous link back to the laws and customs of the original inhabitants deprives those activities of the character of traditional laws acknowledged and traditional customs observed . . . a necessary element of both the statutory and the common law concept of native title rights and interests.[32]

What matters to the juridical sensibility of cultural distinctiveness is not, however, merely what jurists publicly cite from the record, but what they read but do not necessarily repeat. In his seminal text *Coming into Being Among the Australian Aborigines* (1937) M. F. Ashley-Montague noted, in unwitting foreshadowing of commissioners like Olney, that the colonial ethnologies of R. Bough Smyth, G. Tapin, J. D. Woods, and E. M. Curr were in many ways invaluable compilations of knowledge relating to the Australian Aborigines, representing "almost the sole attempts to record in some sort of systematic way something of the manners and customs, the folklore and linguistics, of the aboriginal tribes." And yet, Ashley-Montague also notes that these texts are replete with allusions to social practices that provoke such delicacy of feeling that writers could only describe them with "some such caliginous epithet as 'disgusting', or 'bestial' " or would only allude to "horrible rites" with the vaguest of descriptive content.[33] These social practices are of the sort that contemporary High Court and tribunal justices would likely continue to consider repugnant to common law and public sentiment.

Reading Yorta Yorta culture transparently off this colonial archive, Olney reads the graphic accounts of indigenous practices which captivated the settler imaginary—perceived instances of rape, forced female child marriage, initiatory bodily mutilation, retaliatory spearing and beatings—and he reads allusions to other practices so repugnant that civilized language expires in their company. This elusive, at times repugnant, textual ground is the performative mirror of contemporary Yorta Yorta culture; it is the real toward which courts drive claimants and against which they judge them—a real beyond words, in this case because their repugnancy impales symbolic representation. Thus, unsurprisingly, Olney found that the native title rights and interests of the Yorta Yorta had been extinguished through lack of maintenance of beliefs and practices giving these rights their content. The Yorta Yorta suffered from the discomfort of the cultural uncanny in a multicultural state. The case is under appeal.

Hayes v. Northern Territory (1999)
Unlike the Yorta Yorta, the Central Australian Arrente people represented under the native title claim of *Hayes v. Northern Territory* did not present Justice Olney with the problem of distinguishing degrees of cultural difference. He does note at the beginning of his decision that the evidence presented before him would have to demonstrate "what laws, customs, practices, and traditions, stretching way back, are still acknowledged and observed" and whether these laws, customs, practices, and traditions are "integral to a distinctive culture" or "only a description of how people live" or once lived.[34] Still, Olney seems quite satisfied that the Arrente maintain a distinct cultural law that squares with standardized accounts of "the Dreaming," an account he himself summarizes in the following way:

> The course of creation consists of the spontaneous awakening and movement of ancestral figures, beings with supernatural and human-like qualities and typically associated with specific types of animals, plants, or other natural phenomena (totems). . . . Apart from creating the landscape itself and the forms of

art associated with it, the ancestors also brought into existence all the other features of contemporary human existence — hunting and gathering, the making and use of tools, rules of kinship, language and dialect variation, and so on. Collectively, and in conjunction with totemic beliefs and ceremonial action, all these features may be glossed in English as the Law. While the Law is often narrowly defined in terms of ceremonial activity, it may also be construed as a more general system of rules and regulations through which people define their rights and interests.[35]

When Olney cites real Aboriginal customary law he is citing not only Arrente history but the textual presuppositions of that history mediated by Australian anthropology and Aboriginal politics, its mass cultural circulation, and its juridical precedents. In other words, Aboriginal law is the collectivity of a minimal number of commonsense coordinating features — kinship, ceremony, and hunting and gathering. As a nonlocal supertext, secreted within legal, popular, and legislative texts, it is dense and complex, a distillation of social theory and professional norms. But this is the real text of Aboriginal customary law: the conditions of its stereotypical iterability, of its deep citational possibility and institutional allegiance. The textual density of such descriptions are what allows ceremony and initiation to be "indicative of spiritual attachment to the land." Feeling this exterior textual law supporting the interior interlocutionary texts he heard, Olney found that the Arrente retained the type of customs that give native title its content. But he also found that native title rights gave claimants the ability to exclude only other Aboriginal groups from their lands. Non-Aboriginal groups could continue, or could begin, to use Arrente lands without compensating Arrente people.

In what sense, however, could Olney recognize the law of the Arrente even if it were their law he saw? On the one hand, even when Olney and other jurists recognize contemporary Aboriginal beliefs as traditional in origin and substance, they themselves do not believe the beliefs that provide Aboriginal law its content and form. Aboriginal beliefs are legally productive not because they are perceived to be "true" but in large part because they are untrue, unbelievable, and thus truly distinctive and different — the type of thing to which the contemporary law can demonstrate a liberal reconcilement. In a very different setting, the analytic philosopher W.V. Quine uses "native's outlandish rites and beliefs" to ground his insight that radical communication should "maximize the psychological plausibility of . . . attributions to the native rather than the truth of the beliefs attributed."[36] It is exactly their measurable distance from western-based truth-generating epistemologies, the substance and proceduralisms of public reason, that makes this law not merely a description of how people live.[37]

On the other hand, other forms of difference may all too rapidly switch to an all too recognizable truth repugnant to the law. Remember that customary law has never been a recognized part of Australian common, statutory, or criminal law, neither before nor after *Mabo*.[38] Some of the same "traditions" Olney reads off the historical archive as indicative of customary law and spiritual attachment to the land in the *Yorta Yorta* claim and the *Arrente* claim are prohibited in the contemporary Australian criminal code. Which is to say that the very practices that provide robust evidence of the continuing existence of traditional law, so vital to the proof of native title and land rights cases, may be grounds for criminal prosecution. In its review in the mid-1980s of the possibility of reconciling Aboriginal customary law to Australian criminal law, the Law Reform Commission reiterated this fundamental opposition of common law (and public morality) to repugnant social practices citing as examples Aboriginal practices of polygamy, spearing, child marriage, gender-based physical abuse.

Criminal courts are periodically presented with cases that query the distance between forms of justice within "indigenous customary law" and forms of justice under criminal and common law—thereby opening the process to questions about fairness within a multicultural nation. In *Barnes v. the Queen* (1997), for instance, the court refused bail to an Aboriginal applicant charged with the manslaughter of another Aboriginal man. The Aboriginal man had requested, through his counsel, to be released on bond in order to return to the indigenous community, Lajamanu, to receive traditional punishment for his acts. The applicant's counsel described to the court the content of traditional punishment for murder in terms not foreign to Edward Curr's own description of the Bangarang: "Spearing of both of the applicant's legs four or five times, using sharp and shovel-nose spears; punches with fists to the applicant's face and chest; blows to the applicant's head and back with the use of large heavy wood boomerangs; and similar boomerangs being thrown at the applicant, who would have a small shield with which to protect himself."[39] The court found that bail in this case would be an unlawful act—the tacit authorization of an assault intended to kill or cause grievous harm to the victim. As Max Weber and others have noted, intentional acts of grievous bodily harm remain the legally sanctioned privilege of the state.

Critical reflection on indigenous law does not merely occur within the juridical field, to borrow a phrase of Pierre Bourdieu's. But these cases do provide critical discursive grounds and language for public debate about fairness, cultural difference, and evil. Cases like *Barnes v. the Queen* circulate in the mass-mediated public sphere, reanimating already existing archives of public memory, prejudice, and sensibility, inciting public debates about what indigenous law, ceremony, and culture are really all about and whether the nation and its institutional bodies should protect, enhance, or support them.[40] They continually reopen the question of who and what "we" are and are as a nation; where "their" customs, beliefs, and practices fit in; and on what basis and in what contexts "we" can judge "them."

Whether merely different or either too uncannily similar or starkly repugnant to state law, Aboriginal culture is hardly indifferent to the nation that consumes it. Ritual group sex, murder, certain marriage practices, and genital operations shame the common law and the nation's core values. These Aboriginal traditions have no legal standing; they are allowed to exist only as nostalgic traces of a past, fully authentic Aboriginal tradition. As traces, neither fully forgotten by law or public nor ever fully present to them, these prohibited practices continue to haunt all contemporary representations of Aboriginal tradition, casting an aura of inauthenticity over present-day Aboriginal performances of their culture. In other words, although the court may engage history, Aboriginal Australians express at their own risk their engagement with the democratic form of capital and governance within which they live; the memorial forms of their own histories; and their ambivalences toward and debates about these traditions, identities, and identifications. Even at the moment of their inclusion into the liberal multicultural state imaginary, specific indigenous histories, memories, and practices are irrelevant. Instead, these diverse and sometimes fragmentary elements have to be reformulated to fit the uneven terrain of common and statutory law, criminal codes and common values.

That the court confined its ruling to a legal recognition of only those traditions not already prohibited by common and statutory law in no way seems to have cast a shadow of doubt around the common law's claim that in the *Mabo* decision it recognized the value of Aboriginal law to native title.[41] But it was still faced with the difficult job of separating the common law and Aboriginal law at the historical moment when cultural interchange defined the global system; when anxieties about national identity, status, and power dominated public discussion; and when an older means of distinguishing cultural types was widely held to be racially intolerant. If a group's culture is to be the object

of juridical inquiry, then laws, cultures of law, and cultures that have produced systems of law have to be theoretically separable and the act of separation must signify a (post)racist practice. Gone, the court claims, are the days
when the other's law could be univocally deemed "barbarian" and discarded
as legally irrelevant. For the state to base contemporary social policy and law
on such colonial frameworks exposes it to international charges of racial and
cultural intolerance.

The techniques of cultural discrimination established by the court have
a fairly straightforward structure. First, they separate and make relative Aboriginal and non-Aboriginal cultural systems even while establishing a formal
relationship of value among types of Aboriginal cultural performance. Next,
they differentiate the site from which European-based and Aboriginal legal
systems obtain their value and seek their telos. And, finally, they bind the at-
tainment of native title rights to the successful judicial performance of this
fantastic separation, origination, and destiny.

The court's achievement of a commonsense (post)racist separation is in
part an effect of the recursivity of pronominal reference. By referring to the
shame of "our" law and "our" nation and the good of recognizing "their"
laws, "their" culture, and "their" traditions, the court is able to cite and en-
trench an understanding of the nation as confronting its own discriminatory
practices and facing up to and eliminating a dark stain on its history even as
it reproduces the nation as Anglo-Celtic and "ours."

The former Labour Prime Minister Paul Keating's public statements supporting the legislative implementation of the *Mabo* ruling mirrored the court
in critical ways. In a speech commemorating the Australian launch of the
International Year for the World's Indigenous People, Keating trumpeted the
"historical . . . reconciliation" between Aboriginal and non-Aboriginal Australians and announced his government's intention to use *Mabo* to establish
"a prosperous and remarkably harmonious multicultural society."[42] According to Keating, this "socially just," new multicultural society could be pain-
lessly achieved with no serious costs or losses for "Australians" — that is, "we"
non-Aboriginal Australians.[43] Moreover, it would not challenge, threaten, or
set into crisis the basic values of Australians (including "our" right "to enjoy beaches and other recreation areas, including national parks"[44]). Reconciliation and the socially just, new multicultural society to which it would
be a testament simply meant "acknowledging" and "appreciating" Aboriginal
Australians and providing a "*measure* of justice" for *them*.[45]

Lest we think his position the idiosyncratic discourse of the center-Left,

Liberal Coalition Prime Minister John Howard, who deposed the Keating government and firmly rejected its multicultural policy, similarly distributed nationalism across racially inflected pronominal indexes. In his 1999 parliamentary address supporting the motion of reconciliation, Howard voiced his imagined nation: "We say to the indigenous people of our community that we want you in every way to be totally a part of our community. We want to understand you. We want to care for you where appropriate."[46] Like the High Court and mass media, Keating and Howard, in their public addresses and policy papers and across the political and social spectrum of Australian political leadership, framed the legal dilemma of *Mabo* and historical discrimination as a symbol of the moral dilemma that multiculturalism posed to Anglo-Celtic Australians—the "plight of Aboriginal Australians continues to be *our* failure"[47] and the common law and the social and judicial values under threat are "ours," as is the cultural system into which Aboriginal law (their law) is being accommodated.[48]

The deictical field the court cites and iterates ("ours" and "theirs") to separate Australian and Aboriginal laws and cultural practices makes it possible, even expected, to differentiate the sites from which these "legal systems" obtain their value and seek their telos, and to represent this differentiation, this cultural discrimination, as a nondiscriminatory project. For instance, the court confidently states that native title obtains its value from its ability to signify fixity, stasis, and resistance to a historical dialectic: "Native title has its origin in and is given its content by the traditional laws acknowledged by and the traditional customs observed by the indigenous inhabitants of a territory."[49] In contrast to native title, common law's value arises not from a fixed, locatable territory but from its historical dialogue with elite international institutions. As opposed to the origin and telos that it assigns native title, the court locates the preeminent value of common law doctrine in its ability to "reflect" a historically progressive dialectic of nationality and internationality and, in reflecting this dialectic, to embody truth and justice. It is in this purified air that the history, culture, and social worth of Australia (and Western humanism more generally) is said to originate and proceed; only the common law's own history threatened the legitimacy of its present and its future: "If it were permissible in past centuries to keep the common law in step with international law, it is imperative in today's world that the common law should neither be nor be seen to be frozen in an age of racial discrimination."[50]

But noting this pronominal play does not directly answer the question of what allows the court its optimism, what allows it to cast out historical knowledge, that they, like their predecessors, live in prejudicial time, that such is merely the condition of social discourse? Turning to the *Wik* court helps to illuminate the internal textual techniques by which law is saved from its own advanced forms of discrimination, keeping the repugnant in the other, while assigning past repugnances to the history books. The internal textual pragmatics I describe is not the entire means of cultural discrimination. But it is a vital part of what opens law to a positive articulation with broader discursive fields.

WICKER MAN

The question before the court in *The Wik People v. the State of Queensland* (1996) was whether the granting of a pastoral lease necessarily extinguished native title.[51] The *Wik* decision was crucial to indigenous land aspirations because the vast hectares under pastoral lease were those parts of Australia where Aboriginal beliefs and practices stereotyped as traditional are most likely to be found.[52]

In answering the question of whether pastoral leases extinguished native title, members of the court remade Australian national law in recognizable ways. They argued that as the British law took "seed" in colonial soil, statute law adapted to its new material and social conditions. Certain "archaic" concepts receded slowly into the twilight of historical memory. Other "novel concepts" and "fictions" were grafted onto the common law. Pastoral leases were an example of a novel concept of property arising from the specific nature of Australian settlement. Other novel concepts included the removal of Aboriginal children from their parents, the outlawing of certain indigenous marriage and ritual practices, and the forced internment of indigenous people on missionary and government settlements. All of these benevolent and malevolent adaptations of British law to the social and spatial history of *terra Australis* made Australian common law *Australian* in content, quality, and form. All the good and all the bad were part and parcel of what distinguished and delimited the Australian legal tradition.[53]

Although Australian law's specificity was said to be derived from this history of good and evil, the court claimed that only the good designated the real being of the common law. To distill this good they leaned on a liberal legal apparatus — specifically the distinction between common and statutory law in accordance with the traditionally understood separate origin of judiciary and legislative law in liberal democracies. That is, they not only separated the origin and telos of black and white law, but distinguished the different origins and ends of common and statute law. The justices argued that statutory laws were creatures of parliament and, thus, popular will. As a result, "there is nothing to suggest that it was necessary or convenient" for statutory law "to conform to the common law."[54] Their legislative origin enmeshed statutory law in the political life of the nation and gave voice to the prevailing prejudices of public opinion.

At the time they were passed, these legislative creatures may not have been considered repugnant by members of the judiciary, but that too can be accounted for by the perverting power of public opinion.[55] After all, *Wik* suggests, judges are social creatures too. But these prejudiced, though well-intentioned, people are not the common law. It lies outside them and can be intuited from the iterative trace of a Good discernible not in but through actual human writings. If, for instance, state and federal legislation once allowed the forcible removal of children from their parents, this law reflected the political and social beliefs of the time not the ideals of the common law, even though, *at the time,* justices themselves would have considered these laws just and right, and aimed at the social good. How did the *Mabo* and *Wik* decisions and their public mediations inspire a nation to see themselves as acting fairly and justly in forging a new (post)modern settler ideology? Or, if common law is not in persons or even in the context of the writings, but in some felt perduring formal aspiration within these texts, what is that form? What is its aspiration?

We can begin to answer this seemingly simple question by examining the repeated assertions of the court that native title is not of the common law and the common law is not of native title.[56] Note, as example, a passage first from *Mabo,* then from *Wik:*

> Native title has its origin and is given its content by the traditional laws acknowledged by and the traditional customs observed by the indigenous inhabitants of a territory. . . . Native title, though recognised by common law, is not an institution of the common law and is not alienable by the common law. Its alienability is dependent on the laws from which it is derived.[57]

> This Court, established by the Constitution, operates within the Australian legal system. It draws its legitimacy from that system. Self-evidently, it is not an institution of Aboriginal customary law. To the extent that native title is recognised and enforced in Australia by Australian law, this occurs because, although not of the common law, native title is recognised by the common law

as not inconsistent with its precepts. This does not mean that, within its own world, native title (or any other incidents of the customary laws of Australia's indigenous peoples) depends upon the common law for its legitimacy or content. To the extent that the tide of history has not washed away traditional laws and real observance of traditional customs, their legitimacy and content rest upon the activities and will of the indigenous people themselves.[58]

In these and other textual moments the High Court seems to acknowledge the formal equivalence and independence of customary and common law. And, notably, these moments are what captivate public attention, are deemed noteworthy and quotable; that is, detachable from the stream of public discourse and reinserted with a specific density as "quoted speech" in other legal texts and public media. In statements like "legitimacy and content rest upon the activities and will of the indigenous people themselves," readers sense that the justices are treating the laws equally; that they are being fair and epitomizing liberal tolerance. But I want to suggest that what they sense is a meta-linguistic *form* subtending these discursive tokens—it is the form that seems detachable. *We are not of them* and *they are not of us* is abstracted by readers into the form "*x* is not of *y*" and "*y* is not of *x*." These forms are then made equivalent by a further abstraction into "*a* is not of *b*."

At these levels of textual abstraction, the particular and competing content of Aboriginal and European customary laws is bracketed and, instead, a textual token of formal equivalence is at the foreground. The compelling nature of this token derives from its articulation to the problem faced in liberal multicultural law and nation; namely, how to reconcile, fairly and justly, institutions and ideologies of abstract citizenship with difference, of equal opportunity and structural discriminations in fields of competing cultural injunctions—especially when some of these differences are experienced as moral imperatives. In other words, in the midst of technical juridical language, the court writes and readers hear the reassuring form of classical liberal democratic citizenship buried in the rubble of national cultural differences. It is the survival of this subtending liberal formation—*not* the actual content of traditional law or native title—that Beazley and the public find so necessary, even inspirational.

In actual legal fact, no more than did the *Mabo* court does the *Wik* court consider the Australian common law and Aboriginal customary law to be equivalent, formally or substantively, in power, reach, or authority (nor, probably, would most non-Aboriginal Australian citizens, if asked). Any attempt to posit a relation of identity between the two laws is not only absurd, but *self-evidently so*. Switching genres from law-talk to parental-talk ("because [I] said so"), a member of the *Wik* court, Justice Kirby, outlined a clear hierarchy of legal enforceability. It is "self-evident," writes Kirby, that although Aboriginal customary law is an institution of the common law, the High Court "is not an institution of Aboriginal customary law. . . . Theory accepted by this Court in *Mabo* was not that the native title of indigenous Australians was enforceable of its own power or by legal techniques akin to the recognition of foreign law. It was that such title was enforceable in Australian courts because the common law in Australia said so."[59] The court locates the source of this propositional power — the performativity of "Australia says so" — in colonial history. Colonialism happened. "It is too late now to develop a new theory of land law that would overthrow the whole structure of land titles based on Crown grants into confusion."[60]

We should pay heed to how a naturalized hierarchy of moral and legal authority is reestablished at the very moment common and customary laws are being formally equated. Remember: an invisible asterisk, a proviso, hovers above every enunciation of customary law: (provided [they] . . . are not so repugnant). This proviso interprets specific instances of cultural practices and indexes the monoculturalism of multicultural tolerance in liberal settler societies. For, although the court demands "real acknowledgement of traditional law and real observance of traditional customs" as the basis for a successful native title claim, *real* customary being must be free of any sense of a repugnant that would "shatter the skeletal structure" of state law, that would provoke an affective relation to a cultural or social otherwise, an experience of fundamental alterity. The cunning of recognition lies exactly in this play of the parentheticals: Be (not) Real; Be (not) Alterior.

But the High Court is not exempt from the very problem it poses to Aboriginal subjects: the dilemma of capturing real justice in real discourse and narrative time without prompting the appearance of the same interpretant hovering over native title or criminal law judgments. This judgment is just (unless[although] . . . it may appear retrospectively as repugnant or shameful). As courts cite the vast historical trail of their own mistaken bigotry and malice, they open themselves up to a reading of their present judgments as little more than dumb repetitions of the past. They face, in short, the problem of how to account for justice in the breach and shadow of their own repugnant, shameful history. It is useful, therefore, to examine in some detail the ways the *Wik* court spans the breach of history it cites and widens.

We begin by noting that the High Court has written copiously on the relation between native title and the common law (distinct and hierarchical), on the form native title must take (more or less traditional), and on the type of traditional practice excluded from recognition (the repugnant). It has done so, however, without ever saying what the real content of the customary, the good, or the repugnant is. Quite the contrary: the *Mabo* and *Wik* decisions refuse to mandate the content of the customary or the repugnant, couching this refusal in an ideology of recognition and patient listening.[61]

Rather than defining the content of social goods or evils, the court relies on commonsense understandings of them as formally distinct and discernible states, the former the ultimate and true aspiration of law and nation, the latter that beyond which acceptable cultural difference cannot go. The recognition of difference starts at the doorstep of the customary and stops at the abyss of the repugnant. But the substance of the repugnant and the good are to be announced or to be debated in the open forum of the public sphere. What is not to be debated is whether or not the repugnant and good *are;* whether they are *distinct states;* and how they are related to the common law.[62] The court takes the answers to these questions to be self-evident: moral codes change but the repugnant, whatever it is, is and is always presumed to be a stranger to the *real being* of the common law. No matter that the common law is, or usually is, concerned with fact and reasoned argument—justice in a more modest and narrow legal sense. And, no matter that the common law's origin may come from a set of now archaic social beliefs and practices. Nevertheless, its ultimate end is undeniably and commonsensically principled justice, because this is what legal scholars and the public say it desires—and desire it to desire.

Forming and distributing social goods and evils across temporal and social space depends on a complex set of temporal, aspectival, and metaphorical framings; that is, these are the textual productions, textual sources and scaffoldings that hold desire's form and ideology's optimism in place. The court's use of alluvial metaphors—frozen and flooded cultural fields—helps illuminate how these textual sources of desire and optimism work. Take the following few examples from the *Mabo* decision.[63]

them: The common law can, by reference to the traditional laws and customs of an indigenous people, identify and protect the native rights and interests to which they give rise. However, when the tide of history has washed away any real acknowledgment of traditional law and any real observation of traditional customs, the foundation of native title has disappeared. A native title which has ceased with the abandoning of laws and customs based on tradition cannot be revived for contemporary recognition.[64]

The traditional law or custom is not, however, frozen as at the moment of establishment of a Colony. Provided any changes do not diminish or extinguish the relationship between a particular tribe or other group and particular land, subsequent development or variations do not extinguish the title in relation to that land.[65]

us: If the international law notion that inhabited land may be classified as *terra nullius* no longer commands general support, the doctrines of the common law which depend on the notion that native peoples may be "so low on the scale of social organisation" that it is "idle to impute to such people some shadow of the rights known to our law" can hardly be retained. If it were permissible in past centuries to keep the common law in step with international law, it is imperative in today's world that the common law should neither be nor be seen to be frozen in an age of racial discrimination.[66]

As before, we see the court switching between a veneer of formal equivalence and a substructure of definitive hierarchy. Compare the statements "the true being of their culture adjusts in time" and "the true being of our culture adjusts in time" is translated "as their law adjusts to history it looses its true being" but as our law adjusts to history it gains its true apotheosis. The authorizing temporal frame of customary law is a past-perfect ideal form. The authorizing temporal frame of common law is a future-perfect ideal form. But we also see how the court uses tense, aspect, modality, and pronominal indexes to figure "knowing" as a temporal and social location distal from the here and now of their production of the truth. The law *was* mistaken *then.* *Those* justices *were* enmeshed in a set of social prejudices. In positioning past justices as mistaken, the court positions itself as knowledgeable about the mistake — and thus on its way out of *this moment of intolerance.* In other words, *Wik* and *Mabo* rely on pragmatic features of language to frame the failures of real justice in real time as past-tense problems of past-tense people.

The pragmatics of textual intolerance allow the court to acknowledge mistaken judgment in juridical history even as it incites a future-oriented amnesia about present judicial judgment. These linguistic coordinating agencies forestall two other obvious interpretations of how every judgment of intolerance will appear in the future: First, they will have been wrong *at this exact moment* from the perspective of future time, but they will have judged anyway.

And they will have framed their judgment as a compulsion ("we must make a judgment no matter its contingency"). And, second, they will have been compelled by and will have based their judgment on nothing more than the agentless will of the commonsense discourses and everyday powers of "our time." They will have acted on behalf of an abstract machine whose organic qualities they cannot now see. Not surprisingly, the jurists back away from any such clear metarepresentations of what they are in fact describing.

But if the court forestalls its own fall into the breach of history, it does so by pushing Aboriginal persons over the cliff. In actual given instances of historical time, if the court feels "repugnance" it understands it to be generated from, or be an essential part of, Aboriginal customary practices rather than understanding the feeling of repugnance to be generated from the discursive mandates and contradictions of liberal injunctions. The Good and the Just, whatever they are, *are:* they are . . . they remain; . . . their remainders are the private abstract capital of the common law. When past statutory laws or common law decisions are in contradistinction to contemporary standards of the Good and the Just and the Decent and Right, their authors, not the common law, are claimed to have been mistaken — retrospectively repugnant. Sacrificing justices, lawyers, and politicians — being willing to be placed on the bier of the past, a grand conflagration — is the necessary means of abstracting the Thing that is common law and then safeguarding this abstraction from the long, soiled history of its usage.

Telling the story this way highlights why the *Mabo* and *Wik* decisions are generally considered to have aligned common law with the lofty ideals of Australian multiculturalism. The willingness of the court not only to recognize the fact that an ancient law predated the settler state but to acknowledge that the legitimacy of this law came from "its own world" seemed to usher into national time a truer, deeper form of liberal multiculturalism. But telling the story this way also highlights the textual ideology necessary to produce good common law and to distribute its repugnant history across time and social space. The syntactic plays I have diagnosed in the *Mabo* and *Wik* judgments are, therefore, not so much the games of bored theory as the necessary textual procedures of harried law. The common law justices lean on such linguistic props as the future-perfect "will have been" to orient their and their readers' interpretation of the failed ideals of the nation. They elide and incite an elision of the time and space of justice for the time and space of linguistic form. So confused, these linguistic features critically organize and distribute commonsense feelings and languages of who and what is responsible for the ongoing structural conditions of social discrimination such that Kirby can write: "To the extent that the tide of history has not washed away traditional laws and real observance of traditional customs, their legitimacy and content rest upon the activities and will of the indigenous people themselves."[67]

These discursive and textual features of legal judgment incite specific social practices. They dictate that every time an Aboriginal group performs its local traditions in order to substantiate a native title or land claim it is drawn into playing out the conditions and limits of multicultural law in late modern democracies. First, multicultural law demands that a discriminable (distinct) cultural difference be presented to it in a prepackaged form. In this case, indigenous performances of cultural difference must conform generally to the textually mediated imaginary of Aboriginal traditions and more specifically to the legal definition of "traditional Aboriginal owner." But this demand for a preformed cultural difference generates second-order demands — in main a demand for the law to be cautious and suspicious of the indigenous traditions presented to it. This suspicion is inscribed in the heart of the law's form and purpose: "The nature and incidents of native title must be ascertained as a matter of fact by reference to those laws and customs" and "must not be repugnant."[68] To ascertain cultural difference, the law demands that the Aboriginal suppliant face and speak to it. And the court looks at these suppliants speaking to it, not speaking among themselves where their "true" beliefs and feelings are imagined to be expressed. In other words, in a juridical setting, indigenous people are not a representative of objective cultural difference, but rather a membrane of cultural difference, a membrane that could be hiding a fullness of difference or an absence thereof — hiding a black face, a white face, or a face whose color and/or culture cannot be discerned and totalized.[69]

The already abandoned or hidden artifacts of a previously disciplined indigenous practice haunt every performance of cultural difference. Genital operations, retribution killers, and ritual group sex always draw the law's eye toward a nostalgic but disciplined past, making it just ever so suspicious of the authenticity of present traditions. No Aboriginal subject and performance before the law escapes this suspicion. All irritate it because all mark the law's limit: the impossibility of achieving what it imagines is possible but is not, a form of legal cultural performance not oriented to power, not already an alterity whose internal composition is the hybridized history of colonial identifications, prohibitions, and incitements and continued postcolonial prohibitions and desires.

Even if a form of pure cultural difference untouched by and not oriented to state colonial history did exist, the law itself negates the discursive and affective productivity of its legal agency. For the law must be able to comprehend the cultural narrative presented before it, be able to encompass it in its understanding of what is "indicative of spiritual attachment" in Aboriginal society even as it experiences this narrative as *other than* the cultural narratives it commonsensically understands as its own (or our own) cultural narratives. This is the aporia of the cultural difference the court iterates and faces: resist being (Australian) for me / do not resist me; to discriminate against you is not to discriminate socially / to discriminate against you is to discriminate socially; to understand you is to suspect you are me (Australian, engaged in history) / to not understand you is to suspect you are not (human; Australian). As if using post-Fanonian theory as a handbook, legal practitioners in actual land claim cases produce not quite black / not quite white subjects before the law.[70]

Finally, every native title or land rights case must bear the burden of national anxieties it cannot solve. The law is not simply scrutinizing local traditions, their genealogy and trajectory, but the meaning of recognizing every particular traditional performance in terms of national aspirations. In seemingly remote land claim hearings, national fantasies, frustrations, and anxieties flood legal interpretations; unfix critical reading; catch actors up in imaginaries of national redemption and national shame, national tolerance, and national intolerance; and lead the eye to a sublime object. In doing so, they distract national critical consciousness from the law's actual aim: the re-subordination of Aboriginal society and law vis-à-vis European law and society.[71]

I always pause here. Publics and politicians were moved by the High Court's breathless moral confidence. The justices wrote as if they were circus performers, able to walk suspended in analytical air, cutting the ropes to cultural discrimination while confidently walking along them. The court marked all previous discriminations as ideological without casting doubt on their own eschatological evocations of the Good Society toward which their discriminatory practices aim. It is as though they truly believed that their discriminations would resist history, that their acts represented the lifting of necessity and the allowance of freedom. The present can be good, even if the past was bad. Their good intentions, unlike those of the justices who sat before them, would resist the relentless unfurling of discourse. And it is as if the repetitive failure of past eschatological images never decreases the power these images hold over the present: the New Deal, the New Society, the New Left, the New Right, the New Covenant. All seem to fix critical thinking, on the Left and on the Right, on the abjected and civilized and redeemed. What is it about this moment in national time that allows the law to incite national and subaltern memory on behalf of a new collective self-understanding in a way that makes the rewriting of history seem a recognition of and accounting for that history; that allows the (re)entrenchment of cultural discrimination as a technology of state power; and, as if these were not enough, makes this new technology of state power seem like a means of liberating subalterns from the state?

The answer demands that we break the ideological frame of the court itself. We need to hinge the High Court's claim that the common law was shamed by its own racist history and an international legal gaze to other national mortifi-cations of state, capital, public and counterpublic realignments and struggles. The law's ability to distract the eye depends not only on the internal textual dynamics of legal decisions and proceedings, but on the broader discursive fields (discussed in earlier chapters) that make these discursive techniques performative. The court itself points to these broader horizons of discourse — the gaze of the international legal community — as the essential ground of its own actions and readings. In particular, we should pay attention to the justices' concern that the Australian common law be brought "up to date" with other "civilized," first-world Euro-American nation-states that had long ago recognized the mutual compatibility of native title and the state's radi-cal title.[72] But what is at stake in *Mabo* is not simply a nation's shame at its past as a colonizer. At stake is its future. Will the historical significance of the Australian nation be that it bore an impotent Western humanism, a barren liberal democracy, the only "white" nation on earth unable to produce wealth and status — "the good life" — for its citizens? Will it bear the shame of em-bracing forms of abhorrent social practices that lie outside civil decency or of discriminating against mere cultural difference?

When *Mabo* and *Wik* are placed in these contexts, native title appears as a fetish of national anxieties about the status, role, and future of the Australian nation and helps explain the widespread public debates resulting from the judgments. Native title condenses and stands in for Australian aspirations for first-worldness (symbolically white, Euro-American) on the margins of Euro-American and Asia-Pacific domination, with the Aboriginal subject (indige-nous blackness) standing as the material to be worked over for the nation to maintain its place in (Western) modernity, an organic barometer of national redemption. The court's use of the shamed Anglo-Celtic Australian fixed the ideal image of the nation as a white, first-world, global player in the national imaginary.

Mabo's politics of shame, is not, however, simply a nightmare about the nation's marginality. Instead, shame allows the law to perform the adjustments necessary to recuperate its authority and values in a "postideological" (post)colonial moment. By "postideological" I do not mean to suggest that capital and state relations are now transparent. Rather I mean to point to a characteristic of the contemporary moment, in which a feeling, shame, displaces arguments over power, hegemony, and social contradiction. Shame's political pleasure, its sublime politics, lies in conjuring an experience "beyond ideology" in a moment saturated with ideological readjustments of state discrimination.

When the court evoked a shamed nation whose redemption depended on an acknowledgment of past wrongdoings, it accomplished what a mere change of law could not. It created a focal point beyond politics for both business and subaltern antagonists of the state and the law's multicultural project, the former who might see the project as too radical, the latter as too reformist. The fantasy of shame and reparation created an experience of intimacy—intimate holding, intimate understanding, intimate knowledge—between those who control access to and those excluded from critical rights. Right-wing business leaders, who opposed the decision, had little recourse but to return the court's own rhetoric as a preideological barometer of national well-being. So, for example, a coalition of business interests emphasized the shame of a white nation forced into an unnatural structural adjustment by a nonwhite coalition of transnational and subaltern groups. Rather than manipulating other nations, as a true first-world nation would, Australia was like those other nations in being controlled by international forces unknown.[73]

Subordinate groups and the Left, perhaps surprised by the public pseudo-recognition of their position, were seduced toward the headlights of the law—supporting the judgment and the legislation that was modeled on it. In other words, by deploying a weapon once effectively wielded by the weak (subalterns, colonial subjects, African American civil-rights activists, feminists, gays and lesbians), those who controlled access to resources and rights were able to bind oppressed groups more tightly to the state and to looking to state law as the site from which a nondiscriminatory politics could proceed.[74] They did so not by refusing to accept the shame, but by embracing, foregrounding, and using it as a source of identification for their political projects. They did not simply trumpet the good of state law but lamented its villainy, as if the state were not a part of its own institutionality. And in doing so they showed how institutions are claimed to have feelings and how these feeling institutions translate liberation struggles against them into their own legitimation.[75]

CONCLUSION

The juridical struggle to formulate a legally valid multicultural form of common law provides a particularly important perspective on late liberal forms of power. Legal decisions bring into sharp relief the disjunction between ideologies of recognition and the practices and pragmatics of the distribution of rights, materials, and institutions. In the first place, law is one of the primary sites through which liberal forms of recognition develop their disciplinary sides as they work the hopes, pride, optimisms, and shame of indigenous and other minority subjects. The law is a significant site where local languages are diverted into juridical languages, atrophying imaginations of alternative forms of collective action. Second, Australian legal multiculturalism is exemplary of late modern liberal understandings and institutionalizations of difference and alterity. In this liberal imagination state apparatuses, as well as its law, principles of governance, and national attitudes need merely be *adjusted* to accommodate others. Dominant subjects do not need to experience the fundamental alterity of, in this case, indigenous discourses, desires, and practices or their potentially radical challenge to the nation and its core institutions and values such as "democracy" and the "common law." Likewise, the state administrators and normative publics can imagine that their experience of radically other cultures and practices can be unhinged from their experience of horror and abjection. Alterity is not seen as a threat or challenge to self- and national coherence, but is seen, instead, as compatible with an incorporative project, "an invitation to absorption."[76] And, finally, no one must examine the injunction on indigenous subjects to stage for the nation this sublime scene—not too much and not too little alterity. In this liberal imaginary, the now recognized subaltern subjects would slough off their traumatic histories, ambivalences, incoherencies, and angst like so much outgrown skin rather than remain for themselves or for others a wounded testament to the nation's past bad faith.[77] The nation would then be able to come out from under the pall of its failed history, betrayed best intentions, and discursive impasses. And normative citizens would be freed to pursue their profits and enjoy their families without guilty glances over their shoulders into history, or the slum down the block.

These new legal models of the multicultural nation and its citizenry have not displaced classic liberal models of the state and citizenship, nor do many state and public spokespersons intend them to. These older models of citizenship continue to inform state function, public discourse, and individual feelings about what is right and wrong to demand from the state and its normative publics. Australian courts have always had and continue to reserve the power to discriminate — and to discriminate against — those social and cultural differences considered harmful to individual citizens or the nation's so-called core values. Rather than displacing this classic disciplinary power, Australian legal multiculturalism has added a new dimension to its function. The courts have recognized the state to have both the right to sanction "harmful" social practices and identities, to sanction cultural difference, and the right to discern when a social or cultural difference has ceased to function as a difference as such. The courts, in other words, have expanded the state's discriminatory powers, not restricted them. The court is now empowered to prohibit and to (de)certify cultural difference as a rights- and resource-bearing identity. Yet Australian state apparatuses and public discourses continue to ground citizenship in abstract juridical identities supposedly neutral in relation to social identities, identifications, and practices. Once the state decertifies an individual or community, once it no longer recognizes the form of cultural difference they possess, these persons and communities are "liberated" *back into* the community of abstract citizenship.

In the end, *Mabo* and *Wik* are no more about Aboriginal people, their laws, and customs than are mass cultural objects like *Mutant Message Down Under*. Nor do the *Mabo* and *Wik* courts pretend to be about actual Aboriginal people, their laws, or their experiences of injustice, corporeal trauma, and genocide. These decisions are, instead, about the linguistic and textual mediations necessary for the continual coercions of liberal law to seem either a temporary confusion of those people administering it or a moment of cultural misrecognition. In other words, the *Mabo* and *Wik* decisions are about protecting and advancing Australian common law principles. And this, in the end, is also what the liberal law asks Aboriginal subjects to do.

The people themselves believe that they are descendants of certain great spirit ancestors whose names and deeds are well known; they arrived at identified places and they moved about the land doing various things at various places. Whether or not they were the creators of the physical world, they were certainly the ordainers of the system of life which the Aboriginals accept.

—*Milirrpum v. Nabalco Pty Ltd.*

5 / The Poetics of Ghosts: Social Reproduction in the Archive of the Nation

DEATH RITE FOR MABALAN

In this chapter I describe the attempt of a group of Aboriginal women and myself to translate an audio tape of a death rite held in 1948 in order to examine how indigenous members of the Belyuen community experience, grapple with, and try to produce a legally and morally felicitous form of locality. This production often means they must articulate local social processes, which they themselves at times contest, with the federal law of land rights and cultural difference. In other words, I try to show how these women, and other Belyuen women and men, make their community a socially viable place as they engage the legal and social forms within which they live, along with the archived memorial forms of their own histories, the national and transnational circulations of these forms, and their own ambivalences toward the traditions held in the historical archive.

Insofar as they demonstrate these issues, this chapter and the next return to the central themes explored in chapters 2 and 3 but from an ethnographic perspective; that is, the disciplinary nature of the archive in the context of liberal discourses of difference and morality. How do Belyuen persons at once orient their discursive, emotional, and corporeal natures toward the state's definition of the traditional Aboriginal person at the same time that they ghost this being for the state and sustain their own social imaginaries? In this chapter, I concentrate in particular on liberal approaches to sexuality and social organization because of the central role they play in land claim and native title deliberations. To this end, I first examine in some detail two Belyuen modes of territorialization, the descent and ascent of physical substances through everyday and ritual practices. I then embed these local processes in larger-scale processes of cultural and legal recognition, specifically, how the law of recognition continually refers to local bodily practices as (and converts them into) instances of heterosexual (human) and nonheterosexual (spiritual) forms of community-building.

At this point I should briefly say how I am using the terms "local," "localize," and "localization." A number of scholars have recently attempted to model the extralocal nature of localities, not the least of whom is Arjun Appadurai in his groundbreaking volume *Modernities at Large*.[1] These scholars have noted that the nominal form "local" differs from the verb forms "localize" and "localization" on the basis of the two suffixes, which signal the manner in which a local is produced; that is, how a nominal abstraction, the local, is manifested or projected as a specifiable state. Emphasizing the processes by which locals are produced allows scholars entry into the pragmatics of social production and reproduction that seem at the surface transparent processes of self (and social) revelation and disclosure. Rather than reveal what local social structures are, I ask how they are produced, under what constraints, and by what technologies of affect, force, and discourse. As should become clear, I am arguing that structural and semantic approaches to textual meaning are, in fact, part of the process by which a local is produced as an abstraction that the law of recognition can apprehend. And I am arguing that this abstraction of the pragmatic life of social texts is a critical moment in which national ideologies are localized.

These moments are especially troublesome for indigenous subjects. Indigenous persons face the demand that they desire and identify in a way that just so happens, in an uncanny convergence of interests, to fit the national imaginary of the traditional Aboriginal person. With the help of lawyers and anthropologists like me, they face the task of making the incommensurate discourses, desires, and imaginaries of the nation and its subalterns and minorities arrive at a felicitous, although unmotivated, end point. If they slip, if they seem to be opportunistic, to be speaking to the law, public, or capital too much or not enough or in a cultural framework the public recognizes as its own, they risk losing the few judicial and material resources the state has made available to them.

I also circle around the conversation I had with a group of Belyuen women about a sound recording as a method for demonstrating that the places where the public rhetoric of national support meets the local production of social communities are often nondramatic, quotidian, in nature. They include verandas, shopping malls, and shady trees. Although ordinary, these places are critical to how local beliefs and feelings are shaped into opinions about who is responsible for present-day social maladies, such as the state's failure to curb the excesses of capital and to provide equitable health, housing, and education; and how the failures of public sympathy, state institutions, and lawful forms of property become the failures of local people to maintain their "culture."

A quick caveat. This chapter does not distill, through the alchemy of the social sciences, an authentic if skeletal indigenous tradition still operating across the Darwin Harbor. Quite the contrary, it highlights the contested nature of the production of locales within and between specific indigenous and nonindigenous social networks. Moreover, although I emphasize Belyuen processes of localization and territorialization under the shadow of the Aboriginal Land Rights (Northern Territory) Act, 1976, other Aboriginal groups working within its framework are no less, if differently, engaged in such processes.

DEATH RITE FOR MABALAN AND THE DESCENT OF ANTHROPOLOGY

6 July 1996, Belyuen. As if conspirators in a political intrigue whose historical measure had yet to be determined, we huddled around my small tape recorder under the veranda of the Belyuen women's center: Marjorie Bilbil, Ester Djarem, Gracie Bitbin, Alice Djarug and her daughter Patsy-Ann, Ruby Yarrowin and her daughter Linda, and I. Marjorie, Ester, Gracie, Alice, and

Ruby were the critical remainders of the language and history of the community; their daughters were beginning to "pick it up" in the local colloquial creole. Alongside this tape were a collection of academic and popular writings from the 1930s to the 1960s, most importantly the works of the anthropologist A. P. Elkin, who I discussed in chapter 3, and of Colin Simpson who wrote several short, popular accounts of the ancestors of these women. On the audio tape in the recorder that lay in the center of our loose circle was a recording of a *kapug* (a mourning rite held a year after a death colloquially known as a rag-burning ceremony) held at Belyuen in 1948 when these older women were young adults, my age, Patsy's age, Linda's age.[2] The *kapug* had been held for Mabalan, Ester Djarem's deceased husband's first wife. Several *wangga* were sung during the *kapug; wangga* are a regional musical genre in which song and dance are accompanied by didjeridu and clapping sticks. We had heard that Mabalan's brother, Mosec Manpurr, could be heard on the tape singing a *wangga* referring to the Belyuen waterhole as a *durlg* (totemic Dreaming site). Why did these women and I care that Mosec might have received this type of song text from a *nyuidj* (an ancestral spirit) emerging from Belyuen *durlg?*

For events like the one in which we were engaged, Betty Bilawag would usually have been with us. Her absence was especially marked because Mosec Manpurr and his brother Ginger Moreen were Bilawag's first and second husbands. On this day she was too sick, suffering through the last stages of respiratory failure, confined to a portable electric respirator, slowly dying from the fluids daily dripping into her lungs related to (as spokespersons of tobacco companies like to say) but not proven to be caused by the cigarettes she still smokes, and certainly exacerbated by a lifetime spent by wood-burning fires. By the time I begin writing this chapter in 1998, she will have drowned in the viscous mucus invading her lungs and the secondary infections resulting from this condition. Her closest friend and cousin (or, at that time, colloquially, her "wife"), Maudie Bennett, the sister of her two late husbands, died from the same condition in 1990. As in other interiors of the first world, at Belyuen the national statistics of indigenous ill health are embodied in people, materialized corporeally. Poverty leaves its mark, mottling most people with the scars of endemic streptococcal sores and exhausting some people with diarrhea, diabetes, kidney failure, and other degenerative diseases that alter body chemistries and change mental faculties. Many of those people who survive bear the physical and psychic mourning scars of generations of dead and dying.

As the papers of Elkin and Simpson were kicked about by dry season winds, those of us sitting on the veranda heard the footsteps of Ester Djarem's older sister, Agnes Alanga, rustling the grass around the east side of the building. Agnes Alanga is dead, but her *nyuidj* (spirit, ghost) often visits the women's center when we go there to discuss "culture" and "traditions" or to hold women's ceremonies. She was the ceremonial leader of local women's ritual ("women's business," in the colloquial) before she died of kidney failure in 1994, a cause of death then all too common in the community. At Belyuen, as elsewhere in the Daly River coastal region, human bodies not only physically "absorb" and express their material conditions, they are also thought to be absorbed into the physical environment in the course of both everyday and ritual practices. The substances of human bodies—sweat, language, blood—are continually seeping into surrounding soils, waters, and air in the countless ritual and quotidian interactions that make up a person's life. In this extraordinarily literal way Agnes has become a part of the countryside, has been attached to this place and to those of us who survive her and are drawn to this place in part to be near her.

Agnes's specific identity will persist while those of us who knew her remain alive—the rustling we hear will bear the name of a person we knew; a proper noun (a rigid designator) will tether sounds to a specific face, to a set of memories, to marks she left in the landscape, to the things she used.[3] As we die this specificity will slowly dissipate, mediated by local speech practices such as the avoidance of the proper names of recently deceased persons. Over time, we will witness a reversal of how a name comes to represent, in the words of Charles Peirce, "pretty fairly what it would mean to an acquaintance of the man."[4] But the meaningfulness of the rustling will not vanish if people remain who, although knowing nothing of Agnes, know nevertheless "some *nyuidj* this place." Perhaps in the future people who hear a similar rustling of grass will attribute the sound to the *nyuidj* of a once-living woman, but will no longer be certain who this woman was. In other words, the rustle of grass will no longer indexically signal a particular person, though it might continue to signal a more generic relation—"my grandmother," "his ancestor," "her family." Possible future listeners may forget the humanness of Agnes altogether and instead attribute the sound to the nearby Belyuen *durlg,* suggesting that the Belyuen *durlg* sent a *nyuidj* here for some reason.

Similar processes of abstraction and rereferentialization have occurred elsewhere in the region. In the coastal country south of Belyuen, at a site called Yirrkunwana, an old woman *nyuidj* walks around the coastal mangrove and in the jungle with her two dogs—one brown, one black with a white nose (or so some people describe these dogs). People disagree about who she once was, if she was ever human, if Yirrkunwana is her name or the name of the site, and if she is part of the story for a dog Dreaming (*durlg*) track in the area. No matter the position they take on these issues, most Belyuen who discuss Yirrkunwana delicately qualify their remarks by mood, tense, or evidential markers: "werra" "yi" "before" "must be" "might be but I never been there."

In a like manner but a different situation, once every memory trace of Agnes's particularity might have vanished. Having been transformed into a *nyuidj,* Agnes might have been transformed into a *durlg* or *durlg*-related being; namely, an ancestral presence related to a Dreaming (totemic) site belonging to a particular group of persons in the logic of a clan.[5] Geographical space might have become inlain with the form of Agnes—her movement to and from a place. In losing her particular identity she might have become a type of *durlg*—*Alanga durlg*—structurally equivalent to Belyuen *durlg.*

These transformations of Agnes Alanga, or of Yirrkunwana, are not the result of faulty mental faculties or a dysfunctional culture. They are the result of local processes of semiosis; how sign-activity is locally understood and practiced and its effects on social life.[6] Of particular importance is the local avoidance of proper names and an injunction against using the name of the recently deceased, even their European names. Those who share a European name with a recently deceased person change it. Michael becomes Adam, only later to become Tony. Now, however, some archived signifying potential Alanga as "Agnes" the younger sister of "Chapata" and daughter of "Chunbuk" and "Moorambil," will persist unless every last copy of this page burn in a historically unimaginable conflagration. Until then this page will remain as an archived potentiality, dormant until someone finds and reads it years or decades from now. And, into the fire must go not only this book but also Colin Simpson's *Adam in Ochre,* which describes Agnes as bearing the Aboriginal name "Allunga" and as having "learned some hymns at the mission, where she is called Agnes."[7] And into the fire also must go Elkin's essay "Ngirawat," which describes "Alanga (Agnes) and Mada (Ruby)" Yarrowin as having a ritual relationship based on a shared name (a *ngirawat* relation); and into the fire must go any video and audio tape that Agnes's children and grandchildren might own of her *kapug.* And not only these audio and video tapes, but also the master tapes recorded by the ethnomusicologists Allan Marett and Linda Barwick and the linguist Lyz Ford and their memories and all the archived references they have produced of them.

We were not preparing for a book and recording barbecue, however. Quite the contrary; we gathered to mine the archive of memory held in this tape to bolster their territorial claims over the lands, islands, and waters surrounding the community. It is very uneven terrain. Let me begin with its most local contours. Off in the grass to the left of us lay the ashes of some nondescript half-burnt logs, the remainders of various women's ceremonies slowly seeping into the surrounding soil. Under them are the ashes of numerous other fires. The ground behind the adult education center slopes away to a creek. In Colin Simpson's popular travelogue *Adam in Ochre,* he describes this mythic landscape: "[it was] a creek with a very deep waterhole. Every Waugeit knew that in that waterhole Beluin [Belyuen] once lived, Beluin the Rainbow Snake."[8] Simpson's work was first published in 1951, the same year that the minister for the Territories, the Honorable Paul Hasluck, counseled the nation not only to tolerate but to take full "enjoyment" of the traditions of its indigenous "full-bloods."[9] In the same section of *Adam in Ochre,* titled "Mosek's People," Simpson described how the "Waugeit" attempted to drive the first white settler, Benjamin Cohen De Lissa, off the sacred Belyuen Rainbow waterhole and how De Lissa fired off flares to drive the "Waugite" off his sugarcane farm.[10] "Mosek" refers to Betty Bilawag's first husband, Mosec Manpurr.

A. P. Elkin, the second chair of anthropology in Australia who conducted fieldwork in the community, also mentioned the Rainbow Snake Dreaming as important to the Wagaitj—and Mosec as an important ceremonial leader—in his 1950 essay "Ngirawat, or the Sharing of Names in the Wagaitj Tribe, Northern Australia." Rather than refer to the location of the Belyuen Dreaming (or *durlg*), as Simpson did, Elkin refers to the role the Rainbow Snake played in annual local Inawana (Big Sunday) ceremonies. The Wagaitj held these Inawana ceremonies to " 'call up' Waran [another Dreaming site on the northwest coast] and all the *dorlks*" until the "Government told the old men not to hold the ceremony any more, because natives from other parts working in Darwin blamed this ceremony, performed by almost local natives, for any sickness or other ills which befell them."[11] These Big Sunday ceremonies were the same ones that Harney, Murray, and Turner helped the government suppress, as discussed at the end of chapter 3.[12]

"Waugeit" (now Wagaitj) is a term from the Batjemal language referring to the coast and to coastal people. Since the settlement of Darwin in 1869, it has been a common way of referring to the Aboriginal groups living along the coastline stretching from the Cox Peninsula—where Belyuen is located—to Cape Dombey. Elkin believed that "Wagaitj means beach people, and includes three, and possibly four, linguistic groups."[13] The four groups he mentions in his essays and field notes are the Kiyuk, Wadjigiyn, Amiyenggal, and

Marriamu. Most Aboriginal and non-Aboriginal persons would now supplement his coastal register with two other linguistic (or "new tribal") groups — Mendayenggal and Marritjeban. As for the peninsula on which Belyuen is located, Elkin described it as having been "formerly the country of the Laragia (Larrakia) tribe, which is now nearly extinct. Its survivors are coalescing with one of the Wagaitj groups, the Wadjigiyn."[14]

In modern kinship terminology, Wagaitj, Wadjigiyn, Kiyuk, and so forth are ways of referring to different kinds, levels, and amalgamations of regional descent structures. To what a "descent group" refers is a matter of some dispute within the anthropological community. In Australia, at the time of my fieldwork in 1996, this definition of descent had considerable play: according to Roger M. Keesing, descent is "a relationship defined by connection to an ancestor (or ancestress) through a culturally recognized sequence of parent-child links."[15] The relationship defined by these parent-child links is the presuppositional grounds for a number of other social relations — for example, property, affect, ritual, and economy.

Charles Peirce might consider the kinship diagram a nice example of extreme abduction. The referential truth of descent, and the elegance of its modeling, seems beyond the necessity of justification. Figure 9 and the others that follow are examples of descent forms, in these cases, patrilineal and cognatic forms of descent. These diagrams seem to rely on nothing more than two very simple and seemingly indisputable facts of human being — sex difference and generation (heterosexual reproduction). Of course, figure 9 itself has a history. In 1910, the British psychologist W. H. R. Rivers announced a major methodological breakthrough in the study of "savage" societies.[16] One of his students, Radcliffe-Brown, the first chair of anthropology in Australia who did fieldwork in the Daly River region, would argue that all social organization extended from the kernel of kinship, a father, mother, and their children. According to this perspective, all societies narrow or expand these two "social facts" — sex and generation — to create the various features of social rights, duties, and responsibilities that comprise the skeletal order and function of society. These social facts are often encrusted with linguistic and cultural material. In the instance of patrilineal descent (in figure 9), an Aboriginal group may "phrase" descent as determined by the passage of a *durlg* (or, extralocally, a totem, sacred site, or Dreaming) through the father line — or may say that a Dreaming is "picked up" from fathers or grandfathers, which is usually understood as saying the totem is passed down through the male line.[17]

The locality of this group, what makes it a *local* descent group, derives

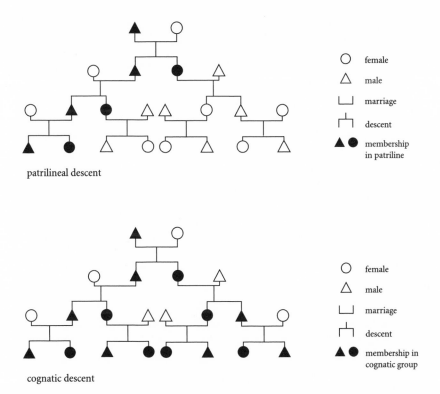

patrilineal descent

cognatic descent

FIGURE 9. Patrilineal and cognatic descent.

from the nature of certain types of *durlg* Dreamings — the fact that *durlg* are located in a specific place.[18] Belyuen, for instance, have *durlg* — dog, whale, devil, stingray — that connect them to various territories along the coast south of the Cox Peninsula. Various combinations of *durlg* groups also refer to language as shared among themselves. Wadgigiyn, Kiyuk, Emi, Mentha, Marriamu, and Marritjeban are terms referring to a collection of *durlg* groups sharing the materiality of language, which, like *durlg*, passes down or is picked up from the fathers (figure 10). The local descent group is thus a complex indexical symbol, anchoring people to places and to each other.

The social implication of this diagrammatic argument was clear to Claude Lévi-Strauss. The atom of kinship was not the father, mother, and children as Radcliffe-Brown had proposed, but those persons and the other father, the uncle who provided the means for exchange between two groups and thus for the emergence of culture qua culture (figure 11). The principles of affinity — generalized and restricted exchange — were added to sexual difference and

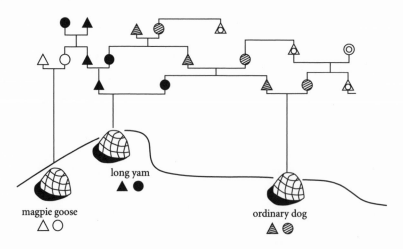

FIGURE 10. Patriclan and estate with symbols of marriage, consanguinity, and descent inverted.

generation as the necessary presuppositional grounds for a complex unfolding of human social organization and symbolization. Words, women, goods: these were possible only after the addition of the uncle.

All of the ideas above, of course, were at the time the subject of heated anthropological debate. Were Australian Aboriginal territorial groups based on principles of descent or affinity? Were all Australian Aboriginal territorial groups based on the estate model? Were Aboriginal men and women, according to L. R. Hiatt, "automata machines following tribal law in everything they do," or were they people with politics?[19] In either case, demonstrating the regular and rational family-based grounds of territoriality was critical to the rhetorical emergence of land rights in Australia. Specifiable indigenous people owned specifiable lands and had specifiable principles for the management of its resources and its title. This process of abstraction was the necessary condition of territorial recognition within the property regimes of the state.[20]

And yet the classical literature was also replete with references to indigenous forms of localization—a different question to the ahistorical framework of the "local." Reporting on Gidjingal territoriality in the mid-1960s, Hiatt noted that the Gidjingal and their neighbors sometimes abandoned their estates and became "permanently associated with a unit in another locality. . . . The descendents retained their group identity but displayed little interest in the land of their migrant fathers." These groups attached themselves to a

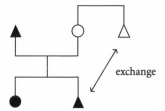

FIGURE 11. The atom of kinship.

local Dreaming site through the process of identification with it, and came to be considered from it in a "company relation" with the descent groups that predated them.[21] Over time the two descent groups came to share the same Dreaming. Elkin likewise reported changes of territorial association and identity in the Cox Peninsula region. In "The Complexity of Social Organisation in Arnhem Land," for instance, Elkin noted the then-remarkable anthropological fact that a high incidence of "meeting and mixing" among the Wagaitj resulted in the "fluidity of [land-owning] boundaries, and even changes of clan countries." Indeed, Elkin characterized the entire coastal region comprising the countries of the Wagaitj as socially dynamic and fluid rather than socially static, countering "the textbook description of local organisation."[22] Elkin did not explain the principles that determined how or why these changes of land-owning boundaries and clan territories occurred other than to observe the fact that an Aboriginal person could change "his local group or horde by residence or initiation or both." He did, however, provide a clue to the underlying processes through which residence and initiation became productive of territoriality in his discussion of the two major forms of totemism in the region, *durlg* and *maruy,* so-called cult totemism and conception totemism respectively.

What provided the mechanism of this social transduction? Why was it persuasive? Or, asking the same questions in a somewhat different way, how did local processes of abstraction and particularization intersect with these anthropological models? To address these questions, let me return to the veranda.

PRAGMATIC DESCENT

We had gathered on the veranda of the Belyuen women's center to listen to an event that occurred in 1948. Some of those recorded in "Death Rite for Mabalan" would be featured in other national broadcasts. Tom Barradjap would eventually become the senior songman and men's ceremonial leader for the region and, as such, be featured on a 1980 segment of the ABC television show "Nationwide Report," about the progress of the Kenbi Land Claim. The Kenbi Land Claim had national significance because of its proximity to the city of Darwin, the only major white settlement in the Northern Territory at the time (with a population then of approximately sixty thousand). The ABC television special shows Tom Barradjap seated on a coastal Dreaming site, Ngalwat, where Belyuen young men are taken as part of their initiation rites. He speaks a language the audience is not expected to understand. The reporter, Murray McLoughlin, translates for the show's imagined public: "This old man is speaking of the importance to Aboriginal people of the land now known as Cox Peninsula and of the importance of breeding places about here. He is mourning the destruction and desecration of the land and those places significant in his culture which occurred since white occupation of this Top End of Australia." Other Belyuen men and women are shown performing a *wangga,* and three are broadcast speaking to McLoughlin: Roy Yarrowin, Ruby's since deceased husband; John Singh; and Olga Singh. Three non-Aboriginal persons speak: Maria Brandl, the senior anthropologist for the aboriginal claimants at the time; Paul Everingham, then chief minister of the Northern Territory; and John Isaacs, the Labour opposition leader. (Figure 12 presents one of the standard representations of the regional landscape inlain with the kinship and marriage relations of some of these men and women and with some of their totemic, clan estate, and language affiliations.)

"Death Rite for Mabalan" was broadcast in 1948 on Australian national radio as part of "The Australian Walkabout Show." It was narrated by the same Colin Simpson who, three years later, included a modified version of the event in his *Adam in Ochre.* Allan Marett, the same ethnomusicologist who videotaped the *kapug* of Agnes Alanga Lippo (and whose fine research on *wangga* provides the basis of much of the discussion in this chapter[23]), found the recording at the Australian Institute of Aboriginal and Torres Strait Islander Studies in Canberra as he worked in the sound archives of Alice Moyle, another ethnomusicologist who worked among the Wagaitj in the 1960s. Moyle recorded several Belyuen performing *wangga* in other contexts, including Tom Barradjap and Billy Mundjimainmain, Marjorie Bilbil's father's brother. Marett informed the Northern Land Council and me of his discovery that the now-deceased Mosec Manpurr, Mabalan's elder brother and Bilawag's first husband, sings a Belyuen *wangga* at the very end of the broadcast "Death Rite for Mabalan." Why was this archival fact of interest? I begin to answer this question with another: What is *wangga?*

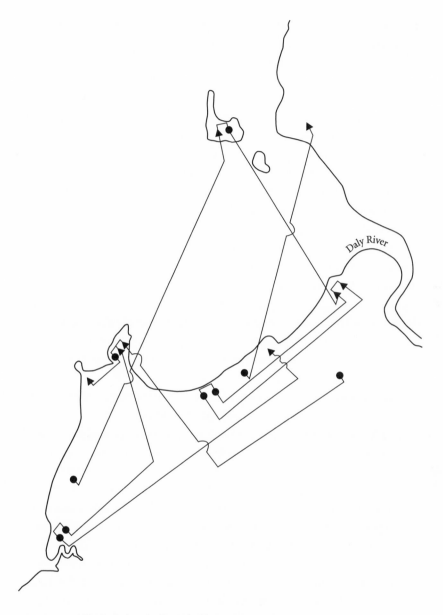

FIGURE 12. Affinal relations in the Daly River Region, 1850–1950.

As noted in general terms earlier, *wangga* refers to a regional musical genre in which song and dance are accompanied by didjeridu and clapping sticks. *Wangga* are public songs, openly sung in a variety of ritual and nonritual contexts. A songman composes a *wangga* text typically either out of material presented to him by a *nyuidj* while he is Dreaming or out of the ordinary events of daily life. *Nyuidj* who present songs to songmen may be a specific human ancestor known to the singer (often the songman's own teacher), or may be the humanlike manifestation of a nearby *durlg*. Elkin alluded to this latter form of text acquisition in his essay "Ngirawat." He observed that after his initiation "a young man is taken by his father to visit his *dorlk* center and is told the myth connected with it. Perhaps he too will dream a song about it." [24] Songmen also inherit specific song texts and inherit or are given the right by their human relations to compose songs for an area. [25]

Although men publicly authorize other men to sing their song texts and to compose and sing songs for specific territories, *durlg*-associated *nyuidj* rather than humans act as the ultimate authorizing agent of song composition. In the case of *nyuidj*-authorized *wangga,* the *nyuidj* not only signals the right of the composer to compose songs about a country but also signals the ancestral composition of that country. In other words, the appearance of a *nyuidj* in a place "says" something about the *durlg* ontology of the place by acting as an indexical hinge between human and *durlg* ontological realms. I use the indefinite modifier "something" purposely because although the indexical hinge between human and *durlg* domains is present in the act of *wangga* composition and song, the meaning of this hinge necessitates higher-order arguments of a type I discuss below.

For those steeped in a Western narrative tradition, analyzing *wangga* may disappoint them, may seem to them a meager, minor literature. *Wangga* may even exasperate them, because the songs may seem to be minor literatures needlessly embedded in complex syntactic structures and impenetrable linguistic registers. [26] When viewed from the perspective of semantic and narrative sense and meaning, *wangga* threaten to reward laborious analytic effort with little return. Not much seems to be there. *Wangga* usually consist of only a few short sentences, whose morphological structure has been "tangled-up" or "twisted" in Belyuen terms. In linguistic terms, normative syntactic structures have been purposively violated in order to force listeners to reconstitute the message by rearranging morphemic units if they want to make sense of the text.

But perhaps the negative evaluation of the song genre results from approaching *wangga* from a narrative and semantic perspective. As much as *wangga* are sense oriented, they are technically and precisely non-sense oriented. By non-sense I refer merely to how Belyuen understand the performative, indexical, function of *wangga*. The linguistic code of *wangga* is not simply, or perhaps not even primarily, a vehicle for expressing sense-meaning; it does not simply or primarily convey a narrative about a place. Rather in the act of composition and singing, *wangga* construct an architectural space of sorts among the ontological realms of singer (and his extendable kin), the territory commonly associated with the language of the song, and the territory to which the song refers. It entails a space in the act of composition and performance. From one perspective, the spatial form (social, geographical) that every *wangga* lays out is neutral in relation to its sense and social meaning. This space simply becomes present in the act of singing. But in being present, this laid-out non-sense space can be (note: may not be) drawn into social work by social agents who, often unknowingly, regiment these actualities into higher-order social meanings and who then make broader arguments about the social consequences of these meanings—the how, who, when, and where of *proper* action.

All this becomes clearer when we look at an actual *wangga* composed for the region and, more specifically, at the semantic and pragmatic features that structure receptions of it. Along with clarifying local semiotic practices, looking at an actual text begins to answer the question of why these women and I cared that Mosec might have sung this type of song about Belyuen. Let us take as example a *wangga* that Billy Mundjimainmain sang about the island Duwun, which is located off the Cox Peninsula and within the area under claim. The first six "lines" of the Duwun song are in *nyuidj mal* (spirit language). The first two lines of the untangled Duwun song are:

dagan mele dagaldja
dagan mele mele

dagan brother dagaldja
dagan brother brother

"*Dagan mele dagaldja*": most Belyuen say that *nyuidj* language is impenetrable, untranslatable. Rather than a vehicle for semantic meaning, *nyuidj mal* indexes a quality of *djewalabag*—the cleverness of men, and women, who can understand and speak these words. Evidential and ontological markers index the origin and authorizing agency of the song—this song came from *nyuidjalag,* a quasiparallel ontic realm that *djewalabag,* "clever persons," access through dream and song, as did Billy Mundjimainmain, and as might have Mosec, who the 1948 radio broadcast stated "is also a *djewalag.*"[27] Rather than diminishing the authority of the *nyuidj* or singer, the semantic opacity of *nyuidj* language intensifies it, signaling the ontic reality of *nguidjalag* while maintaining its epistemological impenetrability to all but those who have the nature of *djewalabag.*

The indeterminate content of the *nyuidj* message is complemented by the indeterminate status of the vocalization itself. Is "*dagan mele dagaladja*" an instance of reported speech (*game,* "he said" nonfuture)? Are we who sit and listen to taped recordings of this song hearing about an event or hearing the event itself — are we hearing Billy Mundjimainmain engaging in an instance of (sung) reported speech or are we hearing the *nyuidj* singing, we in the dream with the songman hearing what he heard?[28] The tense of *game,* nonfuture, influences the undecidability. The answers to these questions cannot be secured or settled once and for all, especially when *wangga* are performed within a locally determined context in which norms against direct interrogatives are in place (say, against asking, "what that meaning?"). Two different problems present themselves. First is the problem of interpretation. What the songman sings and what he intends to convey are understood to be potentially two very different things. The best songmen are understood to encode a secret, or several secret, levels to their song text. Second is the problem of performance and performativity. Even if a songman is presumed to be the medium of a *nyuidj,* in every specific instance someone could claim that he failed to achieve this role. In any case, it is not the definitive answers to the above questions per se that is important here, nor even the possibility of saturated context, but rather that these are conditions of and for argument: the possibilities that the intersections of these two ontological orders, human and *nyuidj,* provide for the making of human sociality, corporeality, and meaning. To understand these possibilities we need to return to the poetics and grammar of *nyuidjalag.*

While most Belyuen and their regional neighbors say that *nyuidj* language is semantically impenetrable, embedded in this language are local human linguistic nominals and particles, most typically kinship terms and phatic and emotive particles. For instance, the first two lines of the Duwun song contain a possible kin address, *mele* (brother), which then figures a set of social relations between the *nyuidj* and the singer and, via the songman, between the *nyuidj* and listeners. Kinship literally extends out from the initial address into the audience of listeners and potential listeners. Extending outward with these kinship relations are other social identities — linguistic, estate, clan affiliations, ceremonial. An entwining of these multiple identities ensues, creating "tracks" or "footsteps" that can be followed and infused with other social meanings, obligations, and identities (see figure 13).

Even when a *wangga* text does not present an explicit kinship relation between singer and *nyuidj,* the understood address of the *nyuidj* to the songman and the formal arrangement of other semantic orders metapragmatically constructs a formally meaningless but coherent and cohering apparatus into which meaningful arguments can be inlaid and, more abstractly, a feeling of the concrete integrity of an alternate worldly authority produced. We have already seen how the linguistic code of the *wangga* structures spatial and social relations. Other linguistic functions build into the *wangga* other semiotic orders into which meaning is laminated. For instance, in the next four lines of the Duwun song the poetic function of the particles *karra* and *yagarra* cohere and regiment the *nyuidj* utterance into segmentable units (*-arra*), while maintaining listeners' attention (the phatic particle "Hey!"), and orienting their emotional states (the emotive lamentative particle "Oh no!"). In other words, the poetics of particles orders the text into higher order segments and thus a *nyuidj* syntax as such.[29]

karra, nyele wewe
yagarra, nyele wewe
karra, nyele wewe
yagarra, nyele wewe

Hey! nyele wewe
Oh no! nyele wewe
Hey! nyele wewe
Oh no! nyele wewe

This pseudosyntax makes the text feel coherent even though sense meaning cannot be extracted from it, and it makes it seem durable and detachable from its local context even though its coherence depends on that local context. The *wangga* can be experienced as something from somewhere nonhuman — if, of course, the listener can interpret the various indexical orders built into its structure. Meanwhile, the meaning of *nyele wewe* remains a placeholder, inciting speculation and motivating contextualized and contextualizing interpretations. For instance, when discussing this text, women and men have asked themselves: What might the *nyuidj* have meant? Why did it appear at

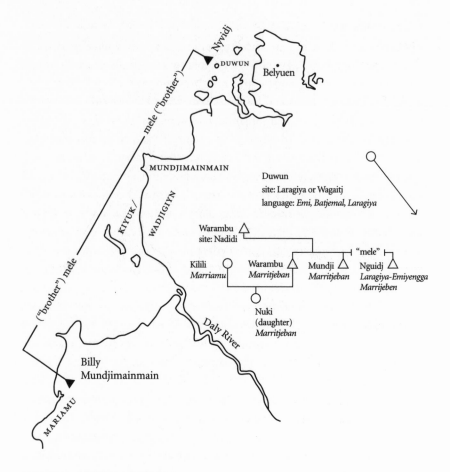

FIGURE 13. Ghostly territorializations.

Duwun? Why did it appear at that moment? To Billy Mundjimainmain? As I argued above, these pragmatic features of the text provide the grounds on which meaningful and persuasive arguments can be made about the social relationship between a social group and a place, and about the "true" substance of a person and, by extension, her kin. In other words, these songs are simultaneously referential, argumentative, and performative acts. But, if this is so, the felicity of these text acts depends only in part on local understandings of evidence and judgment — their institutions, scenarios, and sceneries. It also depends on distally produced and institutionally mediated demands for how evidence and judgment should appear, demands that are now part and parcel of local processes of localization. That is, state laws like the Aboriginal Land Rights (Northern Territory) Act are one of the contexts entailing the ways these texts are excavated. I will come back to this point in more detail later, but here let me remind readers of the conversations found at the end of chapter 1 in which the question of what counted as a real kinship relation in the context of land claim hearings threatened to redefine, narrow, and block processes of local social negotiations.

The propositional and performative potential of *wangga* is clear in the final four lines of the Duwun song when for the first time a human language, Emiyenggal, is used exclusively. This code switch is accompanied by a shift in person, from first to third person, and with this shift a movement from a poetic reliance on *nyuidj mal* to evidential markers (*-yi*). That is, the poetic structure of the Duwun song emerges out of the evidential particles of the now foregrounded, linguistically demarcated composer. Through these evidential markers, Billy Mundjimainmain makes a specific claim about the authenticity of the reported event, his right to sing about the event and the place where it occurred, and the truth value of the authorizing *nyuidj:* Listen! It happened. I was there. *Nyuidj* was over there. You just heard im.

karra game yi
karra duwun ngana yi
gidji dhatdhat mandha ya
karra game yi

Hey! he sang [it happened]
Hey! Duwun I went [it happened]
crawl sit a song away there
Hey! he sang [it happened]

The geographical referent, Duwun, appears only in this final segment of the *wangga,* and with it appears a potential ordering and anchoring of specific persons in specific mythic and geographical spaces. Before I briefly suggest how this might be, I should note that the identity and status of geographical referents can be no better secured from culturally mediated processes of re-memorialization and rethematization than the identity and status of *nyuidj* events — such as was the case for Agnes Alanga discussed above. Mundjimain-main, for instance, simultaneously refers to a person, Billy Mundjimainmain, and to a place, Mundjimainmain. So does Duwun. Therefore, like personal references to Agnes Alanga Lippo ("*Alanga there*") might slowly be trans-formed into geographic referents ("that place Alanga is there"), so might those to Mundjimainmain. And vice versa. Some Larrakia say Duwun refers to a female ancestor of theirs and link themselves to Duwun the place through the common name. Other Aboriginal persons say Duwun is "just a place." In other cases, a personal name derived from a site name has been lifted up from that geographical referent and moved to another geographical place through the movement of the person who was given that name. In any case, the persua-siveness of any particular claim emerges from the multiple "tracks" the person making the claim can muster — residential, linguistic, affective, ceremonial, and so forth.

This is the invaginatory nature of arguments — every claim about the refer-ent of a proper name must be anchored in some evidentially accepted archive of memory, practice, and action and must be attached, if ever so delicately, to whatever new texts and contexts exist at the time the argument is being made. And every effective argument becomes the ground condition for new argu-ments. Even if people all agree that a *nyuidj* did give this *wangga* to the person Billy Mundjimainmain at the place Duwun, this agreement only stands as the grounds for an infinite series of questions and arguments: Why did a *nyuidj* give Billy Mundjimainmain a song about this place in this language? What does it indicate about the two sites, Mundjimainmain and Duwun, about the countries associated through Mundjimainmain the person, his estate, the code of the song, and Marritjeban and Emiyenggal lands and peoples? Who has rights to this song and, thus, responsibilities for this place? Not that the best argument always prevails, or even usually prevails; sometimes the most persistent and consistent arguments figure the scene.

This said, the geographical referent "Duwun" reveals and builds into the Duwun *wangga* a still more elaborate scaffold on which arguments about the spiritual status of this place and this person are built, arguments such as the country in which Duwun is found "speaks" Emi; the country has absorbed Emi people, or Mundjimainmain was secretly Larrakia; the entire territory stretching from Nadidi to Duwun is somehow related, is somehow Wagaitj. Particular persons like Marjorie Bilbil can use the geographical and social architecture of this *wangga* to move backward in time and space, tracing her relationship to Duwun-the-place through her father's brother's relationship to this *nyuidj*, reconstituting the substantial nature of her body in the process. Rather than through heterosexual reproduction in the first or even last instance, corporeality and territoriality is (re)produced through the intercourse of the living and the dead, the textual and corporeal. If, that is, people remain who know how to read the semantic and pragmatic codes embedded in songs like Duwun, and if these cultural practices of interpretation are themselves embedded in contexts that afford them performative force. In other words, although these semiotic practices may be rooted in local understandings of the corporeal exchanges between human and *durlg* ontologies, and although they may provide a basis for the production and reproduction of human lineages, families, and bodies, their social felicity now depends as much on the archive of the nation, legal precedent, public record, and state law as on the archive of local ritual and face-to-face persuasion and incitement.

With this in mind let me return once again to the question I raised above. Why did these women and I care that Mosec might have received this type of song text from a *nyuidj* emerging from Belyuen *durlg*? And, as important, what transformed our interest into an activity, laborious at times? What prompted us to abandon whatever other pressing or passing concerns cluttered our lives, to meet under this particular veranda, and to concentrate on translating *wangga* songs from an old, scratchy tape?

LEGAL DISSENT

"Aboriginal" means a person who is a member of the Aboriginal race of Australia.

"Aboriginal tradition" means the body of traditions, observances, customs, and beliefs of Aboriginals or of a community or group of Aboriginals, and includes those traditions, observances, customs and beliefs as applied in relation to particular persons, sites, areas of land, things or relationships.

"traditional Aboriginal owners", in relation to land, means a local descent group of Aboriginals who:

> (a) have common spiritual affiliations to a site on the land, being af-
> filiations that place the group under a primary spiritual responsibility for
> that site and for the land; and
>
> (b) are entitled by Aboriginal tradition to forage as of right over that
> land.[30]

There seems to be a very obvious answer to the questions posed at the end
of the last section — the ethnomusicologist Allan Marett thought that a translated version of the Belyuen *wangga* might provide the Belyuen useful evidence to support their land claim. The Belyuen had recently decided to put
themselves forward as the nonexclusive "traditional Aboriginal owners" of the
land surrounding the community under the Aboriginal Land Rights (Northern Territory) Act, 1976 (hereafter LRA).[31] In a very simple sense this is why
the women and I had gathered: to be recognized as the "traditional Aboriginal
owners" (a term of statutory law) for the land under claim, the Belyuen and
their lawyers and anthropologists needed to convince a land commissioner
that they satisfied the specific requirements of the LRA; namely, that they were
a "local descent group" who have "common spiritual affiliations" to a site on
the land that place them under "primary spiritual responsibility for the site"
and for the land.[32] The LRA not only enacted a textual limit to the form of
an argument, the legislation also established a number of regional land councils charged with administering Aboriginal land claims. In 1995 I was asked to
act as senior anthropologist for the Belyuen by the Northern Land Council,
having worked with the community since 1984.[33] It was my job to demonstrate the anthropological basis for this thing called a "local descent group."
What, then, is the meaning of the juridical concept of local descent group?

At the time the Kenbi Land Claim was first submitted in 1979, three land
claims had been heard under the auspices of the LRA. In his very first land
claim report, the first land commissioner, Mr. Toohey, accepted the argument by W. E. H. Stanner that all traditional Aboriginal societies reckoned
the descent of territorial rights through the father and father's father (patrilineality), and that an Aboriginal person could belong in a full sense to only one
local descent group and thus to only one territory. For Stanner the patrilineal
"totem" (*durlg*) acted both as a symbol (or emblem) of clan solidarity and as
an index of the proper territorial location of a social group. As it descended
from father to children, the totem functioned as an indexical hinge between
human group and the place where the totem was located. Stanner understood
the transmission of the totem to be a fairly straightforward heterosexually

mediated process by which the sign passed from father to children (with adoption understood as analogous to heterosexual reproduction). In short, Toohey recognized as a matter of legal fact a (disputed) anthropological model of indigenous land ownership—the patrilineal clan-estate group.

In so accepting this academically mediated model of indigenous social organization, Toohey instantaneously cast all other means by which "traditional Aborigines associate identifiable groups of people with particular 'countries' " as distortions of or supplements to the heterosexual machinery of human descent.[34] Ties to country based on corporeal exchanges discussed above and in earlier chapters—quotidian experiences of living in and moving through space and nonquotidian events of conception, ritual, death—were excluded as the legitimate major means by which local descent groups could be formed, or, if formed, found to be legally felicitous territorial groups. The spiritual and material relationship that Aboriginal men and women had to land, to the dead, and to the unborn was reduced *in the last instance* to the heterosexual reproduction of blood, *symbolically* narrowed and demarcated by the patrilineal totem. But this anthropological model also provided the persuasive means to sway a court and public to recognize indigenous land rights. From 1976 to the time of this writing, forty percent of land in the Northern Territory has been granted to indigenous groups under the auspices of the LRA.[35]

Prior to the 1989 Kenbi hearing a number of land commissioners had recognized a restricted form of "spiritual descent" as satisfying the LRA requirement that claimants be a local descent group.[36] In the Nicholson River Land Claim report (1985), for example, Justice Kearney stated that " 'descent' is not limited to biological descent; it means socially recognised descent."[37] Kearney was satisfied that "descent from a common mythic ancestor is a principle of descent deemed relevant by the claimants and sufficient with their other ties to constitute" a finding of traditional Aboriginal ownership.[38] However, in contrast to the Belyuen case, the majority of the claimants in the Nicholson River claim were members of human descent groups (patrilineages or matrifiliates to a patrilineage). Only two claimants, Ned Dambambat and Brady Bates, were said and found to be claimants based on moiety classification, ritual responsibility, and, critically, descent "from the same mythic ancestors as the other members of these groups."[39] That is, spiritual descent supplemented human descent as the primary mechanism of group construction— it did not determine it.

The land commissioner who followed Kearney, Michael Maurice, similarly accepted the concept of spiritual descent as a supplemental mechanism of inclusion to the major human descent group.[40] However, in the Ti Tree report (1987) Maurice refuses to accept spiritual descent—the "assertion that the claimants gain membership into the local descent group through descent from Altyerrenge (Dreaming) ancestors"—as the primary principle on which the local descent group was formed.[41] In the Ti Tree claim, not only were the descent lines by which claimants were said to gain rights to country expanded by "an additional qualification for membership of the local descent group: 'spiritual descent', was asserted and claimed to be of more importance than any of the four genealogical links."[42] In other words "spiritual descent was set apart from the descent from human ancestors . . . and was given a priority in defining the land of the traditional owners."[43] For Maurice this belief was simply inconceivable.

Although having restricted "descent" to include only heterosexual reproduction (and its symbolic equivalent, adoption), since 1979 land commissioners have moved significantly away from viewing the "local descent group" as a strict anthropological concept to viewing it as an ordinary concept and phrase.[44] Toohey himself would reverse paths in his 1981 Finniss River report, stating that the land commissioner should base his understanding of recruitment into a local descent group "on a principle of descent deemed relevant by the claimants" not on anthropological theory or debate. Land Commissioner Michael Maurice also argued that legal judgment should be oriented to local beliefs when he stated in his 1985 Timber Creek report: "It is [a] religious bond with the world . . . that the Parliament has endeavored to recognize by its definition of traditional Aboriginal owner with its three elements: family ties to land; religious ties; and economic rights, i.e., to forage."[45] The most generous reading of this legal genealogy would understand these land commissioners to be attempting to liberate indigenous practices of local descent from the vice grip of anthropological theory. And yet the commonsense family of land claim legislation remains the classical lineage model developed and refined during the heyday of British structural functionalism. This lineage model has not been displaced but merely expanded to include a more diverse set of filial principles—matrilineality, ambilineality, and cognation.[46]

But even these expansions had yet to occur in 1979. Not surprisingly, then, the 1979 Kenbi claim book stated that the traditional Aboriginal owners of the Cox Peninsula and Islands were the seven surviving members of a small patrilineal clan group, the Danggalaba. *Danggalaba* is a Larrakia term in most accounts used to refer to a crocodile Dreaming (*durlg*) on the northwest coast of the Cox Peninsula. The Belyuen refer to this same durlg as *Kenbi*. According to the authors of the Kenbi land claim book (1979); before European settlement, the territory, or "estate," of the Larrakia-speaking Danggalaba clan may well have included only a small northwest section of the peninsula, a claim later disputed by a number of Larrakia claimants. As surrounding patrilineal estate groups died out, were killed, or moved away from the area as a result of the settlement of Darwin, their estates were gradually absorbed by the Danggalaba. At the same time that the Danggalaba clan was slowly absorbing abandoned Larrakia estates, various Wagaitj clans were moving up from their southern estates onto the increasingly depopulated Cox Peninsula to avoid settler violence in their southern countries and to take advantage of the white settlement of Darwin. As did Elkin, the authors of the 1979 Kenbi claim book represented the Danggalaba and Wagaitj as slowly coalescing—marked by the authors' decision to title the claim book *The Kenbi Land Claim* rather than *The Danggalaba Land Claim*. Like all good legal narratives the Kenbi claim book did not overly complicate the case it advanced. The authors make no mention of any of a number of historical records referring to the Cox Peninsula and surrounding islands as Wagaitj country.

Even though they deleted these countermappings, the authors of the Kenbi claim book did something remarkable for the time. They suggested not only that the land commissioner expand the basis of land ownership to include one-step matrifiliates (rights to a person's mother's country, though not to a person's mother's mother's country) of the Danggalaba clan, but also, and more radically, that he recognize the Wagaitj people living at Belyuen (Delissaville) as belonging to and owners of the country under claim on the basis of what they considered to be a wholly different model of corporeality and sociality than that of kinship and descent. The authors observed that it was evident "that people associated with the claim recognized more generalized connections to country than those of patrifiliation."[47] They emphasized the rights and obligations the Belyuen Wagaitj had accrued to claim lands on the basis of their historical, ceremonial, and birth relations to the country; that is, forms of attachment altogether outside a lineage-based model of descent. Invoking Stanner, the authors argued that in the extreme conditions of colonial depopulation "Aboriginal life . . . crossed a threshold . . . [where] the regime was so harsh that estate-range distinctions were near or at a vanishing point."[48] What replaced the estate-range was a territoriality based on ceremonial, birth, death, and name ties to the land.

In so arguing for the expansion of the basis of land ownership from heterosexual reproduction to other forms of corporeal intercourse between human and *durlg* ontological orders, the authors of the Kenbi Land Claim provided an anthropological foundation to the public statements of the Wagaitj. On 12 September 1973, Ginger Moreen, Tom Barradjap (Mosec's younger brother), and Rusty Moreen (Agnes Lippo's older brother), chaired a meeting with Justice Woodward, who was investigating if and how federal legislation should be drafted to recognize the land rights of Northern Territory indigenous groups. In this meeting senior men are recorded telling Woodward that it was "alright" for the Wagaitj and Larrakia to own this peninsula together, and, moreover, that the peninsula should be part of a larger land grant including their southern coastal territories.[49]

Thus it was relatively unsurprising at the time that on 29 July 1975 and 17 December 1975 the Larrakia and Wagaitj Belyuen proposed that two claims be lodged over the peninsula, one of which covered the far northern section where several important Larrakia *durlg* were said to be located. Imabulg, the father of Olga Singh and the senior resident Danggalaba man, was named trustee. Another claim would be lodged over the rest of the peninsula and held in trusteeship by the "Delissaville Council."[50] At this point in time, local sentiment seemed explicitly opposed to territorial claims based on Western models of human descent: "At a meeting it was said that singling people out according to their father and mother divides people. Where land is concerned they would prefer as a community to state, with evidence, their relationship to the claim area and their interests in it."[51]

These proposals were written, however, during the initial drafts of the LRA when it appeared that the federal legislation would provide multiple bases for lodging an indigenous claim. In its final form, however, the LRA stipulated that to be found to be a "traditional Aboriginal owner" a person must be a member of a "local descent group."[52] It was in this legislative context that the authors of the Kenbi claim put forward the smaller Danggalaba group as the "traditional Aboriginal owners" of the claim area.

Several legal challenges postponed the hearing of the Kenbi Land Claim until 1989. Most of the initial indigenous claimants had died by then (and certainly by 1995 when it was reheard) — ten years is a fifth of the average lifespan of Aboriginal men and women. This issue presented a grim vital statistic with political significance — opponents of the claim could count on the debilitating physical and mental health effects of poverty on the claimants. By the time the Kenbi claim was finally heard for the first time, three of the seven members of

the Danggalaba patriclan had died, as had numerous other key Wagaitj informants. So many Wagaitj and Larrakia men and women had passed away that
the senior anthropologist at the time, Michael Walsh, compiled a list of dead
he lodged into the legal record as "Kenbi Necrology." Of the four survivors of
the Danggalaba patriclan, a senior man had suffered an incapacitating stroke
while dancing *wangga* for a young men's initiation ritual at Belyuen; a senior
woman who lived in Darwin had publicly ceded her rights to the Belyuen; a
junior woman had died; another junior woman expressed no interest in the
land claim; and another junior woman knew little about the country, although
she expressed a desire to learn.

If historical time had reduced the Danggalaba patriclan, political time had
increased the resolve of urban-based Larrakia women and men to consolidate
an identity-based political and social program. Having suffered through the
long history of state welfare practices (many urban-based Larrakia or their
parents were part of the Stolen Generation; placed in foster homes because
of their biracial heritage) Larrakia men and women living outside the claim
area took statements such as Elkin's that the "Larrakia tribe" was "now nearly
extinct" not only to be wrong, but to be a dangerous conflation of racial and
cultural being and identity. In 1983 the Darwin-based Larrakia Association
was founded and, around the same time, a "group of urban Larrakia wrote
to the NLC [Northern Land Council] seeking to be added to the list of claimants."[53]

The LRA, however, demanded more than a simple list of claimants; it
required that a specific social configuration be produced—a local descent
group. Agreeing to represent the larger Larrakia group, the Northern Land
Council abandoned the Danggalaba patriclan as the claimant group in 1989
and, instead, advanced a much larger descent group, the "Larrakia language
group." The Larrakia language group was said to be composed of multiple lineages—the families of anyone who identified as Larrakia, could demonstrate
he or she had a Larrakia ancestor, and wished to be a part of the claim.

In order to be legally recognized as a traditional Aboriginal owner, however, it is not sufficient just to be found to be a member of a local descent
group; claimants must also demonstrate "common spiritual affiliations" to a
site on the land that place them under "primary spiritual responsibility for
the site" and for the land. At the time of the hearing only a handful of Larrakia
lived on the peninsula. The Belyuen Wagaitj were the ceremonial leaders for
the country and were considered most knowledgeable about the land's spiri-

tual and material features. Because few people within this larger Larrakia group knew the cultural and economic contours of the land under claim—an unknown number had never visited the area before the claim commenced—lawyers acting on behalf of the Darwin-based Larrakia and the Belyuen decided that the Belyuen Wagaitj would lead the evidence as "custodians" of the land and its spiritual heritage for the Larrakia.

In 1989 I was conducting my dissertation field research and helping with the running of the claim. By 1998 I was testifying in court about my recollection of why, in the middle of the 1989 hearing, the Belyuen were put forward as traditional Aboriginal owners in their own right and, when put forward, why they were presented as three Wagaitj "boxed-up language groups" (the Kiyuk-Wadjigiyn, the Emi-Mentha, the Marriamu-Marritjeban) rather than as a single Belyuen local descent group, the way they had been presented in the 1995 hearing.

> PROF. POVINELLI: No, it was probably not correct to call it a Marriamu/ Marritjabin [Marritjeban] language group because, in fact, it's only a number of what I would call patrilineal fragments of all patri-clans and certainly not the entire Marriamu/Marritjabin [Marritjeban] language group. There are a number of lineages that didn't appear then—no, didn't appear then and don't appear now [as part of the claimant group].
>
> MR. KEELY: Why was it characterised in that three double-named group way in 1989. Why was it advanced and packaged in that manner?
>
> PROF. POVINELLI: It was decided, in the middle of the claim, that these new groups would be—that the Belyuen would be advanced, or the Wagaitj—I think there are various ways in which they were described—would be advanced as a claimant group and then the question was how they should be advanced, what model of descent.
>
> What we were going to say was that the local descent group of the people then—you know, and again I'm using language that people used then and that I would not use—of the people who so clearly demonstrated common spiritual affiliations and primary spiritual responsibility for the place, for the area under claim.
>
> I said, "Well, they say they're all joined up," but I didn't have the time, nor was my research at the time, focused on teasing out that, what I would now call a cognatic descent group. So rightfully, I think, in some ways we had a day to put this together—
>
> MR. KEELY: A single day?

PROF. POVINELLI: Maybe two. I mean, it was really quite short. I forget. I mean, I actually forget the details how long it was, but it was—I think it [was] just [two days].[54]

When the 1989 hearing was over, the fourth land commissioner, Justice Olney, found that no traditional Aboriginal owners existed for the land under claim. Based on his reading of the juridical, legislative, and anthropological archive, Olney argued that Stanner's earlier model of strict patrilineal descent was the correct model of traditional descent. According to Olney no one satisfied the requirements of the LRA: the Larrakia language group was an infelicitous form of descent; the Danggalaba patriclan had only one member who demonstrated primary spiritual responsibility for the land (and one person did not make a "group"); and the Belyuen expressed "very little enthusiasm" and "generally lacked conviction" about their status as claimants.[55] In relation to the Wagaitj claim, he and others were bothered by two facts; first, "the various [Wagaitj] family groups who are put forward in this claim have common spiritual affiliations with sites elsewhere than on or near the claim area and in some cases continue to actively maintain those links by visiting their countries."[57] More troubling to some was the fact that Belyuen seemed to base territoriality to southern countries on principles different from those on which they based their ties to the peninsula.[58] Second, the Wagaitj resisted using the phrase "traditional Aboriginal owners" to refer to their relationship to the land under claim. What had happened between the early 1970s and the late 1980s such that the Belyuen Wagaitj could be described as expressing "very little enthusiasm" and "generally lack[ing] conviction" about their status as claimants?

I had five years to mull over this question before the Kenbi Land Claim was scheduled to be reheard in 1995. In the interim, the Supreme Court overruled the grounds of Olney's decision, referring to the mandate that the land commissioner base his findings of local descent on principles deemed relevant to the claimants.[56] In 1995, an even larger number of Larrakia were once again forwarded as the traditional Aboriginal owners. The criteria for membership remained similar to that in 1989, but the anthropological model of descent changed. The Larrakia were now said to be a cognatically defined "new tribe" rather than a "language group." The practice of the hearing also changed. In the first hearing, the Belyuen were afforded a preeminent status as those who were the knowledgeable people about the land and who held ceremonial knowledge for the claim lands. During the second 1995 hearing, lawyers representing most Larrakia believed that members of their claimant group would have to prove their own independent knowledge about the claim lands to be recognized as "traditional Aboriginal owners." Once again, but this time in the middle of the 1996 claim, the Belyuen asked their legal counsel to advance them as the nonexclusive "traditional Aboriginal owners" for the Cox Peninsula and surrounding islands. This time, however, they insisted they be presented as "Belyuen, all same, together."

When the Kenbi claim was reheard in 1995–96, yet another land commissioner, Justice Gray, not only was faced with deciding what were the recruitment principles deemed relevant by the claimants (what constituted a "local descent group" locally) but he also had to contend with competing, often hostile, claims by groups with significantly different cultural knowledges and sociological practices.[60] The Belyuen claim angered many Larrakia. They believed the Belyuen were trying to steal their country, a country theirs by a Dreamtime mandate, or as some put it, a "blood-right" whereby blood descent from a Larrakia ancestor gave them ownership rights to Larrakia land irrespective of the density of economic or ceremonial practices in relationship to it. The Larrakia claim angered some Belyuen who believed many of the "town Larrakia" to be too genealogically and socially removed from the country and its "Aboriginal culture" to be "for it" in a way superior to themselves.

By the time new lawyers arrived in 1995 to discuss the rehearing of the claim with Belyuen, most people sitting in the meeting hall had heard all they had to say before, had watched history unfold, and had grown up or old with the Kenbi claim. The problems these lawyers outlined had been outlined by other lawyers when the claim was first run and rejected in 1989–90, and, before that, when the claim was first being prepared in 1974. So many lawyers, so many anthropologists, so many research consultants had reviewed these problems that the Belyuen and I sometimes passed the time in the oppressive heat remembering all their names and telling stories about their personal passions, sexual predilections, legal styles, fashion, and eating habits: "Beth tell the time when . . ." "Wulgamen [old lady] Nuki tell the time when. . . ." We reviewed who among the Belyuen had talked in the last hearing or had gone on the endless proofing sessions, who had panicked before the "hard look" of the white lawyers and land commissioner, who had stumbled with the elaborate tape-recording apparatus, pinning the microphone upside down or thinking that it amplified rather than simply recorded and so mumbled inaudibly. We talked about people who had been crippled by shame and fear because of their lack of knowledge, their poverty, their nonstandard English. We noted who had died fighting for this land, who had given up, who was still going. Who the Belyuen were as a community and as a set of individuals was now to some significant degree a fold of the practices, identifications, and discourses of the Kenbi claim.[61]

CONSPIRACY THEORIES

I brought with me to our meeting at the women's center not only the various archival materials mentioned above but also a copy of the genealogies I had made based on senior Belyuen women and men's repeated urging that I line up the families from Marriamu side to Kiyuk side, coast way in order to demonstrate how they had become one family, all Belyuen. If the social history of the Belyuen is examined from the vantage point of marriage alliances between *durlg* groups, a relatively delimited "family" does emerge from the multiple and multiply determined histories of sexual reproduction. This history supports Belyuen description of themselves as "one family" and illuminates why the men who sat with Woodward wished to lodge one large claim over the coastal lands stretching from the Cox Peninsula to Cape Dombey. Based on what the men and women I have worked with remember, between 1850 and 1950 marriage consolidated ("joined up") proximate estates within a linguistically defined territory, followed by proximate language territories, then, through the marriages of Betty Bilawag and Mosec Manpurr, the sisters Agnes Alanga and Ester Djarim and the brothers Tom Lippo and Tom Barradjap, and Maudie Bennett to Tom Imabulg, the two ends and middles of this coastal landscape. Figure 14 presents a sketch model of this process.

It is a mistake, however, to view the figure as regimented by heterosexuality or *that which the diagram diagrams* to be heterosexual descent—although it is perfectly reasonable to describe them as a local descent group. That which the ancestors of present-day Belyuen figured and cohered was not so much sexual as textual in nature, a diagrammatic abstraction made possible by socially mediated understandings of spatial proximity, directionality, and seriality; that is, reproducing a group in the local context is primarily a matter of textuality not sexuality. Like the Duwun *wangga* reveals, and provides a basis for, arguments about the spiritual status of places and person (a pragmatically entailed architectonic palimpsest if people remain who know how to read and manipulate its pragmatic codes) so the semiotically mediated territory subtending these kinship and marriage diagrams reveals and provides

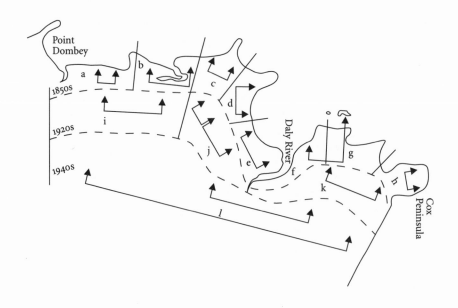

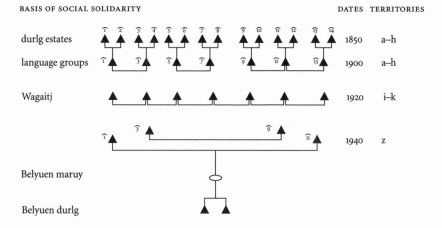

FIGURE 14. Textual transformations of territorial organization in the northwest coastal region, 1850–1940 (*durlg* into *maruy*).

the basis for understanding how to initialize, punctuate, and serialize the syntax of alliance. This spatial architecture of sexuality is not the only architecture (nor even the most important) for building a human component into country. But, like the felicity of the Duwun *wangga,* the felicity of these territorialized kinship diagrams now depends as much on the legislative and public commonsense status of "the family" abstracted from space as on the possible local semiotic architectures embedded in them.

It is a mistake, I think, to understand the fact of this large cognatic group as explaining how contemporary Belyuen came "to be." Indeed, lawyers and anthropologists opposing the claim did not consider it sufficient explanation. Anthropologists representing other groups argued that the information in figure 14 was an artifact of the land claim process. If, opponents argued, one listened to the Belyuen describe how and why they belonged to local claim lands, one would hear the Belyuen referring to their conception (*maruy*) from the Belyuen waterhole, to their life history in the area, and to their ceremonial obligations, not to the history of their biologically human descent. In other words, the entire cognatic apparatus outlined in figure 14 only becomes "local"—Belyuen—on the basis of *maruy,* conception beliefs. Land Commissioner Michael Maurice found this argument inconceivable in the Ti Tree claim. He returned as a lawyer representing a Larrakia group during the second hearing, still unconvinced. In the following he cross-examines a Belyuen claimant during the 1995–96 hearing.

> MR. MAURICE: Wadjigiyn, Kiyuk. You said that the people who belong to this country are the Belyuen and those three kids. Is that right? Why do those three kids belong to this country?
>
> TREVOR BIANAMU: Well, they follow their mother's footsteps, and their grandfather.
>
> MR. MAURICE: Why do the Belyuen belong to this country?
>
> TREVOR BIANAMU: Well, they born here, raised up here. Been living all our life here.[62]

Opponents to the Belyuen claim argued that "the Belyuen" were not *really* Belyuen as such but a cluster of presumptively patrilineal clan groups whose real estates lay south of the claim lands. *Maruy* and *durlg* were said to be contrastive and qualitatively different types of territorial markers.[63] Nor were critics wrong in their observations that neither the social organization of the Belyuen nor their relation to the Cox Peninsula is reducible to an ahistorical, spatially abstracted diagram of heterosexual reproduction. Indeed, geographical time was critical to the formation of the Belyuen as such.

The marriage alliances diagrammed in figure 14 emerged in the context of two contingent geographical conditions: on the one hand, the coastal orientation and geographic proximity of the southern estates, and, on the other, the government consolidation of the Wagaitj onto the Delissaville reserve. It was onto these semiotically mediated spatial and temporal architectures, built by the ancestors of the Belyuen, that contemporary Belyuen, their lawyers, and I built a new supertext of their groupness and locality. This supertext depended on the Belyuen belief that the "Wagaitj" had been reformed into "Belyuen" through their *maruy* relation to Belyuen *durlg*. This argument demanded an understanding of *durlg* and *maruy* as simply temporal characterizations of formally equivalent concepts. Simply put: every *durlg* descent group is a *maruy* relation extended through the bodies of the next generation. And, it demanded understanding the transformation of *maruy* into *durlg* as always already a part of the traditional Wagaitj culture.

Thus, although Elkin would write that older Wagaitj men in the 1930s stated of their children: " 'Got no other *dorlk* or *maroi* for these, because they down here' (that is, interned at Delissaville),"[64] by 1979 the senior members of the Danggalaba clan and of the Belyuen would refer to a Belyuen *maruy* as the basis of Belyuen territorial rights and obligations. The authors of the Kenbi Land Claim quoted Topsy Secretary: "We asked her (on 28 February 1979) if she approved of a joint claim by people from a number of linguistic and dialect groups to the claim area and she replied, 'Yes, because they all were born at Delissaville. No matter that they Ami, Manda, Wadjigiyn, Kiyuk, they born at Delissaville.' "[65]

The structural elegance of the transformation of the southern Wagaitj into the Belyuen through the spatiotemporality of *durlg* and *maruy* was mirrored in the historical emergence of the form, location, and orientation of Belyuen men's and women's initiation rites. Edmund Leach's argument that ritual should be "regarded as a statement in action" of the social organization of a community seems a particularly appropriate point to remember.[66] As the southern Wagaitj increasingly understood their children to be the *maruy* of Belyuen *durlg,* they reoriented their initiation practices away from southern territories and toward the waterhole.

MR. KEELY: All right. How central is this waterhole to the region?

HARRY SINGH: Very important in relation to initiates, young men's ceremony, their—after taking to Ngalwat, which is the manta ray Dreaming they are brought back here and washed in this particular waterhole here.

MR. KEELY: All right. So they wash her; do they wash in the salt water too?

HARRY SINGH: Yes. Taken there first and brought back here.

MR. KEELY: And what notion do the group here believe in as far as sweat is concerned? Can you explain how it works?

HARRY SINGH: Very strongest part of that washing ceremony introduces that, the sweat that goes back to the dreaming, gives them protection when they're travelling, if they happen to travel by boat or out hunting there, so that sweat is very important in that respect.

MR. KEELY: When you bogey [bathe] in the waterhole, does your sweat just stop here or does it travel?

HARRY SINGH: No, it travels.

MR. KEELY: How does it travel?

HARRY SINGH: Travels through that, the hole, the tunnel underground.[67]

MR. MAURICE: Yes, if they come from somewhere else, how do you say those ancestors of yours were traditional owners for this country?

MARJORIE BILBIL: Well, they been here living long time, they participated in cultural, doing culture, all those things. Can I say something?

MR. MAURICE: Yes, please.

MARJORIE BILBIL: I'll put it this way: If Tommy Lyons was gone, and there was no Wadjigiyn, Mandayenggel, Amiyanggel, Marriamu, Marritjabin [Marritjeban] people, we wouldn't have that culture for our children.

MR. MAURICE: Well, which culture are you talking about?

MARJORIE BILBIL: Belyuen. Belyuen people.

MR. MAURICE: Does that culture come from Tommy Lyons?

MARJORIE BILBIL: No, it's past, buried and finished.

MR. MAURICE: Passed from whom?

MARJORIE BILBIL: Old Tommy Lyons has gone.

MR. MAURICE: Passed it on?

MARJORIE BILBIL: No, he has gone and our people then took it over and—

MR. MAURICE: What did they take over?

MARJORIE BILBIL: Songs, telling stories about places, about all this Cox Peninsula, teaching us.

MR. MAURICE: Yes. Who did they take it over from?

MARJORIE BILBIL: Well, they been here long enough, all them Wadjigiyn people.

MR. MAURICE: Yes. Who did they get it from? You said they took it over; who did they take it over from?

MARJORIE BILBIL: Our people had their culture like, like Wadjigiyn, Manda, all those different language, all came one, together, as a family group.

MR. MAURICE: Oh, I see. So is that culture which they brought from those other countries which they originally came from?

MARJORIE BILBIL: No, here, at Belyuen, yes.

MR. MAURICE: Here. Well, who had that culture in the first place?

MARJORIE BILBIL: Everybody.

MR. MAURICE: Who do you mean by everybody?

MARJORIE BILBIL: Everybody that live here.

MR. MAURICE: Yes. Are you talking about the six language groups that now live at Belyuen, are you?

MARJORIE BILBIL: Yes.

MR. MAURICE: But before they came here, who had that culture?

MARJORIE BILBIL: The Larrakia and that old Tommy Lyons.[68]

But the ritual immersions to which Harry Singh, Marjorie Bilbil, and others refer are not simply symbolic statements. They are also corporeal acts, repeating and extending the physical intercourses between the ontological order of *Nguidjlag* and Belyuen such that Marjorie Bilbil can say that the "culture" to which she is referring is Belyuen in nature, form, and orientation.

At this point, it should be fairly obvious why we had gathered to translate the Belyuen *wangga* that Mosec sang at the end of "Death Rite for Mabalan." We were hoping that the Belyuen *wangga* will contain a text that we can re-form into a diagram whose shape would present an argument of a specific order and magnitude as suggested in figure 14.

If we, along with Allan Marett, had hoped that the Belyuen *wangga* would provide an unambiguous narrative or diagrammatic account of how the Wagaitj had been transformed into the Belyuen through the authorizing agency of a ritually invested relation between *nyuidj, maruy,* and *durlg,* we were to be sorely disappointed. After laborious work, and with Allan Marett's and Lyz Ford's additional research, the Belyuen song of Mosec Manpurr emerged as:

karra nyele wewe
yagarra nyele wewe
karra ngadjanung bende
be ngave ngave ngave ngave ya

karra nyele wewe
yagarra nyele wewe

Hey! nyele wewe
Oh, no! nyele wewe
Hey! for me now
Oh! I go, I go, I go, I go away there
Hey! nyele wewe
Oh, no! nyele wewe

The *wangga* did not provide *in the text* even the clear extensions of locale and kinship that the Duwun song had. On the tape Mosec Manpurr can be heard telling Colin Simpson and the nation that Belyuen gave him the Belyuen song in a dream ("I give you one song I get from Belyuen. Belyuen been give me this one song in dream"). But Belyuen is not named in the text; nor is any particular territorial relation between the place Belyuen and the people Belyuen narrativized; nor is any specific kinship relation between Mosec and Belyuen mentioned; nor is any grammatical marker indicating definitively who said "be ngave ngave ngave ngave ya." *Karra! Yagarra!* Worse, "Death Rite for Mabalan" ends rather than begins with the Belyuen *wangga*. The first *wangga* heard on the tape is a lamentation of dislocation sung by the last member of a Emiyenggal *durlg* group, Bitop, an elderly man interned on the Delissaville settlement.

theme ngaburru
ngama nganitudu nu
ngaburru nu
theme ngana nthi mala
ngana nthi

Where did I come from
How will I track
my way back
How will I to go there long way
I go back somewhere

Even if Belyuen or Bitop had sung to our desire it is unclear at this point whether his tune would have been recognized within the framework of the LRA for several reasons. First, as noted above, although Toohey eventually reconsidered Stanner's narrow definition of the "local descent group," this ex-

pansion of the legally recognizable "family" did not displace a human hetero-
normative notion of descent and reproduction but merely speciated its form.
The third land commissioner, Justice Maurice, who would eventually serve
as legal counsel for the Laragiya tribal group during the 1995 hearing, would
close the door on attempts to displace human descent with spiritual descent.

In any case, the *wangga* now appears in the shadow of another, forebod-
ing ritual space that deauthorizes it, that resignifies it as a legitimate mode of
territorialization. Long before we convened on the Belyuen veranda, anthropologists had differentiated "individual songs," which *wangga* were understood to be, from clan songs and cult songs. Clan songs, but especially cult
songs, lay in a doubly restricted archive. They are part of the historical archive
discussed in chapters 2 and 3, a domain of a superanimated prohibitive interest, of men's "high ceremonies" — Big Sunday and other services. These songs
represent for nonindigenous and many indigenous people, the real "hard law"
of Aboriginal culture. This real law drags local tradition from local conditions and inserts it into other national and transnational frames. In his expert
evidence, Allan Marett was asked several times to comment on "accepted"
anthropological distinctions and rankings of song genres in relation to territorial claims. For example, Mr. Dalrymple refers Marett to Alice Moyle's
research conducted in the 1960s.

> MR. DALRYMPLE: I'll come back to that in a little while. You're familiar with
> Doctor Alice Moyle's works on Aboriginal music and song?
> PROF. MARETT: Yes.
> MR. DALRYMPLE: Now she presents a fairly uncomplicated division of Ab-
> original music into types, doesn't she? . . . I'm not trying to say that this is
> a simplistic division but it certainly does characterise the songs into indi-
> vidual songs, clan songs, and cult songs.[69]

The fact of an anthropologically accepted ranking of song genre lessens
the local practice of localization, no matter that the clan songs these lawyers
seek are recognized as having been "buried" — that is, formally ended through
local rituals. And, remember, some of these so-called cults and cult songs
were stopped because of government intervention. But, although gone ("past,
buried and finished"), these other ghost songs echoed throughout the hearing. These terrifying spectral images resignify *wangga* as soft law, as a precur-
sor to the real thing, taunting this court as it had that of a previous generation
with glimpses of what it truly desires — a superceded but still signifying an-

cient society shimmering there just beyond settler time and emergent national history.

> MR. DALRYMPLE: As regards the use of wangga in initiation ceremonies, would you agree that the way that they're used is as a precursor for the initiation itself? Something that happens earlier on, developing up towards the more formal initiation ceremony itself?
>
> PROF. MARETT: Yes, that—in my experience that's the case.
>
> MR. DALRYMPLE: And it's purpose is to set the stage in an open and public way?
>
> PROF. MARETT: Well, I do suggest that it is rather more than that, than simply setting the stage in a rather public way.
>
> MR. DALRYMPLE: I'll leave that.[70]

THE FAILURE OF THE LOCAL

For the last time I return to the question I posed above: Why did we care about the tape recording sitting in front of us? Is it enough to refer to the fact of the law and instrumental reason to explain why we sat at the Belyuen women's center struggling to make sense of this vast, fluttering archive? The force of liberal law is, I think, more insidious and cunning in its processes of ensnarement. As we waited for tea water to boil and for the tape to rewind, the women who I sat with meditated, as they often did, on the consequences of failing in our discursive endeavor, of "being wrong," of "not fitting the law," of making "mistakes." As she often did, Marjorie Bilbil asked me whether, in the event that they failed to convince the land commissioner that they were the traditional owners of the land, the entire community would be sent to southern countries. From these women's perspective, this seemingly fantastic communal apocalypse is not so far-fetched. Soon after the Japanese bombing of Darwin in 1942, the government transported the community to relocation camps in Katherine. Closer to the present, these women have watched other communities displaced in the wake of lost or disputed land claims. The Wagait dispute, the Kamu and Malakmalak dispute, the Kungwarakang and Maranunggu dispute: these are the well-known names of current, bitter intra-Aboriginal arguments, arguments battled out in courts and bush camps, over what a "traditional Aboriginal owner" entails, over who are the "proper" traditional Aboriginal owners for specific regions.

In other words, it is not simply the fact of the law's existence that explains why the women and I sat on the veranda of the women's center. Rather, the anxiety that material and social insecurity generates drives these women into a legal process, attaches their hopes to a legal text and practice, to juridical forms and abstractions, and influences the syntax of their language of success and failures. The structural nature of local poverty provides other incentives for moving toward the law. What happens if we fail? When asked by a lawyer why she and her family did not "pack up and go back" to Banagula and Mabalan, two sites in Emi and Wadjgiyn country, Ruby Yarrowin dryly answered, "Only birrrrrd that place, only pig, only pig and birrrrrd boss that place today." Those who were present laugh when they remember the story, savoring the long, drawn-out onomatopoeic soaring of Ruby Yarrowin's "birrrrrd." But they also ponder the implications of Ruby Yarrowin's answer. How will they live in a place without hospitals or houses, without plumbing, electricity, or roads during the long wet season? Where would Betty Bilawag go, chained as she is (was) to a respirator? Can they point to these needs and desires in a claim hearing without deauthorizing their status as traditional Aboriginal subjects? What would happen to ceremony for this land?

But the functional force of the law depends not merely on material motivations. It also depends on ordinary human emotions and desires to be recognized as having personal and social worth and value. Ruby Yarrowin, Ester Djarem, Alice Djarug, Marjorie Bilbil, and Gracie Bitbin were as eager to listen to "Death Rite for Mabalan" in order to test their own hermeneutic skills as to secure their and their children's material future. They remembered Mosec as a *djewalabag*, a "clever man," a man steeped in sacred law. They remembered national and international celebrities and media traveling to Belyuen to record his singing and dancing.[71] They shared camps, food, argument — history — with him. And they remembered other things, things not recorded on tape — for example, their parents' cleverness in joining up and fitting together the disparate, often disputing groups thrust together at Delissaville. These women who sat with me sought to derive value for themselves in a similar way, piecing together black and white land and law, people and countryside, in order to build a people into a place. And they measured their own personal worth in part against their skill in doing so.

And me? I also measured my worth against this vast national archive, against my anthropological skills, against my guilt for not having devoted more time to genealogical analysis in 1989. I worried that my suspicion of a model of social anthropology has harmed the women sitting before me, that the model of land tenure I planned to propose may have serious negative

ramifications on other claims in the region; that I will fight the legal hegemony of one anthropological tradition only to install another. But I do not
simply worry, I also want. As much as these women want to be the thing, a
local descent group, on which their and the imagined futures of their families
depend, I want to give it to them — in part so that I can repay a debt, in part
because I wish for them to recognize my value, in part so that I was the one
who finally figured out the great Kenbi puzzle. All these noble and banal desires drive me like them deeper into legal forms, values, processes. Sure, I also
attempt to refigure the parameters of national law, but as I am more or less
influenced by these legal forms, more or less distracted by the social diagrams
I am able to extract from historical processes, I am more or less worried about
the social reality of this thing, this cognatic descent group, these two principles
of land tenure — *durlg* and *maruy* — that I have lifted out of the multitude of
corporeal intercourses, human intimacies, and social travails that compose
Wagaitj-Belyuen histories.

But even these necessarily ordinary desires cannot account for why we turn
to this tape, why we seek our argument in Mosec's song, in the archive of
the nation. To understand why we turn to an archived localization returns
us to a matter of law if not a matter reducible to the law — the procedures
for constituting valid, unmotivated, and objective evidence in liberal state
contexts, the discursive forms that validate argument as truth. Two points
seem relevant. First, one often-unarticulated condition of legally felicitous
evidence is that the principle operating to determine the social group must
itself be determinate in two specific senses: first, that the principle of group
cohesion and membership must allow anyone to be able to determine the
group on the basis of that principle and to determine it in such a way that a
judgment of ownership is uncontestable, certain, concrete, decontextual — in
short, monumentalizing abstractions.[72] (Leave that business of cleverness; of
"line-im up," "might be something." Just tell us what it is now.) Second, while
a number of land commissioners have recognized the flexibility of Aboriginal
tradition, the Australian High Court has ruled that "the governing descent
principle in operation in a particular group" cannot be "changed by them at
whim so as to fit the circumstances of a land claim."[73] Thus, we sit and face
the archived past because we need someone other than ourselves to repeat
what we desire, but someone whose words cannot be tarnished by the present
because they are unmotivated by the present, by our desires to be worthy, to
live. *Karra!* We point to the Belyuen *wangga,* to Elkin, to Edmund Leach, to
all those who never would have imagined this claim, or us. *Gameyi* ("he said,

it happened"). This tape was there (*-ya*). *Yagarra!* In other words, we alienate our practices through a national archive in such a way as to make our motivations mysteriously disappear, and make the diagrams we produce appear detachable from the very context that produced them, to be the unmediated force of a subjectless history of tradition.

But even if the law recognized spiritual descent as a principle of descent deemed relevant by the claimants, the bureaucratic nature of the land councils might find it difficult to reconcile this form of territoriality with its legislative mandate to negotiate contracts and capital endeavors on Aboriginal lands. Land councils are charged with passing out royalty payments and negotiating multiyear contracts with small business and multinational corporations. What type of contract would emerge at the interstices of capital and Belyuen social space? And what of other social institutions now constituted on the basis of the commonsense machinery of the local descent group? After all, the local descent group is no longer merely an anthropological object, or fact of law. Today, this conceptual object provides the skeletal structure of progressive policies of welfare distribution, health care, and housing. The local descent group *is* now, no matter whether it was not then. Finally, the hyper-pragmatic nature of this text makes figuring the interpretation of it as "disinterested" difficult. This disinterested figuration is, however, essential to the manifestation of truth in Australian courts of law.

Because there cannot be an interested subject writing Aboriginal history, opponents of the Belyuen claim repeatedly dragged this subject into court, especially during the expert evidence of Allan Marett. Again and again, lawyers representing other Aboriginal groups tainted his interpretation of the territorial significance of *wangga* by linking it to present-day Belyuen persons. The pragmatic nature of *wangga*—the lack of a recognizable narrative and semantic content and structure—deauthorized its viability for producing a locally socially felicitous place. Take, for example, questions that Blowes and Dalrymple put to Marett.[74] Dalrymple refers to a local *wangga* about a buffalo dancing at Benindjila, now the site of tourist resort on the northwest coast of the peninsula, where the *wangga* is sometimes performed. As with Marett, most Belyuen women and men have described the buffalo to me as a *nyuidj*. But the *wangga* does not specify the buffalo as either "normal" animal or *nyuidj*. Blowes refers to the Belyuen song we have been trying to translate.

MR. DALRYMPLE: If in fact—if it were, in fact, the case that this buffalo song is about a buffalo hunt in the vicinity of Benindjila, then while certainly it has a geographical reference, it wouldn't indicate any particular spiritual attachment to country, would it?

PROF. MARETT: No, but all the information that—well, let me backtrack a minute. One has to be—one has to be aware of the fact that with almost all Aboriginal songs there are levels of exegesis. What I would suggest is that the hunting level, which is the level that gets tied up with the presentation of the songs to tourists, is actually very much—what Catherine Ellis actually calls a "false front."

It actually obscures what is the real meaning of the text, which I have absolutely no doubt about, having spent a lot of time talking about this text with people who have rights to sing it. The real—the real meaning has to do with the appearance of the buffalo as a nguidj. The buffalo is not a normal buffalo, the buffalo was a nguidj. So it's you know—

MR. DALRYMPLE: And that's very much the understanding that you've derived.

PROF. MARETT: Mm.

MR. DALRYMPLE: Is the understanding that you've been given in the recent past, is that right?

PROF. MARETT: Yes, that's the—within the last year.[75]

MR. BLOWES: I won't take that one any further. On page 11, you begin—you go through the text to page examples. The first reference you had at example one was about Mosec Manpurr's song of the—for the Belyuen waterhole. Take you to the text of that song. The transcribed portion of the song reads in its entirety "as for me, I'm going back now."

PROF. MARETT: Yes.

MR. BLOWES: And I think elsewhere you said—you referred to on page 5 to the same wangga, and you made reference there to Elkin. So when did you get this information from Ruby Yarrowin and others that you refer to there?

PROF. MARETT: Last year.

MR. BLOWES: Last year, when?

PROF. MARETT: July. Or possibly August.

MR. BLOWES: Now the song itself doesn't refer to the Belyuen waterhole.

PROF. MARETT: No.[76]

Anxious and fascinated we turn to and are transfixed by this thing in front of us, its spinning sprockets and thin brown tape, and the song Mosec promises to sing. Maybe he will sing a song undermining what we claim. But maybe, just maybe, Mosec will sing a song Belyuen gave him for us, a song that will make our present desires "traditiona": before all this, before us, before. The reader now knows the outcome: what the songs actually were, what we are. He disappointed us. The songs were disappointing. We disappointed ourselves. The description of Mosec, of these songs, of ourselves as disappointing suggests the delicacy with which local affective structures are embedded in publicly mediated judgment. These songs did not disappoint or upset us. They were disappointed. They were upset. They were transformed into a quality, a mood, produced as a site of failure, not simply by the explicit demands of statutory law but by subtler expectations about how narratives should work through elaborated decontextualizable semantic content, rather than multilevel contextualizable pragmatic form. And the more these women identify with this cultural product, the more they are not only disappointed by the *wangga* but are disappointed in themselves. Like the text itself, they are produced as a site of failure no matter their extraordinary resilient histories, no matter the mental and physical labor that these histories, these texts, and they themselves represent.

By wishing Mosec had sung otherwise, in digging up and translating the texts, these women and I were not just gathering "proof" that what we say is true. We were not simply engaged in an evidential adventure. Instead, we were engaged in the delicate processes by which local identities are constituted and mediated by the coercive politics of liberal recognition, its technology of the archive, its institutions of force and desire, simple desires like to live and be recognized as being worthy and having personal and social value. In other words, we were engaged in the delicate extensions and reenforcements of liberal legal ideology—that formal and informal legal hearings are primarily dispassionate, objective, noncontextual judgments of social facts rather than the primary means by which social facts are produced. In this rather ordinary archival moment we see the dual processes by which, at once and the same time, translocal law and material structures work in and through local personal passions and optimisms even as the conditions of their translocal nature are erased.

The extraordinary delicacy with which local protocols for evidential claims are worked through state protocols for evidence should not blind us to the power of liberal law, to the cunning of current forms of liberal recognition. These simple desires and dramatic coercions lodge the social machinery of heterosexuality into local structures of language and corporeal practice, displacing other forms of corporeal intercourse as infelicitous, failed social attachments. To pay attention to these delicate restructurings is not to deny the mediating nature of the local, but merely to acknowledge that these delicate calibrations occur in vastly different and multiply structured regimes of power.

The irony of Olney's evaluation of the Belyuen claim in 1989 as generally lacking in conviction derives from his assumption that the source of this lack is local and traditional, that the truth of local social history can be read off this lack. Instead, the Belyuen reluctance, their "very little enthusiasm," is an accurate reading of the hegemonic force of heterosexual descent in the determination of national justice, citizenry rights, material restitution, and subjective constitution.

EPILOGUE

> theme ngaburru
> ngama nganitudu nu
> ngaburru nu
> theme ngana nthi mala
> ngana nthi

> Where did I come from
> How will I track
> my way back
> How will I to go there long way
> I go back somewhere

Of all the *wangga* on the tape, "Death Rite for Mabalan," Bitop's *wangga* was particularly hard to hear and translate. A few days after we listened to the tape, I took many of these same women to Darwin to shop. In the afternoon I went to a meeting at the Northern Land Council. When I returned in the evening to pick up everyone, Marjorie Bilbil told me that while she was shopping she heard Bitop singing a clearer rendition on a tape being played in a nearby store. Perhaps, she suggested, I could buy it so that we could study it. Because I was worried how Bitop's lamentation of dislocation would play in court, I did.

Bitop's song is reproduced as "Nomad," the feature first track on a tape whose title is also Nomad (see fig. 16). The tape consists of a collection of indigenous Australian, African, and Native American spiritual texts, mixed and synthesized with contemporary percussion instruments and produced in 1994 by Australian Music International and Yalumba Music, with production

FIGURE 15. Australian Aborigines: An Aborigine performs the ancient skill of making fire. (Courtesy of Murray Views, Gympie, Queensland.)

and distribution centers in New York City and Melbourne. In the liner notes, the producers state, as had their predecessors in the 1930s, their "gratitude . . . to early explorers, missionaries and others who loved the Aboriginal people and saw a richness in their law and tradition. Without these people, a wealth of cultural heritage would have been lost forever." The music on the tape is "dedicated to the support and rebuilding of the Aboriginal culture so that it can be free and respected in the 'modern world.' "[77]

There is something wonderfully clear about these embracing frames. The unique sounds and rhythms of the didjeridu are no longer merely constitutive of a settler modernity, a new multicultural form of nationalism, but the circulation of transnational capital. As business, nation, and law chase economic capital, national fantasy, and global humanities, they grind out ever more artifacts, archives, and histories through which locals and capital will emerge. When I began this chapter by describing the women sitting on the veranda as the "remainders" of local culture I used this term advisedly. What was once the nation's cultural debris is now the local's cultural mines. These women are the last fluent speakers of Emiyenggal, Mentha, and Wadjigiyn — the languages of the *wangga*. But the very linguistic expertise that these women will use to unlock the riddle of the Belyuen *wangga* shines a bright light on the tenuous, even scandalous, nature of their land claim. Emi, Mentha, Wadjigiyn, Marriamu: these are languages of countries to the south. Most anthropologists, lawyers, the interested public, and Aboriginal persons believe that the historical "language" of this country was Larrakia.

As we drove back to Belyuen we listened to Bitop sing accompanied by hybrid New Age and techno rhythms. Later, on 30 May 1999, flying back to Belyuen, this same song played on the Qanta Airline intercom. This pirated version of "Death Rite for Mabalan" never appeared in court nor did a postcard showing Ruby Yarrowin's father performing the ancient skill of making fire (fig. 15). But these texts do provide the cultural capital that can be transformed into economic capital by businesses who mine the national archive for reasons other than my own or those of the Belyuen women.

August 19th [Tennant Creek] Bar. 28.870 Aneroid IIoo. A.T. 72. Cloudy, overcast and like rain [sic] until 11 A.M. and then the sun shone again. Spent day with niggers. Completed extension of table of relationships and recorded a tradition about a certain pelican about which I shall have something to say later on. The gentleman here depicted is one of our staff, . . . a first rate fellow, called Thanmaru, whose only fault is that he would dearly love to be a white man with the consequence that he is a little ashamed of some of his tribal customs and would therefore like to tone them down. In doing work such as we are engaged upon one has to be careful not to let the savage perceive that you disapprove of or disbelieve in his ideas for if he once gets that idea into his head he will shut up like an oyster and wild horses will not drag reliable information out of him.

—Frank Gillen to Baldwin Spencer, *"My Dear Spencer"*

6 / The Truest Belief Is Compulsion

Throughout the transcript of the Kenbi Land Claim readers encounter the comment, "restricted women's session." This metatextual ellipsis indicates that the conversational time of the text has been foreshortened, that the reader faces an abridged version of the public record as it points to and characterizes the portion of missing text as secret, (indigenous) female. The conversation has not been lost to the archive of history. Conversational time and text have merely been relocated to the Northern Land Council and other authorized spaces, a supertext produced that includes a manila envelope stamped "for women's eyes only" in which lies the restricted evidence. Elsewhere and restricted in circulation, the restricted text remains a formal part of the public record of the Kenbi Land Claim and, formally, part of the transcript of the Kenbi Land Claim. The public does not, however, have access to this missing portion of the transcript. Similar ellipses refer to men's restricted evidence and are found in virtually every contested land claim heard in the Northern Territory and in many native title claims heard throughout Australia.

These techniques for constructing a public transcript can seem odd given a general set of liberal ideals concerning the public sphere and civil society. Benjamin Lee has argued, for instance, that in its ideal form, modern civil society is to be governed by two principles: "The first is that all deliberations that affect the people should be accessible to public scrutiny. The second is what [Michael] Warner has called a principle of negativity. The potential validity of what one argues stands in negative relation to one's self-interest; the more disinterested a position is, the more likely it is to be universally valid and rational."[1] It is certainly true that interestedness is the emergent ground of authoritative claims in some identity-based movements. In the United States, for instance, some people will say that experience should determine the authority of a statement. Still, both principles circulate in legal hearings and public debate. And to them should be added a third; namely, that in certain contexts principled public debate ought to give way to a collective moral sense, and not only should public debate give way but collective moral sense should be protected from the procedures of critical reason. From the point of view of this principle, the aim of public reason is not understanding, let alone agreement, but the sequestering of some often inexpressible (moral) thing from reflexive judgment. In other words, in its ideal form civil society continually invokes three ordering principles often in tension with one another: public scrutiny, individual disinterest, and collective moral limits.

In this chapter I address the fate of Aboriginal belief in the shadow of these principles. I return to Belyuen men and women's attempts to construct and interpret the archive of traditional local social organization. How do they produce "true beliefs" about their traditions in light of these three principles and the application of them in multicultural law? To answer this and other questions I seek a sociology of belief ascription. I do not seek so much the referential content of beliefs, nor the correspondence between belief ascription and truth. Instead I seek the manner in which belief is formed as believable, true, and accurate, and the manner in which the believable is hinged to national senses of justice and the justifiable distribution of rights and material goods. I ask therefore a set of simple questions: how do various indigenous people produce beliefs that are judged to be true? Why must they do so? How does the demand that they produce true beliefs place indigenous persons at the grinding point of competing and irresolvable public injunctions? For example, how do they creatively navigate the public and legal injunction that on the one hand they make public all material that is essential to public matters, and on the other hand they demonstrate a loyalty to local customs including those that prohibit the public discussion of certain matters? Likewise, how do they make their beliefs seem justifiably linked to the redistribution of public goods when, if put into practice, some of these beliefs violate state law? In this discursive environment what is true? How can one tell what is believable, believed? What is seen as fabricated, a lie? What are the material consequences of telling or not telling secrets? How much alterity can various social actors bear and in what contexts?

To be sure, the transcripts of the Kenbi Land Claim are not the only texts pockmarked by elliptical references to conversations that lawyers, anthropologists, and activists have had with indigenous men and women about unspeakable beliefs or inexpressible feelings. My own notebooks are littered with encoded conversations (names deleted, changed, or encrypted to safeguard certain people and places) and with references to other notebooks with similarly encoded interpretive enclosures or to other archived and published materials. They are minor discursive monuments to my and my interlocutors' sense that certain beliefs must be protected from the public record and from public circulation. Some of these other beliefs, however, cannot be found in the texts I have produced because I do not refer to them, not even by elliptical references. Moreover, indigenous men and women at Belyuen and throughout Australia have their own conversations and leave behind their own texts in the form of notes, audio tapes, and drawings. They rely on local conventions for indicating ellipses and encrypting texts to safeguard or exclude portions of their conversations, thoughts, and practices. One safeguard is to cease speaking, to burn or bury material to insure that it will never be found again. And, of course, ellipses occur in another sense throughout the texts. The meaning of utterances is heavily context-saturated; a portion of the conversation or scene necessary to interpret an utterance will by necessity be missing in retrospect, another inserted. (Of course, context exists itself only as a phantasmatic stable background; it is itself a stabilized effect of the here-and-now social processes of negotiated entailment.)

Indeed, no direct correlation exists between the archive of traditions and the interpretation of the communicative intention of the original builders of that archive when it comes to discerning the traditional history and beliefs of an Aboriginal group. In other words, the referential text is of a separate order from the interpretative text and this difference becomes socially meaningful in Aboriginal struggles for recognition. The lack of explicit reference to cultural materials or practices in my or others' texts may be said, retrospectively, to indicate the secret-sacred or otherwise sensitive nature of material and practices. In this sense even the most surface-level explicit text can be opened out into other texts and contexts. The controversy over the claim of some Ngarrindjeri women that sacred sites existed in the seas over which the Hindmarsh bridge was to be built hinged exactly on this problem of reference, predication, and intertextuality.[2]

In April 1993 Binalong Pty. Ltd. was granted a contract to build a bridge between Goolwa and Hindmarsh Island in South Australia. In October of the same year, a group of Ngarrindjeri women sought to stop the construction of the bridge in order to protect sacred women's sites said to be threatened by its construction. They appealed for protection under the Aboriginal Heritage Act (1988). The federal minister for Aboriginal and Torres Strait Islander Affairs, Robert Tickner, reviewed the claim and issued a twenty-five-year building ban. The developers, then in liquidation, appealed the ban to the federal court, which quashed Tickner's decision. Accusations that Ngarrindjeri women had fabricated the stories about sacred women's business sites began circulating in the press in 1995. Soon after, other Ngarrindjeri women denied the existence of any women's sacred sites in the area. A Royal Commission was then appointed by the South Australian government and it published, on 19 December 1995, a report stating that the whole "women's business" had been fabricated. The Royal Commission relied heavily on anthropological research done by earlier anthropologists in the area, especially the work of Ronald Berndt and Catherine Berndt, which did not mention the existence of women's ritual business or sites in the area.

Those who sided both for and against the claim that a sacred site existed in the Hindmarsh area argued about how to interpret the absence of historically documented references to these sites. Did the absence of references to the women's sites in the written archive mean that they did not exist (the women had fabricated their evidence); that the sites were so sacred that Ngarrindjeri women had refused to discuss them with anyone until now; or that the anthropologists with whom they had discussed the sites had carefully excluded the conversations from their texts? If women's business did exist, how could Ngarrindjeri women publicly discuss its content and maintain its sacred status as for women's eyes and ears only? Hindmarsh Island was just the latest of a series of national public debates about what Francesca Merlan has described as "the limits of cultural construction."[3]

In order to understand the social and subjective throes into which belief- and obligation-based reparative legislation place Aboriginal persons and communities it is helpful to distinguish among the concepts of the inexpress- ible, the unspeakable, and the indeterminate. I use the term "inexpressible" to refer to a felt orientation to some social or ideational state. The linguistic notion of propositional attitude certainly captures aspects of the inexpress- ible in ways useful to me here. A propositional attitude includes all statements with verbs denoting belief, doubt, intention, and the like, including inten- tional attitude-ascribing locutions of the type "believes that" and "intends that" and intentional attitude-ascribing locutions of the type "believes of." The inexpressible refers not to the referential content of the statements, but to a second-order experiential relationship to them. A speaker might say some- thing like, "I believe that children should not be abused." But if asked why, all subsequent explanatory statements ("because I believe that . . .") are pro- visional in the sense that, in the final moment, the explanatory ground is an inexplicable sense-feeling, whose phenomenological type can be character- ized as a moral feeling but whose referential content cannot be characterized without loss.

The inexpressible should therefore be distinguished from the "unspeak- able." In the following, the unspeakable refers to instances in which something can be described with a perfectly reasonable degree of accuracy, but can never- theless not be described because of explicit social prohibitions, whether these prohibitions are legal, religious, or personal in nature or whether they are local or nonlocal in origin. Both of these terms are distinct from the notions of "indeterminacy" and "incommensurability."[4] Scholars in the philosophy of language have used the term incommensurability to refer to a state in which an undistorted translation cannot be produced between two or more deno- tational texts. Indeterminacy is used to refer to the condition in which two incompatible translations (or "readings") are equally true interpretations of the same text. In these contexts, deciding which interpretation of the text is the more accurate cannot be based on evidence in the text, but must be found elsewhere, say, what we believe about the integrity of the person who wrote or interpreted the text. This seems to be a good place to start.

"I'M DIFFERENT"

We can begin developing a robust sociology of belief and obligation ascriptions and their role in redistributing material goods and social rights in multicultural Australia by noting two typical ways that philosophers have distinguished belief ascriptions from truth ascriptions. A person can assess another person's beliefs to be true, or she can hold a more circumscribed view that the other person truly believes her beliefs even though what she believes is "glaringly false," as W. V. Quine put it.[5] Analytic philosophers have argued for decades whether it is reasonable to take a charitable interpretation of the belief worlds of others and whether the belief worlds of others are largely true. From a sociological perspective, legal and social judgment seem to conform more closely to a weaker version of the notion of radical communication; namely, that in multicultural contexts state courts and normative publics need merely believe that the culturally other truly believes what she says, and can leave to the side questions of the immediate or ultimate truth of her belief.[6] In the practice of land claims, for instance, lawyers and land commissioners, if not the legislation itself, require Aboriginal claimants to explain the principles on which their social organization and spiritual beliefs are based as a prerequisite for the acquisition of state-based rights and goods. Why are you what you are or claim to be? Why must you do what you do or claim you should do? What does it mean? What is it for? As long as indigenous persons' accounts of their beliefs and practices are relatively coherent and the content is about "culture" rather than "morality," their beliefs might be, strictly speaking, nonsense to nonlocal Aboriginal or non-Aboriginal participants and yet still be legally persuasive.

Toward the end of chapter 2, I noted that it is unlikely that Baldwin Spencer and Frank Gillen believed that the ritual acts they witnessed actually reproduced human life, let alone that Arrente men and women ceased being men and women in the *Temps de Rêve*. These local beliefs remained for them (as they remain for most non-Aboriginal subjects) phantasmatic or metaphoristic. Various Aboriginal claimants in the Kenbi Land Claim described a similar set of fantastic beliefs. Take, for instance, the Belyuen proposition that they were born from a *durlg* (Dreaming ancestor) that lives in a local waterhole (Belyuen); that this birth-relationship (*maruy*) fashioned their bodies and sweat from the material of that Belyuen dreaming; that their ceremonies center on this belief; and that when they die their spirits (*nyuidj*) return to that waterhole.

MR. YOUNG: Okay and are there Aboriginal people who belong to this country, the Cox Peninsula and islands?

LESLIE NILCO: Yes.

MR. YOUNG: Yes? Who?

LESLIE NILCO: The three kids and all the Belyuen people right through.

MR. YOUNG: Well, why do the Belyuen people belong to this country?

LESLIE NILCO: Well, they're born from the waterhole. All our sweat went right through out the dreamings. We've been to ceremonies.

MR. YOUNG: Your sweat is throughout the dreamings and you mentioned ceremonies. Okay. You were telling me about one of those ceremonies before, you were going to tell me about burn'em rag. You know that burn'em rag ceremony?

LESLIE NILCO: Yes.

MR. YOUNG: What does that do? Sorry, I'll withdraw that. When do you have burn'em rag ceremonies?

LESLIE NILCO: When someone passed away.

MR. YOUNG: Yes, and what does that burn'em rag ceremony do? What's it for? What's the reason for burn'em rag ceremony?

LESLIE NILCO: That's for the spirit, you know, when your family passed away and the spirit keeps coming out to the kids and all that and all your sweat goes back to the waterhole and then goes out to the dreamings and all that and you know that your—talking probably let the dreamings know that you have gone away.[7]

We might ask: How does the unbelievable nature of these indigenous beliefs constitute and authenticate the believers as bearers of a legally felicitous cultural difference? When do ascriptions of the fantastic veer into ascriptions of the fabricated? How do these Aboriginal subjects navigate the shores of the unbelievable and the fabricated?

Most anthropologists would consider Leslie Nilco's statements a local variant of a widespread indigenous belief in the spiritual impregnation of women by totemic child spirits; colloquially, a belief in conception dreaming.[8] Since Spencer and Gillen published *Native Tribes of Central Australia* (1898) the self-evident nonsense of this belief from a Western point of view captivated scholars and publics and inspired extended debate about whether indigenous people knew that a form of heterosexual sex ("intercourse") made babies and, if they did not, what this implied about their (primitive) mentality. Carefully couching his example of Christian mentalities in the past, W. Lloyd Warner reminded scholars and the public in *A Black Civilisation* (1927) that the "relationship existing between the primitive men of north-eastern Arnhem Land and me as a field worker would be the same as that of the traditional visitor from Mars who might have come to study the Puritans of Massachusetts in colonial days. Had he asked Cotton Mather or any other member of the community 'where babies come from,' he would have discovered that they came from heaven and that God sent them and that it was the special duty of the church to look after them. He might be told that the stork brought them and discover totemic 'spiritual conception.' "[9] In short, according to Warner, totemic beliefs were not an index of indigenous persons' lack of physiological knowledge nor a sign of their primitive mentality, but rather a mark of their cultural interest in locally defined, sociologically significant structures: "The ordinary savage is far more interested in the spiritual conception of the child, which determines its place in the social life of the people, than he is in the physiological mechanism of conception."[10]

What matters at this point is not the specific content of indigenous conception beliefs, nor how anthropologists and publics debated the sociological and subjective implications of these beliefs, but rather how, in having conversations with Aboriginal subjects on this topic, a host of settler subjects demonstrated to indigenous Australians the meaningful linkages Europeans made between belief ascriptions and truth ascriptions, rationality and humanity, humanity and citizenship. Warner traced the territorially dispersed track, and interactional density and intensity, of these communicative practices. In the same book, he quotes a passage from Spencer and Gillen in which the use of adjectival intensives ("firmly," "time after time," "always") indexes the degree, range, and persistence of their inquires: "We have amongst the Arunta, Luritcha and Ilparra tribes, and probably also among others, such as the Warramunga, the idea *firmly* held that the child is not the direct result of intercourse, that it may come without this, which merely, as it were, prepares the mother for the reception and birth also of an already formed spirit child who inhabits one of the local totemic centers. *Time after time we have questioned them* on this point and *always* received the reply that the child was not the direct result of intercourse"[11] (my emphasis).

Spencer and Gillen were hardly the only settlers circulating the intensity of public and academic interest in local conception beliefs. Anthropologists, pastoralists, missionaries, police, and other figures of colonial settlement held formal and informal conversations with indigenous persons throughout Australia. Warner is himself compelled to ask the Murngin a similar set of questions with a similar degree of intensity in order to counter popular public beliefs in the primitive mind and more firmly and convincingly ground his argument for a "black civilization": "An occasion arose in which I could inquire directly of certain old men just what the semen did when it entered the uterus of the woman. They all looked at me with much contempt for my ignorance and informed me that 'that was what made babies.'" [12] Again, the content of the conversation about human sexuality and physical reproduction is less important here than how, in the long process of having these conversations, settler Australians communicated to indigenous Australians, in the logic of prohibited interest, that a specific coordination of the unbelievable and the true mattered to whether and how they were accorded full status as rational human beings and national citizen-subjets. Indigenous persons opened, in turn, a wedge of doubt about the limits of the possible in any actual settler world, forcing scholars, administrators, farmers, and pastoralists to inspect their own beliefs, or more minimally, to be irritated not only by the thought but by its practical implications.

Similar conversations could be heard at Belyuen throughout the mid-1980s and the 1990s, but with one modification: Belyuen women and men often queried the belief capacity of nonindigenous persons. For example, when in the course of the Kenbi Land Claim hearing a legal counsel for some of the Belyuen, Jessica Klingender, became pregnant, local Belyuen women reckoned the child to be from the Belyuen waterhole. After I returned to Belyuen from a visit to Melbourne to see Jessica's then-small son, I was asked by some Belyuen women whether Jessica knew her child had a *maruy* from the waterhole and whether she could believe that such a thing could be true. Could she? Did she have the capacity for belief? To be sure, ascribing a conception relation to a person is analogous to ascribing a kinship relationship to a person — it binds the resources of persons to local communities and is thus a type of instrumental reason. But this explanation is interpretively seductive and reassuring, exactly insofar as it brackets the question that the Belyuen women raise: the capacity of settler belief and its implications on the way others evaluate them. Did Jessica have the capacity for mental and physical conception? If not, what did she think about their beliefs? How was she able to represent them in court?

Given the long duration of this conversational form perhaps we should not be surprised that contemporary indigenous persons regiment beliefs that they know appear unbelievable to others, or to themselves in the company of others, to concrete but amazing aspects of modernity. To explain to land com-

FIGURE 16. *Nomad,* Australian Music International. (Courtesy of Australian Music International Inc., 253 West 18th Street, Ground Suite, New York, New York 10011.)

missioners, anthropologists, and themselves how the Belyuen (*durlg*) Dreaming communicates to other *durlg* in the region, older men and women often describe as a telephone system the underground Dreaming tunnels (*kenbi*) connecting certain *durlg*. Belyuen-the-*durlg* communicates to other *durlg* through underground tunnels. Belyuen travels through these underground "cables" "ringing up" other Dreaming-sacred sites in its reach, telling them, "Hey these are my kids. You must not harm them. You must take care of them." Belyuen-the-people communicate to this *durlg* environment through song, ceremony, and other bodily practices. During evidence given in 1996, Marjorie Bilbil used the concept of the telephone to describe to Mr. Young how the Belyuen waterhole communicates to other Dreamings in the region.

MR. YOUNG: Can you tell the Judge how ceremony is for dreamings?

MARJORIE BILBIL: When we have ceremony, we just come here and give bath to younger boys and younger girls. Their sweat goes to the fresh water first and then they go down to the salt water. We take them down to the salt water and their sweat goes through the salt water as well goes to all those sites that I have called today.

MR. YOUNG: All the sites you've called?

MARJORIE BILBIL: Yes, it's like a, say, when their sweat's gone through those sites, it's all Belyuen now. Those people going to send this message back like a telephone; they going to ask this fella here. They've got to say "Where these kids from?" and this old man going to say "This is all from Belyuen" and they'll be right, they won't get sick or anything like that.

MR. YOUNG: All right. You mentioned the kids coming out of the waterhole from that old man Belyuen. Is there some ceremony for that? For that old man, that old Belyuen?

MARJORIE BILBIL: Oh yes, when we have ceremony we pay respect back to Belyuen when we have ceremony for girls or young men.

MR. YOUNG: Who do you pay respect back to?

MARJORIE BILBIL: Belyuen.

MR. YOUNG: What for?

MARJORIE BILBIL: For what he have done, like all the girls, like us mob, or our younger ones like today, they got children, they've got their children from that waterhole.

MR. YOUNG: So is it that you're paying respect back because you've got the kids out of the waterhole, is that what you're saying?

MARJORIE BILBIL: Yes, yes.[13]

These short exchanges generate ethnographic and legal support for the Belyuen claim insofar as the beliefs that inform them can be described as having a cultural specificity and directionality. The telephone is embedded in a specific tropic field through which I and Belyuen women and men think about the meaning, truth, and efficacy of their local beliefs and practices. Belyuen is the subject-force of the interlocutionary moment, and the Belyuen community's social power is "measurable" in terms of the nodal reach of its lines, not only in terms of the homogenized space between them, but also in the eruption of "Belyuen power" at a distance.

In other words, western technology, its global reach, is a metaphor for *locality*. Marjorie Bilbil figures the Belyuen in a dislocated location, in a strange trajectory that has led her and her community's self-identity and social relations to be most meaningfully expressed through that blue Belyuen waterhole. The Belyuen draw on technology not for itself but for themselves. We who represent them do not push or question too hard whether Belyuen and *kenbi* are telephones and telephone wires, so that the case focuses on the nature of their believing rather than on the nature of the beliefs themselves. Not questioning the metaphorical status of the metaphor we can use these examples as prima facie evidence of the resistance of local culture to the global, and fit Belyuen into stereotypes embedded in the Aboriginal Land Rights (Northern Territory) Act, 1976 (LRA) and in the Native Title Act, which borrowed much of its language from it. In the reinterpreted world of the *Mabo* decision, the trajectory of the local I have just sketched—outward from the local to enclose nonlocal "foreign" objects—can reinforce the romance of native fixity and mythic thinking and the bent of the law in rewarding local resistance to change. Of course, all of us engaged in this complicated communicative event rely on culturally hybrid communicative technologies to mitigate the legal effects of the dislocated location that Marjorie Bilbil describes. These communicative technologies include faxes, email, and telephones that coordinate strategies across continents and communities; their ability (and my ability) to find a legal language of persuasion; and the Belyuen waterhole's ability to communicate the sweat and spirit of local people into regional claim lands.

But the reality of any of these technologies is not at issue. Rather what is being calculated is whether the Belyuen believe in what they describe; whether they organize their actions on the basis of these beliefs; whether these beliefs may be said to be "local"; and what these local beliefs are said to be capable of producing. This last point is critical. Even if the contents of the beliefs are local, their legal felicity depends on the discursive environment into which they are placed. At a minimum, local beliefs are intelligible as local only insofar as they are embedded in a widespread, longstanding, and well-known anthropological and public debate about the "strange" nature of Aboriginal beliefs about human reproduction and ceremonial practices and insofar as they are embedded in "conceivable" arguments.

For instance, as I noted in the last chapter, one of the key questions put to the Belyuen case was whether or not spiritual descent was capable of fulfilling the requirement that traditional Aboriginal owners be a "local descent group" and whether it was "conceivable" on the part of expert anthropological witnesses that Belyuen could maintain a tenure system based on human descent for one territory and on spiritual descent for another territory. Take, for instance, Peter Sutton's evidence about the Belyuen (Sutton was testifying on behalf of a Larrakia group opposing the Belyuen claim):

I'm not suggesting that it (spiritual descent) couldn't be a social and land tenure formation that people arrive at some time. It's conceivable that a coastal group in north Australia could change its land tenure system from the ancient type that I've been talking about, or its more or less natural children, the cognatic descent group, et cetera, et cetera, with a language identity, a strong interest in descent as a pathway in to tenure and the rest of it. It's conceivable that they might relinquish that kind of system and go for another system. It's much less conceivable to me that they would still have their hearts in both at the same time for a long period, or indeed, I would find them very, very difficult to put together.[14]

In large part the difficulty for Sutton in conceiving the Belyuen claim was its seeming disparity from the anthropological literature on kinship and descent and his own experience in other Aboriginal communities. Justice Maurice, who would work with Sutton on the Kenbi Land Claim, also viewed spiritual descent as an inconceivable basis for a local descent group in the Ti Tree Land Claim. The inconceivability of the claim in that case pushed Maurice to question its source and status as outright fabrication or naïve misunderstanding.

Questions about fabricated culture take us directly back to judgments about believability and belief ascriptions, but with an additional qualification of the person's or group's character. We can simply accept as true that it is inconceivable that indigenous people would use, and believe in, two land tenure systems (or two components of one land tenure system, as argued in the previous chapter) or that they would believe in spiritual conception. But, if we do not accept this as true, then Sutton's and Maurice's commentary suggests that the legal felicity of the unbelievable is constrained by the social use to which it is put, and by another, always lurking, discourse of interestedness. Interestedness acts as metapragmatic interpretant, a switch-point of sorts, transforming the unbelievable into the fabricated (the untruthful). In land claims, ascriptions of interestedness play in a complex, racially inflected social terrain.

Aboriginal subjects are usually portrayed as disinterested truth-tellers, whose beliefs are manipulated by well-intentioned, though overly invested, anthropologists.[15] In Ti Tree, for example, Maurice strongly intimates that arguments of the primariness of spiritual descent did not come from local claimants, and did not refer to their actual beliefs, but rather came from esoteric and naïve anthropological arguments and rivalries: "It seems that the researchers may have taken too literally a set of very complex metaphorical references and this having resulted in considerable confusion about meanings."[16] But the evidence for the metaphorical status of these beliefs returns Maurice and his anthropological consultant, John Avery (who would also serve as the anthropological consultant to the land commissioner on the Kenbi Land Claim), to the anthropological and legal record. Avery and Maurice cannot believe that it is possible to believe in physical descent from a Dreaming—let alone that such could be the basis for a community of people—because the accepted views of anthropological social theory preclude it; because social-scientific notions of parsimony reject it; and because prior cases had not been formulated on this basis. For Avery only the fact of kinship-mediated heterosexual reproduction can clarify the scene: sex makes generations; kinship and descent principles form these generations into social types; and spiritual conception supplements these when they falter. Of course these "facts" of kinship are the grounds of longstanding anthropological debate. But having been accepted as the proper way of viewing spiritual descent in the Ti Tree claim, this proper reading can be cited in subsequent cases like Kenbi as the generally accepted view. The novel is, after all, the anathema to good law. It is what must be denied in the scene.

> MR. RILEY: And in recent times, say in this area, there has been—when I say "this area", I'm talking about the claim area—there's been perhaps a move away from looking at strict patrilineal descent because of the exigencies of the times?
>
> PROF. POVINELLI: No, I think that misrepresents a land tenure system in the area and I tried yesterday to give my understanding of the land tenure system. One aspect, one component of which was the transmission from the father to the children of a durlg substance; what we summarise as blood. That's one—that's one component of the land tenure system.
>
> MR. RILEY: And this is—
>
> PROF. POVINELLI: And I imagine you don't want me to go on.
>
> MR. RILEY: No, I certainly don't want you to. This is what you describe, I think elsewhere, as a sort of a new concept that you're putting forward?
>
> PROF. POVINELLI: A new concept? No.
>
> MR. RILEY: You wouldn't call it that? Well, a radical concept?
>
> PROF. POVINELLI: No.[17]

The novelty of alterity is not the only limit to good legal reasoning in the politics of recognition: cultural similitude becomes an uncanny difference to the law. In cases in which the racial and class background of an indigenous claimant veers toward the sociological profile of mainstream non-Aboriginal

Australia, the claimants themselves can become the magnet for charges of interestedness—their beliefs liable to being transcoded as fabrications. The difficulty of safeguarding the unbelievable from resignification as the fabricated in the (de)authorizing shadow of miscegenation and class is suggested by a comparison between Belyuen and Larrakia beliefs in cultural telecommunication.

In a 1955 essay on Arnhem Land music, A. P. Elkin described the *Nguidjalag* as referring to a perduring mythological realm that Wagaitj people (including the Belyuen) access through ceremonial songs and practices. Ritual events act as communicative technologies with the *Nguidjalag* insofar as they "expressed and strengthened the bond between the individuals and group on the one hand, and with their country on the other hand."[18] Forty years later, an urban Larrakia family, the Fejos, tried to describe their spiritual relationship to the land under claim by referring to a different communicative technology: their family's Christian evangelicalism, ESP, and the New Age spirituality. In sweltering heat, on the northern coast of the Cox Peninsula with Darwin visible across the harbor, the sound of Qantas airplanes often thundering overhead, and a crowd of fifty Aboriginal and non-Aboriginal men and women surrounding him, Wally Fejo told the land commissioner about "Larrakia . . . spirituality" and how through this spirituality he learned about sacred sites in the claim area.

Wally Fejo was the spokesperson for his family and a well-known and respected minister who headed Nanggalinya, a missionary training school in Darwin. During a long personal and family history, he described his changing Christian evangelical beliefs and practices and, among other metaphorical associations, likened the Larrakia and Hebrew diasporas. At one point he described having "within my life span, a lot of mountaintop experiences, a lot of valleys, a lot of creeks, and a lot of hurt feelings."[19] One of the mountaintop experiences he described was of "telecommunicating" with now-deceased Belyuen and Larrakia:

> I don't want to talk for too long. I'd like others to express their story as well but, might I go quickly yet slowly. I came over to Delissaville many times as a young person between the age of 18 and 25 for many reasons. And that was part of my search and putting down on paper as well as keeping it in my mind the kind of depth of spirituality Larrakia people's spirit have. I've been amazed, I've been amazed at what eventuated. I—some of the people who here today, who've met me more who've come to my place or we somehow, somehow even prior

to that we've been thinking of each other. And that's the kind of relationship and telecommunications that we have. You know, we've—Telecom [a phone company] have come so far, technology, but we've had it years and years.[20]

On cross-examination, a lawyer representing Fejo and his family as part of the Larrakia group pressed him to be more site-specific, a specificity commonly understood to be required by the LRA's definition of traditional Aboriginal owners. He asked Fejo whether specific now-deceased Larrakia men had told him about specific sacred sites in the claim area. Wally Fejo answered that they had not taught him "in a verbal way in which you and I are talking now." The deceased men didn't teach him the names of places or the mythic stories about places. They "didn't point out and say, look, here's the demarcation, this is New South Wales, this is the Northern Territory. . . . No we had a better way of communication, as well as of teaching."[21] These better ways were evangelical and telepathic.

Wally Fejo's sister, Christine Fejo King, led the women's side of the family's evidence. She told the land commissioner that her "special job," her "spiritual role," for the Fejo family was "recordkeeper." She then described sacred places she believed existed by referring now and again to a ledger-like set of books she held in her lap. At one point, heard by all in the background, Mirella Fejo urged her sister Christine King to tell the land commissioner about a seance they had held in which they called forth spirits of the dead. Telling Mirella she would have her turn to talk, King continued her evidence. On cross-examination, Tony Young, a non-Aboriginal lawyer hired by the Northern Land Council to represent the Belyuen, asked King whether she thought that dangerous sacred sites existed on the Cox Peninsula, sacred sites past which or over which one could not travel. "Yes," she answered. In an attempt to demonstrate the primariness of the Belyuen's responsibility for the claim lands (again something demanded by the LRA), Young proceeded to ask King whether she knew where the sites were located or how to treat them; and if she did not know would she be dependent on the Belyuen who did:

CHRISTINE KING: I was told but I can't tell you on a map. I don't know the names. But I was told that if I went there, I would feel that it was wrong.

MR. YOUNG: I see. So, do you believe that if you went to one of these dangerous places, you might be in danger, or other people might be in danger?

CHRISTINE KING: You don't—you go there, and the back of your hair, neck on the back of your hair stands up. It's—, you know.[22]

A ripple of laughter and snorts passed through some of the non-Larrakia audience after that last "you know." King turned to Young and said that her feelings and beliefs were like his, like something he himself would know, like how we all "get a feeling." The intimacy of the mimetic knowing she and Young experience dissembled the scene of cultural difference. The land commissioner, lawyers, anthropologists, and some Aboriginal subjects could not *feel* the specific membrance of alterity authorizing multicultural rights. Instead, they felt themselves to be abject, to be what must be purged from this scene of law. The metaphoricity of all moments of translation dissolved too fundamentally, and the law was forced to see too clearly its own and the colonial handprint in the scene. It is the indigenous telling settlers "we share the same feelings" that made whites uncomfortable, that prompted the audience to question the presence of an authentic indigenous difference. This mimetic knowledge made the scene a tense moment of the cultural "difference": it is you seen in me who is making yourself uncomfortable.

During her turn, Mirella Fejo took up the theme of ghosts and the speaking dead and deepened the abjection and shame of settler modernity. She began by saying, "I just have one thing really of importance that I want to tell the Judge."[23] This was that the Fejos had "a gift" on "the spiritual side." They can speak to the dead: "I really don't care what anybody says about seeing ghosts or talking to ghosts or spirits or whatever you want to call it, but I do."[24] When pushed by her lawyer to be more site-specific—to relate her powers to the land under claim—Mirella Fejo spoke of Aboriginal women's ceremony. She had earlier introduced a null relationship between such ceremony and her family's powers: "We have a gift in that we can speak to the dead. I talk with my uncles and my grandfather often. They come and visit. Now, I'm not a ceremony woman. I have never gone through any ceremonies, but they come and visit, not only me, they come to my sisters."[25] In cross-examination, Mirella Fejo embedded her ceremonial beliefs in the language of the LRA ("spiritual affiliation") and in Jungian-inflected notions of "four elements":

> In regards to women's ceremony, as I said before, talking to the spirits of the ancestors, I've never gone through a ceremony but I am aware that, to have a proper women's ceremony, you have to have the artifact or whatever it is, to go ahead and have a proper woman ceremony. You just can't have a women's ceremony like that. That's certain—you've got to have the spiritual affiliation, you've got to have the medicine man there. There's certain things. There's four

elements that have to be there in place for you to have a proper ceremony. Now, where it all is, I don't know.[26]

Finally, Jessica King, Christine King's daughter, took the microphone. Merely a teenager, surrounded by her extended family, she said she wanted to describe to the land commissioner her special relationship to her guardian bird, the sea eagle: "I have a special relationship with a creature in this country. It is a bird. And it is my guardian and I follow it because it'll take me to safe places. And wherever I go it will guard me. . . . And I also found that I can talk to the bird like I'm talking to you now. And I can understand what he says to me back. And if I concentrate I can hear everything he says in detail."[27] Mimicking the young girl, the lawyer for the government opposing the claims of all the Aboriginal groups prodded her to say more about her strange abilities. As she did comments from non-Aborigines on the scene referred to "New Ageism," "earth mothers," and "crystal culture." Other moans and voices of censure stopped the cross-examination. This censure was not simply prompted by the horror and shame of witnessing a Northern Territory government lawyer bait a young Aboriginal woman, but by the evidence itself. In other cases, the claimed beliefs of witnesses were more directly challenged as pure fabrications.[28]

With Jessica King's evidence, we might say that the simulation and drift of signs of indigenousness have reached profound proportions. It is as likely that the cultural images and referents she relied on came from places like Santa Fe, books like *Mutant Message Down Under,* and films like *The Last Wave* as from the land under claim. As such, the "cultural obscenity" of the evidence, as one non-Aboriginal person put it, was its "posture" as local, as "Aboriginal," and, in the climate of competitive Aboriginal claims, as generating rights superior to those of the Belyuen based on nothing but a human descent link to a Larrakia ancestor. But at another level this reappropriation and redeployment of a cultural signifier, a hybridization of cultural hybridity, is a profound meditation on the meaning of urban Aboriginality's relation to its traditional localities under the disciplinary surveillance of settlement history and state governance. That is, there is a deep truth to these beliefs as a genre, as a stitching together of incommensurate national discussions of indigeneity. Like Belyuen telecommunications, Fejo telecommunications are profoundly local mediations on the conditions of the local in transnational times no matter what their inflection or origin in New Age and pop psychological forms of spirituality.

We see in these two brief examples how jurists interpret law as a demand that cultural beliefs be intelligible (that they be like known and accepted principles of Aboriginal social organization and culture) but not too believable (the difference remains the mythopoetic); that they lie within a set of preexisting legal frameworks but not be oriented to them (opportunistic, interested). In other words, the local must be translatable into a certain form and a certain content, but it must speak the truth of itself for itself even though speakers know other laws and agencies are sitting not far away ready to discipline any enunciation that strays "too much" toward or against the nonlocal. "Too much," "by and large," "more or less": these are the strategic nonmeasures, tracked throughout this book, that have defined the state's relationship to Aboriginal "traditions" since settlement. And these nonmeasures continued to haunt, bracket, and qualify local cultural traditions. But we also see how this evidence stresses the generic enclosures of the law—how in struggling against the law's enclosures indigenous men and women continually pry it open. Trapped between too much and not enough cultural difference, Belyuen and Larrakia dilate preexisting parameters of the law and make legal practitioners uncomfortable handling it.

The difficulty the Larrakia and the Belyuen faced figuring their beliefs in the right mode of unbelievableness has been and is being faced by other urban, suburban, and rural indigenous people througout Australia. In this case, Belyuen and Larrakia must both find a way of making the incommensurateness of local and state-mandated discursive and corporeal beliefs seem coherent and commensurate but not opportunistic. Belyuen understandings of *maruy* (conception), *ngunbudj* (sweat), and *nyuidj* (ancestral spirits) are a locally produced reaction to the historical contingencies and brutalities of the colonial period. The Belyuen use these concepts to rearticulate people, places, and bodily inhabitations—desires, dreams, and aspirations. But, at the same time, they and I work to articulate these discourses and embodiments in response to the state demand that they *be* in relation to specific laws, social policies, and state identities and, simultaneously, *erase* any suggestion that these cultural beliefs are an opportunistic *being for* these laws, policies, and identities—*and* erase, yet again, any local traditions sanctioned by statutory and common law. Larrakia men and women likewise work with lawyers and anthropologists to make modern culture not appear as a mutant message in a court of recognition.

THE COMPULSIVE

In land claim contexts, the believable is articulated to the fabricated (negative valence) and to the unbelievable (positive valence) not only on the basis of the degree to which the discursive forms of beliefs and the believers differ from an imagined non-Aboriginal mainstream, but also on the basis of a calculation about the degree to which an interior disposition matches an exterior propositional claim. In simple terms, land commissioners and other jurists must decide whether indigenous subjects believe what they say and whether they are likely to act on those beliefs. The demonstration of such an attitude (interior and dispositional) is demanded by legislation that links material reparation to true belief—that is, to obligation. The LRA requires, for instance, that traditional Aboriginal owners "have" (a form of "be") common spiritual affiliations to a site on the land, and that these affiliations be of a type that "place" a collectivity under a primary spiritual responsibility for the site and the land.[29] It also requires the land commissioner to assess the "strength or otherwise of traditional attachment by the claimants to the land claimed."[29] Although the land commission is required by law only to assess the strength of attachment claimants have to the land, in legal practice most land commissioners assess the strength of attachment claimants have to their beliefs, which are seen to constitute the grounds of their attachment to place. Thus, under this piece of legislation supplicants before the law must present evidence in such a way that others can calibrate the degree and intensity to which their belief is experienced as a necessary (binding), or merely a potential (possibility), source of action. Put another way, claimants must produce belief in such a way that someone else can calibrate the compulsive hold that the belief has on them and, by extension, the collectivity they represent. In short, the law mandates a story about interiority. And the most robust evidence of the interiority of belief is compulsion.

For instance, in his Timber Creek Land Claim report, Commissioner Michael Maurice noted that the "essence of spiritual affiliations to sites is, of course, a system of beliefs about those sites, about the nature of man, and about his relationship to them. They are beyond proof in any conventional sense; but in any event, the nature of Aboriginal religion perhaps like any other, is that proof is everywhere—no inquiry is necessary."[31] With the phrase "beyond proof in any conventional sense" Maurice describes the conventional means by which he arrived at his sense of the truthfulness of the claimants. He calibrated the degree of similitude between what claimants said and what they did; or, more precisely, what claimants said and did within his range of observation: "Whether people possess the necessary beliefs is largely a matter of impression. I have dealt with my impression of various key figures in this claim; it remains only to round it off by saying that the claimants whom I had a chance to speak to and observe satisfied me that they had strong spiritual affiliation with the sites on and around the claim area."[32] As an aside, Maurice evokes the type of difference that designates true cultural beliefs — the curiosity of embodied customs: "Curiously, the claimants did not seem to mind us walking on and around the graves of their relatives behind the pensioners' camp."[33] The curious nature of the claimants' actions serves simultaneously to index their difference from Maurice's culture and the degree to which their statements could be said to index an internal disposition: "Perhaps this was explained by Duncan who, in response to the question, 'Those people who are buried here, are they still here?', replied, 'Only bones. Spirit gone.' One cannot, I suspect, divorce the mysticism concerned with country from the mysticism concerned with other aspects of life. Each is part of a total religious culture."[34] The orientation of law to the compulsory degree of local belief was continually evidenced in the Kenbi Land Claim hearings.

10 October 1996: several lawyers and I arrived at Belyuen early in the morning toward the end of the presentation of Belyuen traditional evidence for the Kenbi Land Claim. During traditional evidence, Aboriginal women and men sit day after day in front of a land commissioner, a sizable contingent of non-Aboriginal lawyers, anthropologists, staff, and other Aboriginal people, describing the sacred geography of the land that they are claiming; the principles of marriage, birth, ceremony, or descent that organize them into a land-holding local descent group for and from this land "according to Aboriginal traditions"; and the customary sacred laws that place them under a sacred obligation to maintain this land and its laws.

Throughout the Kenbi Land Claim hearing, lawyers asked junior and senior Belyuen men and women if there remained a traditional, ritually sanctioned law for the claim lands; if the Belyuen were obliged to act according to this law; — if it was a "hard law"; if violation of this hard law would result in physical punishment; and if such punishment occurred inside or outside ritual contexts. Day in and day out most senior and junior members of the Belyuen answered in the affirmative to all these questions. The law remained in the land and in the people who in turn remained under an obligation to keep the law going generation after generation. Punishment for violating the law could happened anywhere, at any time, but was especially likely to occur in men and women's ritual business. No one asked for or provided details of the specific form that this ritual punishment took in open public segments of the evidence. An exchange between a lawyer representing the Belyuen, Tom Keely, and one of the Belyuen claimants, Alexander Nilco, can stand as typical of these exchanges:

TOM KEELY: Yes. Now do the people who look after the dreaming sites in this country, can they stop doing it?

ALEXANDER NILCO: No, they still running, I think, still going.

TOM KEELY: Under your law though, are they allowed to stop or do they have to keep going?

ALEXANDER NILCO: No.

TOM KEELY: They keep going.

ALEXANDER NILCO: Keep going.

TOM KEELY: That law, there's an Aboriginal law that applies to the way people behave in this country?

ALEXANDER NILCO: Aboriginal law.

TOM KEELY: And how do you get to be inside that law?

ALEXANDER NILCO: Can you explain again?

TOM KEELY: Is there a way—is there something that happens to Aboriginal people as they grow up that puts them inside that law?

ALEXANDER NILCO: It's pretty hard there.

TOM KEELY: Okay, perhaps it's a bad question. But, when you go through ceremony, what does that do for you? Do you have to follow the law, follow that ceremony?

ALEXANDER NILCO: You got to follow the law, yes.

TOM KEELY: Okay, and what happens if you don't follow the law?

ALEXANDER NILCO: Well you get punished for that, from our side, Aboriginal law.[35]

As this brief exchange suggests, claimants are pressed to assert and calibrate—to make a judgment about—their own internal subjective states and those of others in a variety of past, present, and future possible worlds. In effect, witnesses are pushed to lace their testimony with a minor philosophy of the ought.

Analytic philosophers and linguists have sought to determine the logical and semiotic principles expressed in European languages by mood and modal terms such as "ought," "must," "may," and "might," and in non-European languages by various lexical, grammatical, or prosodic markers that semantically express judgment, evidence, obligation, capability, and commitment.[36] This interest in the logical and semantic structure of mood and modality has provided us with a rich comparative understanding of how languages allow speakers to express varying levels of commitment to a statement or action.

But although languages provide speakers with the delicate means for calibrating and asserting the obligation, knowledge, belief, and capacity of sentient and nonsentient beings toward various states, conditions, and events, it is not language that demands that witnesses deploy these various linguistic technologies. Lawyers seeking to aid or impair claimant cases urge speakers to draw on these grammatical, prosodic, and lexical features of language to fine tune their characterizations of past, present, and future states of being, about the beliefs and obligations that will be or have been incumbent on persons in these states — these other possible, probable, even improbable worlds. In other words, languages provide the delicate means for calibrating and asserting obligation but institutional structures pressure Aboriginal subjects to make constant and rapid judgments about others and themselves.

This is not to say that Belyuen women and men do not judge or are not capable of judgment, nor that they do not calibrate their own and others' beliefs and compulsions based on their own intensional and extensional worlds. As an example, take the explicit and tacit attitudes that various Belyuen expressed in the Kenbi Land Claim about the compulsory quality of their relationship to the land under claim. I am not interested here so much in the cultural logic of embodiment they describe, but rather in the stance the Belyuen speakers take toward their obligations. The *inability* of persons to leave a place or a people — their compulsive return — signals for many Belyuen their proper being from and for a people and place. Indeed, a critical index of the proper person for and from a Dreaming site and its general territory is the pattern of human movement — the movement of bodies, desires, and language.

MR. MAURICE: Can you tell me how do you get to be an owner for this country?

ALICE DJARUG: We know for Belyuen people, we know this Belyuen.

MR. MAURICE: What happens if someone from Belyuen moves away and they maybe go down to Port Keats and has children and lives down there.

ALICE DJARUG: No.

MR. MAURICE: They're not an owner?

ALICE DJARUG: Mm. They can't leave this Belyuen.[36]

MR. YOUNG: Who taught you the dreamings on this country, the Cox Peninsula and the Islands?

BETTY BILAWAG: Well, my husband.

MR. YOUNG: Which husband was that?

BETTY BILAWAG: First husband, Mosec.

MR. YOUNG: Now, these dreamings on the Cox Peninsula and the islands we've been talking about over the past few days, who looks after those dreamings?

BETTY BILAWAG: All the Belyuen. Us mob got to look after them.

MR. YOUNG: Does ceremony look after country?

BETTY BILAWAG: Yes.

. . .

BETTY BILAWAG: We got islands, we got to look after them. Kids come and go them camping. I'm going camping. My mother sitting down here going camping. We still going to look after them. We go down to the beach, camping, weekend, take down kids with us. We got to teach them down, grandchildren. And I know I can stop to Milik and my kids don't want to leave that country. Me, I can't leave that country myself.[37]

Freedom from corporeal compulsion is not the ground of a local ethics of territoriality. Particularly instructive is the request of Robert Blowes, legal counsel assisting the Larrakia, to Betty Bilawag, a member of the Belyuen, that she evaluate the type of obligations she, her children, her deceased mother, and other Aboriginal persons had, have, and will have to the country and its Dreamings. (From a non-Aboriginal perspective, Banadjirr and Ngalgenbena were the classificatory grandparents of Betty Bilawag, who was about seventy years old when she gave the following testimony.)

MR. BLOWES: All right. And what about some of these old people we have been talking about yesterday and today. Might be that—first we started with, sorry, Mr. Keely started talking about Banjidjirr [Banadjirr] and Ngalgenbena and people like that. Were they owners for this country?

BETTY BILAWAG: No, they were just stopped, staying here all the time, you know. See, people who look after this country, we've have got to stay in Belyuen and we look after this country and dreamings. We got to look after dreamings else it's gone and we know that dreaming gone so.

MR. BLOWES: So, you've been looking after country?

BETTY BILAWAG: Yes. And kids, all the boys, they can't get away. They got to look after the dreaming Mother got to look after them, kids and dreaming and the way we walk around. It's really our country back long way. We been keep it for Larrakia people but I don't know. Larrakia people don't know this country. I know. I just must be know, but others—

MR. BLOWES: Some Larrakia people know this country?

BETTY BILAWAG: I don't know.

MR. BLOWES: Well, like Raelene?

BETTY BILAWAG: Yes, Raelene know, Zoe.

MR. BLOWES: Some of your family, like Patrick Briston?

BETTY BILAWAG: Yes, that's my family and my sister's kids, Alice Briston.

MR. BLOWES: They know.

BETTY BILAWAG: Might be they know but he don't know much, because I know him. And kids know too, this country.

MR. BLOWES: Which kids?

BETTY BILAWAG: Briston. They always come down here camping on weekend, they always come back. But the others, I never see them. Nobody knows this country, I think. I know.

MR. BLOWES: Is that all you wanted to say about that?

BETTY BILAWAG: I don't know, but must be they know some. Alice know this time. I showed them this country. I said, your grandfather country and your father's country, I said to them, but other people don't want to come back and look after the place any way, camping, no. They don't want to come, I don't know why they never come back. I said, "why?" And they don't like it.[38]

We can account for Belyuen statements like Bilawag's ("They don't want to come, I don't know why they never come back. I said, 'why?' And they don't like it") as political in the most instrumental of senses. Bilawag uses the lack of an action-based commitment to claim lands to assert an internal attitude toward that land and thereby underscore the illegitimacy of the Larrakia claim. But if we extend the same charity to Bilawag and other Belyuen that we extend to other Aboriginal groups testifying in this case, not to mention the lawyers and anthropologists aiding them, then she is, at least some of the time, trying to reconcile her beliefs and knowledges about the relationship between her territorial heritage and her present-day compulsory territorial practices to the territorial aspirations and practices of other Aboriginal people. And, significantly, she is attempting to reconcile beliefs and practices within the genre-specific requirement of a legal hearing. In other words, when placed within the communicative environment of the LRA and other belief-and obligation-based pieces of state legislation, the Belyuen struggle to make sense of the strange fact that people who claim to own or be for and from a country do not exhibit any compulsion to return to it. This in light of the fact that the Belyuen perceive themselves as unable to leave the country from which they were born, even as they find themselves also returning to their southern countries. Why? What accounts for this discrepancy? What is the basis of their attachment?

MR. YOUNG: They [the Larrakia] take this country?
RUBY YARROWIN: Yes.
MR. YOUNG: Yes. Why is that?
RUBY YARROWIN: I don't know. Bit hard.[39]

"Why"? In Emiyenggal, Ruby Yarrowin's first language, "why" translates the term *eminu,* which can also be translated as "what from" or "what caused," with the suffix *-nu* a purposive, future deontic marker. What compelled you to do this? You will be compelled by what? When asked these questions in relation to the land claim, Belyuen men and women provide multiple reasons for why they are bound to the claim lands and its ceremonies. Sometimes people will answer, "We think for this place and come back"; sometimes, "No matter we try go away can't." If pushed, they might add that they cannot leave the country because they have "always been living" there; because their parents passed on to them *maruy* from the Belyuen *durlg;* because their parents' spirits (*nyuidj*) are still in the land; because their ceremony is there. At still other times, in answer to the origin of their obligation to remain in the land, to abide by "our side, Aboriginal law," Belyuen speakers will simply refer to the "Dreaming."

Such citings of the Dreaming refer less to the content of a cultural order than to the fact of its compulsory obligation. The Dreaming, a lexical (nominal) item, acts like a modal "must." To be sure, they might say that they must keep the law going to keep the land going. But most Belyuen do not say that they obey the law because they understand its rationale or the social, moral, and ethical principles underlying it. They are compelled to obey because it is the law and it is "still running . . . still going." And it is still going because people still feel they must . . . or should. Certainly, persons learn more as they progress through ceremonies, as they constantly intercalate ritual and quotidian knowledges. But to explain the reason for the compulsion of the law, they refer to the fact that *the deepest law is compulsion.* To be Belyuen as such is to be compelled to be as such, to find oneself in the returning, again and again to particular places, practices, people; in the knowing that one should be doing certain things—returning, staying—even if one is not; or in the being bothered by the fact that one is not. Indeed, finding the proper place of the self through observing one's compulsive, patterned, actions interprets the truth of all proper connections — affective, linguistic, legal, territorial, and practical.

At this point, it would seem that I have retreated to the high water mark of modernist representations of primitive subjectivity — the logical necessity of totemism as described by Emile Durkheim and Marcel Mauss.

> When Stewart asked a native to which division the bull [totem] belonged, he received, after a moment of reflection, the following answer: "It eats: it is Boortwerio," i.e. of the tea-shrub clan, which probably comprises all grassland and herbivores. But this is very probably an *ad hoc* explanation to which the black has recourse in order to justify his classification to himself and to reduce it to general rules by which to be guided. Quite often, moreover, such questions take him unawares, and he is constrained, in answer to everything, to invoke tradition.[40]

Two points. First, early modernist ethnological accounts sharply distinguished so-called primitive allegiances to cultural forms from civil allegiances to the same. They engaged in what Lévi-Strauss would later call an archaic illusion. Following Lévi-Strauss's general insight if not his model, I have elsewhere argued that all subjects of discourse are subjected to some law of compulsion, although its location, form, and content are liable to historical change. This is to say little more than what critical western social theory has already described as doxa and hegemony.[41] The terms *doxa* and *hegemony*, and the theories supporting them give speakers the sense of having contained the spread of nonfreedom, of coercion, even though the terms cannot and do not pretend to describe the content of the domains to which they refer. The hegemonic, the real, the doxic, and related terms create a feeling of freedom through a referential practice as tautological as the Dreaming, justice, and freedom. All these nouns do is name and point to modal feeling — the inexpressible thing that binds our actions.

The distinction then between Belyuen and Enlightenment stances toward compulsion is not the fact of its presence or absence in subjectivity but the manner in which this fact qualifies social practice. A surface reading of Enlightenment liberalism might find a Western abhorrence of the compulsive, contrasting sharply with Belyuen attitudes toward the same. After all, as humanists creep closer to the categorical imperatives of everyday life — the inexpressible of modal *feelings* rather than the speakable of social propositionality — they inch ever nearer to the conditions that negate liberal definitions of freedom. But Enlightenment rationality, and the state and public institutional structures that have risen up with them, in practice, if not in ideology, abhor the compulsive only in certain contexts. There are many situations in which politicians and publicans refer to moral compulsion (moral sense) as the basis of freedom or freedom's restriction. In personal or state-mediated encounters with the deontic, the facility and bravado of Enlightenment manifestos for liberty or death dim.

Second, subjective compulsions are state mandates. As I mentioned earlier, the legislative language of the LRA requires the land commissioner to take into regard "the strength or otherwise of the traditional attachment by the claimants to the land claimed."[42] The subsequent Native Title Act requires the register of native title claims, and also requires the tribunal that eventually hears them, to assess whether or not the claim group continues to "hold" the "traditional laws" and "traditional customs" that subtend native title according to the state.[43] A claim is, therefore, maximally legally felicitous when claimants exhibit a maximal compulsory relation to land and its law — when they "hold" the land and law without question, abide by it for little reason more than because it is.

THE SECRET

All the above calibrations of legally mandated difference and obligation have referred to instances in which an indigenous person seems to be referring to culture rather than morality, or to cultural practices considered morally neutral. When the traditional practice being described seems to non-Aboriginal listeners to be about morality rather than culture (that is, when the compulsory nature of indigenous law strongly conflicts with the compulsory nature of settler law) the explanations that claimants give about why they believe cannot simply be sensible. They must also seem true, right, just: human(e). The Belyuen themselves, and Keely and myself as their apologists, can present explanations of local moral systems that are coherent and recognizable as such, are socially productive and recognizable as such, and yet still be considered to be mere justifications for immoral — worse, abhorrent — practices. How do indigenous persons discuss the customary when it is prohibited, or considered abhorrent, especially when their livelihood and the livelihood of their social networks seem to rely on this discussion? In what ways does the law's emphasis on difference push claimant culture toward the secret thing lurking in difference and sequestered from the public under the sign of "the secret"? In these moments the inexpressible sense of moral compulsion changes the form in which the speakable is spoken. That is, something strange happens to sense when a person is forced to speak and write about the abhorrent in the genre of the unspoken.

10 October 1996, approximately 7:30 A.M.: Because the ferry from Darwin had been delayed, we were behind schedule and worried that the land commissioner and his entourage would arrive before we had time to speak with key senior men and women who had recently flown in from Port Keats (Wadeye), an Aboriginal community to the south of Belyuen. Tom Keely wished to speak to Alexander Nilco and Paul Smiler in particular. To maximize our time, Keely and I decided to separate. I would speak with the elder women, he with the elder men. Having finished talking with the women, I walked over to the house where Keely had gone. As I approached the driveway, a Toyota troop carrier rapidly backed out and then drove quickly away. The brother (I will call him Fred) of the man whose driveway I was about to enter was driving and was clearly upset. As I turned back into the driveway, Alex Nilco stumbled out of the yard. Against his forehead he was holding tightly what had once been a white rag. It was now soaked with fresh blood. "You right?" I asked. "Me, right. Brother yours just been kill me belonga funeral," he replied. "Mmm, sorry wulman [old man], you right for walk up?" I asked, indicating the health clinic not far away:

> NILCO: Yeah, me right. Judge, what time im come?
>
> POVINELLI: Soon. You talk today?
>
> NILCO: Must be. Lawyer, I been talk le [to] im. Im there inside. I go hospital first, stitches.
>
> POVINELLI: You sure you right?
>
> NILCO: Yeah, me right. What's wrong?
>
> POVINELLI: Neh, nothing.

We laughed, shook our heads and turned away from each other.

Once again I turned into the driveway and once again someone rushed out. This time I faced Tom Keely. He was clearly upset, verging on being beside himself, saying that Fred was out of control. Keely proceeded to describe what had occurred minutes before I arrived. Fred had stormed into the courtyard yelling that no one from the Nilco family had bothered coming to the recent funeral of his eldest brother, the senior ceremonial leader for the area, and yet they dared come to give evidence in the land claim. Fred then picked up a *nullanulla* (fighting stick) and hit Nilco across the forehead. "Hmm," I replied to Keely, "That's true about the funeral." I probably appeared callous and distant to Keely—indeed eerily so considering the blood on the driveway. In response to his unease about my attitude or to my own unease about how it might appear to him or to me on reflection, I continued the conversation. Here is a selection from notes I wrote down later in the day:

> POVINELLI: It's the law, Tom, remember, "It's hard; it can happen anytime." What did you think that meant?
>
> KEELY: Right. Right. Ok, but he was furious, in a rage. This was no rational ritual punishment.
>
> POVINELLI: Whether this is rational or passionate it's what you've been defending day after day. "Any time, anywhere, anyone in your family." No one's kidding. I didn't hear anyone ask if you have to be rational in the delivery system for it to be traditional. This isn't easy. It's not just hard on one end of the stick. You try to hit your brother, mother, daughter, because you're obliged to.
>
> KEELY: You think this is how punishment should be carried out—in a rage?

This was not an easy question for me to answer for personal and conceptual reasons. It was later in this same day that Keely asked Nilco whether or not he had to follow the law, and what would happen if he did not. Nilco replied to this line of questioning with stitches latticed across his forehead.

Tom Keely was experienced in land claim procedures and practices, in the discourses of Aboriginal law, and in representations and some practices of indigenous men's ritual. As was I. And, no less than Daly River's Constable Turner was forced to reflect, hone, and shape his critical judgment in the proximity of ritual law, were Tom Keely and I affected in our practices of truth. Both of our first visceral responses might have been critical. But subsequent reflections focused on the appropriateness of his response and what lay beneath it. Keely came to *understand* the dissonance among his legal practices, his moral beliefs, and his gut responses. I came to understand the strange trajectory of the familial forms of violence I knew at Belyuen and in the United States. Here we seem to have evidence opposing the principle of collective morality. But, on this and subsequent occasions in which we discussed this incident and others like it, Keely remained hesitant to embrace some local practices of truth, law, and justice, no matter what sense they made from a local perspective. I refused to budge on its sensibility. Something nagged at his and my conscience: an ought, a should, an obligatory attitude toward certain types of actors and actions that he and I could not dismiss no matter that neither of us could fully justify its rightfulness in all possible social and cultural contexts. His job and mine, indeed, our desire, was to support the local, the customary; and yet a feeling remained that something about this type of social violence was wrong or right *no matter what sense it might make in its own context.* Something else appeared alongside this ever so delicate feeling that Keely might not have hitherto imagined — the possibility of a truly alterior moral order, an *other* possible world. The possibility of moral alterity irritated the actual world that Keely inhabited and the fantasy world he had imagined in his legal practice.[44] But it also made his practice serious and weighty — indeed, profound. He became more human in the domain of potential inhumanity. And the Belyuen became more authentic; there was a secret or something truly other behind the words they spoke. But this otherness — its truth — is nothing but a feeling of maximal difference from our own; that is, it is not there, in and of itself. This otherness exists in relationship to us.

But land claims do not accidentally run into radical difference. They produce it as the authentic discursive field of indigenous culture. The Kenbi Land Claim is a good example of this. When the case was first run in 1989, little emphasis was placed on the ceremonial side of local indigenous life. And yet, as suggested in Olney's writings summarized in chapter 4, ceremonial activity is widely considered to lie at the heart of Aboriginal culture, to define its difference. Not surprisingly, then, when the claim was reheard in 1995, customary law lay at the foreground. But if we asked ourselves what law is this customary law, we would return to the history of the region as I outline in chapter 3. A history many of the senior members of the Belyuen remember clearly.

We find ourselves at the point where this chapter began: the elliptical nature of Aboriginal testimony. When we reexamine the secret nature of Aboriginal evidence, we now see that indigenous persons are obliged simultaneously to cite and to safeguard the fact of abhorrent beliefs and practices from the public record and from public circulation. Many people inside and outside Aboriginal communities may object to characterizing local secrets as state and public mandates, arguing that from an Aboriginal perspective some information is and should be kept secret, sequestered from the public. And they might further argue that questioning the local origin of practices of secrecy and knowledge feeds into a recent conservative assault on Aboriginal testimony.

So let me be clear. What I'm getting at here is somewhat different from the problem of traditional evidence in land and cultural heritage claims. I am trying to understand the function of the secret in restricted and public sessions as a demand on, not an accommodation to, local epistemological practices. This does not mean that Aboriginal people do not and should not consider their ritual and quotidian practices as involving varying degrees of exclusivity and inclusivity or that they should not be allowed to maintain these degrees in the context of hearings. Rather, it means that a secret is a mandated marker of authentic indigeneity and reminds us that the truth of this secret is already circulating in public.

As a result Aboriginal subjects face the task of deciding not only what to tell non-Aboriginals, but also how deeply they must establish an abject relation to traditions and identifications that are deemed legally and publicly abhorrent. For example, the performance of secret-sacred male and female initiation ceremonies on the land under claim is considered a primary index of land ownership under the LRA in this case and others. But the content of these ceremonies might be immoral from the perspective of the very lawyers presenting the Belyuen case, if not illegal under existing Australian statutory laws. In the context of land claims, indigenous women and men must, therefore, consider once again the morality and legality of their ceremonial identities and identifications, bodily performances and sensualities.

This corporeal anxiety and reflexivity is intensified by the material and psychic needs of the land claim process itself—the need to produce in claimants a belief that, no matter the long, tortured history of state and public repression and laissez-faire neglect, change is possible. To assuage Belyuen doubts and overcome the weight of the historical failure of the Kenbi Land Claim, Belyuen lawyers dangled hope, reason, and the progress of white Australia, emphasizing the evolving nature of law and interpretation, the changing mood of the nation, the moral claim of the Belyuen, and my presence as someone who knew them and cared. The Belyuen were asked to forget failure and indifference and instead focus on history in the making. Lives and generations hanging in the balance, the Belyuen and I stretched to reach the law's demands and to hide from it those traditions that might shame us in order to increase the chances we would be free to live our lives.

Little should be surprising here. All people will find that some customary laws go too far (but we may rely on the facts that the elders will have enough common sense not to go too far or not to publicize practices crossing this line of common sense). At some point, the experience of alterity will capitalize the empty concepts of human justice, human decency, and human right and will act as a commonsense differentiator between difference and evil, the cultural and the moral. But, in all multicultural contexts, difference teases with alterity; it does so especially in contexts in which the distribution of material resources are linked to cultural expression.

Go. Walk into the law.

THE COST OF RELAXATION

It is no surprise to people who have had any land claim experience that the law of recognition imposes certain requirements on the form in which the local must appear to be recognized as a rights- and material-bearing identity. Most practicing land claim lawyers and anthropologists know the law imposes conditions on the performance of local culture and that these conditions are based on abstracted anthropological models that do not fit any particular Aboriginal group, culture, or practice perfectly. Many lawyers and anthropologists would describe themselves as liberal, or liberal-Left, but few as "idealists." They know that even though the legislative shoe does not quite fit local footing, indigenous claimants must squeeze into it if they are to gain the benefits of the law. But this critical legal reflexivity does not preclude these same persons from also believing that local traditions are "shoe-like"; that the statutory abstractions with which they work were found by an anthropological science before becoming foundational in court, public, and state discourse. That is, juridical and critical publics are seduced by a phrase, *by and large,* a variant of the long history of *more or less.* Most lawyers, land commissioners, and anthropological consultants understand Aboriginal cultural traditions to be like the form the law demands, *by and large.* A "reasonable Aborigine" will *see* in the legislation a shadowy image of her or his culture, though she or he will not *seek* it. This is the reasonable Aboriginal subject.[45]

The willingness of lawyers and anthropologists to leap over rather than tarry in the gap between abstracted anthropological and legal models and local modes of localization is one of the means by which forms of liberal force are extended rather than critically engaged. But we can and should ask what lawyers, anthropologists, and Aboriginal activists should do instead. Lawyers and the anthropologists assisting them do their best to represent their clients, to present the truth of their lives to the court, and, through these representations, to work for social justice. The difference between abstracted anthropological models and local modes of social organization can even be understood as a productive part of this fight for social justice. The difference between them allows lawyers to exploit a certain flexibility in the law. Lawyers can argue that even though a local group does not perfectly match the requirements of a piece of legislation they can nevertheless be seen as fulfilling the spirit of the law. The spirit of the law is, after all, to recognize local traditional social organization, not to use an outdated anthropological model to discipline the local. Such arguments are often made in land and native title claims. And they are effectively made. They win country for indigenous people.

The spirit of the law is what cares for indigenous people. Critiques of liberal forms of domination should not dismiss or take lightly the truth of state, national, and legal caretaking. Persons who work within juridical and state jobs do care deeply about subaltern bodies, desires, and language. They seek to demonstrate their concern and to show that these bodies, desires, and language can be recognized by the law. They beckon them toward the state's remedial institutions. But insofar as they do, they unintentionally reinstate liberal law and desire as the end of difference and they help to saturate locals with this dream.

NOTES

INTRODUCTION: CRITICAL COMMON SENSE

1 W. E. H. Stanner, "Continuity and Change (1958)," in *White Man Got No Dreaming* (Canberra: Australian National University Press, 1979), 50, my emphasis.

2 *Hayes v. Northern Territory 1999, Report of the Native Tribunal Commissioner, Mr. Justice Olney,* (Canberra: Australian Publishing Service, 1999), para. 20.

3 www.aboriginal-art.com. Wadeye was connected to this circulatory system prior to the expansion of the airport and the creation of the art gallery. Several Wadeye barks, painted during the 1960s, were featured in the most recent Sotheby's indigenous art catalog, with prices listed ranging between five hundred and five thousand dollars.

4 See Ghassan Hage, *White Nation: Fantasies of White Supremacy in a Multicultural Society* (Sydney: Pluto Press, 1998); Meaghan Morris, *Too Soon, Too Late: History in Popular Culture* (Bloomington: Indiana University Press, 1998); and Sara Ahmed, *Strange Encounters: Embodied Others in Post-Coloniality* (London: Routledge, 2000).

5 See Stuart Hall, "When Was 'the Post-Colonial'? Thinking at the Limit," in *The Post-Colonial Question: Common Skies, Divided Horizons*, ed. Iain Chambers and Lidia Curti (London: Routledge, 1996), 242–60, esp. 252.

6 I do not mean to indicate a geographical space by the phrase "colonial and post-colonial world." Albert Memmi and Frantz Fanon and, more recently, Homi K. Bhabha have convincingly argued that the colonial subject is a historical epoch rather than a geographical location. See Albert Memmi, *The Colonizer and the Colonized* (New York: Orion, 1965); Frantz Fanon, *The Wretched of the Earth*, trans. Constance Farrington (New York: Grove Press, 1965); Homi K. Bhabha, *The Location of Culture* (London: Routledge, 1994). See also Mahmood Mamdani, *Beyond Rights Talk and Culture Talk: Comparative Essays in the Politics of Rights and Culture* (New York: St. Martin's Press, 2000).

7 Ranajit Guha and Gayatri Spivak, eds., *Selected Subaltern Studies* (Oxford: Oxford University Press, 1992); Dipesh Chakrabarty, "Postcoloniality and the Artifice of History: Who Speaks for 'Indian' Pasts?" *Representations* 37 (1992): 1–16; Homi K. Bhabha, "The Other Question: Stereotype, Discrimination, and the Discourse of Colonialism," in *The Location of Culture* (New York: Routledge, 1994), 66–84; Hall, "When Was 'the Post-Colonial'?"; Kaja Silverman, "White Skin, Brown Masks: The Double Mimesis, or Lawrence in Arabia," *differences* 1.3 (1989): 3–54; Michel-Rolph Trouillot, "Abortive Rituals: Historical Apologies in the Global Era," *Intervention: International Journal of Postcolonial Studies*. 2.2 (2000): 171–86, special issue, "Rights and Wrongs," ed. Homi K. Bhabha and Rajeswari Sunden Rajan.

8 See Slavoj Žižek's discussion of the critical ideological role played by images in which the nation and its citizens appear likable to themselves and images in which they appear to themselves as likable and worthy of love (Žižek, *The Sublime Object of Ideology* [London: Verso, 1989], 105). See also Etienne Balibar's provocative reading of Althusser on ideology: "Just as the accumulation of capital is made of 'living labor' (according to Marx), so the oppressive apparatuses of the State, Churches, and other dominant institutions function with the popular religious, moral, legal and aesthetic imaginary of the masses as their specific fuel" (Balibar, "The Non-Contemporaneity of Althusser," in *The Althusserian Legacy* ed. E. Ann Kaplan and Michael Sprinker [London: Verso, 1993], 13). See also Lauren Berlant, "The Subject of True Feeling: Pain, Privacy, and Politics," in *Cultural Pluralism, Identity Politics, and the Law*, ed. Austin Sarat (Ann Arbor: University of Michigan Press, 1999).

9 John Caputo, *Against Ethics* (Bloomington: Indiana University Press, 1993), 85.

10 Charles Sanders Peirce, "The Three Normative Sciences," in *The Essential Peirce: Selected Philosophical Writings, Volume 2 (1893–1913)*, ed. The Peirce Edition Project (Bloomington: Indiana University Press, 1998), 207.

11 Charles Sanders Peirce, "The Nature of Meaning," in *The Essential Peirce: Selected Philosophical Writings, Volume 2 (1893–1913)*, ed. The Peirce Edition Project (Bloomington: Indiana University Press, 1998), 210.

12 For Peirce's discussion of critical common sense, see Charles Sanders Peirce, "Pragmatism," in *The Essential Peirce: Selected Philosophical Writings, Volume 2 (1893–*

1913), ed. The Peirce Edition Project (Bloomington: Indiana University Press, 1998), 398–433.

13 See Jürgen Habermas, *Between Facts and Norms* (Cambridge, Mass.: MIT Press, 1987); and John Rawls, *Political Liberalism* (New York: Columbia University Press, 1993).

14 Michael Walzer, *On Toleration* (New Haven: Yale University Press, 1997), 5–6.

15 This too was the spirit that animated early deconstructive and genealogical texts. See, for instance, Jacques Derrida, "The Ends of Man," in *Margins of Philosophy* (Chicago: University of Chicago, 1982), 109–36; and Michel Foucault, "What Is Critique?" in *The Politics of Truth*, ed. Sylvere Lotringer (New York: Semiotext(e), 1997), 23–82.

16 For a "critical theory of recognition" and redistribution, see Nancy Fraser, "From Redistribution to Recognition? Dilemmas of Justice in a 'Post-Socialist' Age," *The New Left Review* 212 (July/August 1995): 68–93.

17 John Frow and Meaghan Morris, "Introduction," in *Australian Cultural Studies: A Reader* ed. John Frow and Meaghan Morris (Urbana: University of Illinois Press, 1993), x.

18 For an overview of the recent economic history of Australia in relationship to the Asia-Pacific, see R. Higgott, "Australia: Economic Crises and the Politics of Regional Economic Adjustment," in *Southeast Asia in the 1980s: The Politics of Economic Crisis*, ed. R. Robison, K. Hewison, and R. Higgot (Sydney: Allen and Unwin, 1987), 177–217. Meaghan Morris has also noted this period of economic transformation as a significant moment in the cultural time of Australian nationalism: "By 1986, as the Treasurer began to warn of our 'banana republic' tendencies and burgeoning foreign debt, viewers were in the words of one angry critic, 'treated nightly to the spectacle of *economic* commentators pronouncing on the government's *political* performance. . . . It was as though foreign traders, rather than Australian voters, had become the arbiters of political taste in this country" (Morris, "Future Fear," in *Mapping the Future: Local Cultures, Global Changes,* ed. Jon Bird, Barry Curtis, Tim Putnam, George Robertson, and Lisa Tickner [New York: Routledge, 1993], 33).

19 Gilles Deleuze, *Foucault* (Minneapolis: University of Minnesota Press, 1986), 100.

20 Michael Pusey, *Economic Rationalism in Canberra: A Nation-Building State Changes Its Mind* (Cambridge: Cambridge University Press, 1991), esp. 2–3.

21 Antonio Gramsci, "State and Civil Society," in *Selections from the Prison Notebooks* (New York: International Publishers, 1992), 206–76.

22 Pusey, *Economic Rationalism in Canberra*, 213. The equity of income distribution was celebrated during the 1890 Australasian Federation Conference. See Robin Sharwood, *Debates of the Australasian Federation Conference of 1890 together with Extracts from the British Press Concerning Federation and the Australasian Federation Conference of 1890* (Sydney: Legal Books, 1990).

23 Donald Horne, *The Lucky Country* (Ringwood: Penguin, 1964).

24 See Brian Murphy, *The Other Australia* (Cambridge, Eng.: Cambridge University Press, 1993).

25 After periods of sustained growth from 1960 to 1974, the Australian economy suffered a severe recession in 1974, leading to what some economists have called "stag-flation." Unemployment peaked at 9.9 percent in 1982 but stayed above 7 percent from 1982 to 1988. At the same time, Australia's gross external debt rose sharply from under $10 billion to just under $140 billion. See Barrie Dyster and David Meredith, *Australia in the International Economy in the Twentieth Century* (Cambridge, Eng.: Cambridge University Press, 1990), esp. 269. See also Ken Buckley and Ted Wheelwright, *No Paradise for Workers: Capitalism and the Common People in Australia, 1788–1914* (Melbourne: Oxford University Press, 1988), 247.

26 See Alvin Y. So and Stephen W. K. Chiu, *East Asia and the World Economy* (London: Sage Publications, 1995).

27 Steve Chan and Cal Clark, "The Rise of the East Asian NICs: Confucian Capitalism, Status Mobility, and Developmental Legacy," in *The Evolving Pacific Basin in the Global Political Economy,* ed. Cal Clark and Steve Chan (Boulder: Lynne Rienner Publishers, 1992), 41.

28 See Dilip K. Das, *The Asia-Pacific Economy* (London: St. Martin's Press, 1996), 17.

29 Depending on their theoretical orientation, economists explain this realignment of capital accumulation to have been caused by free-market forces, cultural attitudes (Confucianism), state policy, or relations of dependency. For a good overview, see So and Chiu, *East Asia and the World Economy.*

30 Patrick Walters and Michael Gordon, "We're a Culture Apart, PM Tells Asia," *The Australian,* 18 September 1996, sec. A, p. 1. Michael Millet and Louise Williams, "PM Defends Soft Line on Indonesia," *Sydney Morning Herald,* 18 September 1996, sec. A, p. 1.

31 In the same year, the Immigration Restriction Act imposed an infamous dictation requirement that screened out nonwhite immigrants.

32 John Chesterman and Brian Galligan, *Citizens without Rights: Aborigines and Australian Citizenship* (Cambridge, Eng.: Cambridge University Press, 1997), 81–82.

33 Alan Powell, *Far Country: A Short History of the Northern Territory* (Melbourne: Melbourne University Press, 1988), 161.

34 Ronald Wilson, *Bringing Them Home: Report of the National Inquiry into the Separation of Aboriginal and Torres Strait Islander Children from Their Families,* ed. Meredith Wilkie (Sydney: Human Rights and Equal Opportunity Commissioner, 1997). See also Tony Austin, *I Can Picture the Old Home So Clearly: The Commonwealth and "Half-Caste" Youth in the Northern Territory, 1911–1939* (Canberra: Aboriginal Studies Press, 1993).

35 Powell, *Far Country,* 233.

36 See for instance, J. K. Doolan, "Walk-Off (and Later Return) of Various Aboriginal Groups from Cattle Stations," in *Aborigines and Change: Australia in the '70s,* ed. R. M. Berndt (Canberra: Australian Institute of Aboriginal Studies, 1977). See also B. Attwood and A. Markus, *The 1967 Referendum, or When Aborigines Didn't Get the Vote* (Canberra: Australian Institute of Aboriginal and Torres Strait Islander Studies, 1997); L. Lippman, *Generations of Resistance: The Aboriginal Struggles for Justice* (Melbourne: Longman, 1981); F. Bandler, *Turning the Tide* (Canberra: Ab-

original Studies Press, 1989); and A. Wright, ed., *Take Power Like This Old Man Here: An Anthology of Writings Celebrating Twenty Years of Land Rights in Central Australia, 1977–1997* (Alice Springs, NT: Jukurrpa Books, 1998).

37 The Bondi protests were reported by Fiona Harai, "Beating Our Own Drum," *The Weekend Australian,* 26–27 June 1999, 23; The Indonesian banner was photographed by Bullit Marquez, *Sydney Morning Herald,* 21 September 1999, 12.

38 Jane M. Jacobs and Fay Gale, *Tourism and the Protection of Aboriginal Cultural Sites* (Canberra: Australian Government Publishing Service, 1994).

39 Fred Myers, "Representing Culture: The Production of Discourse(s) for Aboriginal Acrylic Painting," *Cultural Anthropology* 6.1 (1992): 26–62; Nicholas Thomas, *Possessions: Indigenous Art/Colonial Culture* (London: Thames and Hudson, 1999); Elizabeth A. Povinelli, "Consuming *Geist:* Popontology and the Spirit of Capital in Indigenous Australia," *Public Culture,* special issue "Millennial Capitalism," ed. Jean Comaroff and John L. Comaroff. 12.2 (2000): 501–28.

40 Eric Michaels, *Bad Aboriginal Art: Tradition, Media, and Technological Horizon* (Sydney: Allen and Unwin, 1994).

41 "Ms Edgar said [one] way to destroy a people was to detribalize them by taking away their stories and their dreams replacing them with imported ones" (reported in Robert Wilson, "Children's TV Head Blasts 'Sinister' US," *The Australian,* 3 July 1996, 3).

42 See, for instance, Rosemary Coombe, *The Cultural Life of Intellectual Properties: Authorship, Appropriation, and the Law* (Durham: Duke University Press, 1998); Will Kymlicka, *Multicultural Citizenship* (Oxford: Oxford University Press, 1995); William E. Connolly, *Identity/Difference* (Ithaca: Cornell University Press, 1991); Bernard Williams, "Toleration: A Political or Moral Question?," in *Tolerance between Intolerance and the Intolerable,* ed. Paul Ricoeur (Providence: Berghahn Books, 1996), 35–48.

43 For critical discussions of the limits of tolerance, see Susan Moller Okin, *Is Multiculturalism Bad for Women?* (Princeton: Princeton University Press, 1997), 7–24; Stanley Fish, "Boutique Multiculturalism," *Critical Inquiry* 23.2 (1997): 378–95; Alenka Zupancic, "The Subject of the Law," in *Cogito and the Unconscious,* ed. Slavoj Žižek (Durham: Duke University Press, 1998), 41–73.

44 Slavoj Žižek, "Introduction," in *Mapping Ideology* (London: Verso, 1994), 7.

45 John Comaroff, "The Discourse of Rights in Colonial South Africa: Subjectivity, Sovereignty, Modernity," in *Identities, Politics, and Rights,* ed. Austin Sarat and Thomas R. Kearns (Ann Arbor: University of Michigan Press, 1995), 193–236.

46 Charles Taylor, "The Politics of Recognition," in *Multiculturalism: Examining the Politics of Recognition,* ed. Amy Gutmann (Princeton: Princeton University Press, 1994), 25–73, 66.

47 France used already existing legislation prohibiting violence against children to outlaw the practice of clitoridectomy. See Celia W. Dugger, "Tug of Taboos: African Genital Rite v. U.S. Law," *New York Times,* 28 December 1996, sec. 1, p. 1. The French state's discipline of a north African practice has an uncanny relationship to its past war in Algeria and to its present-day political relationship with Algeria. The

New York Times noted: "The war has at times come to bear an uncanny resemblance to the war of Algeria's independence. Then, too, the guerrillas, Algeria's National Liberation Front, used methods of startling savagery—including disembowelment, decapitation and the mutilation of genitals—to shatter the middle ground in society. Then, too, the authorities represented by the French Army responded with torture and indiscriminate killing. Then, too, the war spilled over into France, dividing its society and destroying the Fourth Republic" (Roger Cohen, "Troubled Tie: France Hears Alarming Echoes of Colonial Past from Algeria," *New York Times*, 12 December 1996, sec. A, p. 12.

48 The legislation was sponsored by representatives Pat Schroeder (D–Colorado) and Harry Reid (D–Nevada) as part of the Immigration Act. See Celia Dugger, "Genital Mutilation Is Outlawed," *New York Times*, 12 October 1996, sec. 1, p. 27; and Sharon Lerner, "Rite of Wrong," *Village Voice*, 26 March–1 April 1997, 44–46.

49 Christopher Newfield and Avery F. Gordon, "Multiculturalism's Unfinished Business," in *Mapping Multiculturalism*, ed. Avery F. Gordon and Christopher Newfield (Minneapolis: University of Minnesota Press, 1996), 77.

50 A social geography of the practice is emerging in the mass media. The *New York Times* educates the public on the regions where women are at the greatest risk: "New York and Newark are among the metropolitan areas where the largest number of these at-risk girls and women live" (Celia Dugger, "Genital Mutilation Is Outlawed," *New York Times*, 12 October 1996, sec. 1, p. 27.

51 Antonio Gramsci, "The Modern Prince," in *Selections from the Prison Notebooks* (New York: International Publishers, 1992), 123–205, esp. 132–33.

52 Mass media often conflates a diverse set of non-Western cultural practices and represents these as "premodern" or "precivil." For instance, the *New York Times* writes: "A much broader struggle is taking place across Africa. Throughout much of the continent, from the ritual slavery of the Ewe to female genital mutilation to polygamy, ancient practices that strike both Westerns and many Africans as abhorent coexist side by side with modernity" ("Human Rites: Africa's Culture War—Old Customs, New Values," *New York Times*, sec. 4, p. 1). Public culture is currently struggling over how to understand the (il)legitimacy of these practices when they occur among U.S. immigrants. How should U.S. law treat underaged marriage, polygamy, and wife beating when they occur in immigrant communities? See Nina Schuyler, "When in Rome: Should Courts Make Allowances for Immigrant Culture at Women's Expense?" *In These Times* 21.7 (1997): 27–29.

53 In the wake of the outlawing of social clitoridectomies by the U.S. Congress, the Left and Center mass media reported divisions among social communities affected by the law and among the medical community. For instance, the *New York Times* reported that U.S. health care officials were divided in their opinions on whether it was better to permit moderated and medically supervised clitoridectomies (giving a "ritual nick on the prepuse") or to condemn the practice to untrained persons who would perform the operation illegally. See Celia Dugger, "Tug of Taboos: African Genital Rite v. U.S. Law," *New York Times*, 28 December 1996, sec. 1, p. 1. These

divisions within the medical community and the community of practice are noted
· but underemphasized in Sharon Lerner, "Rite of Wrong," 44–46.

54 Stanley Fish has outlined the contradictions and ambivalences in models of multiculturalism. He and others distinguish weak and strong forms of multiculturalism
by the degree to which *any* moral judgment is seen as based on universal grounds
exterior to the particularities of cultural logics or *all* moral judgments are seen as
excretions of cultural logics or historical discursive positions. Fish argues, however, that both models are incoherently formulated. According to Fish, even the
most critical proponents of multiculturalism eventually stumble on a case of cultural difference that they *feel* they should or *do* refuse to support for reasons that
sound universalizing, but now cannot be defended as such. This is famously illus-
trated by the Salman Rushdie and NAMBL (North American Man-Boy Love) cases.
See Stanley Fish, "Boutique Multiculturalism." For a general discussion on the discursive impasse of multiculturalism in liberal democratic society, see Chicago Cultural Studies Group, "Critical Multiculturalism," *Critical Inquiry* 18 (spring 1992):
530–55; David Theo Goldberg, "Introduction: Multicultural Conditions," in *Multiculturalism: A Critical Reader,* ed. David Theo Goldberg (Oxford: Blackwell, 1994),
1–44; and Avery Gordon and Christopher Newfield, "Introduction," in *Mapping
Multiculturalism* (Minneapolis: University of Minnesota Press, 1996), 1–18. For a
critical discussion of the instability of both universalist and particularist grounds
for moral claims, see Ernesto Laclau, "Universalism, Particularism, and the Question of Identity," in *Emancipation(s)* (London: Verso, 1996), 20–35; and Lauren
Berlant, "1968, or Something," *Critical Inquiry* 21.1 (1994): 124–55.

55 Sigmund Freud, "Mourning and Melancholia," in *Collected Papers,* vol. 4, ed. Joan
Riviere (New York: Basic Books, 1959), 152–70.

56 Ernesto Laclau, "Introduction," in *The Making of Political Identities,* ed. Ernesto
Laclau (London: Verso, 1994), 1–8.

57 See Emile Durkheim, *The Division of Labor in Society* (1893; New York: Macmillan, 1964).

58 Segments of this discussion are drawn from Elizabeth A. Povinelli, "Sexuality at
Risk: Psychoanalysis Metapragmatically," in *Homosexuality and Psychoanalysis,* ed.
Tim Dean and Christopher Lane (Chicago: University of Chicago Press, 2001); and
Elizabeth A. Povinelli and George Chauncey, "Thinking Sexuality Transnation-
ally," *GLQ: A Journal of Lesbian and Gay Studies* 5.4 (1999): 439–49.

59 But see L. Sackett, "Welfare Colonialism: Developing Division at Wiluna," in *Going
It Alone,* ed. R. Tonkinson and M. Howard (Canberra: Aboriginal Studies Press,
1990); J. Collman, *Aboriginal Fringe Dwellers and Welfare* (St. Lucia: University of
Queensland Press, 1988); Jeremy Beckett, "Internal Colonialism in a Welfare State:
The Case of the Australian Aborigines," paper presented at the annual meeting of
the American Anthropological Association, Chicago, 1983.

60 Gillian Cowlishaw and Barry Morris, eds., *Race Matters: Indigenous Australians
and "Our" Society* (Canberra: Aboriginal Studies Press, 1997); Annette Hamilton,
"Fear and Desire: Aborigines, Asians, and the National Imaginary," *Australian Cultural History* 9 (1990): 14–35; Gillian Cowlishaw, *Rednecks, Eggheads, and Black-*

fellas (Ann Arbor: University of Michigan Press, 1999); Jeremy Beckett, *Torres Strait Islanders: Custom and Colonialism* (Sydney: Cambridge University Press, 1987); Diane Austin-Broos, " 'Two Laws': Ontologies, Histories: Ways of Being Aranda Today," *Oceania* 7 (1996): 1–20; David Trigger, *Whitefella Comin': Aboriginal Responses to Colonialism in Northern Australia* (New York: Cambridge University Press, 1992).

1 / MUTANT MESSAGES

1 Lorimer Fison, "Kamilaroi Marriage, Descent, and Relationship," in *Kamilaroi and Kunai,* ed. Lorimer Fison and A. W. Howitt (1880; Canberra: Australian Aboriginal Press, 1991).

2 Ibid., 29.

3 Ibid., 42.

4 "By present usage, I mean that which has been developed by the natives themselves, not that which has resulted from their contact with the white men. This is a factor which must be altogether cast out of the calculation, and an investigator on this line of research needs to be continually on watch against it" (Fison, "Kamilaroi Marriage, Descent, and Relationship," 29).

5 Ibid., 30.

6 Ibid., 59–60.

7 *The Wik Peoples v. the State of Queensland* (Canberra: Australian Government Printer, 1996), 146, 176.

8 Ibid., 146. See also Marshall Perron, "Sacred Sites — a Costly Token to a Dead Culture," *Northern Territory News,* 7 January 1989, 7.

9 *The Wik Peoples v. the State of Queensland,* 182.

10 Wilson, *Bringing Them Home.*

11 See Lisa Kearns, "Armbands Sell Like Hot Cakes," *The Age Melbourne Online,* 21 November 1997 (www.theage.com.au).

12 Silverman, "White Skin, Brown Masks," 3.

13 Freud, "Mourning and Melancholia."

14 I mean "meconnaissance" in the technical Lacanian sense in which "misrecognition is not ignorance. Misrecognition represents a certain organization of affirmations and negations, to which the subject is attached. Hence it cannot be conceived without correlative knowledge. If the subject is capable of misrecognising something, he surely must know what this function has operated upon. There must surely be, behind his misrecognition, a kind of knowledge of what there is to misrecognise" (Jacques Lacan, *The Seminar of Jacques Lacan: Book 1, Freud's Papers on Technique, 1953–1954,* ed. Jacques-Alain Miller, trans. John Forester [New York: W. W. Norton, 1988], 167).

15 Morris, *Too Soon, Too Late.*

16 State policy on indigenous affairs is generally considered to have moved through four broad phases: genocide, assimilation, self-determination, and most recently, reconciliation.

17 Debra Jopson, "Unemployment Rate Set to Soar for Aborigines," *The Age,* 24 August 1998, 7.

18 Matt Price, "Lightfoot on Black Policy Committee," *The Australian,* 11 June 1997, 4.

19 Kim Beazley, "Address to the Nation by the Leader of the Opposition Kim Beazley," *The Age Melbourne Online,* 2 December 1997 (www.theage.com.au).

20 "The former Liberal Prime Minister Mr. Malcolm Fraser yesterday added his voice to community pressure on the Federal Government over its handling of the Wik debate with a warning that a reputation of trying to build a fair and just society was at risk" (Claire Miller, "Just Society at Risk, Says Fraser," *The Age Melbourne Online,* 26 November 1997 (www.theage.com.au).

21 Beazley, "Address to the Nation."

22 Ibid.

23 Among numerous reports, see Michael Millet, "Race Row: Tourists Cancel Trips," *Sydney Morning Herald,* 1 November 1996, sec. A, p. 1; and Peter Switzer, "Hansonism Feeds on Economy's Failings," *The Weekend Australian,* 21–22 June 1997, 54.

24 Ronald Wilson, "Sir Ronald Wilson Address in Canberra," *For a Change Magazine, Online,* February/March, 1998. (www.forachange.co.uk)

25 Taylor, "The Politics of Recognition."

26 As part of National Sorry Day, Australians were urged to write their thoughts in Sorry Day Books.

27 David Nason, "Critics Split on Hanson Tactic," *The Weekend Australian,* 25–26 July 1998, 6.

28 For reports in the northern papers, see Bob Watt, "Flogging a Custom, Court Told," *Northern Territory News,* 28 July 1992, 3; Bob Watt, "Flogging Outside the Law," *Northern Territory News,* 6 August 1992, 3; The Lone Ranger, "Death Laws in Culture," *Northern Territory News,* 8 July 1996, 11; Bob Watt, "Wife Killer Says He Was Cursed," *Northern Territory News,* 18 June 1999, 5; Bob Watt, "Nine Years Jail after Brutal Wife Killing," *Northern Territory News,* 19 June 1999, 3; and "Missionary Weds Girls to Save Them," *Northern Territory News,* 1 September 1999, 18.

29 Stephanie Peatling, "PM calls Hanson 'Sinister' on Black Vote," *Sydney Morning Herald,* 16 July 1998, 5. See also Georgina Windsor, Matthew Abraham, and Maria Ceresa, "PM Attacks 'Abhorrent' Hanson View," *The Australian,* 16 July 1998, 4.

30 Peatling, "PM Calls Hanson 'Sinister' on Black Vote," 5.

31 Liberal Prime Minister John Howard described Hanson's remarks as "sinister" (Peatling, "PM Calls Hanson 'Sinister' on Black Vote"). Victorian Premier Jeff Kennett described her remarks as "abhorrent, undemocratic, ignorant and inaccurate" after a memorial lecture in London in honor of former Liberal Prime Minister Sir Robert Menzies. See "Crush Hanson Peril: Kennett," *The Australian,* 16 July 1998, 1. Other Liberal Party leaders were quoted making similar comments. Liberal Senator Ross Lightfoot claimed, "Aboriginal people in their native state are the lowest colour on the civilisation spectrum" (Matt Price, "Lightfoot on Black Policy Committee," *The Australian,* 11 June 1997, 4).

32 The referendum also removed a section of the Constitution that excluded Aborigines from population counts used to determine the number of seats in parliament.

33 The first land rights statute was passed in 1966 in South Australia as the Aboriginal Land Trusts Act, 1966 (SA). Since then there has been a series of statutes, including Pitjantjatjara Land Rights Act, 1981 (SA); Maralinga Tjarutja Land Rights Act, 1984 (SA); Aboriginal Land Rights Act, 1983 (NSW); Local Government (Aboriginal Lands) Act, 1978 (Qld); Land Act (Aboriginal and Islander Land Grants) Amendent Act, 1982 (Qld).

34 See Andrew Harvey, "Land for Rail: Please Explain," *Sunday Territorian,* 26 July 1998, 15.

35 See Wayne Howell, "One Nation Defines Aboriginal Identity," *Northern Territory News,* 27 July 1998, 2.

36 Patrick Walters and Michael Gordon, "We're a Culture Apart, PM Tells Asia," *The Australian,* 18 September 1996, sec. A, p. 1. See also Ben Holgate, "Cringing Under a Culture Defined," *The Australian,* 27 August 1998, 14.

37 See Michael Bachelard, "First Shots in the Race-Based Election We Had to Have," *The Australian,* 20 July 1998, 13.

38 Benjamin Lee, "Textuality, Mediation, and Public Discourse," in *Habermas and the Public Sphere,* ed. Craig Calhoun (Cambridge, Mass: MIT Press, 1993), 414–5.

39 See, for instance, Kymlicka, *Multicultural Citizenship.*

40 Jacques Lacan, "Agency of the Letter in the Unconscious, or Reason since Freud," *Ecrits: A Selection* (New York: W. W. Norton, 1977), 146–78.

41 "At the Third National Welfare Conference held in 1951 the newly appointed federal Minister for Territories, Paul Hasluck, vigorously propounded the benefits to Aboriginal people of assimilation and urged greater consistency in practice between all states and the Northern Territory," (Wilson, *Bringing Them Home*). See also Geoffrey Partington, *Hasluck versus Coombs: White Politics and Australia's Aborigines* (Sydney: Quakers Hill Press, 1996).

42 *Art of the Hunter: A Film on the Australian Aborigines,* John Endean, producer, with the assistance of A. P. Elkin, circa 1950, Aboriginal and Torres Strait Islanders archives, Canberra.

43 See Andrew Hornery, "Corporate Dreamtime Collides with Reality," *Sydney Morning Herald,* 20 March 2000, 1. The ABC ran an exposé on Aboriginal art in its national news magazine, *Four Corners,* on 31 May 1999. For general discussion, see J. C. Altman, *Aborigines, Tourism, and Development: The Northern Territory Experience* (Darwin: North Australian Research Unit, 1988); Jennifer Craik, *Resorting to Tourism: Cultural Policies for Tourism Development in Australia* (Sydney: Allen and Unwin, 1991); Jacobs and Gale, eds., *Tourism and the Protection of Aboriginal Cultural Sites;* Michaels, *Bad Aboriginal Art;* and Fred Myers, "Uncertain Regard: An Exhibition of Aboriginal Art in France," *Ethnos* 63.1 (1998): 7–47.

44 Peter Garrett, *Diesel and Dust,* Columbia Records, New York, 1988.

45 *Aboriginal Land Rights (Northern Territory) Act, 1976* (Canberra: Government Printer, 30 April 1992).

46 See Wendy Brown, "Wounded Attachments," in *States of Injury, Power, and Freedom in Late Modernity* (Princeton: Princeton University Press, 1995), 52–76.

47 See Lisa Clausen, "The Cruelty of Kindness," *Time* (Australian edition) 9 June 1997, 46.

48 Laura Tingle, "Keating Attacks Wik Plan as Racist," *The Age Melbourne Online,* 12 November 1997 (www.theage.com.au).

49 Clausen, "The Cruelty of Kindness," 46.

50 *The Wik Peoples v. the State of Queensland* (1996), 176, 136.

51 Freud, "Mourning and Melancholia."

52 See Debra Jopson, "One Nation or 301 Nations?" *Sydney Morning Herald,* 9 August 1997, 15.

53 Peter Sloterdjik, *Critique of Cynical Reason* (Minneapolis: University of Minnesota Press, 1983); and Slavoj Žižek, "How Did Marx Invent the Symptom?" in *The Sublime Object of Ideology* (London: Verso, 1992), 11–53, esp. 28–33.

54 Roman Jakobson, with Krystyna Pomorska, "The Concept of the Mark," in *On Language,* ed. Linda R. Waugh and Monique Monville-Burston (Cambridge, Mass.: Harvard University Press, 1990); Roman Jakobson, "Mark and Feature," in *Selected Writings VII* (The Hague: Mouton, 1974), 332–35; and Edna Andrews, *Markedness Theory: The Union of Asymmetry and Semiosis in Language* (Durham: Duke University Press, 1990).

55 See Genny O'Loughlin, "Topsy Secretary—Last of the Larrakia," *Northern Territory News,* 10 December 1989, 16.

56 Linda Pearson, "Aboriginal Land Rights Legislation in New South Wales," *Environmental and Planning Law Journal* 10.6 (1993): 398–422, esp. 399, 400.

57 M. M. Bakhtin, "The Problem of Speech Genre," in *Speech Genres and Other Late Essays,* ed. Michael Holquist (Austin: University of Texas Press, 1981), 68.

58 For one such visit, see the discussion of the American ballet star Ted Shawn's visit to Belyuen in 1947 in John K. Ewers, "Aboriginal Ballet," *Walkabout* 1 December 1947, 29–34.

59 Alan Dearling with Brendan Hanley, *Alternative Australia: Celebrating Cultural Diversity* (Freecyb Publications, 2000).

60 For a fuller discussion of these cases, see Povinelli, "Consuming *Geist.*"

2 / THE VULVA THIEVES (*ATNA NYLKNA*): MODAL ETHICS AND THE COLONIAL ARCHIVE

1 Michael Taussig, "Maleficium: State Fetishism," in *Fetishism as Cultural Discourse,* ed. Emily Apter and William Pietz (Ithaca: Cornell University Press, 1993), 231.

2 Michel Foucault, *The History of Sexuality: An Introduction* (1978; New York: Vintage, 1990), 152.

3 Louis Althusser, "From *Capital* to Marx's Philosophy," in *Reading Capital,* ed. Louis Althusser and Etienne Balibar (1968; London: Verso, 1997), 11–69.

4 Richard Rorty, "Habermas, Derrida, and the Function of Philosophy," in *Truth and Progress, Philosophical Papers* (Cambridge, Eng.: Cambridge University Press, 1998), 309.

5 For an account of Spencer and Gillen's meeting, ethnographic research trips, and impact on the social sciences, see D. J. Mulvaney, "'A Splendid Lot of Fellows'": Achievements and Consequences of the Horn Expedition," in *Exploring Central Australia: Society, the Environment, and the 1894 Horn Expedition*, ed. S. R. Morton and D. J. Mulvaney (Chipping Norton, NSW: Surrey Beatty and Sons, 1996), 3–12; D. J. Mulvaney, "F. J. Gillen's Life and Times," in *"My Dear Spencer": The Letters of F. J. Gillen to Baldwin Spencer*, ed. D. J. Mulvaney, Howard Morphy, and Alison Petch (Melbourne: Hyland House, 1997), 1–22; Howard Morphy, "Gillen—Man of Science," in *"My Dear Spencer": The Letters of F. J. Gillen to Baldwin Spencer*, ed. John Mulvaney, Howard Morphy, and Alison Petch (Melbourne: Hyland House, 1997), 23–50; R. R. Marett and J. K. Penniman, eds., *Spencer's Scientific Correspondence with Sir J. G. Frazier and Others* (Oxford: Clarendon Press, 1932); S. R. Moron and D. J. Mulvaney, eds., *Exploring Central Australia: Society, the Environment, and the 1894 Horn Expedition* (Chipping Norton, NSW: Surrey Beatty and Sons, 1996); and D. J. Mulvaney and J. H. Calaby, *"So Much that Is New": Baldwin Spencer, 1860–1929: A Biography* (Melbourne: Melbourne University Press, 1985).

6 See extracts from Gillen's letters to Spencer in Mulvaney, Morphy, and Petch, eds., *"My Dear Spencer,"* 152, 160, 178, 186, 213, 218, 222, 223, 260, 267, 280.

7 Baldwin Spencer, *The Arunta: A Study of a Stone Age People*, vol. 1 (London: MacMillan and Co., 1927), ix; Baldwin Spencer and Frank Gillen, *Northern Tribes of Central Australia* (London: Macmillan, 1904), 8, 17, 46.

8 Fison, "Kamilaroi Marriage, Descent, and Relationship," 29.

9 See extracts from Gillen's letters to Spencer in Mulvaney, Morphy, and Petch, eds., *"My Dear Spencer,"* 257, 253, 249, 186, 177, 172, 167.

10 Spencer, *The Arunta,* ix.

11 George Stocking Jr., *After Tylor: British Social Anthropology, 1881–1951* (Madison: University of Wisconsin Press, 1995), 94–98.

12 See extracts from Gillen's letters to Spencer in Mulvaney, Morphy, and Petch, eds., *"My Dear Spencer,"* 130.

13 Robert Sharwood, *Debates of the Australasian Federation Conference,* 56. See also Luke Trainor, *British Imperialism and Australian Nationalism: Manipulation, Conflict and Compromise in the Late Nineteenth Century* (Cambridge, Eng.: Cambridge University Press, 1994).

14 Emile Durkheim, *The Elementary Forms of Religious Life,* trans. Karen E. Fields (New York: The Free Press, 1995), 2.

15 See extracts from Gillen's letters to Spencer in Mulvaney, Morphy, and Petch, eds., *"My Dear Spencer,"* 203, 218, 221, 222.

16 Ibid., 260.

17 Baldwin Spencer and Frank Gillen, *Native Tribes of Central Australia* (New York: Macmillan, 1899), 97.

18 Ibid., 46.

19 George Stocking Jr., *Victorian Anthropology* (New York: The Free Press, 1987), 249–54.

20 Stocking notes that on account of his radical sexual politics, Richard Burton, then head of the Anthropological Society of London, "risked prosecution to publish works his wife and most of his contemporaries took for pornographic," in Stocking, *Victorian Anthropology,* 253.

21 Walter Roth, *Ethnological Studies among the North-West-Central Queensland Aborigines* (Brisbane: Edmund Gregory, Government Printer, 1897).

22 Herbert Basedow, "Subincision and Kindred Rites of the Australian Aboriginal," *Journal of the Royal Anthropological Institute* 57 (1927): 123–56.

23 Paola Mantegazza, *Anthropological Studies of Sexual Relations of Mankind* (New York: Falstaff Press, 1932).

24 Anne McClintock, *Imperial Leather: Race, Gender, and Sexuality in the Colonial Contest* (London: Routledge, 1995); Jeffrey Weeks, *Sex, Politics, and Society: The Regulation of Sexuality since 1800* (London: Longman, 1989).

25 M. F. Ashley-Montague, *Coming into Being among the Australian Aborigines: A Study of Procreative Beliefs of the Native Tribes of Australia* (London: George Routledge and Sons, 1937), 49.

26 See extracts from Gillen's letters to Spencer in Mulvaney, Morphy, and Petch, eds., "*My Dear Spencer,*" 201, 340.

27 Ibid., 207.

28 Jakobson, "Mark and Feature," 332–35; Jakobson, "The Concept of the Mark," 134–40.

29 Spencer and Gillen, *Native Tribes of Central Australia,* 97.

30 Ibid.

31 Spencer and Gillen, *Northern Tribes of Central Australia,* 137.

32 Bronislaw Malinowski, "Kinship," *Man* 30.17 (1930): 19–29.

33 Bronislaw Malinowski, *The Family among the Australian Aborigines* (New York: Schocken, 1913), 90.

34 Spencer and Gillen, *Native Tribes of Central Australia,* 98.

35 Spencer and Gillen, *Northern Tribes of Central Australia,* xiv.

36 Sir Henry Sumner Maine, *Ancient Law* (1864; Tucson: University of Arizona Press, 1986), 115–16.

37 For example, Alain Testart has used the works of Spencer and Gillen to reexamine the relationship between Arrente ritual body techniques and sexual difference. Testart argues that men defeat women by becoming them. Testart does not mean to imply by this that a *real* sexual transubstantion has transpired—but merely, if very affectively, a metaphorical metamorphosis. (Testart, *De la necessite d'etre initie* [Nanterre: Societe d'ethnologie, 1992], 133, 206).

38 Durkheim, *The Elementary Forms of Religious Life,* 1.

39 "In the matter of their morality their code differs radically from ours, but it cannot be denied that their conduct is governed by it, and that any known breaches are dealt with both surely and severely" (Spencer and Gillen, *Native Tribes of Central Australia,* 47). Compare Lyotard's discussion of the lessons of the sublime: "Because it is a reflective judgment, the Idea of the absolute is only 'present' and this

presence is that of the 'soul-stirring delight' that thinking feels on the occasion of the object it judges sublime" (Lyotard, *Lessons on the Analytic of the Sublime,* trans. Elizabeth Rottenberg [Stanford: Stanford University Press, 1991], 121).

40 See Richard Rorty, "On Ethnocentrism: A Reply to Clifford Geertz," in *Objectivity, Relativism, and Truth: Philosophical Papers, Volume 1* (Cambridge, Eng.: Cambridge University Press, 1991), 207. See also Taylor, "The Politics of Recognition," 25; and Jürgen Habermas, *The Philosophical Discourse of Modernity* (Cambridge, Mass.: MIT Press, 1987).

41 Fison, "Kamilaroi Marriage, Descent, and Relationship," 59–60.

42 See extracts from Gillen's letters to Spencer in Mulvaney, Morphy, and Petch, eds., *"My Dear Spencer"* for confession, 168; anxiety, 128, 130; excitement, 147, 192, 157; and animated puzzlement, 166, 179, 232.

43 *Northern Territory Times and Gazette,* 25 October 1884.

44 See Claude Lévi-Strauss, *Introduction to the Work of Marcel Mauss,* trans. Felicity Baker (London: Routledge & Kegan Paul, 1950); and *The Savage Mind* (Chicago: University of Chicago Press, 1966), 245–69.

45 Donald Davidson, "Radical Interpretation (1973)," in *Inquiries into Truth and Interpretation* (Oxford: Clarendon Press, 1984), 137, my emphasis.

46 See extracts from Gillen's letters to Spencer in Mulvaney, Morphy and Petch, *"My Dear Spencer,"* 353.

47 Stocking, *After Tylor,* 92.

48 See extracts from Gillen's letters to Spencer in Mulvaney, Morphy, and Petch, eds., *"My Dear Spencer,"* 245, 193, 165, 162, 119, 99, 96, 97: "My Christ, all same Engwura fire today," 245; "Too sorry," 193; "Me askum longa Brian," 165; "Say professa Jack, not Fessa," and "Fessa gone Chappie-Akurna Chappie," 162; "My fader, ze lord Zheesas, dwells in my bosom," 119; "Him all same wild dog, him cant a knowem what name father longa piccaninny," 99; "Pirunngaru blackfellow all same while fellow, him catcham any lubra," 99; "By & bye plenty maken Piraunngaru," 99; "That one very good him makeum walk straight," 96; "All the same wild dog, him catchem him sister, jump longa me fellow mother," 97.

49 Donald Davidson, *Inquiries into Truth and Interpretation* (Oxford: Clarendon Press, 1984).

50 To put this in another way: a subtending indexical non-sense form must be distinguished qualitatively and temporally from a secondary sense-meaning built up from this form. See Michael Silverstein, "Metapragmatic Discourse and Metapragmatic Function," in *Reflexive Language: Reported Speech and Metapragmatics,* ed. John Lucy (Cambridge, Eng.: Cambridge University Press, 1995), 280–84.

51 Here I use "conveyance" in the manner elaborated in Jacques Derrida, "Signature, Event, Context," in *Margins of Philosophy,* trans. Alan Bass (Chicago: University of Chicago Press, 1982), 307–30.

52 Take, for example, this passage from Gillen's letter to Spencer written on 18 June 1897: "Two things baffle every attempt at Solution, 1st Why a man speaks to his Ungaraitcha and not to his Quitia — and 2nd the Umbilyirakira ceremony of the Enwura, the term Umbilyirakira has only one meaning, and that is a child fresh

born, for the life of me I cannot get at the meaning of the Ceremony, but the men who fell down and covered up the Churinga bundle before the women, are supposed to be tumbling dow. [down,] that is they are dying—This thing has worried me awfully and I have spent hours and hours trying to solve it" (Gillen to Spencer in Mulvaney, Morphy, and Petch, eds., *"My Dear Spencer,"* 166).

53 See extracts from Gillen's letters to Spencer in Mulvaney, Morphy, and Petch, eds., *"My Dear Spencer,"* 232.

54 Rorty, "Habermas, Derrida, and the Function of Philosophy," 309.

55 Stocking, *After Tylor*, 91.

56 Gillen to Spencer, 30 July 1897, in Mulvaney, Morphy, and Petch, eds., *"My Dear Spencer,"* 178.

57 Stocking, *After Tylor*, 89, 91.

58 Gillen to Spencer in Mulvaney, Morphy, and Petch, eds., *"My Dear Spencer,"* 343.

59 In 1883, a severe drought intensified by the polluting effects of free-range cattle led to a series of conflicts between blacks and whites, which culminated in a massacre widely reported in northern and southern papers.

60 Mulvaney, Morphy, and Petch, eds., *"My Dear Spencer,"* 119.

61 Ibid., 109.

62 Stocking, *After Tylor*, 90–91. See also Mulvaney and Calaby, *"So Much that Is New."*

63 Stocking, *After Tylor*, 9; Mulvaney, Morphy, and Petch, eds., *"My Dear Spencer,"* 106, 108, 109, 122, 128, 130, 159, 166, 179, 186, 192, 232.

64 Derrida has discussed the double-event structure of this liberal deferral in Jacques Derrida, *Specters of Marx: The State of the Debt, the Work of Mourning, and the New International,* trans. Peggy Kamuf (London: Routledge, 1994).

65 Sigmund Freud, *Beyond the Pleasure Principle* (New York: W. W. Norton, 1961), 33; Cathy Caruth, *Unclaimed Experience: Trauma, Narrative, and History* (Baltimore: Johns Hopkins University Press, 1996), 3–4.

66 Derrida, *Specters of Marx*, 65, 62, 64.

67 Perhaps the totemic dilemma was most famously if not most brilliantly discussed by Lévi-Strauss in his *Totemism*. At the end of his revolutionary treatment of the subject he argued that totemic systems should be considered "religious ideas" and thus "accorded the same value as any other conceptual system," namely, their value as providing "access to the mechanism of thought" and "to the understanding." For Lévi-Strauss, totemic systems like those of the Arrente demonstrated definitively that "the demands to which it responds and the way in which it tries to meet them are primarily of an intellectual kind." Lévi-Strauss admits "sentiments are also involved" but these sentiments function "in a subsidiary fashion, as responses of a body of ideas to gaps and lesions which it can never succeed in closing" (Lévi-Strauss, *Totemism,* trans. Rodney Needham [Boston: Beacon Press, 1963], 104).

68 Nancy Munn noted a similar point in her seminal paper "The Transformation of Subjects into Objects in Warlpiri and Pitjantjatjara Myth," in *Australian Aboriginal Anthropology,* ed. Ronald Berndt (Perth: University of Western Australia Press, 1970), 141–63.

69 Spencer, *The Arunta,* 345.

70 *Australian Parliamentary Hansard, House of Representatives,* 4 June 1976, p. 3082.

71 Spencer and Gillen, *Native Tribes of Central Australia,* 172, 175.

72 Ibid., 326.

73 Ibid., 269, 459–60.

74 Ibid., 216, 464–65, 772–74.

75 Spencer, *The Arunta,* 115–16.

76 Spencer and Gillen, *Native Tribes of Central Australia,* 172.

77 Ibid., 179.

78 Ibid., 268.

79 T. G. H. Strehlow, *Aranda Phonetics and Grammar* (Sydney: Australian National Research Council, 1944), 59.

80 Ibid., 59, my emphasis.

81 David Wilkins, *Mpartne Arrente (Aranda): Studies in the Structure and Semantics of Grammar,* Unpublished PhD Thesis, Australian National University, Canberra, 1989.

82 See, for instance, T. G. H. Strehlow, *Aranda Traditions* (Melbourne: Melbourne University Press, 1947), 14–18, 86–95.

83 In other words, we can ask about the "footing" of the utterances of the grounds. See Gregg Urban, "The 'I' of Discourse," in *Semiotics, Self, and Society,* ed. Ben Lee and Greg Urban (Berlin: Mouton de Gruyter, 1989), 27–51; Alan Rumsey, "Agency, Personhood, and the 'I' of Discourse in the Pacific and Beyond," *Journal of the Royal Anthropological Institute* 6 (2000): 99–113.

84 William Hanks, *Language and Communicative Practices* (Boulder: Westview Press, 1996), 86.

85 Testart, *De la necessite d'etre initie,* 205.

86 Lévi-Strauss, *Totemism,* 103.

87 Spencer and Gillen, *Northern Tribes of Central Australia,* xiv.

3 / SEX RITES, CIVIL RIGHTS

1 Australian Archives CRS F1 Item 36/592, 11 June 1936.

2 Ibid., 12 June 1936.

3 Letter from C. A. Carrodus, Secretary, Department of the Interior, to the Administrator of the Northern Territory. Australian Archives CRS F1 Item 36/592, 18 June 1936.

4 Memorandum sent to the Administrator in Darwin. Australian Archives CRS F1 Item 36/592, 10 February 1936. See also the Administrator's response, Australian Archives CRS F1 Item 36/592, 12 June 1936.

5 E. W. P. Chinnery, Director of Native Affairs to C. A. Carrodus, the Government Secretary. Australian Archives CRS F3 Item 20/32, 16 August 1939.

6 See Craig Calhoun, *Critical Social Theory* (Oxford: Blackwell, 1995), esp. 52. See also Walter Benjamin, "The Critique of Violence," in *Reflections: Essays, Aphorisms, Autobiographical Writings,* trans. Edmund Jephcott (New York: Schocken, 1986),

277–300; and Jacques Derrida, "Force of Law: The Mystical Foundation of Authority," *Cardozo Law Review* 11 (1990): 919–1045.

7 Patrick Wolfe, "Nation and MiscegeNation: Discursive Continuity in the Post-Mabo Era," *Social Analysis* 34 (1994): 93–152; Elizabeth A. Povinelli, "Reading Ruptures, Rupturing Readings: Mabo and the Cultural Politics of Activism," *Social Analysis* 41.2 (1997): 20–28.

8 Jürgen Habermas, *Between Facts and Norms* (Cambridge, Mass.: MIT Press, 1998), 66.

9 Chesterman and Galligan, *Citizens without Rights,* 81–82.

10 Ibid., 88–92.

11 Powell, *Far Country,* 161.

12 Wilson, *Bringing Them Home.* See also Austin, *"I Can Picture the Old Home so Clearly."*

13 Powell, *Far Country,* 161.

14 Chesterman and Galligan, *Citizens without Rights,* 92.

15 Ibid., 93.

16 Patrick Wolfe, *Settler Colonialism and the Transformation of Anthropology* (London: Cassell, 1999).

17 W. E. H. Stanner, "Peril in Racial Crossing," *Sydney Morning Herald,* 18 June 1933, in MS 3752, Box 1, Item 4, W. E. H. Stanner Unpublished Material, Australian Institute for Aboriginal and Torres Strait Islanders, Canberra. See also the Crown Law Officer E. T. Asche's memo to the Administrator of Darwin, "Aboriginals Ordinance 1918–1937, Section 3 — Interpretation of Definition of 'Half-Caste.'" Australian Archives CRS F1 Item 37/734, 23 November 1937.

18 See Gillian Cowlishaw, "Colour, Culture, and the Aborigines," *Man* 22 (1987): 221–37.

19 Chesterman and Galligan, *Citizens without Rights,* 138; Geoffrey Gray, "From Nomadism to Citizenship: AP Elkin and Aboriginal Advancement," in *Citizenship and Indigenous Australians: Changing Conceptions and Possibilities,* ed. Nicolas Peterson and Will Sanders (Cambridge, Eng.: Cambridge University Press, 1998), 55–78, 55.

20 Gray, "From Nomadism to Citizenship," 56; J. McEwen, *Commonwealth Government's Policy with Respect to Aborigines* (Canberra: Commonwealth Government Printer, 1939).

21 See C. K. Thomas, "From 'Australian Aborigines' to 'White Australians': Elkin, Hasluck, and the Origins of Assimilation," M.A. thesis, Monash University, 1994.

22 A. P. Elkin, *Citizenship for the Aborigines: A National Aboriginal Policy* (Sydney: Australasian Publishing, 1944), 12–13.

23 W. E. H. Stanner, "The 'Vanishing' Indian," 11 March 1946, 2FC 9:05 P.M., script approved by Federal Talk Dept. MS 3752, Box 3, Item 80, W. E. H. Stanner Unpublished Material.

24 W. Lloyd Warner, *A Black Civilization: A Social Study of an Australian Tribe* (1937; Glouster, Mass.: Peter Smith, 1969, 10. See also lectures by W. E. H. Stanner, "Moral

Man and Immoral Society: Primitive vs Modern Morality," 6 May 1940, MS 3752, Box 3, Item 60, W. E. H. Stanner Unpublished Material.

25 Although Malinowski and Radcliffe-Brown would engage in a bitter public struggle over the anthropological meaning of the "functionalist" approach to society, they and Elkin shared a general understanding of primitive societies as delicately balanced organisms based on local systems of heterosexual reproduction. Thus it is not surprising that in his highly influential *A Black Civilization* (1937), dedicated to Radcliffe-Brown, Warner discovered that "the whole of the social organization [of Murngin] is built on the pattern of kinship. The kinship system is the fundamental form into which the rest of the social organization has been integrated" (7).

26 A. P. Elkin, "Anthropology and the Australian Aboriginal," in *White and Black in Australia,* ed. J. S. Needham (London: The Society for Promoting Christian Knowledge, 1935), 32.

27 From A. P. Elkin, "Anthropology and the Australian Aboriginal." 32.

28 "Any people whose history, tradition and beliefs are different from our own, is almost sure to have customs that seem strange and puzzling to us. We may even feel that these customs are not so good as ours, that they are degrading and should be abolished, but before we pass such opinions or act on them, we must first understand what those customs are, the traditions and beliefs on which they are based, the meaning which they possess for the individuals who practice them, and the social function which they perform. But while such an understanding undoubtedly makes another people's customs less puzzling to us, it does not necessarily commend them all, and we may still feel constrained to use our influence or authority to have some of them abolished or modified. Here again an understanding of those customs is essential so that we may know what we are doing when working for their abolition or modification" (Elkin, *The Australian Aborigines: How to Understand Them* [London: Angus and Robertson, 1938], 108).

29 From Elkin, "Anthropology and the Australian Aboriginal," 32, my emphasis.

30 W. E. H. Stanner quoting "the amiable Mr. Dredge," the early-nineteenth-century protector who so described his wards (W. E. H. Stanner, "Religion, Totemism, and Symbolism," in *Aboriginal Man in Australia: Essays in Honour of Emeritus Professor A. P. Elkin,* ed. R. M. Berndt and Catherine Berndt [London: Angus and Robertson, 1965], 235).

31 Other anthropologists, such as W. E. H. Stanner, gave lectures to and corresponded with missionary groups. See "Fieldnotes Catholic Mission Docherty," MS 3752, Box 6, Item 143, W. E. H. Stanner Unpublished Material.

32 Andrew P. Lyons and Harriet Lyons, "Savage Sexuality and Secular Morality," *Canadian Journal of Anthropology* 5.1 (fall 1986): 51–64.

33 R. M. Berndt and Catherine Berndt, "A. P. Elkin — The Man and the Anthropologist," in *Aboriginal Man in Australia: Essays in Honour of Emeritus Professor A. P. Elkin,* ed. R. M. Berndt and Catherine Berndt (London: Angus and Robertson, 1965), 18.

34 Elkin, *The Australian Aborigines,* 123, 127.

35 Ibid., 109.

36 A. R. Radcliffe-Brown, "Social Sanctions," in *Structure and Function in Primitive Society* (1933; New York: The Free Press, 1952), 205–11.

37 See, for example, " 'Too Many Missionaries and Too Few Policemen,' Minister Says Inexperienced Clergy Have Made Blacks Idle and Restive," *Northern Standard,* 1 February 1929; "Loafing Blacks, Ogden Blames Missions," *Northern Standard,* 19 February 1929; "Leave the Abo Alone," *Northern Territory Times,* 28 October 1930. In an address to the Anglican Men's movements, W. E. H. Stanner began with a *Sydney Morning Herald* allegation that Christianity "ruins" a native people, and then explored the specific good and bad of Christian missionary work in Aboriginal Australia. Stanner includes the "unconcealed contempt of many missionaries for what they call 'pagan' culture, that is for the native way of life and social organization, even in non-religious fields." W. E. H. Stanner Unpublished Material, 19 February 1953. MS 3752, Box 6, Item 143.

38 "The Aboriginal of the North," *Northern Territory Times,* 1 August 1930. See also "Aborigines Praised," *Northern Territory Times* (reprinted from the *Brisbane Daily Mail*), 10 February 1931.

39 The Law Reform Commission, *The Recognition of Aboriginal Customary Laws,* Vol. 1, report no. 31 (Canberra: Australian Government Publishing Service, 1986).

40 Aboriginal Friend's Association, *Seventy Fifth Annual Report,* 1933, cited in The Law Reform Commission, *The Recognition of Aboriginal Customary Laws,* also cited by Elkin, *Citizenship for the Aborigines.* For a more comprehensive comparative account of the Western Australian system, see Kathryn Helen Autry, "Silence(s) and Resistant (Dis)quiet in the Shadow of the Legal System, Race-ing Jurisprudence in Western Australia by Reference to the Courts of Native Affairs (1936–1954)," Ph.D. diss., La Trobe University, 1999.

41 Joe Croft, "The Old People and Their Tribal Affairs," *Northern Territory Times,* 16 May 1930.

42 W. H. Davies, "The Old People and Their Tribal Affairs," *Northern Territory Times,* 20 May 1930.

43 See also Australian Archive CRS F3 Item 20/32, 16 August 1939. This system was modeled and named after the colonial administration of Sir Hubert Murray, lieutenant governor of Papua. The traffic in ideas, methods, and persons was especially thick between the Northern Territory and the British mandates of Papua New Guinea and Canberra; between the Australian and British ethnological communities; and between the Daly River, Darwin, and Canberra. Chinnery was a trained anthropologist in his own right, lecturing in Australia, the United States, and Britain. It was his scholarly reputation as an anthropologist that earned Chinnery an invitation to accompany the minister of the interior on an advisory tour of the Aboriginal population of the Northern Territory in 1938 and his appointment as first director of native affairs in the Northern Territory. And, it was as the gatekeepers of professional anthropology in the Northern and British mandated territories, that Chinnery, Carrodus, Murray, and other government administrators supported and blocked, at varying times, the research projects of anthropologists who would be directly or indirectly linked to this case, including Malinowski,

Radcliffe-Brown, Elkin, Stanner, and their students. Although Murray encouraged the protection of native customs within the framework of controlled economic development, he became alarmed hearing that, at a meeting in 1930 of the Australian and New Zealand Association for the Advancement of Science, Radcliffe-Brown not only outlined the social integrative function of native customs but also questioned the right of the British Empire to interfere in the "destinies" of the peoples of India and Africa. Chinnery was influential in Radcliffe-Brown's appointment as the first chair of anthropology at the University of Sydney in 1926. He would later oversee Radcliffe-Brown's graduate research appointments in the territories as he would the appointment recommendations of the second chair of anthropology, A. P. Elkin. Both Radcliffe-Brown and Elkin produced influential chapters from extended research trips in the general region of the Daly River (Radcliffe-Brown in particular on social organization of Aboriginal tribes based on work among the Murinpatha) and would formally and informally advise government administrators like Weddell and Chinnery in native affairs. For an account of Elkin's career, see T. Wise, *The Self-Made Anthropologist* (Sydney: Allen and Unwin, 1985). For an account of the Murray System and the dense administrative and academic traffic between Papua New Guinea and Australia, see Andrew Markus, *Governing Savages* (Sydney: Allen and Unwin, 1990); Geoffrey Gray, "'I Was Not Consulted': A. P. Elkin, Papua New Guinea, and the Politics of Anthropology," *The Australian Journal of Politics and History* 40.2 (1994): 195–221; and J. D. Legge, "The Murray Period: Papua 1906–1940," in *Australia and Papua New Guinea,* ed. W. J. Hudson (Sydney: Sydney University Press, 1971), 32–56.

44 W. E. P. Chinnery, Director of Native Affairs, to Government Secretary C.A. Carrodus. Australian Archives CRS F3 Item 20/32, 16 August 1939. See also David Carment, Robyn Maynard, and Alan Powell, eds., *Northern Territory Dictionary of Biography, Volume One: to 1945* (Darwin: Northern Territory University Press, 1990), 56–57.

45 Bronislaw Malinowski, *The Sexual Life of Savages* (Boston: Beacon Press, 1929), 371. See also J. W. Bleakley, *The Aborigines and Half Castes of Central Australia and North Australia: Report by J. W. Bleakley, Chief Protector of Aborigines,* Commonwealth of Australia, Parliamentary Paper 21. Australian Government Publishing Service, Canberra, 1929. See also "Lower than the Abo," *Northern Territory Times,* 13 March 1931: "It is a wonder that the abos did not drown themselves rather than come into contact with some of the whites that disgraced Australia's name in earlier years."

46 "The Aborigines, Special State Proposed, Report to Federal Government," *Northern Territory Times,* 5 April 1929.

47 "Among Our Books: Review of ER Gribble, *The Problem of the Australian Aboriginal,*" *Northern Territory Times,* 13 March 1931.

48 Geoffrey Gray, "Piddington's Indiscretion: Ralph Piddington, the Australian National Research Council, and Academic Freedom," *Oceania* 64.3 (1994): 219.

49 N. Green, *The Forrest River Massacres* (Fremantle: Fremantle Arts Press, 1995); Henry Reynolds, *The Law of the Land* (Ringwood, Vic.: Penguin, 1987).

50 J. A. Carrodus, Secretary Department of the Interior, to Administrator of the Northern Territory. Australian Archives CRS F1, Item 36/592, 8 March 1940.

51 See Ann McGrath, *Born in the Cattle: Aborigines in Cattle Country* (Sydney: Allen and Unwin, 1987); Pamela Lyon and Michael Parsons, *We Are Staying: The Alyawarre Struggle for Land at Lake Nash* (Alice Springs: Institute for Aboriginal Development Press, 1989); and Deborah Bird Rose, *Hidden Histories: Black Stories from Victoria River Downs, Humbert River, and Wave Hill Stations* (Canberra: Aboriginal Studies Press, 1991).

52 *Report on the Administration of the Northern Territory,* 1937–38, p. 22, quoted in J. P. M. Long, *Aboriginal Settlements: A Survey of Institutional Communities in Eastern Australia* (Canberra: Australian National University Press, 1970), 1999.

53 This laissez-faire approach made economic sense, as Pamela Lyon and Michael Parsons have noted, in the large pastoral industry of Northern Territory. Attempts to alter it sparked protests in the Northern Territory. In 1934, J. A. Carrodus, then secretary of the Department of Home and Territories, relieved Weddell for a short period after Weddell had been assaulted after a series of labor agitation — including a communist takeover of the government (Lyon and Parsons, *We Are Staying,* 19). See also Carment, Maynard, and Powell, *Northern Territory Dictionary of Biography,* 311–12; and Powell, *Far Country,* esp. 169–73.

54 "A Plea for the Abo," *Northern Territory Times,* 30 December 1930.

55 Rev. Stanley Jarvis is reported to have told the Methodist Conference Foreign Mission that "our aborigines are a national asset" and called for the establishment of native courts. Rev. Stanley Jarvis, "Aboriginal Welfare, Methodist Minister's Plea," *Northern Territory Times,* 27 March 1931.

56 Newspapers announced anthropologists' imminent arrival, such as the *Northern Territory Times* did for W. E. H. Stanner ("Anthropologist Arrives," *Northern Territory Times,* 19 April 1932).

57 "Quite possibly, the average bushman does not look upon the black with the eyes of romance, and is just as well pleased at his gradual extinction, but his habits, and beliefs have great value to the ethnologist, and it is advisable, therefore, to report, whenever possible, any outstanding items of interest" ("The Territory Abo," *Northern Territory Times,* 8 January 1931).

58 The film concludes: "The rock and bark painting of the Australian Aborigines, together with the songs and corroborees, the myths and legends, represent many centuries of artistic and spiritual development. Unless their ancient way of life is accepted and encouraged to continue within the white society, this cultural heritage may be lost as the future generations become detribalized. The art of the hunter has been an artistic and social contribution to the history of mankind" (*Art of the Hunter: A Film of the Australian Aborigines,* John Endean, producer; Les Tanner, commentator, Aboriginal and Torres Strait Islanders Archives, Canberra).

59 William Hatfield, "Serial: 'Smoke Signals from the Never-Never,' " *Northern Territory Times,* 4 March 1932.

60 "Editorial," *Northern Territory Times,* 1 August 1930.

61 An editorial in the *Northern Territory Times* reported, for instance, that "blacks

appreciate justice and fair-dealing"; that "the most fatal mistake that can be made in dealing with blacks is to laugh at their secret superstitions and beliefs"; and that "the old men are the repositories of the ceremonial lore of the tribes; which would rapidly disintegrate did the old men not keep hold of their reins" (*Northern Territory Times,* 1 August 1930). For an opposing portrait in which a settler's murder is blamed on "a sudden blood lust on the part of the aboriginals," see "Daly River Notes, Reported Murder," *Northern Territory Times,* 10 November 1931; and historically, "Daly River Outrages and Black Morality," *Northern Territory Times and Gazette,* 13 March 1886. These newspapers had a dense intertextual relation to ethnological texts. See, for instance, Herbert Basedow, *The Australian Aboriginal* (Adelaide: F. W. Preece and Sons, 1925), 227.

62 For "mass subject," see Michael Warner, "The Mass Public and the Mass Subject," in *Habermas and the Public Sphere,* ed. Craig Calhoun (Cambridge, Mass.: MIT Press, 1993), 377–401.

63 Jacques Derrida, *Dissemination,* trans. Barbara Johnson (Chicago: University of Chicago Press, 1981).

64 For an overview, see Henry Reynolds, *Frontier: Aborigines, Settlers, and Land* (Sydney: Allen and Unwin, 1987).

65 "The Killed Aborigines," *Northern Standard,* 8 March 1929.

66 MS 3752, Box 7, Item 162(b), W. E. H. Stanner Unpublished Material.

67 A. V. Stretton, Superintendent of Police, to the Administrator of Darwin. Australian Archive CRS F3 Item 36/592, 30 June 1936. In an earlier letter Stretton argued that it was "necessary [to] arrest natives in order that they may be interrogated by chief protector who will decide whether [there should be a] court case" (Australian Archives CRS F1 Item 36/592, 15 June 1936).

68 "It should be competent, however, for any such case to be investigated in the first place by the nearest police officer and a report submitted for the consideration of the Chief Protector of Aboriginals" (J. A. Carrodus to Weddell. Australian Archives, CRS F1 Item 36/592, 13 August 1936).

69 Ibid.

70 Australian Archives CRS F1, Item 36/592, 20 June 1936.

71 A. V. Stretton, Superintendent of Police to the Administrator in Darwin. Australian Archives CRS F1 Item 36/592, 30 June 1936. See also later submission of Coroners ordinance, Section 8. Australian Archives CRS F3 Item 20/32, 15 December 1937.

72 In 1829 the New South Wales Supreme Court advised the attorney-general that it was unjust to apply English law to inter-Aboriginal killings, although in *R v. Jack Congo Murrell,* 1836, the New South Wales Supreme Court ruled it had jurisdiction to try Aboriginal persons who committed crimes no matter whether the crimes were committed within customary frame or not. This would become official colonial policy, with the Colonial Office directing the governor of New South Wales in 1837 (The Law Reform Commission, *The Recognition of Aboriginal Customary Laws*).

73 Their roles were elaborated in the latter half of the nineteenth and in the early twentieth centuries: 1867 in Victoria, 1886 in Western Australia, 1897 in Queens-

land, 1909 in New South Wales, and 1910 in the Northern Territory. There were multiple calls throughout the first thirty years of the Australian federation for the establishment of native courts to hear criminal cases in which no settlers were involved. As early as 1836 defense attorneys argued to no avail that Australian courts did not have the jurisdiction to try Aboriginal subjects. *R v. Murrell Legge, Supreme Court of New South Wales* 72 (1836). For a brief period, after an Aboriginal man was sentenced to death for the murder of a white constable (*Tuckiar v. The King*, 1934), minor short-lived legal reforms were introduced that would have taken into consideration Aboriginal customary law in cases in which no white person was involved (*Tuckiar v. the King, Commonwealth Law Review* 52 [1934]: 335, in The Law Reform Commission, *The Recognition of Aboriginal Customary Laws*).

74 Australian Archives CRS F3 Item 20/32, 28 July 1939.

75 W. B. Kirkland, Acting Chief Protector of Aboriginals, to R. H. Weddell, Administrator of the Northern Territory. Australian Archives CRS F3 Item 36/592, 10 July 1936. In early March 1940, on the advice of Carrodus, the secretary of the interior modified his former directive: "In the future, the direction will only apply in the case of relatively uncivilised natives who live more or less permanently in remote areas, who are not under any form of permanent European control, assistance or supervision, and who depend for internal stability on the free exercise of their own native customs." Who had authority to discern the tribal remained as it had in 1936—the chief protector of Aboriginals in consultation with the police and anthropological advisors (Australian Archive CRS F3 Item 20/32, 8 March 1940).

76 Silverstein, "Metapragmatic Discourse and Metapragmatic Function," 280–84.

77 Gray, "From Nomadism to Citizenship."

78 Georg Simmel, "The Metropolis and Mental Life," in *On Mental Life and Social Forms,* ed. Donald N. Levine (Chicago: University of Chicago Press, 1971), 324–39.

79 Northern Territory Medical Service File of Papers, Australian Archives CRS F3 Item 20/103, 6 September 1940.

80 Australian Archives CRS F3 Item 20/103, 7 August 1940.

81 The performance of Kunapipi drew together a number of neighboring groups, including the Nangiomeri and Madngella (Australia Archives CRS F3, Item 20/103, undated ca. 1940).

82 "The words Secret and Sunday ground are meant for what the Natives call SACRED GROUND, but pronounce it as I have written" (Australian Archives CRS F3 Item 20/103, 8 August 1940).

83 Gillen reports to Spencer that fire-sticks are used to burn the eyes of women and uncut boys who have purposely or accidentally witnessed prohibited men's ceremonies (Mulvaney, Morphy, and Petch, eds., *"My Dear Spencer,"* 7).

84 Bill Harney was a supervisor of Aboriginal settlements and, later, a popular writer, radio personality, and collaborator with the anthropologist A. P. Elkin. In this case Harney wrote: "Contact with civilization tends to make the native women disobey the laws and taboos of the tribe, and they would pass over or near these taboo spots knowing they are protected by the law, or the white people of that part, and so the natives seeing their greatest weapon for law and order (increase, regeneration and

clearing up of tribal disputes) becoming useless by these women, become annoyed and use force" (Northern Territory Medical Service File of Papers, Australian Archives CRS F3 Item 20/103, 6 September 1940).

85 Spencer, *Native Tribes of the Northern Territory,* esp. 214–18.

86 Warner, *A Black Civilization,* 224.

87 Ronald Berndt, *Kunapipi* (Melbourne: F. W. Cheshire, 1951); selections can be found in the Human Relations Area Files, at the Human Relations Area Files, Inc. New Haven, Connecticut. See also Ronald Berndt and Catherine Berndt, *Sexual Behavior in Western Arnhem Land* (New York: Viking Fund Publication, 1951).

88 Berndt and Berndt, *Sexual Behavior in Western Arnhem Land,* 148.

89 W. E. H. Stanner, "Religion, Totemism, and Symbolism," 207–37, esp. 213, 219.

90 Ibid., 233–34.

91 "A host of stylized acts — the whole repertory of theatrical forms, the making and use of fire, the drawing and pouring of human blood, spraying with water and spittle. The use of semen and other exuviae, covering and revealing objects, laying on of hands, etc., etc., — all to be seen performed within ritualized processes or described in the associated myths. All may be classed as vehicles, or symbolising means, of symbolising" (Stanner, "Religion, Totemism, and Symbolism," 232–33).

92 MS 3752, Box 7, Item 158(c); See also "The Dreamings of Wali Wali," MS 3752, Box 7, Item 162 (a), W. E. H. Stanner Unpublished Material. For a published critique of the Freudian account, see W. E. H. Stanner, "On Freud's Totem and Taboo," *Canberra Anthropology* 5.1 (1982): 1–7.

93 W. E. H. Stanner, "Durmugam: A Nangimeri (1959)," in *White Man Got No Dreaming: Essays 1938–1973* (Canberra: Australian National University Press, 1979), 67–105.

94 Ibid., 82.

95 Ibid., 83. See also MS 3752, Box 19, Item 419, and Box 7, Item 158(c), W. E. H. Stanner Unpublished Material.

96 Ronald Berndt, "Law and Order in Aboriginal Australia," in *Aboriginal Man in Australia: Essays in Honour of Emeritus Professor A. P. Elkin,* ed. R. M. Berndt and Catherine Berndt (London: Angus and Robertson, 1965), 167–206, esp. 191–92; W. E. H. Stanner, "Ceremonial Economics of the Mulluk-mulluk and Madngella Tribes of the Daly River, North Australia," *Oceania* 4 (1933): 10–29, 156–75, 453–70.

97 Stanner, "Durmugam," 84.

98 Stanner's field notes make reference to the sexual economy, see "Wali Wali Manuscript," MS 3752, Box 7, Item 162, W. E. H. Stanner Unpublished Material. For a general critical discussion, see Anne Summers, *Damned Whores and God's Police: The Colonization of Women in Australia* (Ringwood, Victoria: Penguin, 1975); Diane Bell and Pam Ditton, *Law, the Old and New: Aboriginal Women in Central Australian Speak Out* (Canberra: Central Australian Legal Aid Service, 1980); and Diane Kirby, *Sex, Power, and Justice: Historical Perspectives of Law in Australia* (Melbourne: Oxford University Press, 1995).

99 Powell, *Far Country,* 188.

100 Nan Utarra, "The Black Bagnio," *Northern Standard,* 18 January 1929.

101 Turner to Director of Native Affairs, "Police Correspondence," Northern Territory Archives F77 Series, 28 March 1942.

102 C. D. Rowley, *The Destruction of Aboriginal Society* (Hammondsworth: Penguin, 1972); Markus, *Governing Savages;* Ted Egan, *Justice All Their Own: The Caledon Bay and Woodah Island Killings 1932–33* (Melbourne: Melbourne University Press, 1996).

103 Australian Archives CRS F3 Item 20/103, 7 August 1940. File includes confession statements of Malakmalak men.

104 Ibid.

105 "This lubra Alice was formerly one of Ex-Tracker Bull-bulls lubras" (Australian Archives CRS F3 Item 20/103, 8 August 1940). In the police reports W. E. H. Stanner collected Bull-bull and Litchfield natives in 1935, him taking other local men's wives (MS 3752, W. E. H. Stanner Unpublished Material).

106 Australian Archives CRS F3 Item 20/103, 8 August 1940.

107 Stanner, "Durmugam," 72.

108 Australia Archives CRS F3 Item 20/103, 8 August 1940.

109 In an exchange with Weddell on 16 August 1935, Turner responds to a charge of neglect of duty under the Public Service Ordinance of 1928–1934. Turner details his duties and the rude dismissal of his "knowledge and . . . experience." "It was like if I had been instructed, 'To go and sit down little boy, I am making all the enquiries I want. I'll show you what should have been done' " "Police Files," MS 3752, W. E. H. Stanner Unpublished Material).

110 See, for instance, "The Territory Abo," *Northern Territory Times,* 8 January 1931, which describes recent issues of the Sydney Mail that contain "some rather wild and woolly tales of the N.T. and its inhabitants" and call on "the real dinkum bushmen from the outback" to tell the truth of "stone age abos." See also "The Aboriginal of the North," *Northern Territory Times,* 1 August 1930; and "Unreliable Natives," *Northern Territory Times* 19 February 1930.

111 Australian Archives CRS F3 Item 20/103, undated, unauthored (probably W. Harney).

112 Ibid., 1 October 1940.

113 Ibid., 8 March 1940.

114 "Delissaville Diary Loose Leaves Jan 1st 1942 to End," Australian Archives CRS F3 Item 1980/111.

115 Murray's superintendent responds to a plea from Murray: "Your isolation at Delissaville is appreciated by myself but little can be done to help you other than to get the car fixed to provide you with transport if required." Northern Territory Accession 1980/111. See for example, Murray's personal letter dated 19 July 1942 in Australian Archives CRS F3 Item 52/570.

116 The Aboriginal Ordinance of 1918 had extended the chief protector's control over indigenous women. Under the ordinance, "Aboriginal females were under the total control of the Chief Protector from the moment they were born until they died unless married and living with a husband 'who was substantially of European origin' " (Wilson, *Bringing Them Home,* 133). The management of black women's sexuality

became a central part of a public debate. If Murray was reading the *Northern Territory Times* as a younger man he might have read a report titled "Gins Get a Few Strokes." The article is about Oenpelli men and women, with which Wagaidj and Laragiya had close ceremonial ties. It outlined for readers and administrators a pedagogy of sexual discipline: "The following report is written by P. Cahill, Aboriginal Protector, Oenpelli, and published in the Administrator's annual report:— The station hands, and their families seem very contented, and all disputes are referred to me. Wife beating at the camps is almost a thing of the past. I have had great trouble in preventing wife beating, and am now sure that the preventing of this practice was the main cause of the Romula poisoning case. At first the whole of the male natives were under the impression that their women were to be their bosses, but a little explaining soon showed them their error. The mode is thus— should a woman become sulky or jealous, the husband, instead of knocking her down with a stick (and then having to fight her relations), brings his wife up before me. Very often I can fix the matter at once. At other times I have to let the husband take a piece of leather, and give her a few strokes. Very often the dispute is settled on the way from the camp to the station. The men now see the matter in its proper light, and often in the camp when a lubra is out for a fight, a voice will call out, 'take her up to the boss,' and she is quiet at once. As a sequel to the above there has not been one fight with clubs or spears this year. The women have a bit of scrap among themselves now and again, but it soon ends" ("Gins Get a Few Strokes," *Northern Territory Times*, 3 January 1920). For Murray's own intervention, see Australian Archives CRS F3 Item 52/570 letters to military base on Talc Head dated 31 July 1942; 8 August 1942; 24 August 1942; and 8 October 1942.

117 See Elkin Fieldnotes, University of Sydney, Folder 1, Box 18, Item 26 and Folder 2, Boxes 30 and 31.

118 "Fieldnotes: Catholic Mission" and "Linguistic Notes and Vocabulary," MS 3752, W. E. H. Stanner Unpublished Material. Box 3, Item b.

119 "E.J. Murray, Delissaville Journal," Australian Archives CRS F3 Item 52/570, 21 October 1942.

120 Ibid., 8 November 1942; 9 November 1942; and 10 November 1942.

121 "Superintendent Katherine Settlement (diary)," Australian Archives NTAC 1980/ 111, 5 January 1945; 15 October 1945; 20 October 1945; and 21 October 1945.

122 V. J. White to Director of Native Affairs, Alice Springs, memo dated 30 September 1943. "E.J. Murray, Delissaville Journal," Australian Archives CRS F3 Item 52/570.

123 See, for instance, Elkin, *The Australian Aborigines*, 25–26, 130–31 and Elkin, *Citizenship for the Aborigines*, 25–27.

124 "Fieldnotes: Port Keats, Daly River," MS 3752 Box 3, Item b., W. E. H. Stanner Unpublished Material.

4 / SHAMED STATES

1 Morris, *Too Soon, Too Late*, 213. A number of authors have tackled the politics of shame in Australian public culture. See Elspeth Probyn, "Shaming Theory,

Thinking Dis-connections: Feminism and Reconciliation," in *Transformations: Thinking Through Feminism*, ed. S. Ahmed, J. Kilby, C. Lury, M. McNeil, and B. Skeggs (London: Routledge, 2000); Haydie Gooder and Jane M. Jacobs, "On the Border of the Unsayable: The Apology in Postcolonial Australia." *Interventions: International Journal of Postcolonial Studies* 2.2 (2000): 229–47; and Sara Ahmed, *Strange Encounters: Embodied Others in Post-Coloniality* (London: Routledge, 2000).

2 For the subjective entailment of capital labor in the realm of fantasy, see Gayatri Spivak, "Scattered Speculations on the Question of Value," in *In Other Worlds: Essays in Cultural Politics* (New York: Methuen, 1987), 154–75.

3 For a critique and response to this particular strategy of approaching Australian state responses to multiculturalism, see John Frow and Meaghan Morris, "Two Laws: Response to Elizabeth Povinelli," *Critical Inquiry* 25.3 (1999): 626–30; and Elizabeth A. Povinelli, "The Cunning of Recognition: Reply to Frow and Morris," *Critical Inquiry* 25.3 (1999): 631–37.

4 Between 1992 and 1995 several Australian Commonwealth commissions were established to investigate both the high rate of Aboriginal deaths in custody and the poor quality of health in Aboriginal communities. In addition, Amnesty International investigated the high rate of incarceration of Aboriginal men as a possible violation of their human rights. See David Biles and David McDonald, eds., *Deaths in Custody, Australia, 1980–89: The Research Papers of the Criminology Unit of the Royal Commission into Aboriginal Deaths in Custody* (Canberra: Australian Institute of Criminology, 1992). From 1999 to 2000, the Howard government faced international criticism for not intervening in a mandatory sentencing law in the Northern Territory, a law which was said to discriminate against Aboriginal people. The volumes written discussing the impact and meaning of *Mabo* on property and sovereignty are too numerous to cite in full here; however, the following works were useful to the preparation of this essay: *Sydney Law Review* 15.2 (June 1993); *University of New South Wales Law Journal* 16.1 (1993); Tim Rouse, ed., *After Mabo: Interpreting Indigenous Traditions* (Melbourne: Melbourne University Press, 1993); Bain Attwood, ed., *In the Age of Mabo: History, Aborigines, and Australia* (Sydney: Allen and Unwin, 1996); and Murray Goot and Tim Rouse, eds., *Make Me a Better Offer: The Politics of Mabo* (Leichhardt, NSW: Pluto Press, 1994). In an insightful reading of the *Mabo* decision and critique of liberal theories of society and justice, Paul Patton highlights the seduction of legal recognition of difference as a path toward a "differential concept of society" rather than as an inhibitor. See Paul Patton, "*Mabo*, Freedom, and the Politics of Difference," *Australian Journal of Political Science* 30.1 (1995): 108–19.

5 *Eddie Mabo v. the State of Queensland, Australian Law Review* 107 (1992): 27.

6 Ibid., 82.

7 *The Wik Peoples v. the State of Queensland, Australian Law Review* 141 (1996): 146. See also Marshall Perron, "Sacred Sites — A Costly Token to a Dead Culture," *Northern Territory News*, 7 January 1989, 7.

8 For one of the most influential critical readings of the common law, see Duncan

Kennedy, "The Structures of Blackstone's Commentaries," *Buffalo Law Review* 28 (1974): 279.

9 Bernard Lane, "Judges Rule Stolen Children Law Valid," *The Australian*, 1 August 1997.

10 *Eddie Mabo v. the State of Queensland*, 26.

11 Robert Manne, "Forget the Guilt, Remember the Shame," *The Australian*, 8 July 1996, 11.

12 See Erving Goffman, "Footing," *Semiotica* 25 (1979): 1–29.

13 Manne, "Forget the Guilt," 11.

14 "Talk of sharing in a collective guilt over the dispossession of the Aborigines is one thing; however, talk of sharing in a legacy of historical shame is altogether another. This distinction is most easily explained by analogy. Conservatives such as Howard and Tim Fischer would have no difficulty in feeling admiration and a kind of pride in, say, the resourcefulness shown by the soldiers at Gallipoli. I am sure, too, that they would hope that other Australians would share in their admiration and their pride. Yet if it is possible and just to feel pride in the achievements of forebears, it surely cannot be regarded as impossible or unjust to feel shame about past wrongs. The case I am making can be put simply. To be an Australian is to be embedded or implicated in this country's history in a way outsiders or visitors cannot be. To be implicated in this history opens — as conservatives easily acknowledge — the possibility of reasonable pride. But to be open to the possibility of pride in achievement is also, necessarily, to be open to the possibility in shame in wrongdoing" (ibid., 11).

15 *Australian Parliamentary Hansard, House of Representatives*, Thursday, 26 August 1999, 7046–47.

16 Ibid., 7048.

17 See Rosemary Neill, "Howard Reconciled to a Curate's Egg," *The Australian*, 4 June 1999, 15; Michelle Grattan and Margo Kingston, "Regrets Divide Nation," *Sydney Morning Herald*, 27 August 1999, 1; and "Editorial," *Sydney Morning Herald*, 31 May 1999.

18 Anne Connolly, "Accentuate the Positive in Our History — Malouf," *The Australian*, 10 July 1996, 38; and David Marr, "Australia — Just Imagine Your Future," *Sydney Morning Herald*, 1, 7.

19 *Australian Parliamentary Hansard, House of Representatives*, Thursday, 26 August 1999, 7047.

20 Ibid., 7047.

21 Ibid., 7049–50.

22 Ibid., 7051.

23 "Where a clan or group has continued to acknowledge the laws and (so far as practicable) to observe the customs based on the traditions of that clan or group, whereby their traditional connection with the land has been substantially maintained, the traditional community title of that clan or group can be said to remain in existence" (*The Mabo Decision 1992* with commentary by Richard H. Bartlett [Sydney: Butterworths, 1993], 48).

24 Ibid., 49. In 1993, during a televised address to the nation presenting and defending his decision to enact legislation based on the *Mabo* ruling, Prime Minister Paul Keating summarized the conditions the court imposed on the legal productivity of Aboriginal traditions: "The Court accepted that native title existed where two fundamental conditions were met:—that their connection with the land had been maintained, unbroken down through the years—and that this title had not been overturned by any action of a government to use the land or to give it to somebody else" (P. J. Keating, "Prime Minister's Address to the Nation," in *Make Me a Better Offer: The Politics of Mabo,* ed. Murray Goot and Tim Rouse (Leichhardt, NSW: Pluto Press, 1994), 236.

25 *Eddie Mabo v. the State of Queensland,* 44. Brennan argued that native title rights and interests would be precluded if the recognition were to fracture a skeletal principle of our legal system (43).

26 *The Members of the Yorta Yorta Aboriginal Community v. the State of Victoria,* Federal Court of Astralia 1606 (1998): para 12. See also Deborah Bird Rose, "Hard Times: An Australian Story," in *Quicksands: Foundational Histories in Australian and Aotearoa New Zealand* (Sydney: University of New South Wales, 1999), 2–19.

27 *The Members of the Yorta Yorta Aboriginal Community v. the State of Victoria,* para. 4.

28 Ibid., para. 106.

29 Ibid., para. 112; Olney is quoting from Edward M. Curr, *Recollections of Squatting in Victoria* (1883; Melbourne: University of Melbourne Press, 1965), 245.

30 *The Members of the Yorta Yorta Aboriginal Community v. the State of Victoria,* para. 14.

31 Ibid., para. 126.

32 Ibid., para. 128.

33 Ashley-Montague, *Coming into Being among the Australian Aborigines,* 49.

34 *Hayes v. Northern Territory, 1999, Report of the Native Tribunal Commissioner, Mr. Justice Olney* (Canberra: Australian Publishing Service, 1999), para. 26.

35 Ibid., para 13.

36 W. V. Quine, "Where Do We Disagree?," in *The Philosophy of Donald Davidson,* ed. Lewis Edwin Hahn (Peru, Ill.: Open Court, 1999), 76. See also Gayatri Spivak on the function of the native informant in philosophy, in her *The Critique of Colonial Reason: Toward a History of the Vanishing Present* (Cambridge, Mass.: Harvard University Press, 1999).

37 Elizabeth A. Povinelli, "Do Rocks Listen? The Cultural Politics of Apprehending Australian Aboriginal Labor," *American Anthropologist* 97.3 (September 1995): 505–18.

38 The Law Reform Commission, *The Recognition of Aboriginal Customary Laws.*

39 Shane McGrath, "Traditional Punishment Prevented: Barnes v The Queen," *Indigenous Law Bulletin* 4.8 (December/January 1997–1998): 18.

40 *Barnes v the Queen* was reported in the *Syndey Morning Herald* as are periodically other cases that strain the easy reconciliation of the law of cultural recognition and the "real" referent of Aboriginal customary law. For news coverage of other cases

in the Northern Territory, see "Initiation for All," *Northern Territory News*, 15 June 1999; Bob Watt, "Wife-Killer Says He was Cursed," *Northern Territory News*, 18 June 1999, 5; Bob Watt, "9 Years Jail after Brutal Wife Killing," *Northern Territory News*, 19 June 1999, 3; Bob Watt, "20cm Blade in Lung: Man on Kill Count," *Northern Territory News*, 22 June 1999, 7; "Missionary Wed Girls to Save Them," *Northern Territory News*, 1 September 1999, 18; Amanda Keenan and Stephane Balogh, "Ethnic Community Leaders Attack Killer's Race Defense," *The Australian*, 13 August 1998, 9; Bob Watt, "Spear Man 'Thought Cop Shot Uncle,'" *Northern Territory News*, 28 August 1998, 7; Bob Watt, "Commissioner Hears of Death: 'Bone Pointed at Him,'" *Northern Territory News*, 31 January 1989, 14.

41 For discussion of the potential of *Mabo* for expanding recognition of Aboriginal customary law, see Rob McLaughlin, "Some Problems and Issues in the Recognition of Indigenous Customary Law," *Aboriginal Law Bulletin* 3.28 (July 1996): 4–9. For a fuller discussion, see The Law Reform Commission, *The Recognition of Aboriginal Customary Laws.*

42 Paul J. Keating, "Speech by the Honourable Prime Minister, PJ Keating MP, Australian Launch of the International Year for the World's Indigenous People, Redfern, 10 December 1992," *Aboriginal Law Bulletin* 3.61 (April 1993): 4–5.

43 "The message (of *Mabo*) should be that there is nothing to fear or to lose in the recognition of historical truth, or the extension of social justice, or the deepening of Australian social democracy to include all indigenous Australians" (Keating, "Speech by the Honourable Prime Minister"), 5. See also Paul J. Keating, "Australian Update: Statement by the Prime Minister, The Hon. P.J. Keating Commonwealth Response to High Court *Mabo* Judgement, Canberra 18 October 1993," *Aboriginal Law Bulletin* 3.64 (October 1993): 18.

44 Keating, "Australian Update," 18.

45 Keating is referring to the Council for Aboriginal Reconciliation. He stated that the mission of the council was "to forge a new partnership built on justice and equity and an appreciation of the heritage of Australia's indigenous people" (Keating, "Speech by the Honourable Prime Minister," 4). For a critical account of the Council for Aboriginal Reconciliation, see Daniel Lavery, "The Council for Aboriginal Reconciliation: When the CAR Stops on Reconciliation Day Will Indigenous Australians Have Gone Anywhere?," *Aboriginal Law Bulletin* 2.58 (October 1992): 7–8.

46 *Australian Parliamentary Hansard, House of Representatives*, 7049.

47 Keating, "Speech by the Honourable Prime Minister," 4.

48 See also M. J. Detmold, "Law and Difference: Reflections on Mabo's Case," *Sydney Law Review* 15.2 (June 1993): 159–67.

49 *The Mabo Decision 1992*, 42.

50 Ibid., 28.

51 Decided concurrently with *The Thayorre People v. the State of Queensland* (1996).

52 *The Wik Peoples v. the State of Queensland*, n. 51, 43.

53 *Eddie Mabo v. the State of Queensland*, 18.

54 *The Wik Peoples v. the State of Queensland*, 109.

55 Ibid., 109, 140.

56 *Eddie Mabo v. the State of Queensland*, 42, 139; *The Wik Peoples v. the State of Queensland*, 28, 34, 70, 176.

57 *Eddie Mabo v. the State of Queensland*, 42.

58 *The Wik Peoples v. the State of Queensland*, 176.

59 Ibid., 198.

60 Ibid., 35; see also *Eddie Mabo v. the State of Queensland*, 18.

61 See, for instance, *The Wik Peoples v. the State of Queensland*, 220.

62 See, for instance, *Eddie Mabo v. the State of Queensland*, 18, 26, 27, 29, 41, 83.

63 "There is no question that indigenous society can and will change on contact with European culture.... But modification of traditional society in itself does not mean traditional title no longer exists. Traditional title arises from the fact of occupation, not the occupation of a particular type of society or way of life" (*Eddie Mabo v. the State of Queensland*, 150). "These comments apply with particular force to Queensland where ... there were approximately 70 different kinds of Crown leasehold and Crown perpetual leasehold tenures. To approach the matter by reference to legislation is not to turn one's back on centuries of history nor is it to impugn basic principles of property law. Rather, it is to recognise historical development, the changes in law over centuries and the need for property law to accommodate the very different situation in this country" (*The Wik Peoples v. the State of Queensland*, 58).

64 *Eddie Mabo v. the State of Queensland*, 43.

65 Ibid., 83.

66 Ibid., 28.

67 *The Wik Peoples v. the State of Queensland*, 63.

68 *The Mabo Decision 1992*, 47.

69 Emmanuel Levinas, *Totality and Infinity* (Pittsburg: Duquesne University Press, 1969).

70 See Frantz Fanon, *Black Face, White Masks* (New York: Grove Press, 1967); and Bhabha, "The Other Question," 66–84.

71 Slavoj Žižek, *The Sublime Object of Ideology*.

72 "Radical title" refers to the form of title that gives the sovereign paramount power to create interests in land by grant of tenure. See Susan Burton Phillips, "A Note: Eddie Mabo v. the State of Queensland," *The Sydney Law Review* 15.2 (June 1993): 121–42.

73 Hugh Morgan of the Western Mining Corporation claimed, "the High Court had plunged property law into chaos and 'given substance' to the ambitions of Australian communists and the Bolshevik left," quoted in Richard Bartlett, "*Mabo:* Another Triumph for the Common Law," *Sydney Law Review* 15.2 (June 1993): 178–86. For a discussion on Aborigines and mining in Western Australia, see Richard Bartlett, "Inequality Before the Law in Western Australia: The Land (Title and Traditional Usage) Act," *Aboriginal Law Bulletin* 3.65 (December 1993): 7–9; and R. A. Dixon and M. C. Dillon, eds., *Aborigines and Diamond Mining: The Politics of Re-*

source Development in the East Kimberley, Western Australia (Nedlands: University of Western Australia Press, 1990). See also Paul Kauffman, *Wik, Mining, and Aborigines* (Sydney: Allen and Unwin, 1998).

74 James Scott, *Weapons of the Weak* (New Haven: Yale University Press, 1986).

75 While Drucilla Cornell's discussion of the normative grounding of juridical interpretation in implicit and explicit references to "the good" has been helpful to my understanding of the technology of discrimination, more attention needs to be paid to the traffic of dominant hegemonic projects in legal shame. See Drucilla Cornell, "From the Lighthouse: The Promise of Redemption and the Possibility of Legal Interpretation," *Cardozo Law Review* 11.5–6 (1990): 1688.

76 Brown, "Wounded Attachments," 53.

77 Several critical essays on identity, difference, and democracy have critically attended to the politics of "wounded" subjects in late modern liberal societies. See, for instance, Brown, "Wounded Attachments"; Berlant, "The Subject of True Feeling," in *Cultural Pluralism, Identity Politics, and the Law*, ed. Austin Sarat and Thomas R. Kearns (Ann Arbor: University of Michigan Press, 1999), 49–84; Fish, "Boutique Multiculturalism"; and Trouillot, "Abortive Rituals."

5 / THE POETICS OF GHOSTS: SOCIAL REPRODUCTION IN THE ARCHIVE OF THE NATION

1 Arjun Appadurai, "The Production of Locality," in *Modernity at Large* (Minneapolis: University of Minnesota Press, 1996), 178–99; Michael Silverstein, "Contemporary Transformations of Local Language Communities," Annual Review of Anthropology 27 (1998): 401–26.

2 "Death Rite for Mabalang," *Australian Walkabout Show*, ABC radio program, 1948.

3 For the concept of "rigid designator," see Saul Kripke, *Meaning and Necessity* (1972; Cambridge, Mass.: Harvard University Press, 1980).

4 For Peirce, subject terms and proper names are indices. Thus the "whole burden of the sign," including proper names, "must be ascertained, not by closer examination of the utterance but by collateral observations of the utterer" (Peirce, "Pragmatism," 406–7). See also Benjamin Lee, *Talking Heads: Language, Metalanguage, and the Semiotics of Subjectivity* (Durham: Duke University Press, 1997), esp. 98–99.

5 This meaning of *durlg* is also recorded by Elkin in his "Ngirawat, or the Sharing of Names in the Wagaitj Tribe, Northern Australia," in *Sonderdruck Aus Beitrage Zue Gesellungs und Volkerwissenschaft* (Berlin: Verlag Bebr. Mann, 1950), 67–81.

6 For discussion of these sign-process, see Stanner, "Religion, Totemism, and Symbolism"; Fred Myers, *Pintupi Country, Pintupi Selves: Sentiment, Place, and Politics among Western Desert Aborigines* (Washington, D.C.: Smithsonian Institution Press, 1986); Deborah Bird Rose, *Dingo Makes Us Human: Life and Land in an Aboriginal Australian Culture* (Cambridge, Eng.: Cambridge University Press, 1992); and Ian Keen, *Knowledge and Secrecy in an Aboriginal Religion* (Oxford: Oxford University Press, 1997).

7 Colin Simpson, *Adam in Ochre* (Sydney: Angus and Robertson, 1957), 168.

8 Ibid., 171.

9 Partington, *Hasluck versus Coombs.* Simpson also mentions Hasluck in *Adam in Ochre,* 187.

10 Simpson, *Adam in Ochre,* 164.

11 Elkin, "Ngirawat," 77.

12 *The Elkin Archives,* University of Sydney. See Folder 1, Box 18, Item 26.

13 A. P. Elkin, "Arnhem Land Music," *Oceania* 26.2 (1955): 146.

14 Ibid.

15 Roger M. Keesing, *Kin Groups and Social Structure* (Fort Worth: Harcourt Brace Jovanovich College Publishers, 1975), 148, quoted in Peter Sutton, *Native Title and the Descent of Rights* (Perth: National Native Title Tribunal, 1998), 25. Also influential is Harold Scheffler's understanding of descent, descent-phrased constructs, and descent-phrased rules for group understanding, even though Scheffler does not consider Australian indigenous forms of social organization to be based on descent but rather on affiliation. See Harold W. Scheffler, *Australian Kinship Classification* (Cambridge, Eng.: Cambridge University Press, 1978).

16 W. H. R. Rivers, "The Genealogical Method of Anthropological Inquiry," *Sociological Review* 3.1 (1910): 1–12; see also Elizabeth A. Povinelli, "Notes on Gridlock: Genealogy, Intimacy, Sexuality," *Public Culture* 14.1 (2002): 215–38.

17 See the discussion in 15.

18 The territory to which the descent group's totem is found is usually referred to as an estate, thus the phrase "an estate group." For a review of the study of Australian Aboriginal kinship, see Ian Keen, "Twenty-Five Years of Aboriginal Kinship Studies," in *Social Anthropology and Australian Aboriginal Studies: A Contemporary Overview,* ed. Ronald Berndt and R. Tonkinson (Canberra: Aboriginal Studies Press, 1988), 79–123.

19 L. R. Hiatt, *Kinship and Conflict* (Canberra: Australian National University, 1965), 20.

20 Ian Keen has described the relationship between the definition of "traditional Aboriginal owners" and "the 'orthodox model' of Aboriginal land tenure," in his "A Question of Interpretation: The Definition of 'Traditional Aboriginal Owners' in the Aboriginal Land Rights (NT) Act," in *Aboriginal Land-Owners: Contemporary Issues in the Determination of Traditional Aboriginal Land Ownership,* ed. L. R. Hiatt (Sydney: University of Sydney, 1984), 24–45. See, more recently, L. R. Hiatt, *Arguments about Aborigines, Australia, and the Evolution of Social Anthropology* (Cambridge, Eng.: Cambridge University Press, 1996).

21 Hiatt, *Kinship and Conflict,* 18.

22 A. P. Elkin, "The Complexity of Social Organization in Arnhem Land," *Southwestern Journal of Anthropology* 6.1 (1950): 1–20.

23 Allan Marett, "Wangga Songs of Northwest Australia: Reflections on the Performance of Aboriginal Music at SIMS 88," *Musicology Australia* 15 (1991): 37–46; Allan Marett, "Wangga: Socially Powerful Songs?" *The World of Music* 1 (1994): 67–81; Allan Marett and JoAnne Page, "Interrelations between Music and Dance in a Wangga from Northwest Australian," in *Essence of Singing and the Substance of*

  Song, Recent Responses to the Aboriginal Performing Arts and Other Essays in Honour of Catherine Ellis, ed. Linda Barwick, Allan Marett, and Guy Turnstill (Sydney: University of Sydney Press, 1995), 27–38.

24 Elkin, "Ngirawat," 76.

25 Allan Marett has mapped a genealogy of human authorization for the country surrounding Belyuen.

26 Gilles Deleuze and Felix Guattari, *Kafka: Toward a Minor Literature,* trans. Dana Polan (Minneapolis: University of Minnesota Press, 1986).

27 "Death Rite for Mabalan."

28 "Death Rite for Mabalan" describes the voice of Eliang as the effect of pain caused by *wingmalang,* but might also have been voice of the *wingmalang* pained by Moseck's trickery. Elizabeth A. Povinelli, " 'Might Be Something': The Language of Indeterminacy in Australian Aboriginal Land Use," *Man* 28.4 (1993): 679–704.

29 John Lucy has noted: "In a like manner, structural parallelism in poetry sets up formal equivalences that tell listeners that certain things are to be compared with one another" ("Reflexive Language and the Human Disciplines," in *Reflexive Language: Reported Speech and Metapragmatics,* ed. John Lucy [Cambridge, Eng.: Cambridge University Press, 1993], 10).

30 *Aboriginal Land Rights (Northern Territory) Act, 1976* (Canberra: Australian Government Printer, 30 April 1992).

31 The land on which the Belyuen community is located is already defined as Aboriginal land under the Aboriginal Land Rights (Northern Territory) Act, 1976.

32 The Aboriginal Land Rights (Northern Territory) Act, 1976, also stipulates the traditional Aboriginal owner must be entitled to forage as of right, but this entitlement has never been the basis of a decision.

33 The Aboriginal Land Rights (Northern Territory) Act, 1976, and the Native Title Act, (Commonwealth) 1993, stipulate that every claim be accompanied by an anthropological report.

34 *Australian Parliamentary Hansard, House of Representatives,* 4 June 1976, p. 3082.

35 See C. Athanasiou, "Land Rights or Native Title," *Indigenous Law Review* 4.12 (1998): 14–15.

36 Since then a number of land commissioners have accepted spiritual descent from a mythic ancestor, with some stating that claimants must also be members of a human descent group. Dr. M. Reay in the Borroloola Land Claim described spiritual descent as the basis of all forms of descent from an Aboriginal perspective: "Aborigines collapse history and assimilate the remote Dreamtime into the present. Transformations of quasi-ancestral beings are visible in the landscape. Ceremonies re-enact their adventures and their paths are recorded in song. The remote past is ever present. An individual's connection to it is his Dreamings and the land in which his Dreamings are located. The quasi-ancestral beings he shares with father and the land establish his descent through spirits located in that land from the first people those beings originated" (*Borroloola Land Claim, Report by the Aboriginal Land Commissioner, Mr. Justice Toohey* [Canberra: Australian Publishing Service, 1978], exhibit 45). In the Uluru Land Claim report, Toohey accepted that a claimant

could inherit rights from the estate in which he or she was born: "In that case the rights are in a sense inherited because they derive from the ancestral being who becomes the individual's personal tjukurr or tjukurrpa, his dreaming or totem. Thus a child may belong to two or even three estates. He does so actually not potentially. But the rights are inchoate: more is required before they can be exercised in respect to any one estate" (*Uluru Land Claim, Report by the Aboriginal Land Commissioner, Mr. Justice Toohey* [Canberra: Australian Publishing Service, 1979], para. 27). Justice Kearney stated that this type of kirda link gives no more than a secondary interest in the Yulumu estate and is not passed on to children, *Uluru Land Claim* (para. 46). Justice Toohey argued in the Alyawarra and Kaititja Land Claim report that conception dreaming provides only individual not group rights to country (*Alyawarra and Kaititja Land Claim, Report by the Aboriginal Land Commission, Mr. Justice Toohey* [Canberra: Australian Publishing Service, 1978], paras. 28, 29). However, he accepted Stanner's argument that every member of the patriline is in some sense animated by the "patri-spirit" of the clan to which he is affiliated (ibid., para. 45). In the Warlpiri, Kukaja, and Ngarti Land Claim report, Kearney once again addressed spiritual descent, finding that persons conceived on a Dreaming track within the claimant country are linked with the country, being animated by its spirit; and, given this spiritual connection to the country, if the persons reside with other (descent) members of the group, acquire the necessary knowledge of the Dreamings and sites, perform the required duties, and are recognized by other members of the group they can be found to be members of the local descent group (*Warlpiri, Kukatja, and Ngarti Land Claim, Report by the Aboriginal Land Commission, Mr. Justice Kearney* (Canberra: Australian Publishing Service, 1985), paras. 30, 31.

37 *Nicholson River (Waanyi/Gaeawa) Land Claim, Report by the Aboriginal Land Commissioner, Mr. Justice Kearney* (Canberra: Australian Publishing Service, 1985), para. 57.

38 Ibid., para. 68.

39 Ibid., para. 63. Kearney also noted in Nicholson River report that because Dr. Reay was dealing in Borroloola Land Claim only with patrilineal descent groups, she limited her discussion to the "father" (see *Nicholson River Land Claim,* para. 66). Dr. Chase commented more broadly in Nicholson River that "the positing of a common descent among people from a mythic ancestor in any case presents no problems . . . the phenomenon is commonly found by field workers elsewhere in Australia. In Cape York Peninsula, for example, the term for dreamings, or totems, is a derivative of the term for father's father, and in societies with shallow generational depth in genealogies, the generations immediately above that of grandfathers are commonly fused into the time period of mythic ancestors and their activities" (*Nicholson River Land Claim,* exhibit 58, p. 12). In the Cox River Land Claim report, Kearney found that persons who based their inclusion in a local descent group solely on vaguely phrased relations through the Dreaming or through ceremony should be excluded. They must in addition be related to the relevant local land-holding group by a principle of descent (*Cox River (Alawa-Ngandji)*

Land Claim, Report by the Aboriginal Land Claim Commissioner, Mr. Justice Kearney [Canberra: Australian Publishing Service, 1984]. In the Mount Allan Land Claim report, Mr. Justice Kearney addressed the question of whether "spiritual genealogy" would satisfy the requirements of local descent group under the LRA. Kearney first noted Toohey's finding that a local descent group may be recruited on a principle of descent deemed relevant by the claimants (*Mount Allan Land Claim, Report by the Aboriginal Land Commissioner, Mr. Justice Kearney* [Canberra: Australian Publishing Service, 1985], para. 48). Kearney stated that "perceived descent from a common mythic ancestor is a principle of descent which conveys the notion of common ancestry" (*Mount Allan Land Claim,* para. 48). In the case of Judy Napaljarri, and Tiger Japanangla and his siblings, there was no evidence of any actual genealogical link between them and members of the local descent group for the Yulumu and Ngarlu estates (*Mount Allan Land Claim,* para 45). Moreover, Tiger Japanangla's father's estate was located over one hundred kilometers to the west of the claim land. Tiger Japanangla was, nevertheless, found to satisfy the definition of a traditional Aboriginal owner because the claimants deemed as relevant a principle of a shared "spiritual genealogical link" to the local descent group and claim land on the basis of a shared descent from a common honey ant ancestor. Dr. Peterson described this spiritual genealogy in the following way: "All Honey Ant kirda groups that are in contact and know each other and that lie on common dreaming tracks . . . are seen to be related as from common Honey Ant ancestors—that all the Honey Ant ancestors are themselves related" (*Mount Allan Land Claim,* 134).

40 *Timber Creek Land Claim, Report by the Aboriginal Land Commissioner, Mr. Justice Maurice* (Canberra: Australian Publishing Service, 1985).

41 *Ti Tree Station Land Claim, Report by the Aboriginal Land Commissioner, Mr. Justice Maurice* (Canberra: Australian Publishing Service, 1987), para. 99.

42 Ibid., para. 96.

43 Ibid., para. 100.

44 In his report on the Lander, Warlpiri, and Anmatjirra Land Claim to the Willowra Pastoral Lease, Toohey stated: "The words 'local,' 'descent' and 'group' are ordinary English words to which a meaning can be attached, given a context which in this case is the Land Rights Act. The matter should not be approached with some preconceived model in mind to which the evidence must accommodate itself. Rather it is a matter of the conclusions to be drawn from the evidence. A local descent group may be 'recruited on a principle of descent deemed relevant by claimants.' If the evidence so dictates, a local descent gruop may be unilineal or non-unilineal" (*Lander, Warlpiri, Anmatjirra Land Claim, Report by the Aboriginal Land Commissioner, Mr. Justice Toohey* [Canberra: Australian Publishing Service, 1980], para. 89).

45 *Timber Creek Land Claim,* para. 92.

46 *Northern Land Council and Others v. Aboriginal Land Commissioner and Another, Australian Law Review* 105 (1992): 539, para. 60; See also *Finniss River Land Claim, Report by the Aboriginal Land Commissioner, Mr. Justice Toohey* (Canberra: Australian Publishing Service, 1981), para. 161.

47 *Kenbi (Cox Peninsula) Land Claim, Report by the Aboriginal Land Commissioner, Mr. Justice Olney* (Canberra: Australian Publishing Service, 1991), para. 7.2.3.

48 Maria Brandl, Adrienne Haritos, and Michael Walsh, *Kenbi Land Claim* (Darwin: Northern Land Council, 1979), 152.

49 See Elizabeth A. Povinelli, *Belyuen Traditional Aboriginal Owners (Kenbi Land Claim)* (Darwin: Northern Land Council, 1996).

50 See Povinelli, *Belyuen Traditional Aboriginal Owners.*

51 Brandl, Haritos, and Walsh, *Kenbi Land Claim,* 31.

52 For a concise history of the political events that led to the establishment of Woodward's Commission and the narrowing of its recommendations, see Graham Neate, *Aboriginal Land Rights Law in the Northern Territory* (Chippendale, NSW: Alternative Publishing Cooperative, 1989), esp. 1–40.

53 *Kenbi (Cox Peninsula) Land Claim,* para. 7.2.4.

54 *Kenbi Transcripts* (Indooroopilly: Transcripts Australia, 1995–1998), 7061.

55 Oleny reviewed at length legal precedent for viewing the "local descent group," especially discussion of the Woodward report before parliament: "The paragraphs from the first Woodward report which are reproduced as Appendix A to this report draw a clear distinction in Aboriginal social organisation between a 'tribe' or 'linguistic group' on the one hand, and a 'local descent group' on the other. Given that the form of subsection 50 (4) has its origin in clause 27 of the draft Bill in the second Woodward report, there is a strong inference to be drawn that the meaning to be attributed to 'tribe' or 'linguistic group' was quite different from the idea of a 'local descent group' " (*Kenbi [Cox Peninsula] Land Claim* [Australian Publishing Service, 1991], paras. 8.40–8.49).

57 Ibid., para. 9.6.

58 As an anthropologist opposing the Belyuen claim pointed out in the second hearing.

59 The Supreme Court hearing an appeal of his findings ruled that Olney had erred as a matter of law—he had imposed an outdated anthropological model on local forms of social recruitment rather than considering, as required by law, recruitment principles "deemed relevant by the claimants": "The point is that the principle of descent will be one that is recognized as applying in respect of the particular group. Further, there is no reason the particular principle of descent traditionally operating may not change over time." The Supreme Court advised future land commissioners to first look at contemporary local beliefs, not at anthropological models, and at the degree they have deviated from traditional (read: precontact) beliefs and practices, and then see whether they fall within the meaning and intentions of the Aboriginal Land Rights Act (and likewise, for claims lodged under the *Native Title Act, 1993.* The court also reiterated that the act should be "broadly construed so as to give effect to the beneficial purposes of the Act." But the Supreme Court did not overturn the direction that the assessment (and through it power) flowed. By defining a "local descent group" as a subdivision of a linguistic or dialect group with clan (or "totemic") ties to particular sacred sites on the land claimed, it entrenched

the a priori status of national definitions of sociality functioning before the law enters the locale of its discriminations. See *Northern Land Council and Others v. Aboriginal Land Commissioner and Another, 539.*

60 The land commissioner, Justice Gray, had not as of the writing of this essay written his report on traditional Aboriginal ownership in the Kenbi Land Claim.

61 Others have noted the differential effects of hegemonic formations on social groups. See the still-compelling analysis of family in France in Jacques Donzelot, *Policing of Families,* trans. Robert Hurley (New York: Pantheon Books, 1979).

62 *Kenbi Transcripts,* 5294.

63 Peter Sutton, a senior anthropologist representing one of the Laragiya claimant groups (but having done no ethnographic research among the Belyuen), insisted that the land commissioner distinguish between territorial rights based on bloodlines, a principle of territoriality he considered "traditional," and the personal ties to country based on historical connections he considered "historical." In his view the Belyuen asserted interests "in ancestral country on one basis" (*durlg*) "and the country of their—for most of them, I would think, their strongest emotional and personal—personalized attachments" on another basis" (*maruy*) (*Kenbi Transcripts,* 6578).

64 A. P. Elkin, "Ngirawat, or the sharing of Names in the Wagalt; tribe, Northern Australia," 68.

65 Brandl, Haritos, and Walsh, *Kenbi Land Claim,* 161.

66 Edmund Leach, *Political Systems of Highland Burma* (London: Athlone, 1964), 13–14.

67 *Kenbi Transcripts,* 4899.

68 Ibid., 5241–42.

69 Ibid., 7332.

70 Ibid., 7349–50.

71 Colin Simpson announces to the audience: "Mosec is dancing solo around the old man and I don't know if I have ever seen finer dancing in my life, he is comparable with a dancer like Le Shine the art of a fine ballet. Really, but don't take my word for it ask Ted Shawn the American dancer who toured Australia and visited Delissaville and who said that Mosec would be a sensation in London or New York" ("Death Rite for Mabalan," *Australian Walkabout Show*).

72 Guidelines written to interpret the amended *Native Title Act* make these conditions explicit:

> The description [must be] clear enough to allow someone else to see whether any particular person is a member of the group. The basic principle is that there should be some objective way of verifying the identity of members of the group. The following are *examples only* of what may be an acceptable description:
> • biological relations of a person named in the native title claim group (and relations by adoption, or according to traditional laws and customs);
> • relations or descendents of a person named in the native title claim group, and people related by marriage to those relations or descendents, including

people in de facto or multiple partnerships, where such relationships are recognised by that group's traditional laws and customs;

· relations or descendents or a person named in the native title group, and people who have been adopted by those relations or descendents;

· people who belong to the group, according to its laws and customs.

Note: a description of the group's laws and customs may be required.

National Native Title Tribunal, "Guidelines to Applicants, Registration Test Information Sheet, no 2," October 1998.

73 *Northern Land Council and Others v. Aboriginal Land Commissioner and Another,* 554. For statements by land commissioners on the flexibility of Aboriginal traditions, see *Daly River (Malak Malak) Land Claim, Report by the Aboriginal land Commissioner, Mr. Justice Toohey* (Canberra: Australian Publishing Service, 1982); *Nicholson River Land Claim;* and *Jawoyn (Katherine Area) Land Claim, Report by the Aboriginal land Commissioner, Mr. Justice Kearney* (Canberra: Australian Publishing Service, 1987).

74 See also *Kenbi Transcripts* 7317, 7320, 7341–43, 7351–55, 7464–69.

75 Ibid., 7341–42.

76 Ibid., 7364.

77 *Nomad,* Australian Music International, New York, 1994.

6 / THE TRUEST BELIEF IS COMPULSION

1 Benjamin Lee, *Talking Heads: Language, Metalanguage, and the Semiotics of Subjectivity* (Durham: Duke University Press, 1997), 342. For a critical comment on the emergence of the notion of distinterest, see Mary Poovey, *A History of the Modern Fact: Problems of Knowledge in the Sciences of Wealth and Society* (Chicago: University of Chicago Press, 1998).

2 Diane Bell, *Ngarrindjeri Wurruwarrin: A World That Is, Was, and Will Be* (Melbourne: Spinifex, 1998); Ronald Brunton, "The Hindmarsh Island Bridge and the Credibility of Australian Anthropology," *Anthropology Today* 21.4 (1996): 2–7; and James Weiner, "The Secret of the Ngarrindjeri: The Fabrication of Social Knowledge," *Arena* 5 (1995): 17–32.

3 Francesca Merlan, "The Limits of Cultural Construction," *Oceania* 61 (1991): 341–52.

4 Lee, *Talking Heads,* 109. In the Peircean tradition two types of indeterminacy are distinguished: indefiniteness, signaled by the quantifier "some"; and generality, signaled by the quantifier "any." In the process of distinguishing his account of translation and interpretation from Quine's, Donald Davidson likewise defines indeterminacy in terms of the quantifier "any." See Donald Davidson, "Reply to W. V. Quine," in *The Philosophy of Donald Davidson* (Peru, Ill.: Open Court Publishing, 1999), 80–86. See also Elizabeth A. Povinelli, "Radical Worlds: The Anthropology of Incommensurability and Inconceivability," *Annual Review of Anthropology* 30 (2001): 319–34.

5 W. V. Quine, *Word and Object* (Cambridge, Mass.: MIT Press).

6 Davidson would likely see this sociologically weak version as the result of the social interest in the "new, surprising, or disputed" rather than "the vast amount of agreement on plan matters" (Davidson, "Belief and the Basis of Meaning," in *Inquiries into Truth and Interpretation* [New York: Oxford University Press, 1984], 141–54, 153).

7 *Kenbi Transcripts*, 5660.

8 For a review of the literature, see Francesca Merlan, "Australian Aboriginal Conception Revisited," *Man* 21.3 (1986): 474–93.

9 Warner, *A Black Civilization*, 24.

10 Ibid., 24.

11 Ibid., 23, my emphasis. Gillen continually refers to the labor of interpretation. See, for instance, his letters to Spencer in which he says the following: "Can't get people to admit [that they exchange women in ceremony]" (128); "I couldn't believe it myself at first but after numerous inquiries" (135, see also 139–40); "Father says they have sex on the graveyard. You can't imagine how I tingled with desire to be upon the spot to probe this strange custom to the bottom" (234). (Mulvaney, Morphy, and Petch, eds., *"My Dear Spencer"*).

12 Warner, *A Black Civilization*, 24.

13 *Kenbi Transcripts*, 4961–62.

14 Ibid., 6613.

15 Merland, "The Limits of Cultural Construction."

16 *Ti Tree Station Land Claim, Report by the Aboriginal Land Commissioner, Mr. Justice Maurice*, paras. 92, 93, 107.

17 *Kenbi Transcripts*, 7184.

18 Elkin, "Arnhem Land Music," 144.

19 *Kenbi Transcripts*, 4190–91.

20 Ibid., 4191.

21 Ibid., 4195.

22 Ibid., 4259.

23 Ibid., 4279.

24 Ibid., 4279.

25 Ibid., 4279.

26 Ibid., 4280–81.

27 Ibid., 4295.

28 See for instance, Ibid., 6086–96.

29 *Aboriginal Land Rights (Northern Territory) Act, 1976*, sec. 3(1).

30 Ibid., sec. 51(3).

31 *Timber Creek Land Claim, Report by the Aboriginal Land Commissioner, Mr. Justice Maurice*, para. 90.

32 Ibid., para. 92.

33 Ibid., para 96.

34 Ibid., para 96.

35 *Kenbi Transcripts*, 5901–2.

36 F. R. Palmer, *Mood and Modality* (1986; Cambridge, Eng.: Cambridge University Press, 1998); J. Barnes, "Evidentials in the Tuyuca Verb," *International Journal of American Linguistics* 50 (1984): 255–71; John Lyons, *Semantics* (Cambridge, Eng.: Cambridge University Press, 1977).

36 *Kenbi Transcripts,* 5389.

37 Ibid., 5881 and 5887.

38 Ibid., 5887.

39 Ibid., 5159.

40 Emile Durkheim and Marcel Mauss, *Primitive Classification* (Chicago: University of Chicago Press, 1963), 17, 20–21.

41 Lévi-Strauss, *Totemism.*

42 *Aboriginal Land Rights (Northern Territory) Act, 1976,* sec. 51 (3).

43 National Native Title Tribunal, "Guidelines to Applicants, Registration Test Information, Sheet no 2," October 1998.

44 In being bothered Keely faced the reverse dilemma of Hilary Putman's philosopher, rephrased by Stanley Fish thusly: "What if the answers philosophers come up with are answers only in the highly artificial circumstances of the philosophy seminar where ordinary reasons for action are systematically distrusted and introduced only to be dismissed as naive? And what if, once the philosopher goes away or ceases himself or herself to be a philosopher, those ordinary reasons return *without* a vengeance and action is just as it was before, if not unproblematic, at least not mysterious" (Stanley Fish, "Truth and Toilets: Pragmatism and the Practice of Life," in *The Revival of Pragmatism: New Essays on Social Thought, Law, and Culture,* ed. Morris Dickstein (Durham: Duke University Press, 1998), 418–33.

45 See *Kwaku Mensah v. the King* (1946) *AC* 83; *Moffa v. the Queen* (1977) 138 *CLR* 601.

SELECTED WORKS CITED

Ahmed, Sara. *Strange Encounters: Embodied Others in Post-Coloniality.* London: Routledge, 2000.

Altman, J. C. *Aborigines, Tourism, and Development: The Northern Territory Experience.* Darwin: North Australian Research Unit, 1988.

Althusser, Louis. "From *Capital* to Marx's Philosophy." In *Reading Capital,* ed. Louis Althusser and Etienne Balibar. 1968; London: Verso, 1997. 11–69.

Andrews, Edna. *Markedness Theory: The Union of Asymmetry and Semiosis in Language.* Durham: Duke University Press, 1990.

Appadurai, Arjun. "The Production of Locality." In *Modernity at Large: Cultural Dimensions of Globalization.* Minneapolis: University of Minnesota Press, 1996. 178–99.

Ashley-Montague, M. F. *Coming into Being among the Australian Aborigines: A Study of Procreative Beliefs of the Native Tribes of Australia.* London: George Routledge and Sons, 1937.

Athanasiou, C. "Land Rights or Native Title." *Indigenous Law Review* 4.12 (1998): 14–15.

Attwood, Bain, ed. *In the Age of Mabo: History, Aborigines, and Australia.* Sydney: Allen and Unwin, 1996.

Attwood, Bain, and A. Markus. *The 1967 Referendum, or When Aborigines Didn't Get the Vote.* Canberra: Australian Institute of Aboriginal and Torres Strait Islander Studies, 1997.

Austin, Tony. *I Can Picture the Old Home So Clearly: The Commonwealth and "Half-Caste" Youth in the Northern Territory, 1911–1939.* Canberra: Aboriginal Studies Press, 1993.

Austin-Broos, Diane. " 'Two Laws,' Ontologies, Histories: Ways of Being Aranda Today." *Oceania* 7 (1996): 1–20.

Autry, Kathryn Helen. "Silence(s) and Resistant (Dis)quiet in the Shadow of the Legal System: Race-ing Jurisprudence in Western Australia by Reference to the Courts of Native Affairs (1936–1954)." Ph.D. diss., La Trobe University, 1999.

Bakhtin, M. M. "The Problem of Speech Genre." In *Speech Genres and Other Late Essays,* ed. Michael Holquist. Austin: University of Texas Press, 1981. 60–102.

Balibar, Etienne. "The Non-Contemporaneity of Althusser." In *The Althusserian Legacy,* ed. E. Ann Kaplan and Michael Sprinker. London: Verso, 1993. 1–16.

Bandler, F. *Turning the Tide.* Canberra: Aboriginal Studies Press, 1989.

Barnes, J. "Evidentials in the Tuyuca Verb." *International Journal of American Linguistics* 50 (1984): 255–71.

Bartlett, Richard. "*Mabo:* Another Triumph for the Common Law." *Sydney Law Review* 15.2 (June 1993): 178–86.

———. "Inequality before the Law in Western Australia: The Land (Title and Traditional Usage) Act." *Aboriginal Law Bulletin* 3.65 (December 1993): 7–9.

Basedow, Herbert. *The Australian Aboriginal.* Adelaide: F. W. Preece and Sons, 1925.

———. "Subincision and Kindred Rites of the Australian Aboriginal." *Journal of the Royal Anthropological Institute* 57 (1927): 123–56.

Beckett, Jeremy. "Internal Colonialism in a Welfare State: The Case of the Australian Aborigines." Paper presented at the annual meeting of the American Anthropological Association, Chicago, 1983.

———. *Torres Strait Islanders: Custom and Colonialism.* Sydney: Cambridge University Press, 1987.

Bell, Diane. *Ngarrindjeri Wurruwarrin: A World That Is, Was, and Will Be.* Melbourne: Spinifex, 1998.

Bell, Diane, and Pam Ditton. *Law, the Old and New: Aboriginal Women in Central Australia Speak Out.* Canberra: Central Australian Legal Service Aid, 1980.

Benjamin, Walter. "The Critique of Violence." In *Reflections: Essays, Aphorisms, Autobiographical Writings,* trans. Edmund Jephcott. New York: Schocken, 1986. 277–300.

Berlant, Lauren. "The Subject of True Feeling: Pain, Privacy, and Politics." In *Cultural Pluralism, Identity Politics, and the Law,* ed. Austin Sarat and Thomas R. Kearns. Ann Arbor: University of Michigan Press, 1999. 49–84.

———. "1968, or Something." *Critical Inquiry* 21.1 (1994): 124–55.

Berndt, Ronald. *Kunapipi.* Melbourne: F. W. Cheshire, 1951.

———. "Law and Order in Aboriginal Australia." In *Aboriginal Man in Australia: Essays in Honour of Emeritus Professor A. P. Elkin,* ed. R. M. Berndt and Catherine Berndt. London: Angus and Robertson, 1965. 167–206.

Berndt, Ronald, and Catherine Berndt. *Sexual Behavior in Western Arnhem Land.* New York: Viking Fund Publication, 1951.

———. "A. P. Elkin—The Man and the Anthropologist." In *Aboriginal Man in Australia: Essays in Honour of Emeritus Professor A. P. Elkin,* ed. R. M. Berndt and Catherine Berndt. London: Angus and Robertson, 1965. 1–26.

Bhabha, Homi K. *The Location of Culture.* London: Routledge, 1994.

———. "The Other Question: Stereotype, Discrimination and the Discourse of Colonialism." In *The Location of Culture.* London: Routledge, 1994. 66–84.

Biles, David, and David McDonald, eds. *Deaths in Custody, Australia, 1980–89: The Research Papers of the Criminology Unit of the Royal Commission into Aboriginal Deaths in Custody.* Canberra: Australian Institute of Criminology, 1992.

Bleakley, J. W. *The Aborigines and Half Castes of Central Australia and North Australia: Report by J. W. Bleakley, Chief Protector of Aborigines.* Melbourne: Government Printer, 1929.

Brandl, Maria, Adrienne Haritos, and Michael Walsh. *Kenbi Land Claim.* Darwin: Northern Land Council, 1979.

Brown, Wendy. "Wounded Attachments." In *States of Injury: Power and Freedom in Late Modernity.* Princeton: Princeton University Press, 1995. 52–76.

Brunton, Ronald. "The Hindmarsh Island Bridge and the Credibility of Australian Anthropology." *Anthropology Today* 21.4 (1996): 2–7.

Buckley, Ken, and Ted Wheelwright. *No Paradise for Workers: Capitalism and the Common People in Australia, 1788–1914.* Melbourne: Oxford University Press, 1988.

Calhoun, Craig. *Critical Social Theory.* Oxford: Blackwell, 1995.

Caputo, John. *Against Ethics.* Bloomington: Indiana University Press, 1993.

Carment, David, Robyn Maynard, and Alan Powell, eds. *Northern Territory Dictionary of Biography, Volume One: to 1945.* Darwin: Northern Territory University Press, 1990.

Caruth, Cathy. *Unclaimed Experience: Trauma, Narrative, and History.* Baltimore: Johns Hopkins University Press, 1996.

Chan, Steve, and Cal Clark. "The Rise of the East Asian NICs: Confucian Capitalism, Status Mobility, and Developmental Legacy." In *The Evolving Pacific Basin in the Global Political Economy,* ed. Cal Clark and Steve Chan. Boulder: Lynne Rienner Publishers, 1992. 27–48.

Chakrabarty, Dipesh. "Postcoloniality and the Artifice of History: Who Speaks for 'Indian' Pasts?" *Representations* 37 (1992): 1–16.

Chesterman, John, and Brian Galligan. *Citizens without Rights: Aborigines and Australian Citizenship.* Cambridge, Eng.: Cambridge University Press, 1997.

Chicago Cultural Studies Group. "Critical Multiculturalism." *Critical Inquiry* 18 (spring 1992): 530–55.

Collman, J. *Aboriginal Fringe Dwellers and Welfare.* St. Lucia: University of Queensland Press, 1988.

Comaroff, John. "The Discourse of Rights in Colonial South Africa: Subjectivity, Sovereignty, Modernity." In *Identities, Politics, and Rights,* ed. Austin Sarat and Thomas R. Kearns. Ann Arbor: University of Michigan Press, 1995. 193–236.

Connolly, William E. *Identity/Difference.* Ithaca: Cornell University Press, 1991.

Coombe, Rosemary. *The Cultural Life of Intellectual Properties: Authorship, Appropriation, and the Law.* Durham: Duke University Press, 1998.

Cornell, Drucilla. "From the Lighthouse: The Promise of Redemption and the Possibility of Legal Interpretation." *Cardozo Law Review* 11.5–6 (1990): 1687–1714.

Cowlishaw, Gillian. "Colour, Culture, and the Aborigines." *Man* 22 (1987): 221–37.

———. *Rednecks, Eggheads, and Blackfellas.* Ann Arbor: University of Michigan Press, 1999.

Cowlishaw, Gillian, and Barry Morris, eds. *Race Matters: Indigenous Australians and "Our" Society.* Canberra: Aboriginal Studies Press, 1997.

Craik, Jennifer. *Resorting to Tourism: Cultural Policies for Tourism Development in Australia.* Sydney: Allen and Unwin, 1991.

Curr, Edward M. *Recollections of Squatting in Victoria.* 1883; Melbourne: University of Melbourne Press, 1965.

Das, Dilip K. *The Asia-Pacific Economy.* London: St. Martin's Press, 1996.

Davidson, Donald. "Radical Interpretation (1973)." In *Inquiries into Truth and Interpretation.* Oxford: Clarendon Press, 1984. 125–39.

———. "Belief and the Basis of Meaning." In *Inquiries into Truth and Interpretation.* Oxford: Clarendon Press, 1984. 141–54.

———. *Inquiries into Truth and Interpretation.* Oxford: Clarendon Press, 1984.

———. "Reply to W. V. Quine." In *The Philosophy of Donald Davidson.* Peru, Ill.: Open Court Publishing, 1999. 80–86.

Deleuze, Gilles. *Foucault.* Minneapolis: University of Minnesota Press, 1986.

Deleuze, Gilles, and Felix Guattari. *Kafka: Toward a Minor Literature,* trans. Dana Polan. Minneapolis: University of Minnesota Press, 1986.

Derrida, Jacques. "Signature, Event, Context." In *Margins of Philosophy,* trans. Alan Bass. Chicago: University of Chicago Press, 1982. 307–30.

———. "The Ends of Man." In *Margins of Philosophy.* Chicago: University of Chicago Press, 1982. 109–36.

———. "Force of Law: The Mystical Foundation of Authority." *Cardozo Law Review* 11 (1990): 919–1045.

———. *Specters of Marx: The State of the Debt, the Work of Mourning, and the New International,* trans. Peggy Kamuf. London: Routledge, 1994.

Detmold, M. J. "Law and Difference: Reflections on Mabo's Case." *Sydney Law Review* 15.2 (June 1993): 159–67.

Dixon, R. A., and M. C. Dillon, eds. *Aborigines and Diamond Mining: The Politics of Resource Development in the East Kimberley, Western Australia.* Nedlands: University of Western Australia Press, 1990.

Donzelot, Jacques. *Policing of Families,* trans. Robert Hurley. New York: Pantheon Books, 1979.

Doolan, J. K. "Walk-Off (and Later Return) of Various Aboriginal Groups from Cattle

Stations." In *Aborigines and Change: Australia in the '70s,* ed. R. M. Berndt. Canberra: Australian Institute of Aboriginal Studies, 1977.

Durkheim, Emile. *The Division of Labor in Society.* 1893; New York: Macmillan, 1964.

———. *The Elementary Forms of Religious Life,* trans. Karen E. Fields. New York: The Free Press, 1995.

Durkheim, Emile, and Marcel Mauss. *Primitive Classification.* Chicago: University of Chicago Press, 1963.

Dyster, Barrie, and David Meredith. *Australia in the International Economy in the Twentieth Century.* Cambridge, Eng.: Cambridge University Press, 1990.

Egan, Ted. *Justice All Their Own: The Caledon Bay and Woodah Island Killings, 1932–33.* Melbourne: Melbourne University Press, 1996.

Elkin, A. P. "Anthropology and the Australian Aboriginal." In *White and Black in Australia,* ed. J. S. Needham. London: The Society for Promoting Christian Knowledge, 1935. 13–37.

———. *The Australian Aborigines: How to Understand Them.* London: Angus and Robertson, 1938.

———. *Citizenship for the Aborigines: A National Aboriginal Policy.* Sydney: Australasian Publishing Co., 1944.

———. "Ngirawat, or the Sharing of Names in the Wagaitj Tribe, Northern Australia." *Sonderdruck Aus Beitrage Zue Gesellungs und Volkerwissenschaft.* Berlin: Verlag Bebr. Mann, 1950. 67–81.

———. "The Complexity of Social Organization in Arnhem Land." *Southwestern Journal of Anthropology* 6.1 (1950): 1–20.

———. "Arnhem Land Music." *Oceania* 26.2 (1955): 127–52.

Ewers, John K. "Aboriginal Ballet." *Walkabout.* 1 December 1947, 29–34.

Eyre, E. J. "Finditur usque ad urethram a parte infera penis." *Journal of Exploration* 1845.

Fanon, Frantz. *The Wretched of the Earth,* trans. Constance Farrington. New York: Grove Press, 1965.

———. *Black Face, White Masks.* New York: Grove Press, 1967.

Fish, Stanley. "Boutique Multiculturalism." *Critical Inquiry* 23.2 (winter 1997): 378–95.

———. "Truth and Toilets: Pragmatism and the Practice of Life." In *The Revival of Pragmatism: New Essays on Social Thought, Law, and Culture,* ed. Morris Dickstein. Durham: Duke University Press, 1998. 418–35.

Fison, Lorimer. "Kamilaroi Marriage, Descent, and Relationship." In *Kamilaroi and Kunai,* ed. Lorimer Fison and A. W. Howitt. 1880; Canberra: Australian Aboriginal Press, 1991. 21–96.

Foucault, Michel. *The History of Sexuality: An Introduction.* 1978; New York: Vintage, 1990.

———. "What Is Critique?" In *The Politics of Truth,* ed. Sylvere Lotringer. New York: Semiotext(e), 1997. 23–82.

———. "The Ethics of the Concern for Self." In *Foucault: Ethics, Subjectivity and Truths,* ed. Paul Rabinow, trans. Robert Hurley and others. New York: New Press, 1997. 281–301.

Fraser, Nancy. "From Redistribution to Recognition? Dilemmas of Justice in a 'Post-Socialist' Age." *The New Left Review* 212 (July/August 1995): 68–93.

Freud, Sigmund. "Mourning and Melancholia." In *Collected Papers*, vol. 4, ed. Joan Riviere. New York: Basic Books, 1959. 152–70.

———. *Totem and Taboo: Some Points of Agreement between the Mental Lives of Savages and Neurotics.* New York: Norton, 1950.

———. *Beyond the Pleasure Principle.* New York: W.W. Norton, 1961.

Frow, John, and Meaghan Morris. "Introduction." In *Australian Cultural Studies: A Reader,* ed. John Frow and Meaghan Morris. Urbana: University of Illinois Press, 1993. vii–xxxii.

———. "Two Laws: Response to Elizabeth Povinelli." *Critical Inquiry* 25.3 (1999): 626–30.

Goffman, Erving. "Footing." *Semiotica* 25 (1979): 1–29.

Goldberg, David Theo. "Introduction: Multicultural Conditions." In *Multiculturalism: A Critical Reader,* ed. David Theo Goldberg. Oxford: Blackwell, 1994. 1–44.

Gooder, Haydie and Jane M. Jacobs. "On the Border of the Sayable: The Apology in Postcolonial Australia." *Interventions: International Journal of Postcolonial Studies* 2.2 (2000): 229–47.

Goot, Murray, and Tim Rouse, eds. *Make Me a Better Offer: The Politics of Mabo.* Leichhardt, NSW: Pluto Press, 1994.

Gordon, Avery, and Christopher Newfield. "Introduction," in *Mapping Multiculturalism,* ed. Avery Gordon and Christopher Newfield. Minneapolis: University of Minnesota Press, 1996. 1–18.

Gramsci, Antonio. "State and Civil Society." In *Selections from the Prison Notebooks.* New York: International Publishers, 1992.

———. "The Modern Prince." In *Selections from the Prison Notebooks.* New York: International Publishers, 1992. 123–205.

Gray, Geoffrey. " 'I Was Not Consulted': A. P. Elkin, Papua New Guinea, and the Politics of Anthropology." *The Australian Journal of Politics and History* 40.2 (1994): 195–221.

———. "Piddington's Indiscretion: Ralph Piddington, the Australian National Research Council, and Academic Freedom." *Oceania* 64.3 (1994): 217–45.

———. "From Nomadism to Citizenship: A P Elkin and Aboriginal Advancement." In *Citizenship and Indigenous Australians: Changing Conceptions and Possibilities,* ed. Nicolas Peterson and Will Sanders. Cambridge, Eng.: Cambridge University Press, 1998. 55–78.

Green, N. *The Forrest River Massacres.* Fremantle, Vic.: Fremantle Arts Press, 1995.

Guha, Ranajit, and Gayatri Spivak, eds. *Selected Subaltern Studies.* Oxford: Oxford University Press, 1992.

Habermas, Jürgen. *The Philosophical Discourse of Modernity.* Cambridge, Mass.: MIT Press, 1987.

———. *Between Facts and Norms.* Cambridge, Mass.: MIT Press, 1998.

Hage, Ghassan. *White Nation: Fantasies of White Supremacy in a Multicultural Society.* Sydney: Pluto Press, 1998.

Hall, Stuart. "When Was 'the Post-Colonial'? Thinking at the Limit." In *The Post-*

Colonial Question: Common Skies, Divided Horizons, ed. Iain Chambers and Lidia Curti. London: Routledge, 1996. 242–60.

Hamilton, Annette. "Fear and Desire: Aborigines, Asians, and the National Imaginary." *Australian Cultural History* 9 (1990): 14–35.

Hanks, William. "The Evidential Core of Deixis in Yucatex Maya." In *Papers from the Twentieth Regional Meeting of the Chicago Linguistic Society,* ed. Joseph Drogo et al. Chicago: Chicago Linguistic Society, 1984. 154–72.

———. *Language and Communicative Practices.* Boulder: Westview Press, 1996.

Heidegger, Martin. *Basic Concepts.* Bloomington: Indiana University Press, 1993.

Hiatt, L. R. *Kinship and Conflict.* Canberra: Australian National University Press, 1965.

———. *Arguments about Aborigines: Australia and the Evolution of Social Anthropology.* Cambridge, Eng.: Cambridge University Press, 1996.

Higgott, R. "Australia: Economic Crises and the Politics of Regional Economic Adjustment." In *Southeast Asia in the 1980s: The Politics of Economic Crisis,* ed. R. Robison, K. Hewison, and R. Higgot. Sydney: Allen and Unwin, 1987. 177–217.

Horne, Donald. *The Lucky Country.* Ringwood: Penguin, 1964.

Jacobs, Jane M., and Fay Gale, eds. *Tourism and the Protection of Aboriginal Cultural Sites.* Canberra: Australian Government Publishing Services, 1994.

Jakobson, Roman. "Mark and Feature." In *Selected Writings VII.* The Hague: Mouton, 1974. 332–35.

Jakobson, Roman, with Krystyna Pomorska. "The Concept of the Mark." In *On Language,* ed. Linda R. Waugh and Monique Monville-Burston. Cambridge, Mass.: Harvard University Press, 1990.

Kauffman, Paul. *Wik, Mining, and Aborigines.* Sydney: Allen and Unwin, 1998.

Keating, Paul J. "Speech by the Honourable Prime Minister, PJ Keating MP, Australian Launch of the International Year for the World's Indigenous People, Redfern, 10 December 1992." *Aboriginal Law Bulletin* 3.61 (April 1993): 4–5.

———. "Australian Update: Statement by the Prime Minister, The Hon. P.J. Keating Commonwealth Response to High Court *Mabo* Judgement, Canberra, 18 October 1993." *Aboriginal Law Bulletin* 3.64 (October 1993): 18.

———. "Prime Minister's Address to the Nation." In *Make Me a Better Offer: The Politics of Mabo,* ed. Murray Goot and Tim Rouse. Leichhardt, NSW: Pluto Press, 1994. 235–38.

Keen, Ian. "A Question of Interpretation: The Definition of 'Traditional Aboriginal Owners' in the Aboriginal Land Rights (NT) Act." In *Aboriginal Land-Owners: Contemporary Issues in the Determination of Traditional Aboriginal Land Ownership,* ed. L. R. Hiatt. Sydney: University of Sydney, 1984. 24–45.

———. "Twenty-Five Years of Aboriginal Kinship Studies." In *Social Anthropology and Australian Aboriginal Studies: A Contemporary Overview,* ed. Ronald Berndt and R. Tonkinson. Canberra: Aboriginal Studies Press, 1988. 79–123.

———. *Knowledge and Secrecy in an Aboriginal Religion.* Oxford: Oxford University Press, 1997.

Keesing, Roger M. *Kin Groups and Social Structure.* Fort Worth: Harcourt Brace Jovanovich College Publishers, 1975.

Kennedy, Duncan. 1974. "The Structures of Blackstone's Commentaries." *Buffalo Law Review* 28 (1974): 279.

Kirby, Diane. *Sex, Power, and Justice: Historical Perspectives of Law in Australia.* Melbourne: Oxford University Press, 1995.

Kripke, Saul. *Meaning and Necessity.* 1972; Cambridge, Mass.: Harvard University Press, 1980.

Kymlicka, Will. *Multicultural Citizenship.* Oxford: Oxford University Press, 1995.

Lacan Jacques. "Agency of the Letter in the Unconscious, or Reason since Freud." In *Ecrits: A Selection.* New York: W. W. Norton, 1977. 146–78.

———. *The Seminar of Jacques Lacan, Book I: Freud's Papers on Technique, 1953–1954,* ed. Jacques-Alain Miller, trans. John Forrester. New York: W. W. Norton, 1988.

Laclau, Ernesto. "Introduction." In *The Making of Political Identities,* ed. Ernesto Laclau. London: Verso, 1994. 1–8.

———. "Universalism, Particularism, and the Question of Identity." In *Emancipation(s).* London: Verso, 1996. 20–35.

Lavery, Daniel. "The Council for Aboriginal Reconciliation: When the CAR Stops on Reconciliation Day Will Indigenous Australians Have Gone Anywhere?" *Aboriginal Law Bulletin* 2.58 (October 1992): 7–8.

The Law Reform Commission. *The Recognition of Aboriginal Customary Laws,* vol. 1, report no. 31. Canberra: Australian Government Publishing Service, 1986.

Leach, Edmund. *Political Systems of Highland Burma.* London: Athlone, 1964.

Lee, Benjamin. "Textuality, Mediation, and Public Discourse." In *Habermas and the Public Sphere,* ed. Craig Calhoun. Cambridge, Mass.: MIT Press, 1993. 402–18.

———. *Talking Heads: Language, Metalanguage, and the Semiotics of Subjectivity.* Durham: Duke University Press, 1997.

Legge, J. D. "The Murray Period: Papua 1906–1940." In *Australia and Papua New Guinea,* ed. W. J. Hudson. Sydney: Sydney University Press, 1971. 32–56.

Levinas, Emmanuel. *Totality and Infinity.* Pittsburg: Duquesne University Press, 1969.

Lévi-Strauss, Claude. *Introduction to the Work of Marcel Mauss,* trans. Felicity Baker. London: Routledge & Kegan Paul, 1950.

———. *Totemism,* trans., Rodney Needham. Boston: Beacon Press, 1963.

———. *The Savage Mind.* Chicago: The University of Chicago, 1966.

Lippmann, L. *Generations of Resistance: The Aboriginal Struggles for Justice.* Melbourne: Longman, 1981.

Long, J. P. M. *Aboriginal Settlements: A Survey of Institutional Communities in Eastern Australia.* Canberra: Australian National University Press, 1970.

Lucy, John. "Reflexive Language and the Human Disciplines." In *Reflexive Language, Reported Speech, and Metapragmatics,* ed. John Lucy. Cambridge, Eng.: Cambridge University Press, 1993. 9–32.

Lyon, Pamela, and Michael Parsons. *We Are Staying: The Alyawarre Struggle for Land at Lake Nash.* Alice Springs: IAD Press, 1989.

Lyons, Andrew P., and Harriet Lyons. "Savage Sexuality and Secular Morality." *Canadian Journal of Anthropology* 5.1 (fall 1986): 51–64.

Lyons, John. *Semantics.* Cambridge, Eng.: Cambridge University Press, 1977.

Lyotard, Jean-François. *Lessons on the Analytic of the Sublime,* trans., Elizabeth Rotten-berg. Stanford: Stanford University Press, 1991.

Maine, Sir Henry Sumner. *Ancient Law.* 1864; Tucson: University of Arizona Press, 1986.

Malinowski, Bronislaw. *The Family among the Australian Aborigines.* New York: Schocken, 1913.

———. *The Sexual Life of Savages.* Boston: Beacon Press, 1929.

———. "Kinship." *Man* 30.17 (1930): 19–29.

Mamdani, Mahmood. *Beyond Rights Talk and Culture Talk: Comparative Essays in the Politics of Rights and Culture.* New York: St. Martin's Press, 2000.

Mantegazza, Paola. *Anthropological Studies of Sexual Relations of Mankind.* New York: Falstaff Press, 1932.

Marett, Allan. "Wangga Songs of Northwest Australia: Reflections on the Performance of Aboriginal Music at SIMS 88." *Musicology Australia* 15 (1991): 37–46.

———. "Wangga: Socially Powerful Songs?" *The World of Music* 1(1994): 67–81.

Marett, Allan, and JoAnne Page. "Interrelations between Music and Dance in a Wangga from Northwest Australian." In *Essence of Singing and the Substance of Song: Recent Responses to the Aboriginal Performing Arts and Other Essays in Honour of Catherine Ellis,* ed. Linda Barwick, Allan Marett, and Guy Turnstill. Sydney: University of Sydney Press, 1995. 27–38.

Marett, R. R., and J. K. Penniman, eds. *Spencer's Scientific Correspondence with Sir J. G. Frazier and Others.* Oxford: The Clarendon Press, 1932.

Markus, Andrew. *Governing Savages.* Sydney: Allen and Unwin, 1990.

McClintock, Anne. *Imperial Leather: Race, Gender, and Sexuality in the Colonial Contest.* London: Routledge, 1995.

McEwen, J. *Commonwealth Government's Policy with Respect to Aborigines.* Canberra: Commonwealth Government Printer, 1939.

McGrath, Ann. *Born in the Cattle: Aborigines in Cattle Country.* Sydney: Allen and Unwin, 1987.

McGrath, Shane. "Traditional Punishment Prevented: Barnes v The Queen." *Indigenous Law Bulletin* 4.8 (December/January 1997–1998): 18.

McLaughlin, Rob. "Some Problems and Issues in the Recognition of Indigenous Customary Law." *Aboriginal Law Bulletin* 3.28 (July 1996): 4–9.

Memmi, Albert. *The Colonizer and the Colonized.* New York: Orion, 1965.

Merlan, Francesca. "Australian Aboriginal Conception Revisited." *Man* 21.3 (1986): 474–93.

———. "The Limits of Cultural Construction." *Oceania* 61 (1991): 341–52.

Michaels, Eric. *Bad Aboriginal Art: Tradition, Media, and Technological Horizons.* Sydney: Allen and Unwin, 1994.

Moron, S. R., and D. J. Mulvaney, eds. *Exploring Central Australia: Society, the Environment, and the 1894 Horn Expedition.* Chipping Norton, NSW: Surrey Beatty and Sons, 1996.

Morphy, Howard. "Gillen—Man of Science." In *"My Dear Spencer": The Letters of F. J. Gillen to Baldwin Spencer,* ed. John Mulvaney, Howard Morphy, and Alison Petch. Melbourne: Hyland House, 1997. 23–50.

Morris, Meaghan. "Future Fear." In *Mapping the Future: Local Cultures, Global Changes,* ed. Jon Bird, Barry Curtis, Tim Putnam, George Robertson, and Lisa Tickner. New York: Routledge, 1993. 30–46.

———. *Too Soon, Too Late: History in Popular Culture.* Bloomington: Indiana University Press, 1998.

Mulvaney, D. J. " 'A Splendid Lot of Fellows': Achievements and Consequences of the Horn Expedition." In *Exploring Central Australia: Society, the Environment, and the 1894 Horn Expedition,* ed. S. R. Morton and D. J. Mulvaney. Chipping Norton, NSW: Surrey Beatty and Sons, 1996. 3–12.

———. "F. J. Gillen's Life and Times." In *"My Dear Spencer": The Letters of F. J. Gillen to Baldwin Spencer,* ed. D. J. Mulvaney, Howard Morphy, and Alison Petch. Melbourne: Hyland House, 1997. 1–22.

Mulvaney, D. J., and J. H. Calaby. *"So Much That Is New": Baldwin Spencer, 1860–1929: A Biography.* Melbourne: Melbourne University Press, 1985.

Mulvaney, John, Howard Morphy, and Alison Petch, eds. *"My Dear Spencer": The Letters of F. J. Gillen to Baldwin Spencer.* Melbourne: Hyland House, 1997.

Munn, Nancy. "The Transformation of Subjects into Objects in Warlpiri and Pitjantjatjara Myth." In *Australian Aboriginal Anthropology,* ed. Ronald Berndt. Perth: University of Western Australia Press, 1970. 141–63.

Murphy, Brian. *The Other Australia.* Cambridge, Eng.: Cambridge University Press, 1993.

Myers, Fred. *Pintupi Country, Pintupi Selves: Sentiment, Place, and Politics among Western Desert Aborigines.* Washington, D.C.: Smithsonian Institution Press, 1986.

———. "Representing Culture: The Production of Discourse(s) for Aboriginal Acrylic Painting." *Cultural Anthropology* 6.1 (1992): 26–62.

———. "Uncertain Regard: An Exhibition of Aboriginal Art in France." *Ethnos* 63.1 (1998): 7–47.

Neate, Graham. *Aboriginal Land Rights Law in the Northern Territory.* Chippendale, NSW: Alternative Publishing Cooperative, 1989.

Newfield, Christopher, and Avery F. Gordon. "Multiculturalism's Unfinished Business." In *Mapping Multiculturalism,* ed. Avery Gordon and Christopher Newfield. Minneapolis: University of Minnesota Press, 1996. 76–115.

Okin, Susan Moller. *Is Multiculturalism Bad for Women?* Princeton: Princeton University Press, 1997.

Palmer, F. R. *Mood and Modality.* 1986; Cambridge, Eng.: Cambridge University Press, 1998.

Partington, Geoffrey. *Hasluck versus Coombs: White Politics and Australia's Aborigines.* Sydney: Quakers Hill Press, 1996.

Patton, Paul. "*Mabo:* Freedom and the Politics of Difference." *Australian Journal of Political Science* 30.1 (1995): 108–19.

Pearson, Linda. "Aboriginal Land Rights Legislation in New South Wales." *Environmental and Planning Law Journal* 10.6 (1993): 398–422.

Peirce, Charles Sanders. "Pragmatism." In *The Essential Peirce: Selected Philosophical Writings, Volume 2 (1893–1913),* ed. The Peirce Edition Project. Bloomington: Indiana University Press, 1998. 398–433.

————. "The Three Normative Sciences." In *The Essential Peirce: Selected Philosophical Writings, Volume 2 (1893–1913)*, ed. The Peirce Edition Project. Bloomington: Indiana University Press, 1998. 196–207.

————. "The Nature of Meaning." In *The Essential Peirce: Selected Philosophical Writings, Volume 2 (1893–1913)*, ed. The Peirce Edition Project. Bloomington: Indiana University Press, 1998. 207–225.

Phillips, Susan Burton. "A Note: Eddie Mabo v. the State of Queensland." *Sydney Law Review* 15.2 (June 1993): 121–42.

Poovey, Mary. *A History of the Modern Fact: Problems of Knowledge in the Sciences of Wealth and Society*. Chicago: University of Chicago Press, 1998.

Povinelli, Elizabeth A. " 'Might Be Something': The Language of Indeterminacy in Australian Aboriginal Land Use." *Man* 28.4 (1993): 679–704.

————. "Do Rocks Listen? The Cultural Politics of Apprehending Australian Aboriginal Labor." *American Anthropologist* 97.3 (September 1995): 505–18.

————. *Belyuen Traditional Aboriginal Owners (Kenbi Land Claim)*. Darwin: Northern Land Council, 1996.

————. "Reading Ruptures, Rupturing Readings: Mabo and the Cultural Politics of Activism." *Social Analysis* 41.2 (1997): 20–28.

————. "Notes on Gridlock: Genealogy, Intimacy, Sexuality." *Public Culture* 14.1 (2002): 215–38.

————. "Radical Worlds: The Anthropology of Incommensurability and Inconceivability." *Annual Review of Anthropology* 30 (2001): 319–34.

————. "Consuming *Geist*: Popontology and the Spirit of Capital in Indigenous Australia." *Public Culture* 12.2 (2000): 501–28. Special Issue: "Millennial Capitalism and the Culture of Neoliberalism," ed. Jean Comaroff and John L. Comaroff.

————. "Sexuality at Risk: Psychoanalysis Metapragmatically." In *Homosexuality and Psychoanalysis*, ed. Tim Dean and Christopher Lane. Chicago: University of Chicago Press, 2001.

Povinelli, Elizabeth A., and George Chauncey. "Thinking Sexuality Transnationally." *GLQ: A Journal of Lesbian and Gay Studies* 5.4 (1999): 439–49.

Powell, Alan. *Far Country: A Short History of the Northern Territory*. Melbourne: Melbourne University Press, 1988.

Probyn, Elspeth. "Shaming Theory, Thinking Dis-connections: Feminism and Reconciliation." In *Transformations: Thinking through Feminism*, ed. S. Ahmed, J. Kilby, C. Lury, M. McNeil, and B. Skeggs. London: Routledge, 2000.

Pusey, Michael. *Economic Rationalism in Canberra: A Nation-Building State Changes Its Mind*. Cambridge, Eng.: Cambridge University Press, 1991.

Quine, W. V. *Word and Object*. Cambridge, Mass.: MIT Press, 1960.

————. "Where Do We Disagree?" In *The Philosophy of Donald Davidson*, ed. Lewis Edwin Hahn. Peru, Ill.: Open Court, 1999. 73–86.

Radcliffe-Brown, A. R. "Social Sanctions." In *Structure and Function in Primitive Society*. 1933; New York: Free Press, 1952. 205–11.

Rawls, John. *Political Liberalism*, New York: Columbia University Press, 1993.

Reynolds, Henry. *The Law of the Land*. Hammondsworth: Penguin, 1987.

———. *Frontier: Aborigines, Settlers, and Land.* Sydney: Allen and Unwin, 1987.

Rivers, W. H. R. "The Genealogical Method of Anthropological Inquiry." *The Sociology Review* 3.1 (1910): 1–12.

Rose, Deborah Bird. *Hidden Histories: Black Stories from Victoria River Downs, Humbert River, and Wave Hill Stations.* Canberra: Aboriginal Studies Press, 1991.

———. "Hard Times: An Australian Story." In *Quicksands: Foundational Histories in Australia and Aotearoa New Zealand.* Sydney: University of New South Wales, 1999. 2–19.

———. *Dingo Makes Us Human: Life and Land in an Aboriginal Australian Culture.* Cambridge, Eng.: Cambridge University Press, 1992.

Rorty, Richard. "On Ethnocentrism: A Reply to Clifford Geertz." In *Objectivity, Relativism, and Truth: Philosophical Papers, Volume 1.* Cambridge, Eng.: Cambridge University Press, 1991. 203–10.

———. "Habermas, Derrida, and the Function of Philosophy." In *Truth and Progress: Philosophical Papers.* Cambridge, Eng.: Cambridge University Press, 1998. 307–26.

Roth, Walter. *Ethnological Studies among the North-West-Central Queensland Aborigines.* Brisbane: Edmund Gregory, Government Printer, 1897.

Rouse, Tim, ed. *After Mabo: Interpreting Indigenous Traditions.* Melbourne: Melbourne University Press, 1993.

Rowley, C. D. *The Destruction of Aboriginal Society.* Hammondsworth: Penguin Books, 1972.

Rumsey, Alan. "Agency, Personhood, and the 'I' of Discourse in the Pacific and Beyond." *Journal of the Royal Anthropological Institute* 6 (2000): 99–113.

Sackett, L. "Welfare Colonialism: Developing Division at Wiluna." In *Going It Alone? Prospects for Aboriginal Autonomy,* ed. R. Tonkinson and M. Howard. Canberra: Aboriginal Studies Press, 1990.

Scheffler, Harold. W. *Australian Kinship Classification.* Cambridge, Eng.: Cambridge University Press, 1978.

Schuyler, Nina. "When in Rome: Should Courts Make Allowances for Immigrant Culture at Women's Expense?" *In These Times* 21.7 (1997): 27–29.

Scott, James. *Weapons of the Weak.* New Haven: Yale University Press, 1986.

Sharwood, Robin. *Debates of the Australasian Federation Conference 1890 together with Extracts from the British Press Concerning Federation and The Australasian Federation Conference of 1890.* Sydney: Legal Books, 1990.

Silverman, Kaja. "White Skin, Brown Masks: The Double Mimesis, or Lawrence in Arabia." *differences* 1.3 (1989): 3–54.

Silverstein, Michael. "Metapragmatic Discourse and Metapragmatic Function." In *Reflexive Language: Reported Speech and Metapragmatics,* ed. John Lucy. Cambridge, Eng.: Cambridge University Press, 1995. 280–84.

———. "Contemporary Transformations of Local Language Communities." *Annual Review of Anthropology* 27 (1998): 401–26.

Simmel, Georg. "The Metropolis and Mental Life." In *On Mental Life and Social Forms: Selected Writings,* ed. Donald N. Levine. Chicago: University of Chicago, 1971. 324–339.

Simpson, Colin. *Adam in Ochre*. 1956; Sydney: Angus and Robertson, 1951.

Sloterdjik, Peter. *Critique of Cynical Reason*. Minneapolis: University of Minnesota Press, 1983.

So, Alvin Y., and Stephen W. K. Chiu. *East Asia and the World Economy*. London: Sage Publications, 1995.

Spencer, Baldwin. *The Arunta: A Study of a Stone Age People*, vol. 1. London: MacMillan and Co., 1927.

Spencer, Baldwin, and Frank Gillen. *Native Tribes of Central Australia*. New York: Macmillan, 1899.

———. *Northern Tribes of Central Australia*. London: Macmillan, 1904.

Spivak, Gayatri. "Scattered Speculations on the Question of Value." In *In Other Worlds: Essays in Cultural Politics*. New York: Methuen, 1987.

———. *The Critique of Colonial Reason: Toward a History of the Vanishing Present*. Cambridge, Mass.: Harvard University Press, 1999.

Stanner, W. E. H. "Ceremonial Economics of the Mulluk-Mulluk and Madngella Tribes of the Daly River, North Australia." *Oceania* 4.2 (1933): 156–75.

———. "Religion, Totemism, and Symbolism." In *Aboriginal Man in Australia: Essays in Honour of Emeritus Professor A. P. Elkin*, ed. R. M. Berndt and Catherine Berndt. London: Angus and Robertson, 1965. 207–37.

———. "Preface." In *White Man Got No Dreaming: Essays 1938–1973*. Canberra: Australian National University Press, 1979. vii–x.

———. "Durmugam: A Nangimeri (1959)." In *White Man Got No Dreaming: Essays 1938–1973*. Canberra: Australian National University Press, 1979. 67–105.

———. "Continuity and Change (1958)." In *White Man Got No Dreaming: Essays 1938–1973*. Canberra: Australian National University Press, 1979. 41–66.

———. "On Freud's Totem and Taboo." *Canberra Anthropology* 5.1 (1982): 1–7.

Stocking, George Jr. *Victorian Anthropology*. New York: The Free Press, 1987.

———. *After Tylor: British Social Anthropology, 1881–1951*. Madison: University of Wisconsin Press, 1995.

Strehlow, T. G. H. *Aranda Phonetics and Grammar*. Sydney: Australian National Research Council, 1944.

———. *Aranda Traditions*. Melbourne: Melbourne University Press, 1947.

Summers, Anne. *Damned Whores and God's Police: The Colonization of Women in Australia*. Ringwood, Victoria: Penguin, 1975.

Sutton, Peter. *Native Title and the Descent of Rights*. Perth: National Native Title Tribunal, 1998.

Taussig, Michael. "Maleficium: State Fetishism." In *Fetishism as Cultural Discourse*, ed. Emily Apter and William Pietz. Ithaca: Cornell University Press, 1993. 217–47.

Taylor, Charles. "The Politics of Recognition." In *Multiculturalism: Examining the Politics of Recognition*, ed. Amy Gutmann. Princeton: Princeton University Press, 1994. 25–73.

Testart, Alain. *De la necessite d'etre initie*. Nanterre: Societe d'ethnologie, 1992.

Thomas, C. K. "From 'Australian Aborigines' to 'White Australians': Elkin, Hasluck, and the Origins of Assimilation." M.A. thesis, Monash University, 1994.

Thomas, Nicholas. *Possessions: Indigenous Art/Colonial Culture.* London: Thames and Hudson, 1999.

Trainor, Luke. *British Imperialism and Australian Nationalism: Manipulation, Conflict, and Compromise in the Late Nineteenth Century.* Cambridge, Eng.: Cambridge University Press, 1994.

Trigger, David. *Whitefella Comin': Aboriginal Responses to Colonialism in Northern Australia.* Cambridge, Eng.: Cambridge University Press, 1992.

Trouillot, Michel-Rolph. "Abortive Rituals: Historical Apologies in the Global Era." *Interventions* 2.2 (2000): 171–87. Special Issue: "Rights and Wrongs," ed. Homi K. Bhabha and Rajeswari Sunden Rajan.

Urban, Greg. "The 'I' of Discourse." In *Semiotics, Self, and Society.* ed. Benjamin Lee and Greg Urban. Berlin: Mouton de Gruyter, 1989. 27–51.

Walzer, Michael. *On Toleration.* New Haven: Yale University Press, 1997.

Warner, Michael. "The Mass Public and the Mass Subject." In *Habermas and the Public Sphere,* ed. Craig Calhoun. Cambridge, Mass.: MIT Press, 1993. 377–401.

Warner, W. Lloyd. *A Black Civilization: A Social Study of an Australian Tribe.* 1937; Glouster, Mass.: Peter Smith, 1969.

Weeks, Jeffrey. *Sex, Politics, and Society: The Regulation of Sexuality since 1800.* London: Longman, 1989.

Weiner, James. "The Secret of the Ngarrindjeri: The Fabrication of Social Knowledge." *Arena* 5 (1995): 17–32.

Wilkins, David. *Mpartne Arrente (Aranda): Studies in the Structure and Semantics of Grammar,* unpublished Ph.D. thesis, Australian National University, Canberra, 1989.

Williams, Bernard. "Toleration: A Political or Moral Question?" In *Tolerance between Intolerance and the Intolerable,* ed. Paul Ricoeur. Providence: Berghahn Books, 1996. 35–48.

Wilson, Ronald. 1997. *Bringing Them Home: Report of the National Inquiry into the Separation of Aboriginal and Torres Strait Islanders from their Families,* ed. Meredith Wilkie. Sydney: Human Rights and Equal Opportunity Commission, 1997.

Wise, T. *The Self-Made Anthropologist.* Sydney: Allen and Unwin, 1985.

Wolfe, Patrick. "Nation and MiscegeNation: Discursive Continuity in the Post-Mabo Era." *Social Analysis* 34 (1994): 93–152.

———. *Settler Colonialism and the Transformation of Anthropology.* London: Cassell, 1999.

Wright, A. ed. *Take Power Like This Old Man Here: An Anthology of Writings Celebrating Twenty Years of Land Rights in Central Australia, 1977–1997.* Alice Springs, NT: Jukurrpa Books, 1998.

Žižek, Slavoj. "How Did Marx Invent the Symptom." In *The Sublime Object of Ideology.* London: Verso, 1992. 11–53.

———. "The Spectre of Ideology." In *Mapping Ideology,* ed. Slavoj Žižek. London: Verso, 1994.

Zupancic, Alenka. "The Subject of the Law." In *Cogito and the Unconscious,* ed. Slavoj Žižek. Durham: Duke University Press, 1998. 41–73.

INDEX

ELIZABETH A. POVINELLI is Professor of Anthropology
and Social Sciences at the University of Chicago. She is
author of *Labor's Lot: The Power, History, and Culture of
Aboriginal Action* and editor of the journal *Public
Culture.*

Library of Congress Cataloging-in-Publication Data
Povinelli, Elizabeth A.
The cunning of recognition : indigenous alterities and
the making of Australian multiculturalism / Elizabeth A.
Povinelli.
p. cm. — (Politics, history, and culture)
Includes bibliographical references and index.
ISBN 0-8223-2853-4 (cloth : alk. paper)
ISBN 0-8223-2868-2 (pkb. : alk. paper)
1. Australian aborigines—Ethnic identity.   2. Australian
aborigines—Claims.   3. Multiculturalism—Australia.
4. Australia—Race relations.   I. Title.   II. Series.
GN666 .P64   2002
305.89'915—dc21   2001007382